T0271096

ROUTLEDGE LIBRARY EDITIONS: THE HISTORY OF ECONOMIC THOUGHT

Volume 13

BRITISH ECONOMISTS AND THE EMPIRE

BRITISH ECONOMISTS AND
THE EMPIRE

JOHN CUNNINGHAM WOOD

Routledge
Taylor & Francis Group

LONDON AND NEW YORK

First published in 1983 by Croom Helm Ltd

This edition first published in 2017
by Routledge
2 Park Square, Milton Park, Abingdon, Oxon OX14 4RN

and by Routledge
605 Third Avenue, New York, NY 10017

Routledge is an imprint of the Taylor & Francis Group, an informa business

British Library Cataloguing in Publication Data
A catalogue record for this book is available from the British Library

ISBN: 978-1-138-29250-5 (Set)
ISBN: 978-1-315-23288-1 (Set) (ebk)
ISBN: 978-1-138-23071-2 (Volume 13) (hbk)
ISBN: 978-1-315-31696-3 (Volume 13) (ebk)

Publisher's Note
The publisher has gone to great lengths to ensure the quality of this reprint but points out that some imperfections in the original copies may be apparent.

Disclaimer
The publisher has made every effort to trace copyright holders and would welcome correspondence from those they have been unable to trace.

BRITISH ECONOMISTS AND THE EMPIRE

JOHN CUNNINGHAM WOOD

CROOM HELM
London & Canberra

©1983 J.C. Wood
Croom Helm Ltd, Provident House, Burrell Row,
Beckenham, Kent BR3 1AT

British Library Cataloguing in Publication Data
Wood, J.C.
    British economists and the Empire, 1860-1914.
    1. Economists——Great Britain   2. Great Britain
    ——Colonies——History
    I. Title
    909'.097124108   DA18
    ISBN 0−7099−2750−9

Library of Congress Cataloging in Publication Data

Wood, John Cunningham
    British economists and the Empire, 1860-1914

Originally presented as the Author's Thesis
(Doctoral——University of Oxford, 1978)
    Bibliography: p.
    Includes index.
    1. Economists——Great Britain——History.
2. Economics——Great Britain——Hitsory.   3. Great
Britain——Colonies——History.   4. Great Britain——Foreign
economic relations. I. Title.
HE103.A3W66   1983   330'.0942   83−3400
ISBN 0−312−10089−2

Printed and bound in Great Britain

TABLE OF CONTENTS

Pages

LIST OF TABLES

ABBREVIATIONS

AER	American Economic Review
CR	Contemporary Review
EHR	Economic History Review
EJ	Economic Journal
ER	Economic Review
EW	Ethical World
HOPE	History of Political Economy
IJE	Indian Journal of Economics
JLE	Journal of Law and Economics
JPE	Journal of Political Economy
JRSS	Journal of the Royal Statistical Society
SEJ	Southern Economic Journal
OEP	Oxford Economic Papers
PR	Propgressive Review
PSQ	Political Science Quarterly
QJE	Quarterly Journal of Economics
UP	University Press

ABSTRACT

Despite the considerable volume of historical research on the era of "new imperialism" in the late nineteenth century, and the importance of the economic issues involved, no attempt has hitherto been made to examine the British economists' ideas on this subject. This study is designed to rectify that omission by reviewing, analysing, and evaluating the economists' writings on a range of economic and non-economic aspects of the British empire during the period from 1860 to the outbreak of World War I. The adoption of an author-by-author approach makes it possible to demonstrate the role of individual personalities, beliefs and allegiances as well as the development of economic ideas and policy proposals. Due attention is also paid to the context of the economists' ideas, including the background of classical economics and the changing historical conditions of the time.

TO THE MEMORY OF MY MOTHER

ACKNOWLEDGEMENTS

This book is the outgrowth of a thesis, first submitted at the University of Oxford in 1978. Its origins can be traced to the University of Western Australia where Dr Robin Ghosh, who first sowed the seeds of my interest in the history of economic analysis, suggested the topic. He, along with Professor R T Appleyard, has remained a constant and reliable source of help in my intellectual endeavours. At Oxford, Professor Peter Mathias initially supervised and nurtured the formative phases of the work and guided the research in a willing and receptive manner. He has continued to read draft material and his opinions have proved invaluable.

The research was propelled and trimmed by the intellectual and social environment of Nuffield College, wherein guidance was offered by my college supervisors, Mr D K Fieldhouse and Dr R M Hartwell. Together with Mr G Gallop, Dr R N Ghosh, Professor T W Hutchison, Dr A Petridis and Mr E D Warner they read and commented upon early drafts. Members of the staff at Brunel, Stanford and New England Universities willingly rendered assistance and advice. During 1981 I benefited particularly from discussions with Professors P J Drake and M L Treadgold. However, my chief debt and deep gratitude lies with Professor A W Coats, my doctorial supervisor. His undying and challenging encouragement, generous spirit of offering knowledge and assistance, and his extensive commentary on draft material significantly refined the study. For his superivsion I am, and shall remain, truly grateful.

I am also extremely appreciative of the efforts of the numerous librarians at the Sheffield University Library, Sheffield, the Bodleian Library, Oxford, the Marshall Library, Cambridge and the Public Records Office, London. In particular, I am thankful to Mr Finkel of the Marshall Library Cambridge who greatly assisted my search for correspondence in the Marshall Papers and Miss Beach of the Search Department, Public Records Office, who persisted at my repeated requests and found Marshall's The Fiscal Problem.

In returning to Perth in 1982 I had no idea that my publisher, Christopher Helm, would produce the book in such rapid time. The production was facilitated greatly by Mrs Patricia Miskelly of the Western Australian Institute of Technology, who typed the manuscript and Mr Don Frearson, Head of the School of Economics and Finance, who assiduously proof-read the work.

Finally, my heartiest thanks are due to my wife, Caroline who has suffered the "economists and the empire" for the past seven years.

Despite all the assistance and advice, I alone remain responsible for any errors and omissions contained in this thesis.

SECTION ONE

INTRODUCTION

Chapter 1

INTRODUCTION

AIMS AND PROCEDURE

There is an abundance of literature, encompassing many disciplines, on the rise and expansion of "new imperialism" in Britain and Western Europe in the late nineteenth and early twentieth centuries.(1) Although the history of the growth and decline of the British empire is widely known, no attempt has hitherto been made to present a systematic investigation of the discussion and analysis of the empire by British economists over the period 1860 to 1914. This neglect is somewhat surprising, for during these years not only did the British empire experience its most rapid growth, but economics itself underwent numerous changes and modifications.(2) This study is primarily concerned with what the economists wrote on a range of economic and non-economic aspects of the British empire, and the reasons for their conclusions. Moreover, an attempt will be made to correct the view, sometimes encountered, that mainstream British economists after 1860 were antipathetic to the concept of empire.(3)

The study will demonstrate that authors such as W S Jevons and Alfred Marshall did not, as Donald O Wagner asserted in 1932, "completely pass over" imperial problems.(4) In addition to these specific aims, the study has four subsidiary concerns: firstly, to compare and contrast the economists' views on empire with those of their classical predecessors; secondly, to note the relationship of the economics of the empire to the core of economic theory;(5) thirdly, to establish whether the economists had anything to contribute to imperial discussion qua economists; and finally, to establish whether the economists' economic analysis of the empire reveals anything about the changing nature of the economics profession over the period 1860-1914.

It is not an aim of the study to investigate the relationship between economic ideas and policy systematically, though occasional references to this matter occur throughout the work.(6) Nor has any consistent or concerted attempt been made to show how economists' ideas filtered through and were popularized, interpreted and modified by politicians and intellectuals. Furthermore, although the discussion refers to the economists' views on Indian problems, it does not deal with their analysis of Indian currency questions.

There is no ideal way of organising the materials in this study for, as T S Ashton once observed, there is the intractable problem of combining the chronological with the logical.(7) Various possible procedures have been considered - for example; (a) by means of a chronology of ideas on imperialism, with special reference to the economists' perception of the issues and the influences of current events; (b) by demonstrating the application of the various theories of imperialism to specific issues and considering the economists' responses, taking account of any personal or intellectual groupings that emerged; (c) by applying one of the available general philosophies of science to the subject; or (d) by sacrificing strict chronology and adopting an author-by-author approach. The third approach is the most ambitious, but it presents considerable difficulties, for "economics and empire" does not fit easily into any of the frameworks suggested by Karl Popper, Thomas Kuhn and Imre Lakatos, each of which has previously been applied to the history of economics.(8) Much of our subject is on the periphery of economics and somewhat far-removed from the theoretical "core" of the discipline, and as any general model necessarily imposes a pre-determined pattern on the economists' ideas it tends to obscure their individual idiosyncracies and the changing influences operating upon them and ignores their broader perspectives and ideas.

The economists with whom we are concerned cannot, in practice, be placed in any neat chronological pattern. But in seeking the logical connections between their ideas, an author-by-author approach has proved to be preferable to a thematic arrangement, which tends to conceal the complexity, subtlety, and interconnections within any given writer's works. A thematic treatment necessitates the parcelling of a given writer's views, whereas the method adopted herein allows more attention to be paid to the role of personality, political beliefs, and individual allegiances and affiliations. It enables us to consider individual contributions against the background of classical economics, thereby highlighting any advances (or retrogressions) in ideas; and it permits us to group authors together, where appropriate. However, because of the constraints of the work, the approach adopted herein does result in some neglect of the complex and varied imperial issues, as seen by contemporaries.

The intellectual background and historical context of the study are provided in Chapters 2 and 3, which deal, respecitvely, with the classical economists' ideas on empire and colonies, and the leading imperial issues and economic developments of the 1860-1914 period. There is no presupposition that these issues and developments were identical for each of the economists, or that events in any strict sense determined the ideas. Throughout the remainder of the work there is frequent reference back to these two chapters, which are designed to present some of the vital logical and chronological developments.

There is also the (largely unresolved) problem of what criteria an analyst utilizes for evaluating the economists' ideas. If one assesses their ideas solely from the standpoint of modern economic theory, then the likelihood of making anachronistic judgements is virtually guaranteed. Yet, there seem to be no unambiguous or of authoritative judgements on the meaning of "anachronistic" or the means of distinguishing between anachronistic and sound judgements in the history of economics.(9) But to deny parallels between early and later ideas, largely because the terminology is different, is to commit what Paul Samuelson has called the reverse of "inverted anthropomorphism".(10) As Michael Polanyi has stressed, there is no literally "transparent language", by which the concepts and terms of one theoretical system can be translated into those of another, and the translation from one native tongue to another inevitably raises subtle questions of meaning or ambiguity.(11)

To this author, the most appropriate sources of criteria for the evaluation of an economist's ideas are in the past, and in this study the economists' works are reviewed in relation to their classical predecessors. We are concerned to establish what the economists said, why they held particular views, whether their statements were internally consistent, rather than critically evaluating their ideas from a perspective of modern economic analysis. The study concentrates on establishing what their beliefs and intentions were, rather than applauding them for their success or correcting them for failure in terms of modern economicanalysis.(12)

Finally, it is worth noting why 1860 was chosen as the beginning of the period to be studied and not 1870, which is traditionally taken as the demarcation date for the end of the period of classical economics as well as heralding a new age in British imperial expansion. Whilst the comprehensive studies of Ghosh and Winch on classical political economy and the empire extend till the 1870's, the contribution of some economists' writing in the 1860's, particularly Henry Fawcett and J E T Rogers has been overlooked, and there is the need to rectify this omission for as will be shown below, their contributions are not without interest. Secondly, recent re-interpretations of British imperial expansion in the nineteenth century suggest that it is incorrect to consider 1870 as representing the start of a new age in overseas expansion.(13)

THE SELECTED ECONOMISTS

Using Professor Stigler's article, "Statistical Studies in the History of Economic Thought" a survey was made of all the "important" economists of the period 1870-1914.(14) However Stigler's definition of an "important economist", namely one who had a substantial influence on the economists of his time as against general public and policy-makers, was found to be too restrictive, since it excluded certain popularizers of the subject (for example, Henry Fawcett) and the pupils of the important economists, who themselves became distinguished academics (for example, A C Pigou).(15) The present survey concentrated on economists who: (i) either taught economics in a University, worked as civil servants associated with economic policy, or were employed as journalists concerned with economic matters (these occupational restrictions imply a professional status and incorporate the important recognized economists of the period); and (ii) published substantive, if not necessarily original work, either in economic theory, economic history or applied economics, which contained material relevant to the British empire. Mere volume of output is not in itself significant. Those selected are:

Name	Occupation
Ashley, W J (1860-1927)	Academic
Cairnes, J E (1823-1875)	Academic
Cunningham, W (1849-1919)	Academic, Archdeacon
Fawcett, H (1833-1885)	Academic, Member of Parliament, Minister
Giffen, R (1837-1910)	Civil Servant, Journalist
Hewins, W A S (1865-1931)	Academic, Member of Parliament
Hobson, J A (1858-1940)	Journalist
Jevons, W S (1835-1882)	Academic
Marshall, A (1842-1924)	Academic
Nicholson, J S (1850-1927)	Academic
Rogers, J E T (1823-1890)	Academic, Member of Parliament
Sidgwick, H (1838-1900)	Academic
Smith, G (1823-1910)	Academic, Journalist

Thus, for present purposes, a selected economist is a person who was either an academic, civil servant, or journalist, who published works in economics containing opinions and analysis of the nature, development and significance of the British empire.(16) The exception to this rule is Goldwin Smith, who is correctly perceived as the leading exponent of mid-nineteenth century separatist thought. This, together with his strong influence on the economists writing on imperial matters in the 1860's, notably Cairnes and Rogers, means that it is imperative to outline the leading aspects of his thought.

In addition to the above economists, specific leading ideas of two other economists, T E C Leslie (1827-1882) and H Merivale (1806-1873) have been considered. The former wrote briefly, but incisively, on imperial matters and whilst the latter has been the subject of prior research, certain of his important works have been delineated in the context of a chapter on other economists.(17) Furthermore, there are occasional references to the work of A C Pigou (1877-1959) and L L Price (1862-1950) in relation to the tariff-reform debate.(18)

The work of each economist is considered in either a single chapter or in a substantial portion of one, with the exception of Leslie's and Merivale's specific contributions which have been briefly detailed in the context of a chapter on an individual economist. A biographical sketch and the general leading economic thoughts of each economist have been presented, followed by the discussion of their views on the British empire.

NOTES

1. See, for example, The Cambridge History of the British Empire (Cambridge, CUP, Vol. I 1929, Vol. II 1940, Vol III 1959); Paul Knaplund, British Commonwealth and Empire, 1900 - 1955 (London, Hamish Hamilton, 1956); A L Burt, The Evolution of the British Empire and Commonwealth from the American Revolution (Boston, D.C., Heath, 1956).
2. See Ch. 3, pp.16-18.
3. See, for example, C A Bodelsen, Studies in Mid-Victorian Imperialism (Copenhagen, Glydendalen, 1924), pp.14-42; Donald O Wagner, "British Economists and the Empire, II", PSQ, Vol. 47, 1932, pp.53-74.
4. Ibid, p.62.
5. In a recent article "Core demi-core interaction: towards a general theory of disciplinary and sub-disciplinary growth", HOPE, Vol. II, No. 1 Winter, 1979, pp.30-63, J V Remenyi constructed a theory which owed much to T Kuhn's and I Lakatos' work. Remenyi developed a model and demonstrated, by reference to the emergence of the sub-discipline of development economics, how his theory could be used to analyze the dynamics of endogenous and exogenous interactions within and between disciplines, as well as the relationships which branches of economic theory held to its cores. Whilst Remenyi's model may be applied to a discussion of economists and empire, it tends to a straight-jacketing and narrowing of the economists' ideas, hence potentially obscuring subtleties and peculiarites of their positions.
6. See, for example, Ch. 6, pp.121-132 and Ch. 9, pp.223-230.
7. T S Ashton, "The Relation of Economic History to Economic Theory" reprinted in N B Harte (ed.), The Study of Economic History, (London, Cass., 1971) pp.161-80.
8. Historians of economic thought have utilized philosophies drawn from the works of K Popper, The Logic of Scientific Discovery, (New York, Hutchinson 1968): T Kuhn, The Structure of Scientific Revolutions, (Chicago, CUP 1962, 2nd ed., 1970); I Lakatos and A Musgrave (eds.), Problems in the Philosophy of Science, (Amsterdam, North Holland Publishing Co, 1965). Considerations of the applicability of these philosophies to economics can be found in a number of sources, for example, A W Coats, "Is There a Structure of Scientific Revolutions in Economics", Kyklos, Vol. XXII, 1969, pp.289-96; D Gordon, "The Role of History of Economic Thought in Understanding Modern Economic Theory", AER, Vol. 55, 1965, pp.96-99; Martin Bronfenbrenner, "The Structure of Revolutions in Economic Thought", HOPE, Spring 1972, pp.136-51; M Blang, "Kuhn Versus Lakatos or Paradigm Versus Research Programmes in the History of Economics", HOPE, Vol 7, No. 4, 1975, pp.399-433;

T W Hutchinson, <u>On Revolutions and Progress in Economic Knowledge</u> (Cambridge, CUP, 1978); J V Remenyi, "Core-demi-core interaction: towards a general theory of disciplinary and sub-disciplinary growth", op.cit.

9.   There is little discussion of this problem in the literature. See, for example, G Stigler "Textual Exegesis as a Scientific Problem". <u>Economica</u>, New Series, Vol. 32, No. 128, Nov. 1965, pp.447-50 and A W Coats "The Interpretation of Mercantilist Economics: Some Historiographical Problems", <u>HOPE</u>, Vol. 5, No. 2, Fall 1973, pp.485-95.

10.   P A Samuelson, "Review of Hla Myint's <u>Theories of Welfare Economics</u>", <u>Economica</u>, New Series, Vol. 16, Nov. 1949, pp.371-4.

11.   Michael Polanyi, <u>Personal Knowledge: Towards a Post-Critical Philosophy</u> (Chicago, CUP, 1958).

12.   For an excellent example of the difficulties of applying modern economic analysis to earlier periods, see the debate between T W Hutchinson and Ian D S Ward on the subject of George Berkeley's <u>Querist</u>: T W Hutchinson, "Berkeley's Querist and Its Place in the Economic Thought of the 18th Century", <u>BJPS</u> 14 (May 1953), pp.52-77; Ian D S Ward, "George Berkeley: Percursor of Keynes or Moral Economist on Underdevelopment", <u>JPE</u> 67 (Feb. 1959), pp.31-40; Hutchinson, "George Berkeley as an Economist: A Comment", Ibid 68 (June 1960), pp.302-7; Ian D S Ward, "Reply", Ibid, pp.307-10.

13.   For a discussion of this point see Ch. 3, pp.35-37.

14.   G Stigler, "Statistical Studies in the History of Economic Thought" in <u>Essays in the History of Economics</u> (Chicago, CUP, 1965) pp.31-50.

15.   Ibid, pp.33-35.

16.   Published work considered herein covers not only books and periodical journal articles, but newspaper contributions, magazine articles, speeches, letters and correspondence. Despite long, intensive searches, unpublished letters and notes were only utilized in relation to Hewins, Rogers and Marshall.

17.   See, for example, Ch. 4, pp.46-48. For a discussion of Merivale's work see Ghosh, <u>Classical Political Economy and the Colonies</u>, op.cit, pp.271-295.

18.   See, for example, Ch. 6, pp.122, 132.

Chapter 2

CLASSICAL ECONOMISTS AND THE EMPIRE, 1776-1860

Classical economists' theorising on the empire moved through two fairly distinct stages over the period 1776 to 1860.(1) In phase one, from 1776 to the 1820s, the economists' hostility to colonies was founded on Adam Smith's free trade doctrine and the growth of the United Kingdom's commercial dominance. In contrast, from the 1820s to 1860, the economists' growing concern over the nation's excessive population resulted in the colonies being viewed as outlets for the mother country's surplus population.(2) Wakefield utilised the concept of surplus population in conjunction with his thesis of overproduction to produce a generally accepted theory of colonisation.(3) By 1860, J S Mill's writings combined all the important strands of classical thought and policy prescriptions for the empire.

CLASSICAL ECONOMICS, EMPIRE AND FREE TRADE

The origin of classical free trade doctrine lies with Adam Smith. Viner in <u>Studies in the Theory of International Trade</u> argues that there were only five genuine free trade writers before Adam Smith.(4) In the <u>Wealth of Nations,</u> Smith presented a comprehensive case for the freedom of trade based upon his critique of mercantilism.(5) Smith's basic argument was grounded on the theory of 'absolute advantage', which states that it never pays a nation to produce goods and commodities when it is possible to obtain these items cheaper elsewhere. Trade, in Smith's view, widened the market and extended the scope for the division of labour. It was essentially a means of disposing of surplus produce i.e. the 'vent for surplus' argument.(6) This argument implied that international specialisation was irreversible and part of the development process. Furthermore, it assumed that there is an actual or potential surplus capacity before trade begins.(7) Free trade increased income, resulted in input requirements being at their lowest combinations, and capital flowing to areas where it would be most productive in increasing the demand for labour.

To Smith and the early economists, colonies flourished if they were left free to pursue their own activities. Any retention of political control by the mother country imposed heavy financial burdens on the nation by way of defence expenditure and increased the threats of wars and the possibility of domestic corruption.(8) The monopoly of the colonial trade conferred no benefit on the mother country.(9) Mercantile policy benefited the merchants at the expense of the community.(10) The trade monopoly of the colonial system distorted the allocation of capital, since it raised the profits of the colonial trade and attracted capital from other employments into areas in which its turnover was exceedingly slow.(11) Nevertheless, Smith did argue that one advantage of the colonial trade was that it widened the market and acted as a 'vent for surplus' products. Subsequent mainstream classical writers, under the influence of the Mill-Say law of markets, coupled with Ricardo's theory of international trade, rejected this doctrine. Ricardo utilised the Mill-Say law of markets (i.e. the doctrine of the impossibility of the failure of effective demand - that the production of commodities constituted a demand for commodities) in his growth model, which demonstrated the tendency for profits to decline. Ricardo argued that industry was limited by capital rather than the size of the market.(12)

Ricardo extended Smith's free trade theory by reference to a two world model of England and Portugal.(13) He posited that there was advantage in trade even if one country was absolutely more efficient for both commodities, just so long as it was relatively less efficient in the production of one commodity than of another. Ricardo did not explain how this would be realised and it was left to J S Mill to expound the theory of comparative advantage.(14) Mill demonstrated that where the terms of trade settled depended upon the reciprocal demand of each country for the products of the other. Mill also believed that the theory of international trade was mainly applicable to the trade between countries enjoying more or less similar stages of development. He confirmed Fredrich List's proposition that protection was justified in the case of infant industries.(15)

CLASSICAL ECONOMICS, EMPIRE AND THE MALTHUSIAN THEORY OF POPULATION

Classical economics population doctrine stemmed from T R Malthus' Essay of 1798, though he had a number of precursors.(16) Smith noted that population is dependent on the means of subsistence not so much because fertility varies with the means of subsistence as because the survival rate does.(17) In the first edition of An Essay on the Principle of Population, published anonymously in 1798, Malthus presented his law of population. When unchecked, population increases geometrically; subsistence increases at best only arithmetically. Malthus' basic principle, established in this edition, was founded on two assumptions: (i) Food is necessary for the existence of man, (ii) Passion between the sexes is necessary and will remain unchanged. He identified certain preventive checks, for example, birth control, that reduced the birth rate. The sole preventive check he approved of was 'moral restraint', outlined in his second edition of the Essay in 1803. He did not believe prudence, chastity or abstinence from sex in marriage would be effective in holding down population growth; but he emphasised the postponement of marriage. He also recognised certain positive checks (plagues, famine, war, misery) to population growth which increased the death rate.

Ricardo adapted Malthus' simple proposition on food supply and population, reducing them to an even more mechanistic form than in the first edition of Malthus' Essay.(18) Subsequent classical economists did not hold strict Malthusian opinions; McCulloch and Senior (initially supporters) led the challenge on the Malthusian doctrine. Senior attacked Malthus on two counts. Firstly, he noted that man's desire to increase his standard of living and general position in the world was at least as important as his desire to procreate. Secondly, Senior recognised that agricultural productivity may increase as population increases, so postponing diminishing returns. McCulloch became anti-Malthusian as a result of his review of food and population statistics which did not support Malthus' thesis. Despite McCulloch's and Senior's challenge to the Malthusian doctrine, J S Mill continued to advance the basic Malthusian position, incorrectly asserting that Malthus did not attach much importance to his arithmetic and geometric progression.(19) Though he was aware that technical improvements could outstrip population increases, Mill nevertheless contended that there is a tendency for population to catch up and exceed agricultural output.(20)

Shortly after the termination of the Napoleonic wars there was widespread unemployment, pauperism, a large number of disbanded soldiers, the disorganisation of commercial conditions and the general acceptance of the Malthusian thesis. These factors assisted in generating the new belief that colonies were an outlet for the nation's surplus population. J Wilmot-Horton and E G Wakefield advanced rival schemes by colonisation.(21) Wakefield's scheme was the more ambitious and the one accepted by such classical economists as Torrens, J S Mill, Scrope and Bentham.(22) There were differences of opinion among the classical economists over emigration, and Ricardo and Malthus objected to the various schemes because they felt that the vacuum created in the population by emigration would be speedily refilled by the increase in population.(23)

It is vitally important to stress the theoretical dimensions of Wakefield's scheme. He was not solely or primarily concerned with surplus labour. Wakefield accepted and extended Smith's 'vent for surplus' argument. Smith had noted the possibility of an exhaustion of investment opportunities and the arrival of a stationary state, unless there were continuous outlets for goods. As previously mentioned, the majority of economists rejected this doctrine. Ricardo, arguing in the Mill-Say tradition, contended that domestic investment opportunities were limited by agricultural labour productivity. By contrast, Wakefield argued that the mere existence of hoarding and wasteful speculation indicated the exhaustion of domestic investment opportunities. Despite Wakefield's thesis, the dominant (though dormant) tradition in economics till J M Keynes was the Mill-Say law of markets.

J S MILL AND THE CLASSICAL HERITAGE ON EMPIRE

Doubts have recently been expressed as to whether later classical economists, particularly J S Mill, accepted the Smith-Wakefield position on empire, since it contrasts strongly with the Mill-Say-Ricardo tradition.(24) To the present author J S Mill accepted both positions, but on two separate levels, the theoretical and the practical.(25) Mill accepted the policy recommendations of the colonial reformers, while overlooking the theory on which they were based. From Wakefield, Mill seemed to have attached a new significance to the importance of expanding markets and investment opportunities. Yet, he constantly stated that in allowing markets to play a larger role, he was not abandoning the idea that "a market for commodities does not constitute a demand for labour".(26) On the other hand, he accepted Wakefield's explanation of falling profits, which was based on the explicit rejection of the Mill-Say law of markets. Mill, who was generally sympathetic to Wakefield's policy prescriptions, recognised England's increasing dependency on foreign imports as early as 1829. He realised that the export of British capital to European settled colonies and America provided the means to increase the supply of cheap food to meet Britain's expanding needs.(27) He acclaimed the export of capital, since it arrested the decline of profits in Britain and was invested in colonies which became large exporters of cheap agricultural produce.(28) In return, the colonies purchased British manufactured goods.

> It is to the emigration of English capital that we have chiefly to look for keeping a supply of cheap food and cheap materials of clothing proportional to the increase of our population; thus enabling an increasing capital to find employment in the country, without reduction of profit, in producing manufactured articles with which to pay for this supply of raw produce. Thus, the exportation of capital is an agent of great efficiency in extending the field for that which remains and it may be said truly that up to a certain point the more capital we send away the more we shall possess and be able to retain at home.(29)

Mill accepted the policy recommendations of Wakefield and the colonial reformers while ignoring the theory on which they were based. He constantly stated that he had not abandoned the Mill-Say law of markets, while accepting Wakefield's explanation of falling profits which was founded on the explicit rejection of the Mill-Say law of markets.(30) However, as argued, Mill was primarily interested in the practical aspects of the colonial reformers' schemes. In brief, his synthesis of classical theorising on colonies embodied Wakefield's colonisation theory and the doctrine of free trade.

Besides these more strictly economic considerations, Mill left further legacy for future economists and commentators in his ideas on colonial self-government, the government of subject races, the question of Indian rule and in his more general considerations of the costs and benefits of the empire. Specifically, he contended that Britain did not require the colonies for defence or commerce, and any prestige derived from the empire was, to him, far outweighed by the costs of military and naval defence. Whilst Mill believed that Britain could survive without the empire, he felt that there was a strong reason for maintaining a slight bond of connection with the constituent parts of the empire, namely that control was a precondition for universal peace. By such action, Britain kept the markets of different countries open to each other, with her possessions adding to her moral influence in international affairs.(31) He stressed that the costs of imperial defence had to be borne by the United Kingdom, a position which stemmed from his conviction that the bonds between the constituent parts of the empire could only be continued on an unequal footing. Yet he thought it important "to consider by what means this small amount of inequality can be prevented from being either onerous or humiliating to the communities occupying the exalted position".(32) The prime advantage of such an unequal arrangement was that the mother country decided on matters of war and peace. For this privilege, she had an obligation to repel aggression in the colonies.

Mill also discussed, at considerable length, the complex question of the government of subject races as well as that of the "British population in the colonies". In regard to the former, he argued that regions which were ruled by Englishmen, but were predominantly inhabited by another race (eg, India) were not ready to govern themselves and he considered that the best way to train people to be capable of a higher civilisation was to have a vigorous despotism(33) ie, as the 'barbarous' and 'semi-barbarous' people such as the Indians were not fit to govern themselves, they ought to be governed by a civilised country like Britain. Mill contended that the ideal to strive for was that the "ruling country ought to be able to do for its subjects all that could be done by a succession of absolute monarchs, guaranteed by irresistible force against the precariousness of tenure attendant on barbarous despotisms, and qualified by their genius to anticipate all that experience has taught to the more advanced nation".(34)

He maintained that whatever form the government took, it had to protect the weak from the strong and the rulers had to have "the highest moral standards". In any dependency so much of government's effectiveness depended on the personal qualities and the capacities of its agents. If a free country (Britain) attempted to govern a distant dependency (India), which was inhabited by a dissimilar people, by means of a branch of its own execution, it would almost inevitably fail. In such a situation Mill believed that the only mode of government which had any chance of tolerable success was that which governed through a delegated body of a comparatively permanent character. Arguing in a similar manner to his father, Mill was convinced that Britain's delegated rule of India represented a gain in civilisation. To him, enlightened despotism was the only form of government applicable to such a diverse land.(35) He also maintained that in economic affairs alone, the "backwardness of the Indians" made it necessary for the government to assume larger and more pervasive responsibilities than would have been desirable in a developed and civilised country like Britain.(36)

> This mode of government is as legitimate as any other if it is the one which in the existing state of civilisation of the subject peoples most facilitates their transition to a higher state of improvement.... Under a native despotism, a good despot is a rare and transitory accident: but when the dominion they are under is that of a more civilised peoples, that people might be able to supply it constantly.(37)

When Mill turned to consider the government of the "British population" in the colonies, he argued that regions colonised by Englishmen, such as the British possessions in Australia and America, had a similar civilisation to the ruling country. These areas were capable and ripe for representative government and self-government was an ideal in such regions.(38) Mill, like other colonial reform radicals supported Durham's conclusions that a permanent imperial bond could be forged by granting responsible government to those colonies of European settlement.(39) However, as previously noted, Mill wanted to maintain a slight bond of connection with the colonies and he thought that a complete separation of the English colonies would be a great shock to the English public.

> For my own part I think a severance of it would be no advantage, but the contrary, to the world in general, and to England in particular; and though I would have the colonies understand that England would not oppose a deliberate wish on their part to separate, I would do nothing to encourage that wish except telling them that they must be at the charge of any wars of their own provoking, and that though we should defend them against all enemies brought on them by us, in any other case we should only protect them in a case of extremity, such as is not at all likely to arise.(40)

Mill also claimed that many democratic advances which had not occurred in England could be advanced in the colonies; but he failed to say why this should be the situation. He welcomed the democratic constitution in Victoria and wanted to see women admitted to the vote, but regretted that "the vulgar and insulting expression 'manhood suffrage' has found its way to Australia.(41) He believed that often the conditions in a new country produced, of necessity, a state of society "so much more democratic than our own".(42)

Moreover, Mill was unsure if the British government was wise in giving up unoccupied lands to the colonial government. He felt that in a new colony many important prerequisites of prosperity had to be provided by the government, eg, irrigation, ships, canals, mines.(43) By creating such infrastructure, the government would assist the smooth and efficient operation of private enterprise.(44) If the British government had retained control of the "self-governing" colonies, then they could have used land sales to the advantage of labour.(45) These thoughts were related to his acceptance of Wakefield's scheme of systematic colonisation, to which he remained faithful until his death.(46)

Finally, Mill considered - albeit briefly - the question of imperial federation before it became widely discussed in Britain. He could not foresee "any practical mode of federal government for communities so widely scattered over the globe".(47) Mill dismissed as impractical the ideas of an imperial federation which hoped to transform the empire into a completely equal federation of states with a shared legislature, arguing that the problems of distance were far too great to even consider federation schemes.

NOTES

1. For the classical position on the empire see R N Ghosh Classical Macroeconomics and the Case for Colonies (Calcutta, New Age, 1967) and D Winch Classical Political Economy and the Colonies (London, G Bell and Son, 1965). In addition to these authoritative works a number of others exist, such as Klaus E Knorr British Colonial Theories (Toronto, Frank Cass, 1963) and B Semmel The Rise of Free Trade Imperialism (Cambridge, CUP, 1970); D P O'Brien's The Classical Economists (Oxford, Clarendon, 1975) has a summary of the phases of classical thought, see pp. 288-292.

2. Edward R Kittrell, in The Development of the Theory of Colonisation in English Classical Political Economy, (Chicago University, unpublished Doctoral Dissertation, 1962) adopts a somewhat different position to this breakdown which follows closely the Ghosh-Winch tradition.

3. It must not be thought that the doctrine of free trade was not important in the discussion on colonisation during the second phase. See Edward R Kittrell "The Development of the Theory of Colonisation in English Classical Political Economy", SEJ, Vol. 31, Jan. 1965, No. 3, pp. 189-206, especially pp. 189-193, 200-203.

4. J Viner, Studies in the Theory of International Trade (New York, Harper Bros, 1955), pp. 91-109. The five free trade writers were Gervajse, Joselyn, North, Pateson and Whatley.

5. A Smith, An Inquiry into the Nature and Causes of the

Wealth of Nations, (E Cannan ed., New York, Modern Library, 1937), Vol. 1, pp. 341, 345, 357-8, 413.

6. J S Mill coined the term "vent for surplus" in his Principles of Political Economy (W J Ashley ed., London, Longmans and Green, 1907), p. 577. For two articles on this concept, see Hla Myint, "The Classical Theory of International Trade", EJ, Vol. 68, 1958, pp. 317-331 and the more recent article, "Adam Smith's Theory of International Trade in the Perspective of Economic Development", Economica, Vol. 44, 1977, pp. 231-248.

7. As D P O'Brien says in The Classical Economists, op.cit., p. 171, this is a two edged sword for "on the one hand it suggest that imports are more or less costless; but on the other it also suggests that because of the non-reversibility of specialization, an exporting country is very vulnerable to a reduction of demand for its produce".

8. A Smith, Wealth of Nations, op.cit., Bk. 2, p. 115.

9. See Winch, Classical Political Economy and the Colonies, op.cit., pp. 6-24 and D P O'Brien, J R McCulloch: A Study in Classical Economics, (London, Allen and Unwin, 1970).

10. See Smith, Wealth of Nations, op.cit., Bk. 2, p. 114.

11. Ibid., pp. 96-97, 101-105.

12. See Winch, Classical Political Economy and the Colonies, op.cit., pp. 39-50.

13. David Ricardo, Principles of Political Economy and Taxation, Vol. 1, pp. 135-6, in Vol. 1 of The Works and Correspondence of David Ricardo, (P Sraffa and M B Dobb, eds., Cambridge, CUP, 1951-5).

14. J S Mill,, Essays on Some Unsettled Questions of Political Economy, 1884, (London School of Economics reprint, No. 7), p. 12, and Principles, op.cit., p. 587.

15. See Mill, Principles, op.cit., p. 92.

16. See J Bonar, Theories of Population from Raleigh to Arthur Young, (London, George Allen and Unwin, 1931).

17. See E Cannan, History of the Theories of Production and Distribution, (London, Perival, 1903), p. 81.

18. For a summary of the changing views on Malthusian population theory see D P O'Brien, The Classical Economists, op.cit., pp. 60-66.

19. J S Mill, Principles, op.cit., p. 359.

20. Ibid., pp. 156-166, 561, 702-703, 721-722.

21. See Ghosh, Classical Macroeconomics and the Case for Colonies, op.cit., pp. 228-245, and Winch, Classical Political Economy and the Colonies, op.cit., pp. 5-72.

22. Ibid., pp. 25-38.

23. D Ricardo, Works, op.cit., Vol. I, pp. 99-100; T R Malthus, An Essay on the Principle of Population (1826 ed., Vol. 2, London, John Murray, 1826), p. 49.

24. For an outline of these doubts see O'Brien, The Classical Economists, op.cit., pp. 291-292.

25. For a similar position, see Winch, Classical Political Economy and the Colonies, op.cit., pp. 135-143, especially pp. 139-140.

26. J S Mill, Principles, op.cit., pp. 727-728; Winch, Classical

Political Economy and the Colonies, op.cit., pp. 142-143.

27. J S Mill, Principles, op.cit., pp. 738-43.

28. Ibid., p. 739-41.

29. Ibid., pp. 739.

30. Ibid., pp. 27-8.

31. J S Mill, "Essay on Representative Government" in A D Lindsay (ed.) Utilitarianism, Liberty and Representative Government (London, A M Dent, 1926, ed.), pp. 379-380.

32. Ibid., p. 380. Also see Mill's letter to Judge Chapman (in New Zealand) on 14/1/1870 in H Elliot (ed.) Letters of J S Mill (London, Longmans, 1910) Vol. II, pp. 237-239.

33. Mill, "Essay on Representative Government", op.cit., pp. 302-390.

34. Ibid., p. 382.

35. For an analysis of Mill's views on India see G D Bearce, British Attitudes Towards India 1784-1888, (London, OUP, 1961), Ch. X.

36. Mill, Principles, op.cit., p. 978.

37. Mill, Representative Government, op.cit., p. 364.

38. Ibid., pp. 376-393.

39. See Letters by Wakefield and Mill, quoted in M G Fawcett, Life of The Right Honourable Sir William Molesworth (London, Macmillan, 1901).

40. Letters from Mill to Judge Chapman, 14/1/1858 in Vol. II of H Elliot (ed.) Letters of J S Mill, op.cit., pp. 237.239.

41. Letter from Mill to Judge Chapman, 8/7/1858, Vol. II, Ibid., pp. 200-1.

42. See Mill's correspondence with Arthur Helbro, Vol. II, Ibid., pp. 245-6.

43. Mill, Representative Government, op.cit., pp. 376-93.

44. See Mill's letter to A M Francis, 8/5/1869 in Elliot (ed.) Letters, op.cit., Vol. II, pp. 200-202.

45. Mill, Representative Government, op.cit., p. 238.

46. See Mill's letter to F Sinnet, 22/10/1857 in Elliot (ed.) Letters. op.cit., Vol. I, pp. 198-199, and to A M Francis, 8.5.1869, Vol. II, pp. 200-203.

47. Mill, Representative Government, op.cit., p. 379 and Mill's letter to Judge Chapman on 14/1/1870 in Francis E Mineka and Dwight N Lindley The Late Letters of J S Mill, Vol. XVI (Toronto, TUP, 1972) Letter 1517, pp. 1685-1686.

Chapter 3

THE ECONOMIC STAGE, 1860 - 1914

In addition to being influenced by the classical economists' discussion of colonies the post-1860 economists' ideas were formed by the continuously changing economic, social and political environment in which they wrote. This chapter highlights - albeit briefly - some important economic facts of empire in the period and outlines the leading imperial issues arising from public discussions of the economic and political unification of the empire, namely the complex questions of tariff reform, imperial preference and imperial federation. Moreover, since the economists' analysis was interlinked to the changing nature of economics over the period as well as being associated with a substantial expansion of Britain's overseas territories, the period of neo-classical economics and the framework for the discussion of nineteenth century imperial history has been summarised.

THE PERIOD OF NEO-CLASSICAL ECONOMICS: A SUMMARY

The period 1860-1914 covers the decline of classical economics and the emergence of neo-classical economics in the United Kingdom (and elsewhere).(1) Classical economics' hey-day was from about 1800 to 1850, but it is difficult to date the transition to neo-classical economics precisely. J E Cairnes' Leading Principles of Political Economy, one of the last significant works of classical economics, was published in 1874, the year Fawcett's Manual was in its fourth edition. Fawcett's work was popular as late as 1895, as evidenced by the fact that when Winston Churchill wanted to learn some economics he turned to Fawcett.(2) Unlike neo-classical economics, a leading concern of classical political economy was the formulation of analytical proposals which had more or less immediate policy applications. Micro economic questions and the problem of distribution were not considered to the same extent as macro economic issues, and the focus was on the problems of population increase, capital accumulation and economic growth.

The 1860s and 1870s witnessed considerable attacks on the established methodology and principles of classical economics. There was the growing contradiction between Ricardian theory and the actual operation of the British economy. Increases in population coupled with rising real income strengthened the arguments of those who rejected the Malthusian population doctrine. By the 1870s orthodox political economy was under challenge and in 1876, at the Political Economy's Club centennial celebration of the Wealth of Nations serious questions were raised concerning the validity of the deductive method, the social effects of free competition and the advisability of free trade.(3) J S Mill's Principles had, on matters of economic theory and policy, left considerable latitude for varied interpretations, and the volume included economic theory, moral imperatives, applied economics, sociology and economic history.(4) However, by the late 1870s, the "marginalist" movement was gaining increasing momentum as economic theory focused on analysing the effects of the scarcity of given means in relation to alternative ends as the economic problem.(5) Whilst marginalism resulted in a narrowing of the aims of economic theory, it did not - as Winch points out - result in a more professional recognition of the distinction between art and science, a distinction Marshall pondered throughout his career.(6)

The marginalist school developed in several countries and through the efforts of people working independently of each other. Among the pioneers were Carl Menger in Austria, Leon Walras in Switzerland, J B Clark in America and W S Jevons and Alfred Marshall in England. In the 1870s Jevons, Menger and Walras all published major treaties criticising the classical cost of production theory and offered a new theory of value which placed almost exclusive emphasis on marginal utility. The increasing use of mathematics in economics was resented by some defenders of classical political economy. For example, in the second edition of his Theoretical and Logical Method of Political Economy (1875), Cairnes attacked Jevon's use of mathematics in economics.(7)

However, the use of mathematics in economics continued under Marshall's influence though he assigned it a distinctly subordinate role. Marshall was trained in mathematics, but he came to the study of economics at a propitious time, for it was widely claimed that political economy was disintegrating. He recognised the power of mathematics as a tool of economic analysis and his close study of Ricardo revealed the insights to be gained by building abstract models. Marshall asserted that everything in the economic system seemed to depend upon everything else and he noted that there was often a complex and subtle relationship between the various parts of the system. By 1890, Marshall justly claimed to be an originator of the marginal productivity theory. He fused the recent developments of marginalism into a well rounded theory of households, firms and markets. He applied his new analysis to the ways in which competitive markets allocated scarce resources among alternative uses. Marginal analysis was fundamentally deductive in its approach using abstract models of households and firms, which were assumed to be maximising utility and profits, respectively. Nevertheless, it must not be thought that there was no factual/realistic analysis in Marshall's writings.(8)

Marshall believed that it was possible and necessary to separate the normative and positive elements of economics and busied himself in developing what he regarded as a positive science, which he felt would be achieved at a cost of realism. He therefore argued that theory must be supplemented by descriptive and historical material. Between 1870 and 1900 Marshall formulated a new set of analytical tools which gave microeconomics much of its present content. His brilliant new synthesis of economic theory re-established the position of deductive economics. Marshall's system and his personal influence represent an important chapter in the professionalisation of British economics.(9) Around the turn of the twentieth century, this growing professionalisation was coupled with the increased differentiation of economics from other social sciences.

Towards the close of the period economic theory, applied economics, and economic history began to be recognised as separate, though related, disciplines in British Universities.(10) The newly founded London School of Economics offered an historical economics course in 1903, the same year as the first graduate in the Cambridge tripos and the introduction of a degree in applied economics at Birmingham.(11) Nevertheless, Marshallian ideas dominated theoretical economics throughout the early twentieth century. T W Hutchison observed that Marshall was "the great father figure of English economics, firmly upholding the virtue of respect for one's elders and betters in the family of economists. After the middle eighties there were in England patently no betters than Marshall himself, and, of course, fewer and fewer comparable elders".(12) Economics became through Marshall and the marginal utility movement, increasingly recognised as requiring distinctive intellectual expertise, with its practitioners stressing the scientific and technical aspects of the subject. However, despite this increased professionalisation, there were still no generally acknowledged standards of technical competence in economics, no uniform provisions for the training of apprentices, and no standardisation of examinations.(13) Yet, by 1914 economics was less dominated by the writing of bankers, merchants, administrators and philosophers than in 1860. The standards of rigour and precision in the formation of pure theory were higher than ever before.

BRIEF OVERVIEW OF BRITISH EXPANSION AND ECONOMIC FACTS ASSOCIATED WITH EMPIRE, 1860-1914

The economists' beliefs, ideas, theories and writings were considerably influenced by the scientific community to which they belonged, and their views were not independent of the economic history of their age. This section briefly notes the growth of empire and the important economic developments associated therewith from 1860 to 1914, during which time the British economy itself underwent significant changes.

Suddenly, and almost simultaneously, in the closing decades of the nineteenth century, the European states began to extend their control over large areas of the world.

Table 1
British Colonial Possessions, Area
and Population 1860-1914

Year	Area (millions of square miles)	Population (millions)
1860	2.5	145
1875	8.7	253
1900	12.1	367
1914	13.1	493

Source: Michael Barrat Brown, The Economics of Imperialism (London, Penguin, 1974), pp. 185-186.

Other nations expanded their overseas territories after 1870 and various European nations, especially the French, acquired an empire in Africa, Madagascar and South East Asia. However, it was the German imperial conquests that alarmed the British leaders for Germany suddenly entered the ranks of the colonial powers in 1884.(14) The United Kingdom was now confronted not only by two formidable industrial competitors (Germany and the United States), but also by other colonial empires, and the balance of international power had shifted in a manner posing new problems of military defence for the United Kingdom.

Emigration

The latter half of the nineteenth century witnessed high but declining rates of population increase and the extensive migration of labour to newly established overseas territories. Britain's population increased from 23 million persons in 1861 to 40.7 million in 1911 which was a considerable increase, given the sustained volume of emigration in the period.(15)

Throughout the period 1860 to 1914, most British emigrants travelled to the United States, not to the British empire. However, after 1900 there was a notable relative and absolute increase in emigration to the empire (see Table 3, p.21-22).

Emigration may be the result of push factors, like depression, persecution and governmental policy at home, or pull factors, such as rising incomes, labour shortages and the expectation of a better future abroad, or a combination of the two. It seems undeniable that economic conditions greatly favoured an increase in the migration of labour in the latter part of the nineteenth century. Improvements in shipping made it easier, cheaper, and safer to reach distant countries; railways rapidly transported newly arrived immigrants to developing industrial or agricultural areas. Workers in Britain seemed better educated than elsewhere and shipping companies encouraged them with advertisements of high wages, employment in interesting work, and land ownership.(16)

Table 2
Migration from the United Kingdom
1846-1920

Year	Total emigration from the United Kingdom - each period (millions of persons)
1846-1850	0.3
1851-1860	1.3
1861-1870	1.6
1871-1880	1.85
1881-1890	3.25
1891-1900	2.15
1901-1910	3.15
1911-1920	2.6

Source: W S Woytinsky and E S Woytinsky, World Commerce and Government (London, Allen and Unwin, 1953).

Trade and Investment, 1860-1914

The magnitude of British foreign trade and capital investments overseas in the period 1860-1914 was both unprecedented and remarkable.(17)

After 1860 Britain became increasingly dependent on the importation of foodstuffs. By the end of the 1870s a network of railways had been established in many countries, particularly the

Table 3
Actual Emigration from the United Kingdom to the United States,
to the Empire and to Other Countries 1843-1913

Annual Average (nearest thousand)

Country of Destination

Period	Total	United States	British North America	Australia and New Zealand	South Africa	Total Empire	All Other Countries
	(1)	(2)	(3)	(4)	(5)	(6)	(7)
1843-1852	214	150	41	20	1	62	2
1853-1860	164	100	15	46	2	63	2
1861-1870	157	113	13	27	1	41	1
1871-1880	168	109	18	30	5	53	3
1881-1890	256	172	30	37	8	75	6
1891-1900	174	114	19	13	17	49	9
1901-1910	284	126	85	23	28	136	11
1911-1913	464	123	189	85	28	306	22

Table 3 (Cont'd)
Actual Emigration from the United Kingdom to the United States,
to the Empire and to Other Countries 1843-1913

Percentage Shares

Country of Destination

Period	Total	United States	British North America	Australia and New Zealand	South Africa	Total Empire	All Other Countries
	(1)	(2)	(3)	(4)	(5)	(6)	(7)
1843-1852	100.0	70.1	19.2	9.3	0.5	29.0	0.9
1853-1860	100.0	61.0	9.1	28.1	1.2	38.4	0.6
1861-1870	100.0	72.0	8.3	17.2	0.6	26.1	1.9
1871-1880	100.0	64.9	10.7	17.8	3.0	31.5	3.6
1881-1890	100.0	67.2	11.7	14.5	3.1	29.3	3.5
1891-1900	100.0	65.5	10.9	7.5	9.8	28.2	6.3
1901-1910	100.0	44.4	29.9	8.1	9.9	47.9	7.7
1911-1913	100.0	26.5	40.7	18.3	6.1	65.1	8.4

Source: Official figures taken from I Ferenczi and W F Willcox, International Migrations, Vol. I (New York, National Bureau of Economic Research, 1929) pp. 627-8, 636-7.

Table 4
Geographical Distribution of British Exports, 1870-1910
(Percentages)

Year	N & NE Europe	Western Europe	Central & SE Europe	S Europe & N Africa	Turkey & Middle East
1870	5.5	13.7	11.4	6.5	8.0
1890	5.0	13.0	8.3	7.2	4.2
1910	6.7	11.4	10.2	6.0	4.3

	Rest of Africa	USA	British N America	West Indies	Central & S America
1870	2.3	14.2	3.4	3.3	8.8
1890	5.0	12.2	2.7	2.2	10.8
1910	8.0	7.3	4.7	1.1	12.2

	Australia	New Zealand	India	Western & Central Europe & USA	British Empire
1870	4.2	0.8	9.7	39.3	26.0
1890	7.5	1.3	12.7	33.5	33.1
1910	6.4	2.0	10.7	28.9	34.2

United States, and the accompanying expansion of agriculture, as well as the innovations in steam shipping combined to produce a flood of grain into the United Kingdom. Consequently, between 1874-1900 the home wheat acreage was halved, and the land under cultivation fell from 17 million to 13 million acres between 1874 and 1913.(18) Although there had been a decline in the relative importance of overseas industrial markets over the period 1870-1914, imports were often complementary products to domestic production, rather than competitive - eg, petrol, non ferrous goods, wood and timber products.(19)

Although British trade grew with the empire over the period 1860-1914, imperial trade did not come to dominate British trading patterns. There was relatively little trade with those countries acquired after 1870; imperial trade was primarily confined to the lands of recent settlement - Australia, Canada, New Zealand and South Africa. The composition of imperial trade changed significantly after the 1880s. In 1913, the empire absorbed 44% of textile exports and 42% of Britain's capital goods exports, compared with 33% of a much smaller absolute volume in 1870.(20) In 1901 approximately 20% of Britain's imported wheat came from British possessions; by 1913 the total had risen to almost 50%. This was primarily a result of the 50% growth of Australia's wheat area, while Canadian production increased because of the harder varieties of seed and the introduction of new machinery. As Table 4 (p.23) shows, the empire's share of the United Kingdom's exports expanded after 1895, but at a lesser rate than from 1870-1890.(21)

British dominance in overseas investment activities before 1914 exceeded that in commodity trade. Almost half of the outstanding international investment in 1913 was owned by the United Kingdom. Like her goods, British capital flowed to numerous countries, including the empire, which was not the largest field for its employment. This is not to deny that the importance and magnitude of British investment in the empire increased over the period 1860-1914. However those areas acquired by the United Kingdom between 1860 and 1900 did not receive substantial inflows of capital. From 1860-1890 exports of capital to Europe formed a significant proportion of total British capital exports.(22) Throughout the period, 60% of portfolio foreign investment went to independent countries and approximately 40% to the empire.(24)

British investments in the period 1860-1914 were staggering by comparison with all previous periods and Paish has estimated that British overseas investments rose from a total of 785 million pounds in 1871 to 3500 million pounds in 1911.(24) Exports of capital averaged 61.6 million pounds per annum in 1881-5, 87.6 million pounds p.a. in 1886-1890, moderated thereafter, increased after 1906 to average 145.8 million pounds p.a. between 1906-10 and reached a peak of 206.1 million pounds p.a. between 1911 and 1913.(25) More significantly, over 40% of capital exported from Britain financed railway investment which directly stimulated British export industries supplying the necessary materials and railway equipment.(26)

Simon has recently argued that private firms accounted for almost 55% of new British portfolio investment.(27) The capital was utilised to develop those facilities which increased the primary producing nations' capacity to produce and sell their surpluses, especially in Europe. As he remarks, "... it is abundantly clear that British funds did not directly foster the development of extensive overseas industrialisation as less than 4 per cent of the total capital was invested in manufacturing".(28) Throughout the period Britain lent a great deal to governments and by 1913 the aggregate investments in publicly issued securities amounted to 3,763.3 million pounds, of which 47.3 per cent was invested in the empire. (See Table 5, p.26-27)

Finally, it is important to note that among the important fundamental economic changes affecting Britain in the late nineteenth century were those resulting from the emergence of strong international industrial competitors especially Germany and the United States. The United Kingdom's quasi-monopolistic position of the late 1860s could not be maintained forever as industrialisation marched on in Western Europe and the United States. Britain's declining share of the world trade in the late nineteenth century reflected, amongst other things, the opening up of new countries outside Europe and the entry of an increasingly large volume of non-manufactured products in the world market. Her share in world trade in manufactures declined much less steeply than her share in world manufacturing production.(29)

As the first industrial nation, Britain's chief exports were textiles manufactured from imported cotton, machines, rails, and ships made from her coal, iron and steel. Her economy had essentially come to rely on a few staple industries that were heavily dependent on foreign markets, and her superiority in these industries was steadily diminishing. Britain had done much to create the pattern of world industry, but from the 1870s onwards a new industrial technology emerged with changes in methods and sources of power. Consequently Britain's comparative advantage was steadily undermined.(30)

SCHEMES FOR THE ECONOMIC AND POLITICAL UNIFICATION OF THE EMPIRE

In the closing decades of the nineteenth century questions relating to the economic and political unification of the empire were debated widely in the United Kingdom. Both were related to the debate over free trade versus protection which was a wider issue than imperial and colonial trade policy, and the colonies of recent settlement were generally considered in the light of this broader and long-standing controversy. Nevertheless, the empire occupied an important and

Table 5
British Overseas Investments in Publicly-Issued Securities,
December 1913, by Country

Country	Amount (Pounds S)	Percentage
British Empire		
Canada and Newfoundland	514.9	13.7
Australia and New Zealand	416.4	11.1
South Africa	370.2	9.8
West Africa	37.3	1.0
India and Ceylon	378.8	10.0
Straits Settlements	27.3	0.7
British North Borneo	5.8	0.2
Hong Kong	3.1	0.1
Other British Colonies	26.2	0.7
	1,780.0	47.3
United States	754.6	20.0
Latin America		
Argentina	319.6	8.5
Brazil	148.0	3.9
Mexico	99.0	2.6
Chile	61.0	1.6
Uraguay	36.1	1.0
Peru	34.2	0.9
Cuba	33.2	0.9
Other Latin American States	25.5	0.7
	756.6	20.1

Table 5 (Cont'd)

Country	Amount (Pounds S)	Percentage
Europe		
Russia	110.0	2.9
Spain	19.0	0.5
Italy	12.5	0.3
Portugal	8.1	0.2
France	8.0	0.2
Germany	6.4	0.2
Austria	8.0	0.2
Denmark	11.0	0.3
Balkan States	17.0	0.5
Rest of Europe	18.6	0.5
	218.6	5.8
Egypt	44.9	1.2
Turkey	24.0	0.6
China	43.9	1.2
Japan	62.8	1.7
Other Countries	77.9	2.1
All Foreign Countries	1,983.3	52.7
Grand Total	3,763.3	100.0

Source: H Feis, Europe: The World's Banker, p. 33.

special position in discussions of the future of the United Kingdom's trading policy, especially during the late nineteenth and early twentieth centuries.

By 1850 Britain was firmly committed to free trade as the cornerstone of her external trade policy, and hoped that the rest of the world would folow her example.(31) From 1846, colonies were free to abolish the preferences they had hitherto been forced to give to British goods. Yet after 1870 it became a fact of increasing importance that although Britain pursued a free trade policy the majority of foreign countries and her colonies did not. The granting of self-government to Australia, Canada and New Zealand meant that they now exercised the right of self-determination in all aspects of their external and internal policies, with the sole exception of foreign policy. They enacted tariff barriers against the mother country for the purpose of industrial development. External economic policy-making was considered part of a nation's internal affairs.(32)

Shortly after receiving self-government, Canada became the colonial pace-setter in tariff policy. In 1858 the Canadians enacted their first protective tariff despite the protests of British manufacturers.(33) Colonial protectionism was a novel thing in the 1860s, or at least it seemed so to the British. English public opinion had not yet quite recovered from the shock of seeing their colonies adopt a policy which seemed not only unwise but "sinful".(34) The colonies refused to follow the mother country's lead in establishing free trade, levying protective duties on English as well as foreign goods. In 1879 Canada established high protective duties against the mother country, which caused excitement in the House of Commons but was eventually accepted by the British government.(35) Such action by a colonial government was only one factor contributing to Britain's changed situation during the last quarter of the nineteenth century. From approximately 1870 onwards there was a profound shift in Britain's industrial and trade position for America, France and Germany were emerging as challengers to Britain's position as the workshop of the world. They adopted protection and their tariffs were designed to exclude British producers. After 1866, European duties were gradually reduced until 1873, then there was return to protectionism in the trade depression after the Franco-Prussian war. In Germany the zollverein had began to increase its protective duties under the influence of Fredrich List and in response to the pressures for protection against the overwhelming industrial supremacy of the United Kingdom. The German tariff became protectionist in 1879 and even more so in 1885; France established tariffs in 1882 and increased them in 1892; the United States was well sheltered by the McKinley tariff of 1891 and the Dingley tariff of 1897. Other European nations - Italy, Austro-Hungary, Russia - followed the example of the protectionist powers. As a result of the growth of rival industial powers Britain suffered a decline in the rate of growth of her foreign trade which seemed serious by comparison with the booming expansion of Germany and America. Only in the export of raw materials did

Britain's performance keep pace with that of Germany.(36)

In the latter 1870s misgivings about the permanence of the United Kingdom's position as leader of the world increased. Appeals for some kind of protection against the invasion of foreign goods and supposed curtailment of British markets became more widespread.(37) The National Fair Trade League was formed in 1881 with the direct aim of advancing the cause of tariff reform. The Report of the Royal Commission on the Depression of Trade and Industry in 1886, the Imperial Federation movement and the Colonial Conference of 1887 all gave prominence to schemes for reforming the United Kingdom's trading policy.(38) However, the Fair Trade movement of the 1880s never won the support of more than a minority. Throughout 1880-1900 the members of the largest exporting trade, cotton textiles, remained faithful to the policy of free trade and only in the tariff reform debate of 1903 did some converts appear.(39) Nevertheless, a good many people continued throughout the 1880s and 1890s to question the free trade doctrine while still not abandoning their faith eg, Goshen and Lord Salisbury.(40) In the 1890s as more countries adopted protectionist policies, the imperialist movement became a greater threat to free trade principles. Various societies, like the United Empire Trade League, emerged to advocate imperial unity and the use of tariffs.(41)

In 1896 Joseph Chamberlain, the Colonial Secretary and former radical mayor of Birmingham, cautiously endorsed the movement for protection. After the Boer War he became the leader of the campaign for an imperial zollverein and his speech on 15th May 1903 at Birmingham is usually regarded by commentators as marking the beginning of the tariff reform debate.(42) This speech must be seen against the background of the April 1903 budget in which the new Chancellor of the Exchequer, Ritchie, with the support of Sir Frances Mowat, the Permanent Secretary of the Treasury, repealed the nominal duty on corn imposed a year earlier by Hicks-Beach, Ritchie's predecessor as Chancellor of the Exchequer.

Early in 1902 Hicks-Beach introduced into his budget a shilling-a-quarter tax on corn and flour in an effort to meet the war expenditure. In order to establish reciprocity with Canada and thereby obtain a promised increase in preference, the British government had merely to remit the existing corn duty on colonial produce at the next budget and, if revenue was a trifle short, compensate for the colonial arrangements by slightly increasing the duty on foreign produce. Chamberlain won the provisional consent of the Cabinet to the maintenance of the corn duty and its eventual preferential remission in favour of the British empire.(43) When Ritchie repealed this nominal duty on corn he directly confronted the tariff reformers. Subsequently the issue reached a climax when A J Balfour, the Prime Minister, presented to the Cabinet two documents on fiscal reform - a confidential blue paper and his Notes of Insular Free Trade - which aimed at placating the contending factions within his party.

It is difficult to disentangle the various strands of thought in the tariff debate although it has been argued that four distinct issues were involved in the controversy;(44) (i) A simple protective tariff to reserve the domestic market for British industries; (ii) Justification of tariffs simply as a revenue raising device; (iii) Retaliatory tariffs directed against foreign dumping; (iv) The concept of imperial preference. However, there were many subtle variations of these four themes and there was considerable terminological confusion. Furthermore, important figures, like Goshen and Hicks-Beach, appeared to adopt shifting and inconsistent positions.(45)

Chamberlain was the undisputed leader of the tariff reform movement. When he suffered a heart attack in 1905 the campaign lost much of its impetus. He won the support of the squirearchy of the House of Commons and the leaders of heavy industry. Along with Rosebery and Milner he was a "radical imperialist". They were enthusiastically supported by Liberal imperialists like Cecil Rhodes, Leo Amery, Lord Curzon and Lord Gelborn. All these men belonged to the Tariff Reform League which was originated in 1903 "for the defence and development of the industrial interests of the British Empire". Membership of the League also included Conservative and Liberal politicians, industrialists, journalists and economists.(46)

The defenders of free trade were also a complex group. The Cobdenite Liberals (Gladstone, Morell, Harcourt, Campbell-Bannerman, Lloyd George, Courtney and Bryce) were supported by industrial traders who felt secure despite foreign competition. These industrialists included coal owners, cotton manufacturers, and shipbuilding and engineering employers, the last two of whom enjoyed the advantages of cheap American and German steel. The Trade Union Congress, fearful of an increase in the price of food, lent its support to the free traders.(47)

Several of the leading economists of the period became deeply involved in the tariff reform debate as their advice was sought and their names were invoked on either side.(48) Fourteen economists signed a Manifesto published in The Times in 1903 condemning protectionism in general, and the arguments which had been advanced anonymously by Hewins in a series of articles in the paper over the preceding weeks. Although the fourteen economists sympathized with the objectives sought by the tariff reformers they argued that Chamberlain's fiscal proposals would not achieve the desired ends, and attacked the proposals on both economic and moral grounds.(49) Alfred Marshall and J S Nicholson were signatories to the letter, an action Marshall later regretted.(50) Some economists opposed the manifesto (including Ashley, Cunningham and Hewins) and controversy among economists increased, with their divisions of opinion becoming public knowledge. It has been claimed that economists had damaged their professional reputations by using their academic positions to influence a public controversy, and by claiming competence on matters outside their specialist knowledge.(51)

The Liberal landslide in 1906 dashed immediate hopes for tariff reform in Britain. After the election there was a "tentative" Conservative commitment to some form of protection. However, the British public had a "lively sense of the advantages" of free trade and were reluctant to accept any kind of protection.(52) The principle of freedom of action, as most likely to promote greater imperial trade, was accepted and re-affirmed by electorate in 1911.(53)

Imperial Preference

Intertwined with the Protectionist movement in the United Kingdom in the late nineteenth century and early twentieth century was the renewed and enlarged interest in schemes of imperial preference. This issue is difficult to disentangle from the other subjects of popular discussion and the general pattern of events in the last quarter of the nineteenth century. Imperial preference in the form of differential duties favouring the mother country and empire was one thing, but the "grand conception" - an enclosed domain of empire with no internal tariff barriers fenced against the outside world - was another and larger matter. Few self governing colonies were likely to forfeit national revenue to benefit the empire at large. The proposals for a preferential system originally came from the self governing colonies which had already abandoned free trade. The Canadian tariff of 1859 was based upon protectionist principles. In the 1860s Victoria had adopted a Protective tariff and her example was followed by other parts of Australia. Both Canada and Australia had urged the mother country to inaugurate a preferential system.(54)

The idea of imperial preference was discussed at the Colonial Conference of 1887. At the second conference, at Ottawa in 1894, a resolution was submitted which recommended inter-colonial reciprocity, subject to the United Kingdom's participation. At the third colonial conference at London 1897, presided over by Joseph Chamberlain, a resolution was passed stating that the principle of the preferential tariffs which Canada had implemented that year by granting a 12% preference upon British goods, should be extended.

Not until the conference had ended did the British government accept, and prepare the way for, the general adoption of the Canadian system of preference. As from 1st August 1898 Canada established a British preference of 25% (subsequently raised to 33% in 1900) on products of the United Kingdom and certain of the low tariff colonies. However, it was not until the Imperial Economic Conference at Ottawa in 1932 that comprehensive imperial preferential tariffs were established between the United Kingdom and the self-governing colonies.(55)

Imperial Federation

In the 1850s and 1860s the self governing colonies acquired more and more control over their territories. In 1861 a select committee of the House of Commons held that the supervision and cost of the military defence of the colonies ought to devolve upon themselves. The following year the House of Commons reaffirmed this principle without a division.(56) Yet any tendency to complete self-determination in all colonial governmental activities seemed to stop short in the 1870's. The immense emigration of the earlier decades had created ties across the oceans with new groups in England more sympathetic to colonial society. Popular writers made the colonies widely known. Politicians, poets and travellers spoke of the potentialities of a united empire. The act of granting self-government to the colonies re-awakened their loyalty to the mother country and the case for separation lost its attraction.(57)

The movement for imperial unity had gained increasing momentum by 1870, and the examples of Germany and the United States were instrumental in suggesting a federal solution to colonial questions.(58) During the 1870s it was generally held that if the colonies were not to be estranged from the mother country some positive measures must be taken to attach them. The creation of an imperial federal system seemed to many to be a possible solution to some of Britain's economic and political problems. Imperial federation schemes were widely discussed and societies were formed to promote the idea.(59) One such society was the Imperial Federation League, established in 1884 to secure "by federation the permanent unity of the empire".(60) The League enlisted such men as the Liberal, W E Forster and Edward Stanhope (Salisbury's Colonial Secretary in 1886), J A Froude, the Tory historian of Tudor England and John Seely, the professor of Modern History at Cambridge, into its ranks. Through their meetings, writings, and speeches, these well-known figures popularised the case for imperial federation and assisted in summoning the first Colonial Conference in 1887.

Imperial federation was considered in numerous different forms. Indeed, it became customary to speak of any plan for closer union as a "Federation". Of the 150-200 schemes mooted in the period 1880 to 1900 two were most strongly supported: (i) the admission of colonial representatives to Westminster Parliament. (ii) A federal constitution modelled on the lines of the United States or Canada, and embodying a super-parliament.(61) The former scheme had been widely discussed about the time of the American Revolution when it was primarily viewed as a means of solving the problem of "taxation without representation". It was in this context that Adam Smith had considered the possibility of an imperial parliament: he declared that the old colonial system had caused the nation great losses, and that such a situation could be remedied in either of two ways: a separation or a federation of political powers.(62) Smith explained both solutions, but devoted far more attention to imperial reform since he thought it essential to demonstrate the form of organisation which could remedy the problems of empire.(63) As an alternative to complete separation, Smith held that it was possible to let the colonies assume a proportionate share of the cost of imperial government, especially defence expenditure, by imposing direct taxation on all its members. He advocated colonial representation in parliament in proportion to taxation:

> The parliament of Great Britain insists upon taxing the colonies; and they refuse to be taxed by a parliament in which they are not represented. If to each colony .... Great Britain should allow such a number of representatives as suited the proportion of what it contributed to the public revenue of the empire, in consequence of its being subject to the same taxes, and in compensation admitted to the same freedom of trade with its fellow-subjects at home; the number of its representatives to be augmented as the proportion of its contribution might afterwards augment; a new method of acquiring importance, a new and more dazzling object would be presented to the leading men of each colony.(64)

In the early nineteenth century the scheme re-appeared on several occasions in connection with various proposals for the reform of the House of Commons. It was advocated by Joseph Hume in 1831, by the Colonial Magazine in 1847 and referred to by William Molesworth in the House of Commons in 1850.(65) Other similar schemes were advocated by H Clinton in 1856 and J C Meekins in 1859.(66) The 1880s saw another revival of schemes of imperial federation and Smith's scheme was advanced by Wesgarth, Creasy and Frere.(67)

The second alternative, that of a federal constitution modelled on the lines of the United States or Canada and embodying a super-parliament, was the one favoured by the early imperialists. A comprehensive statement of the scheme was made by W Arthur in 1853 and echoed by Carfax four years later. Such schemes varied widely, ranging from a few basic ideas to elaborate plans involving, amongst other things, the abolition of the House of Lords.(68) Underlying many of them was the notion that the United Kingdom should have the predominant voice in decision-making and the right to control tariff policies. As Bodelsen has argued, it was ironic that the federalists should view imperial federation as a concession to the colonists at the same time as they sought to revoke the colonial power of enacting tariffs.(69)

Amongst the politicians Carnarvon, Forster, Rosebery and Salisbury advocated an extension of the imperial frontiers to meet the foreign challenge. Asquith, Grey, Haldane, Amery and Milner were also sympathetic to imperial unification. W E Henley made the National Observer into the literary organ of imperialism and his paper was strongly supported by the Pall Mall Gazette, which was converted to imperial federation by W T Stead, a friend of Rhodes.

Schemes of unification were opposed by Gladstone, Harcourt, Morley and Ripon amongst the prominent politicians, for they considered the effort to achieve imperial federation as impracticable and reactionary because of colonial nationalism and the immense distances between the members of the empire.(70)

Defence considerations occupied an important place in imperial federation proposals. In particular the mother country's expenditure on imperial defence became of increasing importance especially during the inter-imperial rivalry of the Western European powers in the last quarter of the nineteenth century. This is not to say that the magnitude of British imperial defence expenditure had been ignored till the 1880s. In 1862 the House of Commons had passed a resolution reducing colonial defence expenditure. However, throughout the decade of the 1860s substantial difficulties arose with this topic, especially as applied to New Zealand.(71) Subsequently, Prime Minister Gladstone, wanted to reduce defence expenditure and it has been argued that the dissolution of parliament in 1874 was primarily due to a difference of opinion between the Prime Minister and at least two of his principal colleagues as to the provisions to be made for the Army and Navy estimates of 1874-75.(72)

The retention and expansion of the empire was expensive for the British government. The spate of wars in the 1870s (the Abyssinian, Russian and Kaffir wars) and the troubles in South Africa and India involved substantial outlays. Primarily as a result of the Russian war, a Colonial defence committee was appointed in March 1878. This led to a Royal Commission in 1879 on colonial defence which reported that colonies should undertake the local defence of their own commercial ports.(73) Despite this report the mother country continued to bear the entire costs of imperial defence.

Discussions over the manner in which imperial defence costs should be allocated intensified in the 1880s.(74) Having once conceded the right of self-government, imperial federation was a delicate issue. The British government slowly concluded that the self governing colonies should meet the costs of their respective defences, especially since their total trade and wealth per head were rising very rapidly. Nevertheless, Australia and Canada were very reluctant to agree to any such proposal. In his first budget of 1887 Goshen drew attention to colonial defence arrangements and questioned whether this was "just".(75) To many people, free trade seemed to ignore vital aspects of the problem of defence, particularly since Britain increasingly depended on foreign food supplies and maintained open searoutes for her supplies of essential raw materials.

The rise in defence expenditure was restricted until Gladstone's second ministry ended in 1885, after which it rose by 13% between 1888 and 1913.(76) The main expansion of central government outlay till 1910 was for naval and military purposes, and was the result of the international political rivalry as well as the rapid rate of technical developments.

While the self governing colonies were interested in imperial preferential arrangements, it was in defence matters that most British statesmen felt the need for closer political union.(77) The so-called "small" wars of the 1880s and the 1890s were a significant drain on the mother country's resources.(78) In 1907 a colonial conference resolved to establish a defence committee for the empire, and in 1909 there was a subsidiary conference of representatives of the United Kingdom and the self governing colonies. However, it was not until the outbreak of war in 1914 that the self governing colonies definitely moved towards meeting their own defence costs.

THE FRAMEWORK OF BRITISH IMPERIAL HISTORY IN THE NINETEENTH CENTURY

Historians have recently re-considered the traditional framework for discussing the history of nineteenth century British expansion and it is pertinent to summarise their views.

The Traditional Framework

Until the 1950s, historians of British nineteenth century colonial policy closely followed the work of such contempories as C W Dilke Greater Britain (1868), J A Froude Oceana (1886) and J R Seeley The Expansion of England (1883). Late nineteenth and early twentieth century imperial historians adopted and extended these works, and H E Egerton's pioneering study, A Short History of British Colonial Policy (1897), introduced a legalistic approach to imperial history.(79) Egerton's framework was endorsed by other leading commentators in the field, particularly A P Newton and Sir Charles Lucas.(80) Their conception of the Victorian age was divided between a period of separatism in the 1840s to 1870s and the age of belligerent expansion from 1870 to 1900, the era of "new imperialism". The acceptability of this approach was enhanced by the Publication of C A Bodelsen's Studies in Mid-Victorian Imperialism in 1924 and R L Schulyer's The Fall of the Old Colonial System in 1945.(81)

According to this interpretation of British imperial history after the American war of independence and the widespread acceptance of Adam Smith's ideas, British politicians and commentators stressed the economic and political disutility of empire. Any such advantages as were to be gained from the possession of a large empire (for example, prestige) were greatly outweighed by the defence expenditure on behalf of the colonies. Consequently, some historians labelled the period 1850 to 1870 the "age of separatism". In particular, the 1860s were isolated as the decade when separatist ideas and the doctrines of the Manchester School, of which Goldwin Smith was the leading literary figure, reached their peak. The years 1868 to 1870 have been called the "climax of anti-imperialism" for between these years the Prime Minister, Gladstone and his colleague in the Colonial Office,

Lord Granille, attempted to dismantle the empire. Their efforts provoked an outcry and in 1872 Disraeli defended the empire in his famous Crystal Palace speech.

This approach argues that in the 1870s Britain's global position - politically and economically - was less secure, as Germany and America emerged as major industrial competitors. Moreover, along with other European nations, Germany sought overseas areas for her raw materials and manufactured products. Subsequently, Britain became enmeshed in the late Victorian burst of territorial expansion, and fought a war in South Africa. Supported by merchants, missionaries, and philanthropists, British ministers acquired the largest share of the remaining "unoccupied" regions of Africa and the Pacific.

The New Framework

In 1953, Gallagher and Robinson, two Cambridge historians, challenged the traditional approach in a seminal article, "The Imperialism of Free Trade".(82) Distinguishing between "informal" and "formal" empire, they argued that in any economic analysis it was improper to concentrate solely on the areas "painted red" on a map of the world. Hence, they adopted the term "informal empire" to describe the expansion of British commercial and financial power beyond the boundaries of political jurisdiction. They supported their case by pointing out that British economic expansion had been occurring throughout the nineteenth century, mostly without the need for political control. They posited that British imperial policy followed the dictim "trade with informal control if possible; trade with rule when necessary". In the context of Mid-Victorianism, informal techniques were often sufficient to control these ends and any expense associated with formal political control was considered to be a last resort. In a later publication with Alice Denny, Africa and the Victorians, Gallagher and Robinson supported their thesis by investigating the Victorians' motives for partitioning Africa, regarding "the mid-Victorian period as the golden age of British expansion, and the late-Victorian as an age which saw the beginnings of contraction and decline".(83)

The first serious effort at a rebuttal of Gallagher's and Robinson's ideas came from Oliver Macdonagh in an article "The Anti-Imperialism of Free Trade", in which he denied that free trade advocates had ever promoted the growth of "informal" empire.(84) He asserted that the forcible opening of markets contradicted their pacific interpretations as it had exposed the empire and mother country to the risks of war. Macdonagh quoted from Richard Cobden's writings, arguing that Cobden had opposed imperial growth because of his adherence to free trade. Moreover, he attacked the terminology of "formal" and "informal" empire and concluded that Gallagher and Robinson's approach raised new conceptual difficulties.

Macdonagh's position was supported by D C M Platt in his article, "The Imperialism of Free Trade: Some Reservations".(85) While conceding that the British government sought to open the world to trade, Platt denied that British official policy relating to overseas trade and investment was of the form described by Gallagher and Robinson and asserted that in the early Victorian period the government's participation in imperial expansion was minimal. In subsequent articles, Platt rejected the view that the term "informal empire" could apply to those years prior to 1860.(86)

Despite such attacks on Gallagher and Robinson's thesis, contemporary historians such as Eldridge, Fieldhouse and Porter accept the view that there was a fundamental continuity in British overseas trade and territorial expansion throughout the nineteenth century which occurred in uneven bursts for various reasons at different times and in different places.(87) In 1967 Fieldhouse, for example, asserted that no single theory or explanation of imperialism was satisfactory. Rather, he argued that the only possible approach was to begin by investigating the general forces operating within Europe and elsewhere, and then to study each case of annexation as a special problem and the reasons for colonisation.(88) In a later work, Economics and Empire 1830-1914, Fieldhouse contended that late nineteenth century imperialism covered a multiplicity of diverse European responses to urgent and varied problems which happened to arise on the frontiers of European activity in other continents.(89) Gallagher and Robinson's thesis also received support with the publication of B Semmel's The Rise of Free Trade Imperialism in 1970. Semmel sought to consider the character of the "ideology" which underlay the dismantling of the old colonial system and the construction of the Victorian Pax Britannica.(90) He demonstrated that mercantilist assumptions and objections were embodied in the "classic" pre-1914 imperialism and argued that mercantilist ideas were "far from absent" in the thinking of the economists and politicians who erected Britain's free trade system. He concluded that from the standpoint of ideology and "from the perspective of theory and policy no less than from that of activities, it is possible to see continuity, rather than an interlude of anti-imperialism. Indeed, the period of the fall of the old colonial system may be viewed as one of the rise of a free trade imperialism".(91)

NOTES

1. For a discussion of neo-classical economics, see J A Schumpeter, History of Economic Analysis (New York, OUP, 1954), pp.753-1048 and T W Hutchison, Review of Economic Doctrines, op.cit, and the articles in R D C Black, A W Coats and C D W Goodwin, The Marginal Revolution in Economics (Durham, DUP, 1973).

2. See Randolph Churchill, Winston S Churchill (London, Heinemann, 1967), Vol. 1, pp.585.

3. See the Political Economy Club's Revised Report of the

Proceedings of the Dinner of May 31st (London, 1867) and Sir Francis
Galton, "Considerations Adverse to the Maintenance of Section F",
JRSS, 40, Sept 1877, pp.468-73.

4.   J S Mill remained relatively orthodox in his theory of value
and production, but his conclusions on land reform, the social effects
of unregulated competition, the protection of infant industries in new
countries and state sponsored social reforms were similar to the views
of the economic historians.   On Mill's economics, see M Blaug
Ricardian Economics: A Historical Study (New Haven, Conn, 1958),
Ch. 9, and Pedro Schwartz, The New Political Economy of J S Mill
(London, Weidenfeld and Nicolson, 1968).

5.   For a discussion of the marginal revolution see Black, Coats
and Goodwin (eds) The Marginal Revolution in Economics, op.cit.

6.   See D Winch, "Marginalism and the Boundaries of Economic
Science", Ibid, pp.259-77.   Also see Marshall's "Notes on Art or
Science" in Large Red Box, Bundles 2-5, Marshall Papers, Cambridge
University.

7.   J S Mill had earlier attacked the use of mathematics in
economics.   See N B De Marchi, "Mill and Cairnes and the Emergence
of marginalism in England" in Black, Coats and Goodwin (eds), The
Marginal Revolution in Economics, op.cit, pp.78-97.

8.   See R H Coase, "Marshall on Method", JLE, Vol. 18, April
1975, pp.25-32.   Marshall thought that J N Keynes' Scope and Method
of Political Economy (London, Macmillan, 1917 ed) gave insufficient
weight to the historical elements in economics.   See T W Hutchison A
Review of Economic Doctrines, op.cit, pp.62-85.   Also see the
discussion in Ch. 6, pp.113-115.

9.   See John Maloney, "Marshall, Cunningham and the Emerging
Profession of Economics", EHR, 1976, pp.440-451;   A W Coats,
"Sociological Aspects of British Economic Thought, (1880-1930)", JPE,
75, Oct 1967, pp.706-729.

10.   For present purposes economic theory is considered to be the
derivation of abstract principles from economic phenomena; economic
history the objective study of past economic events; and applied
economics the study of contemporary economic issues for the
formation of economic policy.

11.   For Marshall's feelings at the establishment of the London
School of Economics, see A W Coats, "Alfred Marshall and the Early
Development of the London School of Economics: Some Unpublished
Letters", Economica, Vol. 36, pp.408-417.   For a discussion of the
development of economic history, see N B Harte (ed), The Study of
Economic History: Collected Inaugural Lectures 1893-1970 (London,
Cass, 1971).   On the development of the Cambridge Economic Tripos,
see John Maloney "Marshall, Cunningham and the Emerging
Economics Profession", op.cit, passim.

12.   See T W Hutchison, A Review of Economic Doctrines, op.cit,
pp.63-64.   In 1885 Foxwell claimed that half the economic chairs in
the United Kingdom were occupied by Marshall's pupils.   Quoted in
A W Coats, "Sociological Aspects of British Economic Thought",
op.cit, pp.707.

13.   See A W Coats, "Political Economy and the Tariff Reform

Campaign of 1903", JLE, Vol. 11, April 1968, pp.181-229, especially p.184.

14. See M E Townsend, The Origins of Modern German Colonialism 1871-1885 (New York, Columbia, 1921), passim.

15. B R Mitchell and P Deane, Abstract of British Historical Statistics (Cambridge, CUP, 1962), Table 2, p.6.

16. See R S Walshaw Migration to and from the British Isles, Problems and Policies (London, Jonathon Cape, 1961), pp.32-3. It has also been observed that a complex and changing relationship existed between the fluctuations in economic activity and the flow of emigrants in the nineteenth century. Jerome found that the inflow into the United States was dominated by conditions of employment in America. See Harry Jerome, Immigration and Business Cycles (New York, National Bureau of Economic Research, 1926), p.208. Brinley Thomas argued that evidence suggested that a noticeable change occurred in the American economy just after the civil war, with the effect of changing the direction of the lag between immigration and economic activity in the United States. See B Thomas, Migration and Economic Growth (Cambridge, CUP, 1973) pp.160-4.

17. For a discussion of this see I Kravis, "Trade as a Handmaiden of Growth", EJ, Vol. 80, No. 320, December 1970, pp.850-70.

18. For a discussion of these trends see M B Brown, The Economics of Imperialism, op.cit, p.142.

19. See D H Aldcroft and H W Richardson, The British Economy 1870-1939 (London, Macillan, 1969), pp.30-31, 80; and S B Saul, Studies in British Overseas Trade (Liverpool, LUP, 1960), p.150.

20. W Schlote, British Overseas Trade, op.cit, Tables 20, 22, 23.

21. See Cambridge History of the British Empire, op.cit, Vol. III, p.460 and R Pares, "The Economic Factors in the History of the Empire", EHR, Vol. III, No. 2, May 1937, pp.119-144.

22. See Matthew Simon, "The Pattern of the New British Portfolio Foreign Investment, 1965-1914", in A R Hall (ed), The Export of Capital from Britain 1870-1914 (London, Methuen, 1972), pp.15-45.

23. Ibid, p.26. Another aspect of the development of the international economy before 1914 was that capital outflows from Britain were closely associated with outflows of labour. See B Thomas, Migration and Economic Growth, op.cit. and his Migration and Urban Development, (London, Methuen and Co, 1972).

24. Sir George Paish, "Great Britain's Investments in Other Lands", JRSS, Vol. LXXI, September 1909, pp.456-80.

25. M Simon, "The Pattern of New British Portfolio Foreign Investment", op.cit, pp.25-31.

26. H Feis, Europe: The World's Banker (New Haven, Yale UP, 1930), p.27.

27. See Simon, "The Pattern of New British Portfolio Investment", op.cit, pp.25-31.

28. Ibid, p.26.

29. F Hilgert, Industrialisation and Foreign Trade (London, Longmans, 1945) pp.13.

30. A E Kahn, Great Britain and the World Economy (London,

Pitman, 1946) p.72.,

31. Commentators have frequently argued that the achievement of free trade was a direct result of the principles of classical political economy. However, one should not over-simplify the relationship between economic ideas and policy "for while textbook writers take it for granted that the Repeal of the Corn Laws in 1846 represented a victory for classical doctrine, it can be shown that the prevailing economic orthodoxy was a positive embarrassment to Cobden and his fellow members of the so-called Manchester School". (A W Coats (ed), The Classical Economists and Economic Policy (London, Methuen 1971), p.28) The classical economists were either opposed or indifferent to the campaign launched by the Anti-Corn law league and there "was no close correspondence between the ideas of the Manchester School and those of the classical economists". (W D Grampp, The Manchester School of Economics (London, OUP, 1960), p.33)

32. Tariffs were utilised by colonial governments before full self government was granted to raise revenue for government purposes.

33. See Ronald S Russell, Imperial Preference (London, Empire Economic Union, 1947).

34. See The Times of 27.10.1869 and the Pall Mall Gazette of 2/9/1869.

35. E Parrett, Sixty Years of Protection in Canada (Toronto, TUP, 1961) pp.286, 358-9.

36. Se B Semmel, Imperialism and Social Reform, op.cit, pp.88-9.

37. See Lord Bateman's letter to The Times of 13/11/1877.

38. See Cambridge History of the British Empire, Vol. III, op.cit, pp.413-22.

39. See F W Hirst, From Adam Smith to Philip Snowden: A History of Free Trade (London, Fisher Unwin, 1925), p.46.

40. See for example, G Goshen in Hansard, 3rd Series, Vol. 350, Col. 932-40, 17/2/1891.

41. The United Empire Trade League was founded in February 1891. Its intention was to draw together all elements of British opinion favouring the use of tariffs to serve imperial interests. See Semmel Imperialism and Social Reform, op.cit, p.108.

42. Chamberlain had become the leader of a movement which had gathered momentum for more than a decade. See B H Brown, The Tariff Reform Movement in Great Britain 1881-1885 (New York, Columbia UP, 1943). On Chamberlain see J L Garvin, The Life of Joseph Chamberlain (London, Macmillan 1932-34). Chamberlain's specific proposals were contained in a speech delivered in Glasgow on 6/10/1903. See C W Boyd, Speeches of Joseph Chamberlain (London, Constable, 1943), Vol. 2, pp.158-59.

43. J L Garvin, The Life of Chamberlain op.cit, Vol. 4, pp.523-8.

44. See H W McCready, "Alfred Marshall and Tariff Reform", JPE, Vol. 65, pp.259-67.

45. See A W Coats, "Political Economy and the Tariff Reform Campaign of 1903, JLE, Vol. 11, April 1968, pp.181-229.

46. See Semmel, Imperialism and Social Reform, op.cit, pp.101-102.

47. Winston Churchill believed that tariff reformers would destroy the Conservative party as it was and lead to "corruption at home, aggression to cover it up abroad, the trickery of tariff juggles, the tyranny of a party machine; sentiment by the bucketful; patriotism by the imperial pint; the open hand at the public exchequer, the open door at the public house, dear food for the millions, cheap labour for the millionaire". See Parl Debates, 4th Series, CXXIII 194, May 28, 1903.

48. See A W Coats, "Political Economy and the Tariff Reform Campaign of 1903", JLE, Vol. II, April 1968, pp.181-229.

49. See A W Coats, "The Role of Authority in the Development of British Economics", JLE, Vol. 7, 1964, pp.85-106, especially pp.99-101.

50. See H W McCready, "Alfred Marshall and Tariff Reform", JPE, Vol. 63, June 1955, pp.259-67.

51. See Coats, "The Role of Authority in the Development of British Economics", op.cit, pp.100-101.

52. On this general point see M Barrat Brown, The Economics of Imperialism, op.cit, pp.156-170.

53. See Parl Paper, 1907, LV cd 3406, p.29; Parl Papers, LIV cd 5741, p.17.

54. See The Cambridge History of the British Empire, op.cit, Vol. 2, pp.442-67.

55. J A Marriott, The Evolution of the British Empire and Commonwealth, (London, Nicholson and Watson, 1939), pp.300-310.

56. See Hansard, Third Series, 1165, p.1060.

57. Cambridge History of the British Empire, op.cit, Vol. 3, pp.201-2.

58. See J E Tyler, The Struggle for Imperial Unity 1868-95 (London, Longmans, 1938).

59. See Bodelsen, Studies in Mid-Victorian Imperialism, op.cit, pp.205-14.

60. Ibid, p.208.

61. Ibid, pp.206-214.

62. Adam Smith, The Wealth of Nations, op.cit, pp.207-214, 583-7.

63. For a discussion of this matter see D Winch, Adam Smith's Politics: An Essay in Historiographic Revision (London, CUP, 1978), Ch. 7, "The Present Disturbances", pp.146-163 and Classical Political Economy and the Colonies, op.cit, pp.14-17. Also see the discussion in Ch. 7 pp.156-160.

64. Smith, The Wealth of Nations, op.cit, p.587.

65. See J Hume, Hansard III, 6, p.10, 16/8/1831. Also see Hugh Egerton, Speeches of William Molesworth (London, Tonebridge, 1903), p.315.

66. H Clinton, Suggestions Towards the Organisation of the British Empire by Realising the Parliamentary Representation of all Home and Colonial Interests (London, Smith Elder and Co, 1856). J C Meekins, Parliamentary Reform. Should the Colonies be Represented? (London, Macmillan, 1859).

67. See Bodelsen, Studies in Mid-Victorian Imperialism, op.cit, p.133.

68. Ibid, pp.135-6.

69. Ibid, p.138.

70. On the failure of the imperial federation movement, see Ibid, pp.206-14. Also see the Cambridge History of the British Empire, op.cit, Vol. 3, pp.179-180.

71. Bodelsen, Studies in Mid-Victorian Imperialism, op.cit, pp.20-24.

72. Gladstone believed that colonies should provide for their own defence and be financially self supporting. See J Morley, The Life of Gladstone, (London, Lloyd, 1908), Vol. 1, pp.676-677.

73. See Cambridge History of the British Empire, op.cit, pp.235, 403-429.

74. See Parl Papers, 1887, LVI cd 4091, pp.213-230; Parl Papers, 1888, III, cd 346, pp.369-70.

75. B Mallet, British Budgets (London, Macmillan, 1913), p.8.

76. Ibid, p.466.

77. See Hansard, 4th Series, LXXVI, p.435; LXXXVII, p.831, CXLII, p.805.

78. See Parl Papers, 1890, XIX, CD 5979, p.xxiv; 1888, LXVII, cd 5304; 1904, XL, cd 1789, pp.1333-4.

79. See C W Dilke, Greater Britain (London, Macmillan, 1868); J A Froude, Oceana (London, Longmans, Green, 1886); J R Seeley, The Expansion of England (London, Macmillan, 1883); H E Egerton, A Short History of British Colonial Policy (London, Methuen, 1897).

80. See for example, A P Newton, A Hundred Years of the British Empire (London, Duckworth, 1940).

81. See C A Bodelsen, Studies in Mid-Victorian Imperialism, op.cit, and R L Schulyer, The Fall of the Old Colonial System (New York, OUP, 1945).

82. J Gallagher and R Robinson, "The Imperialism of Free Trade", EHR, 1953, pp.1-15.

83. R Robinson and J Gallagher with Alice Denny, Africa and the Victorians: The Official Mind of Imperialism (London, Macillan, 1961), p.471.

84. O Macdonagh, "The Anti-Imperialism of Free Trade", EHR, 2nd Series, Vol. XIV, 1962, pp.489-501.

85. D C M Platt, "The Imperialism of Free Trade: Some Reservations"., EHR, 2nd Series, Vol. XXI, 1968, pp.296-306.

86. Platt, "Further Objections to an 'Imperialism of Free Trade', 1830-60", EHR, 2nd Series, Vol. XXVI, 1973, pp.77-91, and "The National Economy and British Imperial Expansion before 1914", Journal of Imperial and Commonwealth History, Vol. II, 1973, pp.3-14.

87. C C Eldridge, Victorian Imperialism (London, Hodder and Stoughton, 1978); D K Fieldhouse, Economics and Empire, 1830-1914 (London, Weidenfeld and Nicholson, 1973) and B Porter, The Lion's Share: A Short History of British Imperialism 1850-1970 (London, Longman, 1975).

88. See D K Fieldhouse (ed), The Theory of Capitalist Imperialism (London, Longmans, 1967), pp.192-3.

89. Fieldhouse, Economics and Empire, 1830-1914, op.cit.

90. B Semmel, The Rise of Free Trade Imperialism (Cambridge,

CUP, 1970).
     91. Ibid, p.5.

SECTION TWO

THE SHADOW OF J S MILL: THE 1860s ECONOMISTS

Chapter 4

J S MILL'S CRITICS: GOLDWIN SMITH AND J E T ROGERS

GOLDWIN SMITH

Introduction

During his life-time Goldwin Smith became known as the leading literary exponent of the Manchester School, and in this capacity exerted a strong influence not only on the imperial views of J E Cairnes and J E T Rogers, but also on many writers after 1863, the year Smith's article series in the Daily News were published as a book - Empire.(1) Although most of his life was spent as a journalist, Smith began his working life as an academic and lawyer. After five brilliant years at Eton, he matriculated at Christ Church College, Oxford, in 1841, but transferred to Magdalen the following year when he won a demyship to the college. In 1845 he obtained a first in Literae Humaniores and graduated the winner of several of the available academic laurels, including the Hertford Scholarship in Latin verse and an English Essay.(2) Subsequently he became a Fellow in Civil Law at University College, and was also called to the bar at Lincoln's Inn.

Through his joint-secretaryship on the 1850-1852 Commission of Inquiry into the state of Oxford University, Smith met numerous politicians and influential people including Lord John Russell, Gladstone, Peel, Thackeray and Carlyle. Meanwhile his reputation as a journalist and commentator on questions of the day grew and he became a founder-member of the newly established Saturday Review, which was launched in November 1855. Among his colleagues were Henry Maine, William Vernon Harcourt, James Fitzjames Stephen and Lord Robert Cecil. The editor of the Review, John Douglas Cook, considered Smith the "most brilliant and trustworthy member of his staff with the most effective pen".(3) During these years (1845-1858), Smith not only formulated his radical liberal beliefs, but he also coveted the Regius Professorship of Modern History at Oxford, and in 1859 was elected to the Chair. In his inaugural lecture, he advocated broadening the course of study at the university so as to train students not only in classics, philosophy and mathematics, but also in such modern   subjects   as   science,   jurisprudence,   political economy and history, particularly England's political history.(4) He resigned the Chair in 1866 to care for his father who was suffering from mental illness. Shortly after his father's suicide Smith visited the United States and accepted a Professorship at the newly created Cornell University where he stayed for three years, from 1868 to 1871. Subsequently he settled in Canada and remained there till his death in 1910, although he frequently travelled to the United Kingdom and published widely in the British press.(5)

Smith wrote on a diverse range of social, political, economic and ethical topics. A radical in his political ideology, Smith became the leading literary exponent of the Manchester School. Strictly speaking the Manchester School was a group of businessmen who campaigned for the repeal of the British corn laws and the establishment of free trade. Although the School did not have a complete or consistent doctrine, it had firm ideas about particular problems, the most important of which was the effect of free trade in grain.(6) Its members chiefly attacked any form of protection and their beliefs gave them a strong bias against the maintenance and retention of colonies. The School's leaders, Cobden and Bright, favoured colonial emancipation and advocated financial retrenchment. Bright believed the costs of defence were excessive.(7) To Cobden, the colonies imposed a military burden on the mother country which the nation could not afford.(8) Both were against any form of wars, believing that the best hope for the world's peace and the general happiness of mankind lay with free trade and the gradual erosion of national barriers. Moreover, Cobden's and Bright's personalities and ideas lived on after their deaths, especially in the Cobden Club and through the publication of their speeches.(9) Smith continued to popularise their work, for he accepted the essential ingredient of Manchesterism - the policy of government non-intervention.

Whilst Smith published numerous articles, his most important work, at least in terms of the present study, was Empire.(10) The book, published at Cobden's urgent pleas, combined letters written to the Daily News during 1862-63. In the preface of Empire, Smith carefully distinguished between "empire" and colonies, which he considered to be regions where the inhabitants enjoyed the principles of self-government. By contrast, the term empire was taken "in a wide sense, as including all that nations hold beyond their own shores and waters by arms of dominion, as opposed to that natural influence which a great power, though confining itself to its own territory always exercises in the world".(11) In this definition, Smith was not referring to an accepted terminology; he was attempting to create his own usage, and he viewed empire as including a critical survey of colonial, Indian and external appendages.

Economic Disutility of Empire: Trade and Emigration

In an effort to discredit the leading proponents of empire, Smith attached the view that trade followed the flag, and attempted to demonstrate that colonial trade was not thriving as much as trade with non-empire countries, particularly in the 1860s.(12) Thinking along similar lines to Cornewall Lewis, a former Chancellor of the Exchequer whose book, The Government of Dependencies (1841) did much to revive the early nineteenth century scepticism towards the utility of colonies, Smith contended that the arguments relating to the extent of colonial trade and the capital invested therein proved nothing unless it was possible to show that the trade itself was in some degree dependent on the "continuance of the political connection".(13) In this context, he rejected the Times' analysis of the increased trade with the Australian colonies for he felt that the expansion of colonial trade was a direct result of economic, not political forces.

> The obvious cause of the increase of exports to the Australian colonies is that the group of markets in Australia has been actually undergoing numerical expansion, not to mention the discoveries of gold; while, as new communities these Colonies have necessarily for the time to import every description of manufacture.(14)

Goldwin Smith thus posed the problem of how far the pattern of development of a colonial territory stemmed from its distinctively colonial features. He needed a comprehensive theory of economic development in order to produce a convincing argument. This was not, however, his purpose, as he was primarily interested in demonstrating that the colonies conferred no great benefits upon the mother country, and that she would be better off without them. Smith's arguments on colonial trade - like those of Cobden and Bright - were tied to his political conviction that the colonies should be separated from the mother country.(15) This restricted his economic analysis and resulted in a loss of any extensive interpretation of the nature of the colonial economy and its implications for the United Kingdom.

Like J A Roebuck and Arthur Mills, Smith referred to the migration statistics which, he claimed, demonstrated that most British emigrants travelled to the United States, and not the British Empire.(16) This he believed, reinforced the case for colonial emancipation. Moreover, like Rogers and Fawcett, he regretted that it was the young, vigorous and healthy members of the British population who emigrated.(17)

Smith's discussion on trade and emigration revealed an awareness of the writings of Herman Merivale who, while professor of political economy at Oxford, published his widely acclaimed Lectures on Colonies and Colonization in 1841. Subsequently Merivale joined the Colonial Office where he became permanent Under-Secretary of State for Colonies from 1847 to 1859, and his popular Lectures were re-published in 1861.(18) Smith had accepted Merivale's position that the empire was not an outlet for surplus population, a viewpoint which Merivale subsequently renounced. Towards the end of his life, and after thirty years of substantial migration, Merivale adopted Wakefield's argument, abandoning his earlier views, and in so doing, producing some genuinely interesting ideas. Initially, he did not attempt to construct a dynamic theory, simply stating that emigration was no remedy for over-population unless it was on a large scale and continually repeated.(19)

> Any single emigration, however large, can have no permanent effect in checking the undue increase of numbers unless it be followed either by increased forethought, or by an increase in the productiveness of labour; and either the one or the other of these causes must initially have produced the same effect on the progress of the population only in a somewhat longer time, as if there had been no emigration at all.(20)

By 1862, however, Merivale was arguing that the mother country could derive two direct economic benefits from her colonial empire: "first, the superior productiveness of capital and labour when applied to a new soil; secondly, the relief which emigration affords to the pressure of population on subsistence".(21) He now contended that emigration provided an outlet for the United Kingdom's excess population and, in contrast to the French, the English did not have to place constraints on their marriage by marrying later or having fewer children.(22) Merivale's opinions permanently changed not because of any economic analysis, or awareness of birth rate movements, but as a direct consequence of his Malthusian fears and the American civil war.

> Few, I think, have at all realised the nature and magnitude of the evil which is impending over us from the closing even for a time, of that outlet for our superabundant population. For it is most important to observe that its great value arose not only from its largeness, but from its extensive regularity of action. It was a safety valve always open, and expanding and contracting almost to our wish. Periods of comparative depression here, such as rendered emigration more desirable, were seldom coincident with periods of comparative depression in the United States; and indeed the broad West hardly knew depression at all.(23)

Merivale raises here, in a slipshod manner, a complex and much debated question.(24) He did not elaborate the logic of his ideas and his view of emigration as a "safety valve" went unnoticed, but his opinions on the loss of the United States as an area for the excess of Britain's population did not. Smith attacked Merivale's article in a letter to the editor of the Daily News in October 1862. To Smith, Merivale's position that the colonies were the only sure outlet for emigration was at variance with the fact that emigration from the United Kingdom to the United States was "greater by two-thirds than to all our dependencies (colonies) put together".(25) Smith particularly challenged Merivale's argument that the United States would be closed to British emigrants for a long time because of the civil war. He argued that instead of the falling-off of emigration to the United States, which Merivale assumed, there was a large increase in 1862 in spite of the confusions and ravages of the war. Smith's accurate quotation of the migration statistics to the United States (especially in 1862) may have demolished Merivale's case.(26) However, Smith ignored the potential force of Merivale's ideas and the implications of the civil war for long-term British emigration to the United States.

The General Costs and Benefits of the Colonial Connection

Though he did not make a comprehensive quantitative case against the empire, Smith's work on the value of the British empire covered all the major aspects of the question. Thinking along similar lines to Lewis, Mills and Roebuck, Smith was not simply content to demonstrate the economic disutility of empire by reviewing questions of trade, capital and emigration. Rather, he wished to counter every conceivable argument which had been used to justify the British empire or could so be used in the future. His ideas, which were more political than economic, amounted to a concerted and consistent attack on those wishing to maintain British dominance and political control over the colonies.(27)

Aligning himself with the Mid-Victorian critics of empire, Smith argued that the defence of the empire was a source of great weakness to the mother country, which bore all the costs of the necessary arrangements. The empire exposed the United Kingdom's defensive weakness, as the expanse of empire made it impossible to concentrate military forces in Europe and British possession of other lands constantly involved risk of entanglements with foreign powers.(28) Throughout his work, he re-emphasised the high costs of the empire's defence arrangements, though only in the case of the Ionian Islands and Malta did he stipulate the costs of the defences. Furthermore, he ignored any military or naval advantages which could accrue from the possession of a large empire.

While Smith was a keen and frequent advocate of colonial emancipation, he was extremely hostile to those recently proclaimed self-governing colonies which erected tariff barriers against the mother country, asserting that they "did not obey British law, did not contribute to British armaments and are at liberty even to wage commercial war against the mother country by laying protective duties on her goods".(29) Like Rogers, Smith vehemently attacked J S Mill's application of the infant industry case to the British colonies.(30) Like Cobden, he viewed protection as an act of war, whereas free trade was an article of faith. The only possible justification he saw for protection was the colonies' urgent need for ready cash.(31) Smith's adherance to free trade principles was rooted in Cobdenite orthodoxy and steeped in the essentials of Manchesterism, and his free trade conviction so blinded him that he was unwilling to consider that the doctrine might not be applicable to all times and situations.(32)

In addition to the more strictly economic considerations of empire, Smith also considered the non-economic motives for stressing the colonial connections. Smith's views correspond closely with those of James Mill and Cornewall Lewis, who believed that the ruling classes fostered distant colonies as a source of patronage and a means of providing for their dependents.(33) He also considered the case for empire which involved national pride and, arguing along similar lines to J S Mill and Roebuck, he constantly denounced this rationale, claiming that it was only the militaristic classes who experienced direct pride in empire.(34)

Despite all his cries for colonial emancipation, in keeping with other critics of empire, Smith was proud of the British contributions to the growth of Anglo-Saxonism in the world. He argued that "though the sun may set on England's military empire, morning in its course around the world, will forever be greeted in the Anglo-Saxon tongue and the sun will never set on Anglo-Saxon greatness".(35) Moreover, Smith profoundly believed that the British empire of ideas, literature and political institutions had no peer in history, maintaining that the chief future interest of English history would lie in the fact that Great Britain was the source of political and social institutions transplanted to new lands. This power to establish such institutions was a uniquely Anglo-Saxon gift, and he regarded the United States as the greatest achievement of his race.(36)

Smith did not undertake a systematic study of the rise of new imperialism after 1870.(37) Nevertheless, there is a close parallel between his ideas and those of the late nineteenth century critics of imperialism for he was bitterly opposed to militarism and war.(38) He did not believe that the United Kingdom needed an empire for defence purposes and was extremely depressed by the United Kingdom's role in the Boer War, especially the mass slaughter of African tribes. Moreover, he decried those Americans who were taking up the white man's burden in the Philippines, when they neglected the millions of oppressed blacks in the Southern United States.(39) In short, he believed that no nation was sufficiently moral to be able to govern other peoples for the benefit of the governed.(40)

Imperial Federation and the Union of Anglo-Saxonism

Although Smith was living in Canada when the popular discussion on imperial federation broke out in the United Kingdom in the 1880s, he was a keen and frequent contributor to the debate.(41) Smith postulated that imperial federation was largely an English chimera based on an essential misunderstanding of the real strength of colonial nationalism.(42) Upon this claim of colonial nationalism Smith remained totally opposed to all schemes of political unification refusing either to acknowledge any merits in them or to enter into discussion on the form and content of the various schemes. However, he was particularly scathing towards those commentators who argued that there was an "institutional" unity in the empire:

> If the institutions of the colonies are directly opposed to those of the mother country in religions, in politics and in trade; if, while we have a high electoral qualification, and an aristocratic parliament, they have manhood suffrage and democratic assemblies; if, while we proclaim free trade as the principle of our commercial system, they pass measures of protection, in what does "the unity of the empire" consist?(43)

Using similar arguments to Cobden and Bright, Smith felt that if there was any unity in the empire it was intimately connected to the "bonds of blood and language", and hoped that when the colonies "were nations, something in the nature of a great Anglo-Saxon federation may in substance, if not in form, spontaneously arise out of affinity and mutual affection".(44) In line with both critics and advocates of empire, Smith pointed out that in such an Anglo-Saxon federation the United States would play an important role, since Americans were "intimately related" to the English. In his will, in leaving the bulk of his 700,000 pounds estate to Cornell University, Smith stated his desire

> to show my attachment to the University, in the foundation of which I had the honour of taking part; to pay respect to the memory of Ezra Cornell, and to show my attachment as an Englishman to the union of the two branches of our race on this continent with each other, and with their common mother.(45)

India

Like most commentators on empire, Smith felt that the United Kingdom had a duty to uplift the Indians, although such a task was extremely difficult. He felt that there were numerous problems to be resolved - including how to improve the standard of living, raise the populace to Western values, and infuse the Western spirit of justice and property into the native policemen and legal officials.(46) He believed that the "material value of the possession is, after all, secondary to its moral value as a field of achievement".(47) On the other hand, Britain was directly responsible for substantial gains to the Indian economy.

> To strike the balance of profit and loss, either on the side of the conqueror or on that of the conquered, would not be easy. India has long ceased to be to the conqueror a field of plunder. She has never paid tribute; but she has furnished honourable appointments, with high salaries and pensions, to a great number of Englishmen. Her public works have given employment to others. English capital has been profitably invested in her railways. Her trade, though opened by the liberal policy of Great Britain to the whole world, has been practically for the most part in British hands. That she has supplied England with great men

has been said, but is not the fact, since the man who has spent the prime of his life in India is not good for much when he comes home. Some British generals, Wellington among the number, have been trained in Indian fields. On the wrong side of the balance sheet are the expense and danger of holding and guarding this distant, and in itself defenceless, empire.(48)

In the same way as the Utilitarians had argued, Smith reasoned that the British domestic political party disagreements on Indian policy impaired the government of India. The parties suffered from their connections with India, and engaged in corrupt practices and lavish occasions, and degraded themselves all in the name of uplifting the natives. However, Smith did not want the British to leave India, for that would be followed by anarchy.

About keeping India, there is no question. England has a real duty there, she has undertaken a great work and stands pledged before the world to perform it. She has vast interests and investments. Her departure would condemn Hindustan to the sanguinary and plundering anarchy from which her advent rescued it.(49)

Conclusion

Among the mid-nineteenth century critics of empire, Smith was the most vociferous and popular. A self-proclaimed Manchester radical, he captured Cobden's and Bright's misgivings over the colonial connections and his writings influenced separatist sentiments well into the twentieth century. More often than not, he produced non-economic arguments against Britain maintaining her imperial connections. Moreover, his firm enunciation of the economic as well as the political disutility of empire won supporters in Cairnes, Fawcett and Rogers.(50) But Smith's influence was not confined to his immediate peers, and his ideas on united Anglo-Saxonism, the benefits, costs and complexities of Indian rule, were echoed throughout the nineteenth century by economists such as Marshall and Hobson.(51)

J E T ROGERS

Introduction

J E T Rogers (1823-1890) was "one of the founders of modern British economic history", and "a vigorous and versatile scholar whose forceful personality and uninhibited political partisanship directly affected his academic career".(52) His tertiary education began at King's College London, but he went up to Magdalen Hall (now Hertford College) in 1846 with the intention of entering the Anglican Church. As an undergraduate he was described as "loud, dominating and a rapid talker". This did not stop him from obtaining a first in Greek philosophy and literature in 1848, the year he was ordained a deacon. Six years later he became a priest and married the second daughter of Henry Revell Reynolds, who was the solicitor to the Treasury.(53)

Rogers' quarrelsome personality and his radical political views meant that he experienced great difficulty in finding an Oxford college which would take him as a tutor. His interests had moved from the classics to economics, politics and statistics and in 1859 he was elected as the first Tooke Professor of Statistics and Economic Science at Kings College, London. In 1862, upon the death of Professor Neats, he was elected Oxford's Professor of Political Economy. However, he lost his position in 1868 when a vigorous campaign was mounted against him.(54)

Rogers' bluff manner and radical proposals for university reform caused alarm in more conservative circles and resulted in numerous opponents. A reformer, he urged a larger role for political economy at the expense of classical studies and clashed with Henry Wall, the Wykeham Professor of Logic, who was a staunch opponent of such new studies. Rogers urged that "instutions are to be valued by their direct general utility, and that they should be examined sceptically".(55) Rogers was openly critical of Oxford education and he excoriated landlordism in a University whose colleges were largely dependent on landed endowments. He was a foundation member of the National Liberal Club and was a President of the Oxford Reform Society, which stood for manhood suffrage, a redistribution of seats, the ballot and the payment of all election expenses from the local rates.(56) In short, Rogers' personality, political activities and beliefs led to his adversaries successfully canvassing against his reappointment to the Chair of Political Economy in 1868, despite the belated attempt by Goldwin Smith (the late Regius Professor of Modern History) to win support for Rogers.(57)

After losing the Chair, Rogers campaigned even more vigorously for the radical liberal cause, and was a leading supporter of the Clerical Disabilities Relief Act of 1870, becoming the first former cleric to enter Parliament. After standing unsuccessfully as a candidate for Scarborough and Bermondsey, he became the member of Southwark from 1880 to 1885. He was "neither a conspicuously successful nor active parliamentarian" for he continued to live in Oxford and pursue his scholarly activities.(58) However, he established a number of influential political allies, and upon Bonamy Price's death in 1888 was re-elected to the Oxford Professorship.

It appears the election was in the hands of a small number of persons, of whom the Chancellor of the University, Lord Salisbury was one. In the absence of Mr Goschen, who as Chancellor of the Exchequer is an ex-officio member of the electoral body, the members were equally divided in the choice of two candidates, of whom Professor Rogers was one. When Mr Goschen arrived upon the scene, it is said, he at once declared, without wanting to hear the views of his colleagues, that Rogers was the only man for the Chair.(59)

But Rogers retained numerous enemies and his death in 1890 was greeted by some commentators as "a pleasant event", since he had contributed "nothing to man's well-being".(60) Twenty years earlier, in 1870, an Oxford scholar had written to Rogers, "I don't know you; I don't want to know you ... You have become a public menace, ... But you are not a politician, nor a historian".(61)

Politics and Economics

Rogers' political and economic beliefs were closely intertwined. Politically, he was a follower of Cobden, whose sister had married Rogers' elder brother. To Rogers, Cobden was "the most farsighted statesman the country had produced".(62) Like Cobden, Rogers had a passionate aversion to the landed system, and was hostile to all forms of privilege. He firmly believed in government non-intervention in social and political life, and upheld free trade principles.(63) Generally speaking, there were two grounds for government interference. "1. The protection of the weak against the strong. 2. The development of such national powers and resources as could not struggle into usefulness except under patronage".(64)

> The economist postulates that the law should bestow no exceptional advantage on any industrial agent, should put no hindrance in the way of anyone who would lay out his share to the best advantage. Freedom in opinion, freedom in innocent action, freedom of exchange, are, in my view, personal rights which it is utterly immoral and unjust to violate on any plea whatever but the public safety; and even then the hindrance should be morally and obviously necessary, exceptional and temporary.(65)

As a parliamentarian, Rogers spoke infrequently in the House, though he was often called to order. During his maiden speech, which was in support of Bradlough's refusal to take the religious oath, the speaker reprimanded him for his sharp tongue.(66) Like Cobden, his most characteristic politics were his attacks upon the aristocracy.(67) Rogers was rarely constructive in the House, and his most notable achievement was when he carried an important resolution pledging parliament to reform local taxation. On the other hand, he had found parliament most instructive and felt "profoundly thankful to the Southwark electors for my experience".(68) To Rogers, the economist and politician shared common concerns:

> Now, though an economist should abstain from the criticism of political action, he always has to discuss social motives and practices, to search into the causes which bring about the former, and to predict the consequences which follow from the latter. The economist and the politician are equally busied with human society, but the function of the economist is limited by

observation and analysis, that of the politician is to proceed to action.(69)

As a scholar, Rogers was governed by his strong likes and dislikes and he made numerous scathing and bitter attacks on Ricardo, Malthus and J S Mill.(70) All three were "metaphysical economists", and "the only prediction which you can make about the conclusions of a metaphysical economist, is that he is almost certain to be in the wrong".(71) Ricardo's theory of rent and Malthus' theory of population were examples "of metaphysics and crude economics".(72) By "metaphysics", Rogers meant that the economists had evolved "their conclusions from their own conciousness, or from unproved generalisations, or from vague hints of tendencies".(73) However, Rogers' Manual of Political Economy was only partly heretical, even though he stated in the preface that it expressed widely diverging views from the accepted economics of his day.

> There is, I believe, reason to differ from some of the views generally entertained by economists on the subject of Population, Rent, Wages, Profit, and one or two other cognate terms .... The ordinary theory of Rent is not historically supported by the facts which it has arrived, and the theory of Population is closely connected with that of Rent.(74)

The Manual's arrangement was modelled on Mill's Principles or Fawcett's catechism of Mill. As a free trader, Rogers was more orthodox than Mill.(75) Like Malthus, he felt that a solution for the English poor could only be achieved through thrift and the free-play of market forces. Though expressing adherence to popular political economy in his Manual, Rogers also claimed to reject both the Ricardian theory of rent and Malthus' law of population.(76) He outlined an unsophisticated labour theory of value and provided an implicit defence of the wage-fund theory. He explicitly agreed with Ricardo that distributional problems were the keystone of political economy.(77) In the preface to A History of Agricultural Prices, he noted that it was "to no real purpose to learn the lesson by which wealth is produced unless we are also ready to leave to their natural freedom those agencies by which wealth is distributed".(78)

Rogers published numerous books on a diverse range of economic subjects in which he claimed to have rejected the a priori approach of the Ricardo school and, in its place, invoked 'economic induction'. He wanted to abandon 'that metaphysical approach' to the subject and replace it with an abundance of statistical information. Rogers insisted that there was a need to base economic principles on an exhaustive examination of facts and he felt that the reputation of political economists had suffered because of "their slovenliness in regard to facts"(79) These made him an ally of the historical economists who attacked the doctrines and methods of classical political theory in the 1870s and 1880s.

He claimed that Adam Smith possessed an "inductive mind to the highest degree", and that by applying the historical method, he was following Smith's tradition.(80) Rogers seemed to believe that exhaustive statistical research in economic history would eventually lead to a scientific interpretation of history.(81) In his review of Cliffe Leslie's Essays in Philosophy, he aligned himself with the historical economists and attacked the deductive school's doctrines on wages, population, rent and profit.(82) To Rogers, historical enquiry was essential for solving contemporary problems. In Work and Wages, he pointed out that

> the peoples of this country have become what they are by reason of events and acts which it is the duty of the genuine economist to discover, as contrasted with the economist who constructs a system out of a few axioms and a multitude of postulates.(83)

However, Rogers did not dispense with the deductive method or many of the conclusions of Ricardian economics, despite his attacks on the hypothetical method.

> I have the greatest aversion to the introduction of hypothetical cases into a subject like Political Economy, in which a flaw in the reasoning, an error in induction, has often had serious consequences.(84)

Rogers' dislike of the deductive approach resulted in a great deal of patient statistical research on wages and prices covering six centuries and resulted in the publication of A History of Agriculture and Prices.(85) His interest in the history of prices had at first been aroused by a discussion of wages and prices at an international statistical conference in Brussels in 1860.(86) Subsequently, he published Six Centuries of Work and Wages (1884), which enjoyed a generation of popularity as a text for friendly societies and trade unions.(87)

Rogers' detailed quantitative research led him to argue that the orthodox theory of rent, which was interlinked to that of population, was not historically supported by the facts and he asserted that "rent was originally, and for centuries, a tax (on the 'surplus' of agricultural production), imposed by the strong on the weak". Rent was the result of agricultural productivity and was dependent upon the skill of the tenant and the improvement of the land.(88) Rogers also condemned classical political economy's opposition to labour unions, which was rooted in the Ricardian scheme of distribution. To him, the wages-fund doctrine was hostile to the growth of the labour movement, and on this ground, he opposed the theory.(89) Nevertheless, it would appear that he did not understand the theory behind the rejection, for the wages-fund doctrine is to be found implicity in even his latest writings.(90)

Despite his attacks on the classical economists, Rogers remained a convinced free trader.(91) He was critical of Smith's defence of the Navigation Acts and was appalled at Mill's support for protection of infant industries believing that only an international division of labour would ensure that Britain's naval strength was sufficient for the country's defence and simultaneously permit all nations to develop those industries in which they had comparative advantages.(92) Like Cobden and Goldwin Smith, he argued that free-trade would decrease the likelihood of wars, maintain low food prices and curtail monopolies.(93)

On Empire and Colonisation

In common with other mid-nineteenth century commentators on empire, Rogers divided the British empire into three regions - dependencies (eg, India), military outposts (eg, Malta, Gibralta) and "colonies proper" (eg, Australia, Canada, New Zealand). Throughout his published work, he concentrated upon "colonies proper", though every so often he discussed India.(94) Thinking along similar lines to Wakefield he outlined this definition of colonies:

> By free colonies I understand not only those which, like New Zealand, have been entirely the offspring of voluntary emigration, but those which, though originally conquests, have been made autonomous, and those which have had the courage and success to thwart the administration of the mother country in its attempts to make the colony the means for expelling the least satisfactory part of the native population of the United Kingdom, under a system of perpetual colonisation from the worst part of the criminal classes at home.(95)

Accepting Cobden's and Goldwin Smith's view, Rogers argued that a colony had to be a settlement in which the citizens enjoyed the "ordinary political rights" of Englishmen ie, self-government, political representation, revenue and expenditure functions, and property laws.(96) Ideally a "true colony" was a voluntary settlement.

Clearly influenced by Wakefield, Rogers carefully considered the colonisation of Australia, which he considered was "not the action of government, but of private enterprise".(97) To Rogers, the English government had never colonised "except with convicts but the free settlers soon resented that practice" and it was in this context that he outlined Wakefield's plan of systematic colonisation.(98) In his Manual (1868), he examined the sudden increase of population in the Australian colonies between 1851-1865, believing that it "would have been, however, much scantier had not the colonies adopted the system of assisted emigration, first suggested by Mr Gibbon Wakefield".(99) However, Wakefield's scheme had broken down because of the gold discoveries, which resulted in a great influx of unassisted migrants. Generally speaking, Rogers thought Wakefield's plan had worked well, although he objected to it on four grounds: it took from the land purchaser a portion of his capital at a time when this capital was required for other purposes; it discouraged settlers by fixing a high price on public lands; the regulation price was fixed too high; and he favoured voluntary emigration.(100)

Emigration, Capital and Trade

Rogers outlined the history of emigration since the eighteenth century from the United Kingdom, stressing that, generally, it had been voluntary.(101) Thinking along similar lines to J S Mill he observed that emigration to Australia was very slow because of the considerable distances involved, which was not the case with migration to North America.(102) Moreover, as he was anxious to establish solutions which could alleviate labour's degradation he noted that an obvious remedy was to diminish the number of people competing for the wages-fund.(103) In contrast to Fawcett and the classical economists, he did not examine the theory of whether emigration would reduce the nation's population in the long-term. Nevertheless, Rogers pointed out that irrespective of any benefit which could accrue to the migrant, the nation "must not be weakened".(104) Unfortunately, Britain was losing its best workers "but voluntary migration generally takes away the best, the most thrifty, the most active, the most hopeful of the population".(105) More significantly, he did not accept the commonly held position that there was over-population in the United Kingdom.

If population be excessive - and a general excess of population is almost as great an absurdity as a general overproduction - it could only be relieved by an emigration en bloc. It is no relief to a country to carry off the handiest labourers, and to leave the weak, the thriftless, the stupid and shiftless behind.(106)

Despite his objection to Wilmot-Horton's scheme, he outlined a scheme aimed at relieving the United Kingdom of its pauper children and giving them the opportunity to succeed in the colonies.(107) He hoped that an "arrangement" could be made with the colonies to accept orphan and deserted children, "whose parents cannot or will not maintain them".(108) He foresaw seven advantages from such a programme: 1. children would be removed from pauperism, 2. they would not be restrained by a class system, which Rogers detested, 3. they would receive a fresh career, 4. they could be taught to be wise and provident, unlike their parents, 5. in the long-term, it would relieve various English districts of those who would become adult paupers, 6. their labour was of immediate value in the colonies, where they could serve an apprenticeship, 7. so long as they produced more than they consumed, they would add to the country's resources.(109) Unfortunately, Rogers referred to the scheme in passing and it was more an idea than a fully worked out plan. Yet, mere mention of it reveals his concern with the complex problem of pauperism and a willingness to contravene his laissez-faire principles to solve the problem of inherited poverty.

If Rogers saw any long-term advantage in emigration, it was the settlement of Britons throughout the world.

> Remote regions, hitherto occupied by a few savage tribes, are gradually being peopled by men who bring with them all the appliances and most of the tastes which have been accumulated by the highest civilisation .... Every year of this action is taking away from the risk of barbarism, is giving overwhelming strength to the power of intelligent labour and civil government, so testing the habits and traditions of the old world .... But the course of this progress will be the gain of humanity.(110)

Intertwined with his general discussion of emigration, Rogers referred to the movement of capital and goods from the United Kingdom to the rest of the world and he stressed that colonial markets existed, irrespective of any political dependence, though he accepted the position that an emigrant took with him "the habits, tastes and fashions of the country he has left".(111) However, habits and purchasing patterns did not last forever, especially in a new colony. In contrast to Wakefield and J S Mill, Rogers did not examine the role of capital in colonial development, but noted that the colonies suffered a "dearth of capital" and that the rate of interest was always "high for borrowers".(112)

Protectionism in the Colonies

Rogers claimed with justification, that he had consistently "laboured for free trade for 40 years".(113) He allied himself with free traders and was appalled at the introduction of protective tariffs in the colonies and frequently denounced the passage quoted by protectionists from J S Mill's Principles.(114) To Rogers, Mill's support for infant industries was "mischievous and misused" by the colonists as a justification for their financial system.(115) "The fact is the whole passage is metaphysics, mere political economy, very bad metaphysics, and no political economy at all."(116)

Despite attempting to appreciate the arguments for protective tariffs in the colonies, Rogers rejected them all, claiming that any protective tariff was an act of war.(117) "A protective system differs in form only not in fact, from any other belligerent act".(118) In a similar manner to the Manchester School he asserted that the "refutation of the protective theory" belonged to "the rudiments of economic science" and agreed with the Cobdenites that a tariff led to an increase in the price of articles, which lowered the value of money and produce as well as diminishing labour's purchasing power by lowering the amount of real wages.(119) Tariffs in any colony restrained economic development because all colonies suffered from a lack of capital. In such a situation imposition of a tariff forced capital from a more to a less productive undertaking. This, in turn, resulted in capital wastage, a general increase of prices and losses to the community.(120) In short, industries which received protection were imperfectly productive since they obtained the "artificial assistance of legislative protection in order thay they may exist".(121) Moreover Rogers believed that protection of an infant industry would reduce "the incentives" to labour and industry and he claimed that "The United States people have markedly declined in inventiveness since they adapted the Morrill tariff, and lately influences have kept it going."(122) Furthermore, he thought that there were ominous signs that in countries like the United States and Australia, where there was protection, a movement would evolve under which the immigration of labour would be threatened "with regulation or even prohibition".(123) He consistently argued against any form of restrictions between countries, and demanded the free flow of labour and capital throughout the world.(124) On this basis, he was strongly against any retaliatory action by the English government for the difficulties it encountered from the colonial tariffs.

> The worst offenders against us are our own kinsfolk, whom we have defended in their infancy at our cost, and who retort on us by repudiating all the products of our industry but our money. It is certain that any attempt to retaliate upon them would be resented, and that the result of the attempt would be, that the Imperial Institute and all that it symbolises would be shattered.(125)

Whereas the majority of the Manchester School remained faithful to a position of no government intervention, Rogers was so angered at colonial tariffs that he contradicted his laissez-faire beliefs in wishing the English government had stipulated, with the granting of self-government, that the colonial parliaments could only enact tariffs for revenue purposes and not protect infant industries by "mischievous tariff barriers".(126)

The Disutility of Empire

Associating himself with Cornewall Lewis, J A Roebuck, Arthur Mills and Goldwin Smith, Rogers argued that colonies were of little, if any economic benefit and that their continued possession by the British government involved heavy financial burdens to the British taxpayer.(127) In The Economic Interpretation of History (1888) he recalls his pleas, and those of Goldwin Smith, over the cost of defending the British Empire.

> Almost 25 years ago, Mr Goldwin Smith and myself called public attention to the cost of the British Colonies. Half the English army was being kept in them, at the cost of the British exchequer, and to the profit of colonial statesmen. Every particle of British spirit was absent from the colonial character. Traders were making money fast, planning protectionist tariffs in order to enable them to make money faster, and calling on the British exchequer to relieve them from all risks at the expense of the British taxpayer .... We thought the relationship one-sided

and said so plainly .... our views were taken up and the situation rapidly improved. The colonists recognised that if they were part of an empire, they had duties of self-defence, and a further duty in the direction of general defence, and at the present time, I do not know that there is a British regiment in colonial quarters.(128)

Some nineteen years earlier, Rogers had defended Goldwin Smith's right to comment on colonial affairs and rebuffed Lord Bury's attacks that Goldwin Smith had utilised his professional position to enunciate his views on colonies.(129) In his defence, Rogers allied himself whole-heartedly with Smith's position.

Mr Goldwin Smith never enunciated his doctrines on the colonial question from a professorial chair. He published his statements in the form of a series of letters sent to the Daily News. In common with every professor in this university, he did not use his official position as a means of inculcating his own views on questions of controversial politics.

Nor did Mr Goldwin Smith enunciate the position that our colonial possessions are encumbrances and sources of weakness to the inhabitants of the United Kingdom. What he did enunciate was the fact, uncontested by all but the ignorant and self-interested, that any attempt to govern the colonies in time of peace, or to defend them in time of war, is a transparent absurdity and a real source of weakness. Furthermore, Mr Smith pointed out that the pretence of government and defence induced serious social and political evils in the colonies themselves, and that the charge of this futile and mischievous policy was a heavy additional burden on the overladen taxpayers of the United Kingdom. It is easy to see that colonial possessions may be no disadvantage to a country. It is gratifying to every one who loves the English race, name, institutions, and literature, to watch the rapid occupation of those parts of the earth's surface in which that race and those institutions can thrive, by the descendants of the English people. But it is quite another thing that they should be governed by the Colonial Office and defended by the Horse Guards and the Admiralty. It was against this theory of the colonial empire that Mr Goldwin Smith protested, and with great effect. The fruit of his reasonings has been already considerable. We have given up the Ionian Islands, European justice and the honour of Spain. We have disendowed a Church in Jamaica, and are withdrawing regiments from Canada. We have informed New Zealanders that we are no longer willing to aid them in making raids on the grounds of the Maoris, and Cape settlers that we will have no more Kafirr wars. We have repudiated the Dalhousie policy in India, and are seriously doubting whether the British navy shall be at the discretion of impetuous missionaries and equally impetuous consuls. Nor has our success in enacting the terms of the Canadian Confederation been so marked as to furnish a precedent for detailed as contrasted with permissive legislation.(130)

While in the above quotation, Rogers reveals a keen appreciation of Smith's leading ideas it was incorrect to credit the changes in British policy to Smith's influence. Rogers also accepted Smith's argument that the expenditure on colonial defence arrangements caused a loss to the British community, whilst certain classes gained.(131) Ultimately, the colonies had to protect themselves, but while there were English troops defending their territory, the colonial government should pay the British Government.(132) If there were domestic wars (eg as in New Zealand), the costs should not be met by the British government although millions of pounds had already been spent on maintaining "Canada's colonial independence".(133) In brief, Rogers was consistently and adamantly against British defence expenditure which protected the colonial empire. This stemmed from his concern not to have the working classes pay for the armament expenditure, his more general opinion on the aggressiveness of most government legislation and his desire to foster world peace and his indebtedness to Smith's case on the political disutility of empire.

> The presumed political benefits of the present colonial system are an exploded fiction. The colonial empire adds nothing to the military strength of the home country, but rather diminishes it. The Colonial Office adds nothing to the stability of colonial society, but tends to lower the character of colonial life.(134)

In a similar vein to Smith, Rogers also considered the economic arguments associated with colonial possessions, particularly the proposition that the colonial connection secured "a readier market to British goods, a more obvious field to British capital, a readier outlet for British emigration".(135) The protectionist policy of the colonies meant that the United Kingdom received no direct benefits from its colonial connections. Whilst the colonies were outlets for British capital, Rogers believed that the diversion of capital resulted in greater advantages to the colony than the British "investing public".(136) Furthermore, other countries (eg America, Western Europe) received greater amounts of capital and were larger trading areas than the colonies. He also rejected the view that the colonies were outlets for emigration, claiming that this opinion "appears to have no foundation".(137) Rogers quoted emigration figures from 1857 to 1864, which demonstrated that most emigrants went to the United States where labour was in more regular demand than in the colonies and there was governmental stimulus (land grants) to emigrants. Thus, Rogers agreed with Smith that there were no significant economic and political advantages from colonisation.(138)

The Utility of Empire

Whilst Rogers condemned the costs and expense of empire, he associated himself with other mid-Victorian critics of empire and expressed a pride in the extension of "the British race" throughout the world "A 100 million of people speak the English tongue: in a century they will be quadrupled. A 100 million of people are sensible of a common honour; in a century they will achieve a peaceful victory over barbarism".(139) Moreover, like the mid-Victorian critics he contended that the ties of common blood, language and institutions were sufficient for an alliance of the colonies and the United States.(140)

> But the possession of that social system which this country has developed in the course of its political and economical history, the extension on our part, and the inheritance on theirs, of those memories, laws, municipal institutions, and with them those liberties which our race has won, all of which it is bound to commend to its so-called dependencies, are a tie which is not the less powerful, because it is seldom recognised as the real bond between Great Britain and her distant children. It is, however, just as strong in the United States as it is in the so-called colonies.(141)

However he broke with the ideas of Roebuck, Lewis and Arthur Mill when he claimed that in the self-governing colonies "radical domestic reforms" were far easier to achieve than in the United Kingdom. The colonies greatly benefited from the lack of a church establishment and an hereditary nobility, which were barriers to parliamentary and general reforms within the United Kingdom, and were therefore free to "solve the problems of society under a new and an equal set of conditions".(142) The progressive advances in colonies provided examples for the mother country to follow:

> The British colonists adopted an extended franchise, and there is no doubt that the example was not lost on the politicians of the Old World. They secured the independence of the voter, and the decorum of the content, by the use of the Ballot in Parliamentary elections, and the precedent of the Australian Colonies, nay even their practices, were recommended and accepted by the British legislature. The rule of absolute and unconditional religious equality, the expediency of maintaining civil equality, the grant of secular education, with free religious teaching, and the necessity of keeping the process by which land is transferred simple, are principles in the Colonies. In a short time they will be urged with overwhelming force in the home country, and will be accepted.(143)

Although Rogers argued for colonial emancipation, unlike his mentor, Smith, he was against the severance of all political connections, which if it occurred, would be a great "misfortune".(144) However, he noted Adam Smith's ideas on an imperial parliament and considered the contemporary argument for an imperial federation of the British Empire.(145) Rogers believed that even if the problems of distance could be overcome, and there were colonial representatives in the House of Commons, two grave difficulties would arise: 1. The House of Commons, already an unwieldy chamber, would become more cumbersome; 2. British domestic interests would dominate the debates, and colonial matters would be ignored.(146) He concluded that any system of representation in the British parliament was impracticable as a means of union between the United Kingdom and the free colonies.

India

Rogers was interested in Indian affairs, and he readily offered his services as an examiner for the Indian Civil Service.(147) He advocated more debate in the House of Commons on the Indian budget, although his parliamentary contribution to Indian affairs was slight compared with Fawcett's speeches and activity.(148) In a similar vein to the Manchester School, Rogers explained that the conquest of India was a striking example of British energy and vigour, which had won Britain great acclaim. However, Rogers thought the domination of the East India Company had prevented the acclimatisation of Europeans in India, and checked the development of native produce. In contrast to Smith he criticised the 'present administration' as nothing more than a despotism shared between the Indian secretary and the permanent officials.(149) Despite these reservations Rogers followed Smith's ideas and did not want England to forfeit her control of the world's 'greatest dependency':

> I never believed that the Indian empire was either strength, glory, or profit to England; but I am certain that the history of the world supplies no such example of a determination to fulfil the highest duties of government to a race which has been profoundly debased, but which may be fully civilised, as the policy of the English administration of India has been proved to be.(150)

He was proud of British achievements in India, especially the 'general economic progress', which had been assisted by Government public work programmes. Rogers, like so many other proponents of laissez-faire, considered India an exception to the general rule. Moreover, he was delighted at the changes which opened the Indian civil service to public competition, claiming that this made Indian government more efficient. Whilst Rogers maintained that England had a great responsibility to India, he agreed with Fawcett that this involved tremendous costs to the British taxpayer, especially in regard to defence.(151)

Conclusion

Rogers' discussion of imperial issues contains a jumble of his economic and political opinions, and little of his self-proclaimed inductive methodology and statistical research penetrates his analysis. This was in contrast to two of his contemporary economists, Cairnes and Fawcett, who occasionally utilised imperial examples to bolster their principles of political economy.(152) Thinking along similar lines to other mid-nineteenth century commentators, particularly Goldwin Smith, Rogers was opposed to the political domination of the colonies, although, like Smith, he supported British rule in India. While Rogers stressed the economic and political disutility of empire, in common with all nineteenth century economists, (including Alfred Marshall and J A Hobson) he was extremely proud of the "bonds of blood and language" created by British imperial expansion.(153) A staunch free trader and supporter of laissez-faire, Rogers' strong personal, nationalistic feelings occasionally entered his imperial discussions and, as has been noted in specific instances - the loss of the best British labourers, the granting of colonial self-government, pauper-children emigration schemes - he contravened his principles.

NOTES

1. G Smith, Empire, (Oxford, John Henry and James Parker, 1863). For a comprehensive account of Smith's life and general opinions, see Elisabeth Wallace, Goldwin Smith - Victorian Liberal, (Toronto, TUP, 1957); G Smith, Reminiscences, (ed. by Arnold Hamilton, New York, Norwood, 1910); J Cooper, Goldwin Smith, DCL, (Privately Published Reading, 1912).

2. Wallace, Goldwin Smith, op.cit, p.5.

3. Ibid, p.13.

4. Smith, An Inaugural Lecture, (Oxford, Parker, 1859).

5. Wallace, Goldwin Smith, op.cit, passim. Smith retained a large correspondence with fellow radicals in the United Kingdom. See W H G Armytage, Goldwin Smith: Some Unpublished Letters, Nuffield College Library, Special Collection, Ca. 86.

6. On the Manchester School see William D Grampp, The Manchester School of Economics, (London, OUP, 1960), pp.2-16; C A Bodelsen, Studies in Mid-Victorian Imperialism, (Copenhagen, Glydendalen, 1924), pp.32-39; Bernard Porter, Critics of Empire, (London, Macmillan, 1968), pp.10-16.

7. See J Bright, Speeches of John Bright, (London, Cobden Club, 1859), Speech of 29/10/1858, p.288.

8. J Bright and J E T Rogers (eds), Speeches on Questions of Public Policy by Richard Cobden MP, Vol. I, (London, Macmillan, 1878).

9. Smith was the author of the Cobden Club's motto "Free Trade, Peace, Goodwill Among Nations". See Wallace, Goldwin Smith, op.cit, p.137.

10. Smith, Empire, op.cit.

11. Ibid, p.viii. For a brief discussion of Smith's definition of "empire" see Richard Köebner and Helmut Dan Schmidt, Imperialism: The Story and Significance of a Political Word, 1840-1910, (Cambridge, CUP, 1964), pp.32-34.

12. Smith, Empire, op.cit, pp.88-94; Questions of the Day, (New York, Macmillan, 1893), pp.26-27.

13. Smith, Empire, op.cit, pp.82-103. Also see George Cornewall Lewis, An Essay on the Government of Dependencies, (London, John Murray, 1841).

14. Smith, Empire, op.cit, p.52.

15. On Cobden and Bright, see Bodelsen, Studies in Mid-Victorian Imperialism, op.cit, pp.33-34.

16. Smith, Empire, op.cit, pp.165-187. Also see J A Roebuck, The Colonies of England, (London, Parker, 1849) and Arthur Mills, Colonial Constitutions, (London, Stanford, 1891).

17. Smith, Empire, op.cit, p.179; also see eg pp.58-59 and Ch. 5, p.80-86.

18. H Merivale, Lectures on Colonization and Colonies, (London, Cass, 1967 reprint, delivered at Oxford during 1839-41). For discussions on Merivale see Ghosh, Classical Macroeconomics and the Case for Colonies, op.cit, pp.271-295 and Winch, Classical Political Economy and Colonies, op.cit, pp.49-50, 132-7, 167.

19. Merivale, Lectures on Colonization and Colonies, op.cit. See Lecture V, pp.137-166.

20. Ibid, p.160.

21. Merivale, "On the Utility of Colonies as Fields for Emigration", Journal of the Statistical Society, Oct. 1862, pp.491-496, especially pp.491-492.

22. Merivale demonstrated a remarkable appreciation of demographic movements in France, which seemingly reveal an awareness of changes in the birth rate in that country. See D V Glass and D E C Eversley (eds), Population in History: Essays in Historical Demography, (London, Edward Arnold, 1965).

23. Merivale, "On the Utility of Colonies", op.cit, pp.494-5.

24. See Brinley Thomas, Migration and Economic Growth, (Cambridge, CUP, 1973), pp.1-10.

25. See Smith's letter to the Daily News, 7/10/1862, reprinted as Chapter XI, "Colonial Emigration" in Empire, op.cit, pp.115-189.

26. Ibid, pp.121-129.

27. See Wallace, Goldwin Smith, op.cit, pp.13-32. For a consideration of Lewis, Mills and Roebuck see Bodelsen, Studies in Mid-Victorian Imperialism, op.cit, pp.39-42.

28. Smith, Reminiscences op.cit, pp.2, 106-215; Empire, op.cit, p.128.

29. Smith, England and America, (Manchester, Ireland, 1865).

30. For a brief outline of Mill's position see Ch. 2, pp.10-13 and pp.58-59 of the present chapter.

31. Smith, Empire, op.cit, pp.90-2.

32. For a slightly different interpretation see Wallace, Goldwin Smith, op.cit, pp.205-210.

33. Smith, Reminiscences op.cit, p.146. For a discussion of James Mill's views see Ghosh, Classical Macroeconomics and the Case for Colonies, pp.105-110.

34. Ibid, pp.93-4.

35. Smith, The Schism of the Anglo-Saxon Race, (New York, New Coy, 1887), p.139.

36. Wallace, Goldwin Smith, op.cit, pp.5, 28-38.

37. For a discussion of his views on the matter, see Wallace, Ibid, p,p.194-210.

38. On this general point see B Porter, Critics of Empire, op.cit.

39. Smith, "Imperialism in the United States", CR, No. 401, May 1899, p,p.620-28. The idea of the white man's burden had gained popularity since the trial of Warren Hastings and the investigating of the East India Company, see D C Somerville, English Thought in the Nineteenth and Twentieth Centuries, (2nd ed, London, Macmillan, 1929).

40. Smith, "The Impending Revolution", Nineteenth Century, Vol. XXXV, March 1894.

41. See Wallace, Goldwin Smith, op.cit, pp.202-10. For an introduction to the debate see Ch. 3, pp.   .

42. G Smith, "The Political Aspects of Imperial Federation", Saturday Review, February 1897, pp.287-9. Smith's residence in Canada greatly influenced his opinions on colonial nationalism. See Elisabeth Wallace, Goldwin Smith - Victorian Liberal, op.cit, pp.53-132.

43. Smith, Empire, op.cit, p.45.

44. Ibid, p.6.

45. Quoted in Wallace, Goldwin Smith, op.cit, p.51.

46. Smith, England and America, op.cit, p.421; and Empire, op.cit, p.144.

47. Ibid, p.144

48. Smith, Commonwealth or Empire (New York, Norwood, 1902), pp.66-8.

49. Smith, Essays on Questions of the Day, op.cit, p.131.

50. See for example, pp.59-61 and Ch. 5, pp.74-76 and 80-92.

51. See for example, Ch. 6, pp.132-134 and Ch. 10, pp.250-253.

52. A W Coats, "James Edwin Thorold Rogers", International Encyclopeadia of the Social Sciences, Vol. 13, (London, Macmillan, 1968), p.542. On Rogers' life see, W J Ashley, "James E Thorold Rogers", PSQ, Vol. 4, 1889, pp.381-407; H B Gibbens, "In Memoriam: Thorold Rogers", ER, Vol. 1, pp.86-89; W A S Hewins, "J E T Rogers", Dictionary of National Biography, (London, OUP, 1921), Vol. 17, (1897), pp.122-6.

53. See "J E T Rogers Scrap Book" in Rogers Papers in the Bodleian Library, Oxford, No. 232, d188, 1894.

54. See N B De Marchi, "On the Dangers of being Too Political an Economist: Thorold Rogers and the 1868 Election to the Drummond Professorship", OEP, No. 3 November 1976, pp.364-80, and "J E T Rogers Scrap Book", op.cit, and Rogers Papers, Bodleian Library, Oxford, Oxon c84 (404).

55. See "National Association for the Promotion of Social Science", Transactions, 1864. p.117.

56. See Oxford Reform Society Papers and Rogers Papers, Bodl, GA, Oxon, c84.

57. See De Marchi, "On the Dangers of Being Too Political an Economist", op.cit, and Rogers Papers, Bodl, GA, Oxon, c84 (468), Oxford. Rogers lost the election to Bonamy Price.

58. Coats, "James Edwin Thorold Rogers", op.cit, p.542.

59. See "J E T Rogers Scrap Book", op.cit.

60. Ibid, from newspaper reports towards the end of the scrap book.

61. A B Beavon, Thorold Rogers, the Historical (Tare) -

Gleaner: A Critical Review, printed and published by the author (Pembroke College), 1870.

62. Rogers, Cobden and Modern Political Opinion, (London, Macmillan, 1873), p.V. For a discussion of Rogers' economics, see G M Koot, The English Historical School of Economics, 1870-1920; Economic History, Social Reform and Neo-Mercantalism, (Unpublished PhD Thesis, Stony Brook Library, New York, 1972), pp.126-170.

63. See pp.58-59

64. Rogers, Manual of Political Economy for Schools and Colleges, (Oxford, Clarendon, 1868), p.269.

65. Rogers, The Relation of Economic Science to Social and Political Action, (London, Cassel, 1872), p.24.

66. See Hansard, Third Series, 252, 24/5/1880, pp.347-51.

67. See Hansard, Third Series, 293, 6/11/1884, pp.1164.

68. Rogers, The Relation of Economic Science to Social and Political Action, op.cit, pp.42-43.

69. Rogers, The Economic Interpretation of History, Lectures delivered at Worcester College Hall, Oxford, 1887-8, (London, T Fisher Unwin, 1888), p.503. Marshall outlined a similar position in his "Notes on Method", in Mss Box 9/2, Marshall Papers, Marshall Library, Cambridge.

70. For his attacks on Mill's support of protection for infant industries, see p.58.

71. Rogers, England's Industrial and Commercial Supremacy, (London, T Fisher Unwin, 1892), p.61.

72. Rogers, The Relation of Economic Science to Social and Political Action, op.cit, p.37.

73. Rogers, A History of Agricultural Prices from 1259 to 1793, (Oxford, Clarendon, 1866, (Vol. 1), Vol. 4, published, 1882), p.v.

74. Rogers, Manual of Political Economy, (Oxford, Clarendon, 1863 ed), p.vi.

75. Ibid, pp.231-34, 250-54.

76. Ibid, p.76.

77. Rogers, A History of Agricultural Prices, op.cit, p.viii; Economic Interpretation of History, op.cit, p.xiii; England's Industrial and Commercial Supremacy, op.cit, p.22; Relation of Economic Science to Social and Political Action, op.cit, p.24.

78. Rogers, A History of Agricultural Prices, op.cit, p.viii.

79. Rogers, Relation of Economic Science to Social and Political Action, op.cit, p.4 and Ashley, "J E Thorold Rogers", op.cit, pp.391-2.

80. See Rogers (ed), The Wealth of Nations, (Oxford, Clarendon 1869), p.xii.

81. Rogers, A History of Prices, Vol. 1, op.cit, pp.vi-vii.

82. Rogers, "Review of T E Cliffe Leslie's Essays in Philosophy", The Academy, No. 370, June 7, 1879, pp.489-491.

83. Rogers, Six Centuries of Work and Wages: The History of English Labour, (London, Swan Sonnenschien, 1884), p.435.

84. Rogers, Manual, 1868 ed, op.cit, p.96.

85. Rogers, A History of Agriculture and Prices, op.cit.

86. Ibid, Vol. II, p.xi.

87. Rogers, Six Centuries of Work and Wages, op.cit.

88. Rogers, Manual, 1868 ed, op.cit, p.vi; Economic Interpretation of History, op.cit, pp.180-181; Industrial and Commercial Supremacy, op.cit, p.222; "The History of Rent in England", Contemporary Review, 37, April 1880, pp.673-690.

89. Rogers, Work and Wages, op.cit, pp.400-1, 523; Industrial and Commercial History, op.cit, pp.162-183; Economic Interpretation of History, op.cit, pp.vii, ix, 307-10, 162-183.

90. For a discussion of this matter see Koot, The English Historical School of Economics 1870-1920, op.cit, p.138.

91. See pp.58-59.

92. Rogers, Economic Science and Political Action, op.cit, p.27; "The Colonial Question" in Cobden Club Essays, 2nd Series, (London, Cassel, 1872), pp.447-448; Economic Interpretation of History, op.cit, pp.379, 286-388; Cobden and Modern Political Opinion, op.cit, pp.41-42, 45-6.

93. Ibid, pp.18-19, 230.

94. Rogers, Manual, 1868 ed, p.247; "The Colonial Question" op.cit, p.410.

95. Rogers, "The Colonial Question", op.cit, p.409. For a discussion of Wakefield's definition see Ghosh, Classical Macroeconomics and the Case for Colonies, op.cit, pp.7-8.

96. Ibid, p.410; The British Citizen: His Rights and Privileges, (London, Society for Promoting Christian Knowledge, 1885), p.253.

97. Rogers, The British Citizen, op.cit, p.182.

98. Ibid, p.182; Rogers, Manual, 1868 ed, op.cit, pp.253-254; "The Colonial Question", op.cit, pp.439-440.

99. Rogers, Manual, op.cit, p.253.

100. Ibid, p.254.

101. Rogers, England's Industrial and Commercial Supremacy, op.cit, pp.270-290.

102. Ibid, p.282, for Mill's position see Winch Classical Political Economy and the Colonies, op.cit, pp.135-143, 153-158.

103. Rogers, Manual, 1868 ed, op.cit, pp.99-100. On Fawcett and the classical attitude to emigration see Wood, "Henry Fawcett and the British Empire", The Indian Economic and Social History Review, Vol. XVI, No. 4, December 1979, pp.395-414.

104. Rogers, England's Industrial and Commercial Supremacy, op.cit, p.289.

105. Rogers, Manual, 1868 ed, op.cit, p.100. Also see England's Industrial and Commercial Supremacy, op.cit, pp.289-90; Cobden and Modern Political Opinion, op.cit, p.247.

106. Rogers, "The Colonial Question", op.cit, p.439.

107. He referred to J Wilmot-Horton's scheme as "wild and chivalrous philanthropy". See Letter No. 66 in Rogers Papers, op.cit. On Wilmot-Horton see Ghosh, Classical Macroeconomics and the Case for Colonies, op.cit, pp.132-155.

108. Rogers, "The Colonial Question", op.cit, p.444.

109. Ibid, pp.444-445.

110. Rogers, Manual, op.cit, p.256.

111. Rogers, "The Colonial Question" op.cit, p.435. Marshall also argued along these lines. See "Notes on Immigration", Large Brown Box Mss Box 2, Marshall Papers, Cambridge. Also see Ch. 6, pp.117-118.

112. Rogers, Manual, op.cit, p.232; Also see "The Colonial Question", op.cit, pp.435-36. 448.

113. Rogers, Address in 1885 to the Electors of Bermondsey, (London, Bean Webley and Co, 1895), p.6; "Free Trade and Fair Trade: What Do These Words Mean?", Cobden Club Leaflets, No. XXVIII, (London, 1885).

114. For Mill's statement see Principles of Political Economy, (Ashley, ed, 1907), p.92.

115. Rogers, "The Colonial Question", op.cit, p.425; Cobden and Modern Political Opinion, op.cit, p.245; Manual, op.cit, pp.231-232; The Relation of Economic Science to Social and Political Action, op.cit, p.27; Economic Interpretation of History, op.cit, pp.338-9.

116. Ibid, p.338.

117. Ibid, p.338; "The Colonial Question", op.cit, p.446; Economic Interpretation of History, op.cit, p.338.

118. Rogers, "The Colonial Question", op.cit, p.446.

119. Ibid, p.449.

120. Ibid, p.447. On Cobden and the Manchester School's defence of free trade see W Grampp, The Manchester School of Economics, op.cit, passim.

121. Rogers, Manual, op.cit, p.232.

122. Rogers, The Relation of Economic Science to Social and Political Action, op.cit, p.27.

123. Rogers, Economic Interpretation of History, op.cit, p.316.

124. Rogers, "The Colonial Question", op.cit, pp.447-458.

125. Rogers, Economic Interpretation of History, op.cit, p.380.

126. Ibid, pp.378-379; Cobden and Modern Political Opinion, op.cit, p.245.

127. For a discussion of these commentators see Klaus E Knorr, British Colonial Theories, (Toronto, Frank Cass, 1963).

128. Rogers, Economic Interpretation of History, op.cit, pp.335-336.

129. Rogers, Letter to The Star, 16 March 1869. Also Rogers Papers, Bodleian Library, Oxford.

130. Letter from Rogers to the Editor of The Star, 16/3/1869. Clippings in Rogers Papers, op.cit.

131. Rogers, "The Colonial Question", op.cit, p.432.

132. Rogers, The Free Trade Policy of the Liberal Party, (Manchester, Guardian, 1868).

133. Rogers,"The Colonial Question", op.cit, p.432; Economic Interpretation of History, op.cit, p.334.

134.Rogers, "The Colonial Question", op.cit, p.432. Rogers mentioned in passing that since self-government, colonial expenditure by the British government had risen from 2 to 6 per head. This was due to military expenditure, Ibid, pp.425-426. He did not cite the source for his figures.

135. Rogers, Manual, op.cit, p.250

136. Ibid, pp.252-253. Also See "The Colonial Question", op.cit, pp.435-436; Cobden and Modern Political Opinion, op.cit, pp.246-247.

137. Ibid, pp.437-440; Manual, op.cit, pp.253-254.

138. Rogers, Manual, op.cit, pp.253-254. Although he wrote little on late nineteenth century expansion he was also opposed to the imperialistic conquests of the Western European powers: "It is not our duty to meddle with the affairs of other nations, least of all to league with oppressors, to spend English lives and English money, always wrung in the end from labour in the interests of speculators and loan-mongers .... In and out of Parliament, by speech and in print, I have always repudiated the policy of intervention." See Rogers' Address to the Electors of the Division of Bermondsey, op.cit, p.7.

139. Rogers, "The Colonial Question", op.cit, p.419.

140. Rogers, Cobden and Modern Political Opinion, op.cit, p.258; "The Colonial Question", op.cit, pp.451-455; Manual, op.cit, pp.257-258. Also see C A Bodelsen, Studies in Mid-Victorian Imperialism, (Copenhagen, Glydendalen, 1924), pp.32-60.

141. Rogers, Cobden and Modern Political Opinion, op.cit, p.258.

142. Ibid, p.254.

143. Ibid, p.257.

144. Rogers, "The Colonial Question", op.cit, p.455.

145. Ibid, pp.450-451 and Cobden and Modern Political Opinion, pp.252-253.

146. Rogers, Cobden and Modern Political Opinion, op.cit, pp.258-259; "The Colonial Question", op.cit, pp.451-452.

147. For his exam questions and letters concerning these examinations see Nos. 46, 106, 121 in Rogers Papers, Oxford, op.cit.

148. Ibid, No. 46. On Fawcett and India see Wood, "Henry Fawcett and the British Empire", op.cit, and Ch. 5, pp.

149. Rogers, England's Industrial and Commercial Supremacy, op.cit, p.271.

150. Rogers, The Representation of Scarborough: An Address, (Scarborough, Dennis and Case, 1873), Speech made on 29/4/1873, p.4.

151. Rogers, Manual, op.cit, pp.17, 235, 252.

152. See J E Cairnes, "Colonisation and Colonial Government" reprinted in Political Essays, (London, Macmillan, 1873) and H Fawcett, Manual of Political Economy, (London, Macmillan, 1863), pp.68-73, and Ch. 5, pp.73-76 and pp.80-92.

153. See A Marshall, "Imperialism and Centralisation", 27/12/1907, in Large Red Box, Mss Box 2, Marshall Papers and Industry and Trade, (London, Macmillan, 1933 ed), pp.104-6; and J A Hobson, Imperialism, (London, James Nesbitt, 1902), pp.123, 140, 147-161, 382-3, The Evolution of Modern Capitalism, (London, Scott, 1894), pp.235-6. Also see Ch. 6, pp.132-134 and Ch. 10, pp.250-253.

Chapter 5

J S MILL'S ADMIRERS: J E CAIRNES AND HENRY FAWCETT

J E CAIRNES

Introduction

During his lifetime J E Cairnes became recognised as the leader of British academic economists.(1) In The Character and Logical Method of Political Economy published in 1857, a year after he won the Whately professorship, he attempted to return economics to its first principles and defended the 'science' against the attacks of its critics.(2) He offered a precise and clear exposition of the province and method of economics from the viewpoint of Ricardo and Mill, and urged that political economy was concerned with what is, not with what ought to be. Unfortunately, the science of political economy had suffered from the intrusion of alien elements represented by "considerations of equity and expediency".(3) To Cairnes, political economy was to be regarded as:

> ... standing neutral between competing social schemes; neutral as the science of mechanics stands neutral between competing plans of railway construction, in which expense, for instance, as well as mechanical efficiency, is to be considered; neutral as chemistry stands neutral between the competing plans of sanitary improvement; as physiology stands neutral between opposing systems of medicine. It supplies the means, or more correctly, a portion of the means to identify itself with any.(4)

In Cairnes' view it was necessary to limit economics to a science of wealth that was above policy. Economics should be neutral between different plans of social organisation as mechanics was between different plans of railway construction.(5) He categorically stated that economic laws were rules deduced from "human nature and external facts", not "from the statistics of society, or from the crude generalisation of history".(6)

Furthermore, Cairnes noted that compared to a physicist, an economist had one distinct advantage - "a knowledge of ultimate causes" which centred around the behaviour of economic man and consisted of "uncertain mutual feelings and beings".(7) The proof of an economic law must rest on an appeal to certain principles of human nature, operating under certain physical conditions.(8) Cairnes argued that political economy was a deductive science with empirical premises and so long as the premises were empirical the hypothetical procedures were satisfactory.(9) When conclusions arrived at by deduction were contradicted by statistical evidence, then there had to be underlying tendencies which accorded with the conclusions.(10) As Mark Blaug argues, Cairnes' concern was to warn against those who "would bend economics to political purposes, who would condemn it because it stood for laissez faire and who would refute its abstract principles by factual evidence".(11)

In The Slave Power (1862) which he dedicated to J S Mill, Cairnes applied his deductive methodology when he endeavoured to predict from the known effects and causes of slavery the future pattern of events.(12) He systematically examined and deduced the economic influences of slavery on the course of civilisation, remarking that just as an "anatomist might be able from a fragment of a tooth or bone to determine the form, dimensions and habits of the creature to whom it belonged", so might "a political economist, by reasoning on the economic character of slavery and its peculiar connection with the soil deduce its leading social and political attributes, and almost construct, by way of a priori argument, the entire system of the society of which it forms the foundation".(13) His "Essays Towards a Solution to the Gold Question" are characterised by a similar exhibition of the working of a principle amid a mass of facts.(14) He traced "the consequences which would result from the increased supplies of gold which were pouring into the world from the mines of California and Australia".(15)

Perhaps Cairnes' most important work was his final publication - Some Leading Principles of Political Economy Newly Expounded (1874) - which is often regarded as the last statement of the classical system of ideas.(16) The work is highly theoretical and consists of three broad areas: an analysis of normal and market values; an analysis of supply and demand; and a discussion of the theory of the wages fund or of "average aggregate wages".(17) Leading Principles chiefly sought to correct Mill's heresies on free trade, socialism and the wages-fund doctrine. Cairnes' defence of free trade was more categorical than that of Mill, and he completely rejected Mill's heresies on reciprocity and protection asserting that free trade was both sound for Britain's particular circumstances and was theoretically unimpeachable as a true principle of scientific economics.(18) In the Leading Principles, Cairnes did not expound the Malthusian doctrine on wages, since his earlier works had comprehensively covered the topic.(19) He believed that it was sufficient to note "the influence of Mr Darwin's great work, in which ... the tendency of human beings to increase faster than subsistence ... was shown to be surely a particular instance of a law pervading all organic existence". He added that the objection to the Malthusian doctrine had "for some time come to an end".(20) However, in defending the wages-fund doctrine, Cairnes explained away a great deal of the theory.(21) He emptied the doctrine of almost all its earlier content, so much so that Jevons considered Cairnes had abandoned it.(22)

Cairnes' Leading Principles was the last formal attempt to justify the arguments of the classical economists. In the preface he stressed that his work should not be viewed "in any sense as antagonistic in its attitude towards the science built up by the labours of Adam Smith, Malthus, Ricardo and Mill ... On the contrary, my hope is that it will - should its reasonings find acceptance - strengthen, in some sensible degree, and add consistence to that fabric".(23) However, in reality, Cairnes further exposed the contradictions within the Ricardian structure and denied economics its social applicability and utility.(24) Though a great admirer of J S Mill, Cairnes shared "some of the doubts and uncertainties of the critics of orthodoxy".(25)

Principles of Political Economy and the Empire

Occasionally Cairnes applied the principles of political economy to the empire and cited events in, and evidence from, the self-governing colonies to support and verify the principles.

The Australian Gold Discoveries In a collection of essays published in 1873, Cairnes aimed to apply the principles of economic science to the solution of the actual problems presented by the Australian (and also the Californian) gold discoveries. In the first essay, written in 1858, he examined the effects of the gold discoveries on trade, industry and pecuniary relations.(26) He aimed to deduce that: (1) the increased production of gold tended to alter the distribution of real wealth in the world, rather than increase its amount; (2) the gain to Australia (and California) accrued exclusively through their foreign trade, since cheap gold enabled the purchase of foreign production; (3) there was an increase in the stock of money in foreign nations.

At the outset of the essay, Cairnes noted that gold could often be mined by unskilled workers with little capital and that gold rushes resulted in the general disorganisation of industry and trade. This in turn caused the establishment of new branches of production, a rise in money wages and prices as well as the inflow of labour and capital from the United Kingdom. Thinking along similar lines to Fawcett, Cairnes reviewed the impact of a gold discovery on the agricultural sector, particularly the woollen industry.(27) The rush of labour to the gold fields caused a general shortage of manpower on the farms, which increased the price of wool and adversely affected the export trade. However, the influx of population from abroad increased the demand for meat·and saved the woollen industry. Prior to the gold boom, Cairnes argued, woollen producers depended on the European markets, but during and after the gold discoveries, they relied on the internal demand for meat which was required to feed the increased population. However, the stimulus given to the agricultural sector was only short term, and Cairnes felt that in the long run the mere presence of rich gold fields had to operate unfavourably on the agricultural community.(28)

In contrast to J S Mill, Cairnes claimed that these principles were verified by the Australian experience where there was abundant territory and above average fertility but the importation of a substantial quantity of food. The increase in wages also placed the farmer at a disadvantage in world markets; the gold fields were a barrier to the development of the land.

> The extension of agriculture in Australia has thus, though stimulated for the moment, suffered a real check from the gold discoveries; and the same influence has been felt throughtout every branch of industry in that country, gold mining alone excepted.(29)

Furthermore, he claimed that the gold discoveries had stifled manufacturing production in Australia. To Cairnes, such a result was clearly dictated by an established principle of economic science - the doctrine of comparative cost.

> The true explanation, therefore, of the importation of corn into a country possessing abundant resources from agriculture is that she possesses comparatively still greater resources for the production of gold; so that she finds it profitable to obtain her corn rather through the medium of her cheap gold than by its direct production.(30)

In preparing the "Essay" for publication in 1872, Cairnes added a postscript, which summarised the history of Australian trade since the original essay was written. He elaborated the gradual exhaustion of the richer gold fields and the accompanying rise in world prices. Concurrent with these phenomena, new developments occurred in Australian industry, particularly in Victoria. He claimed that the value of Victoria's foreign trade had steadily declined over the period 1862-1872, and population had rapidly grown. As the colony prospered, there had been a contraction in its external trade. To Cairnes, this demonstrated how foreign trade often failed to reflect the growth and progress in real wealth. Victoria had eliminated its importation of bread, beer, butter and shoes; all were domestically produced.(31)

Colonisation and Colonial Government In a lecture delivered on 26 October 1864 in Dublin, Cairnes brilliantly surveyed the history of colonisation, cited the important works on the subject by E G Wakefield, G C Lewis, Herman Merivale and, finally, argued that the motives for colonisation had completely disappeared.(32) To appreciate the 'critical epoch' in colonial affairs which faced Britain, he reviewed the era of modern colonisation from the conquest of the new world.(33)

He differentiated the period of modern colonisation into three phases: (1) from the conquest of the new world to the American War of Independence; (2) from the American War of Independence to 1830; (3) from 1830 to the present (1864). In summarising the first two periods, Cairnes relied greatly on Merivale's Lectures on Colonies and Colonization.(34) In the first phase Cairnes believed that the "most striking fact connected with the early English colonies is, the extraordinary variety of political institutions which prevailed in them".(35) However, the American War of Independence marked a "change of vital moment" in British colonial policy, a movement towards centralised bureaucracy with penal colonies and absolutism. He also reiterated Wakefield's argument that colonisation was brought into disrepute by transportation, which had also corrupted the "whole tone of English thought" on the topic.(36) Cairnes then outlined the colonial reformers' ideas and evaluated their success.

With this historical context, Cairnes turned to a consideration of "the present situation". In doing so, he adhered to the fundamental propositions of the classical school and the ideas of G C Lewis and Goldwin Smith.(37) He discussed the view that colonies provided tribute, the possibility of commercial monopoly (free trade had removed this ground for colonies) and a region for penal settlements.(38)

> We do not any longer ask - we certainly do not receive - from our colonies any commercial advantages which are not equally open to the whole world, which we should not equally command, though the political connection were severed tomorrow. The commercial reason for holding colonies in subjection, therefore, like the financial one, has passed away.(39)

Furthermore, he quoted Merivale's new position, that the colonies were valuable as fields for emigration. But to Cairnes, this "theory wanted nothing but a basis, in fact. In this, however, it was deficient, as most emigrated to non-empire countries, especially the United States".(40) In this instance, Cairnes contravened his methodology on principles of political economy and utilised facts to disprove a theory, something he condemned in others.(41)

Thinking along similar lines to Smith and Rogers, Cairnes argued that it was also impossible to justify colonisation on the grounds of "the extension of free trade", because with the granting of self-government, nations such as Australia and Canada could dictate their own commercial policy. He agreed with them and asserted that all the grounds for colonisation had completely disappeared.(42) England had never received any substantial tribute from her colonies; most emigrants went to the United States; and the colonies had established high tariff walls against the mother country.

We have abandoned all the objects for the sake of which our Colonial Empire was founded. We are unable to impress our will upon our colonies in any particular manner ... Wholly irrespective of our wishes, they enter into alliance, unite and separate, dispose of their lands, recast their constitutions, and even combine for the avowed purpose of thwarting our design. When things have reached this pass, it seems rather idle to ask - Are we to retain our colonies? Retain our colonies! What is there left to retain? Retain the privilege of spending nearly 4,500,000 pounds sterling on their prohibitive tariffs and 'ironical allegiance'.(43)

Cairnes identified himself with Smith, but not Rogers and Mill, when he stated that he was for colonial emancipation and against any retention of political control.(44) He believed that if the pretence of political unity was given up, then it would be possible to establish a "moral unity" bound together by "blood, language and religion".(45) His political stance was identical to that of Goldwin Smith, whose ideas he totally accepted. In contrast to Smith, however, he confined his discussion to the self-governing colonies, and only referred in passing to India. After his lecture in 1864, Cairnes rarely returned to discuss the question of colonisation, despite his differences with his mentor in economic theory, J S Mill, on the matter of colonial government.(46)

He did, however, expound his opinions on emigration questions, and in this connection also disagreed with Mill. In "Fragments on Ireland", written in 1866, Cairnes considered the magnitude and implications of Irish emigration from 1846 to 1866 on the domestic and international economies.(47) Associating himself with other mid-nineteenth century thinkers he explained Irish emigration as a combination of both internal and external forces, such as the 'seasons of death' (potato famine), gold discoveries, foreign wars, urgent demand for labour in the United States and fluctuations in trade.(48) Whilst these causes had contributed to the general result, four "modern agencies" were primarily responsible - popular education, steam, free trade, and the progress of colonisation. "Popular education has thus supplied the motive, and steam and free trade have not less surely furnished the means".(49) Emigration, which was "one of the most remarkable facts" of the civilised world, was made easier and less repulsive as colonisation extends".(50) As a result of the prosperity in the colonies and in other new settlements, emigration was, and should remain, self-supporting.(51) While Cairnes remained totally opposed to any form of government involvement, J S Mill was favourably disposed to government assistance to emigration.(52)

HENRY FAWCETT

Introduction

Whilst J E Cairnes was the theoretical defender of J S Mill, Henry Fawcett was the popularizer of Mill's Principles.(53) Born in 1833 at Salisbury, to a draper shopkeeper, Fawcett's early life held great promise and it was generally agreed he would have a brilliant future.(54) After successful schooling at King's College, Fawcett went up to Peterhouse, Cambridge and then transferred to Trinity Hall and was elected to a fellowship in 1856. In the following year he lost his sight in a shooting accident, but this did not deter his life-long ambition to enter parliament. In 1860 he stood, and then withdrew as a Candidate for Southwark. Three years later, he was elected Professor of Political Economy at Cambridge and unsuccessfully contested the seat of Cambridge and Brighton.(55) In 1865 he was elected as a member for Brighton and entered the House of Commons as an advanced liberal.(56) Although he was defeated in the 1874 election, an old friend (Sir Charles Reade) resigned his Hackney seat, and Fawcett was re-elected as the member for this constituency and held it till his death in 1884, when he was Post Master General.(57) In Parliament, he became affectionately known as the 'MP for India', and one commentator wrote that his death "deprived the natives of India of a Parliamentary advocate more powerful than any other they had possessed since the time of Burke".(58)

At Cambridge, Fawcett studied mathematics, and his two close friends (C B Clarke and Daniel Jones) were mathematicians. "They were typical Cambridge men; believers in hard facts and figures, admirers of strenuous commonsense, and hearty despisers of sentimentalism".(59) Fawcett's interests were diverse and he was most active in the Union. He spoke frequently, preparing carefully written speeches on national education and university reform.(60) He was an eager participant in an informal discussion group, led by Edward Wilson (the eighth wrangler in 1853) who especially delighted in discussing political economy and vindicating Mill. Fawcett graduated as the seventh wrangler, a disappointment because he was expected to be first.

Economics

Fawcett does not command a place beside the founders of economics, though he was unquestionably a great populariser of the subject. In 1863 he published the first edition of his Manual, which ran eight editions during his lifetime. Fawcett first became interested in political economy at Cambridge, and was urged to read J S Mill's Principles by Edward Wilson. Subsequently, he studied Smith, Malthus and Ricardo, in whose "terse logic he especially delighted", and he confined his theoretical work to expanding and applying the principles of his predecessors, and became Mill's devoted pupil, claiming that "no teacher could ever boast of a more ardent and attached disciple".(61)

He met Mill for the first time in 1860, and they developed a strong friendship.(62) Fawcett frequently invited him to Cambridge, though Mill generally declined the invitations.(63) Fawcett was delighted to sit near Mill in the House of Commons, and after his first day as a member wrote to his father: "The seat I have is as convenient a one as any in the House, and a capital place to speak from. I walked away from the Commons with Mill. He sits on the bench just above me, close to Bright".(64)

Despite Fawcett's early work on the effects of the South American, Californian and Australian gold discoveries and the drain of precious metals to the East, it was his Manual which established his reputation as an economist.(65) The Manual was the result of a proposal by Alexander Macmillan that Fawcett write a popular manual on political economy. Macmillan, a close friend of Leslie Stephen and Fawcett, was frequently in their rooms at Cambridge, "trying rather fruitlessly to stimulate Fawcett's interest in the writings of Carlyle, Maurice and Kingsley".(66) Fawcett commenced work on the Manual in the autumn of 1861 and it was published at the beginning of 1863. It was really an introduction to Mill's Principles, not a substitute. In the preface of the first edition, Fawcett praised Mill's economics and stated his reluctance to publish such a work because it "would withdraw students from the perusal of a more complete treatise. I am, however, convinced that those who become acquainted with the first principles of Political Economy will be so much struck with the attractiveness and importance of the science that they will not relinquish its study".(67)

To Fawcett, political economy was a science, not a code of morality, as it dealt with "laws in the scientific and not the normal sense". Economics was positive, not normative: "It doesn't pronounce the proper ends of man to be money-making, or anything else. It confines itself to showing what are, in fact, the conditions and consequences of money-making and spending".(68) This view of economics was consistently and systematically expounded in the successive editions of his Manual and other publications. However he was always particularly concerned to demonstrate that political economy was closely connected with the practical questions of life. In the first edition of the Manual, he devoted chapters to co-operative societies, strikes and trade unions and the third edition (1869) was substantially revised to take account of changes in the economy and society at large.(69) In the fifth edition (1876), because of the substantial fall in the price of silver, he substituted a chapter on "The Recent Discoveries of Gold and Silver" for "The Recent Gold Discoveries", and in the sixth edition (1883) this was expanded to two chapters on the gold discoveries and the depreciation in the value of silver. Despite taking account of such real world changes and introducing chapters into the Manual not discussed in Mill's Principles, Fawcett generally remained faithful to the leading tenets of Mill's economics. Associating himself with Cairnes, Fawcett adhered to the wages-fund theory after Mill had abandoned it as a consequence of

Thornton's attack. In the first edition of his Manual, Fawcett proved it to be "physically impossible that any permanent rise in wages should take place without a corresponding diminution in profits".(70) In subsequent editions the chapter was re-written and this statement disappeared. Even in the first edition there are explanations which considerably modify the sweeping character of the phrase just quoted. However, in spite of Mill's repudiation of the wages-fund theory, Fawcett remained satisfied with the general validity of the main principles.

Generally speaking, on matters of government intervention, Fawcett believed that every proposed measure had to be considered on its own merits, although he was on the side of government non-interference and to all matters of potential government involvement he asked "Does the remedy tend to raise or to lower the spirit of self-help?"(71) Upon this criterion, Fawcett recognised a number of areas where government could participate usefully in a nation's affairs. On the Irish Land Question, he seems to have justified State intervention on the grounds that the existing sentiment in Ireland denied the existence of the landlord's absolute right on the soil. The situation was abnormal, and this required abnormal legislation. Likewise, he recommended that the cotton tax in India, which was a protective measure, should remain.(72) As Post Master General, he believed that the State could do a great deal to encourage thrift and self-help by supporting savings banks, providing a system of deferred amenities and by facilitating the investment of small sums in national securities.(73)

While Fawcett's economic principles followed those of Mill, in Free Trade and Protection, published fifteen years after the first edition of his Manual, Fawcett rejected Mill's infant industry argument.(74) In his Principles, Mill had argued that the imposition of a protective duty, with the view of promoting a new industry in a recently settled country, could be justified as a temporary expedient.(75) In a manner akin to Cairnes, Rogers and Smith, Fawcett considered that Mill's statement had given "considerable encouragement" to colonial protectionists.(76) When Fawcett considered the arguments propagated by the protectionists, he attempted to both explain and criticise Mill's position:

> There is no-one more ready than I am to recognise the high authority of Mr Mill as an Economist, and I will at once admit that the arguments which he advances in favour of the imposition of protection in a young country would be conclusive if there were a reasonable probability that the solutions under which he supposes that such a protective duty could be imposed would ever be realised.(77)

Fawcett forcibly argued that no amount of theoretical reasoning "as to the desirability of imposing a protective duty" as a temporary expedient in a young country, could contend with the experience that once imposed, such a duty was permanent.(78) In attacking J S Mill's position, Fawcett clearly reveals his firm opposition to all forms of protection, arguing that it was an impediment to progress, which interfered with the free movement of labour and capital, discouraged industrial enterprise by weakening the feeling of self-reliance and fostered "political corruption by inducing various trade interests to use their influence in securing the imposition of duties specially to benefit themselves".(79) Although Fawcett's defence of free trade was orthodox, he did recommend - as will become evident - the retention of the cotton tax in India.(80)

Principles of Political Economy and the Empire

Fawcett frequently sought to verify the principles of political economy by reference to the Australian colonies and India, although his efforts were not as extensive as those of Cairnes. The two countries figure prominently in his numerous examples, which were intended to bolster and support the fundamental principles of political economy.

Australia In the tradition of J S Mill's support for Wakefield's ideas on colonial development, Fawcett noted how in the early settlements in eastern Australia, the migrants had scattered themselves over the land.(81) Thinking along similar lines to Wakefield, Mill and Cairnes, Fawcett was highly critical of such a policy. Given the tendency for population to disperse itself over a colony, it was initially supposed that agriculture would be crippled by gold discoveries as labour would be attracted to gold mines. However, Fawcett argued that Wakefield's theory of colonisation was corroborated by the effects of the Australian gold discoveries.(82)

He noted that gold may have been the primary stimulus to Australia's prosperity, but gold output per se, was an inaccurate measure of the increased wealth since the land had been rendered more efficient and productive as a consequence of the co-operation of labour and the increased population. Before the sudden influx of migrants with the gold discoveries, much of the produce from the land was not required but with the gold rushes there was an increased demand for meat, which in turn stimulated agriculture.(83) Wheat was not as cheap as mutton for it required more capital and labour than wool but the returns were high because of the sheer abundance of land. In this context, Fawcett agreed with Cairnes and argued that there were two main reasons why agriculture and mining flourished in Australia and manufacturing did not, namely: the great abundance of land and the lack of skilled labour and machinery required for manufacturing.(84)

On Emigration Fawcett was aware of Wakefield's ideas on colonial development, Mill's support of systematic colonisation and Cairnes' rejection of State-assisted emigration. Given his close interpretation of Mill's work and interest in Wakefield's ideas on colonial development, it is no surprise to find Fawcett considering the general and popular topic of emigration in considerable detail. However, unlike his contemporaries he did not review schemes of colonisation or devote much attention to questions of State-assisted emigration, but concentrated on the general theory and effects of emigration and was the last classical economist to present a detailed, comprehensive and systematic account of migration theory. In the first edition of his Manual of Political Economy published in 1863 he accepted Wakefield's and Mill's position, arguing that the emigration of labour from the United Kingdom relieved low wages, reduced the nation's excess population, and assisted colonial development. Fawcett contended that over the period 1848-1863, three million persons had emigrated from the United Kingdom thereby reducing the numbers competing for the wages fund - provided that there were no net effects on the natural rate of increase. Moreover, Fawcett adhered to the wages fund doctrine even after Mill's recantation. The concept of the wages fund was only one element in a theory of wages. It was essentially a theory of the demand for labour, according to which demand was a function of the accumulation of capital. It took for granted the principles and forces governing the supply of labour and referred both to the short-run and the long-run. In the short-run the total demand for labour in any given year was seen as a function of the wage fund accumulated in the previous year. In the short-run, labour supply was assumed to be a given stock of workers competing for employment. Thus, short-run wages were the result of dividing two stocks-wage capital and the number of workers. In the long-run the demand for labour was conceived as a function of the rate of accumulation of total capital. In the long-run, labour supply fluctuated according to the revised Malthusian theory of population; it was a function of the standard of living. It increased as the standard rose and diminished as it fell. The natural or long-run rate of wages was, in theory, held to be fixed at that point determined by the infinitely elastic supply of labour.(85)

Fawcett's acceptance of the classical theory of wages and the Malthusian population doctrine provided the basis for his discussion of emigration and he specified four main advantages associated with the migration of people.(86) Firstly, emigrants left an oversupplied labour market and settled in new countries with large underdeveloped natural resources which they were able to exploit for their own benefit and to the advantage of both their adopted country and their nation of origin. Secondly, since labourers received wages in their new country, wealth could be more rapidly accumulated and the new societies could become prosperous. Thirdly, the newly exploited regions produced reliable supplies of cheap food for export to the United Kingdom. Fourthly, and most importantly, emigration averted a substantial prospective decrease in wages.(87) Fawcett's blind acceptance of the wages fund doctrine led to his failure to adequately explore other factors besides emigration which could avert a decrease in money wages.

Emigration, therefore, is not only a very efficient check upon population, but it is in every respect most beneficial in its results; it causes wages to rise, or rather prevents their fall in those countries from which emigration takes place, and by providing supplies of cheap food, it indirectly confers upon the labouring classes another most important advantage.(88)

To Fawcett, the Irish potato famine and the accompanying emigration revealed the beneficial effects of large-scale migration. The Irish were presented with the clear alternative of starving or emigrating, which many did. "This emigration must be regarded as a most happy circumstance; for if it had not occurred, a great part of the nation must have fallen victims to all the horrors of starvation". Not only had an onerous burden of population been relieved, but labour supply had decreased and consequently wages rose.(89) Whilst Fawcett's consideration of the beneficial effects of Irish emigration was consistent with other mid-nineteenth century commentators, the Irish economist, T E Cliffe Leslie, adopted a heretical stance over the effects of emigration on Irish wages and disagreed with the classical economists.(90) At this stage it is pertinent briefly to consider Leslie's views on the matter not only for their own sake but also to highlight Fawcett's orthodoxy on the subject.

Leslie's unorthodox approach to wages underlay his emigration analysis. Wages, to Leslie, were determined by a host of institutional factors, which included customs, habits, and local conditions. He repudiated the wages fund doctrine before Mill's famous recantation, maintaining that even in competitive industries wages were chiefly determined by trade unions and productivity levels.(91) Leslie's challenge to the tenets and methodology of classical economics included criticism of customary terminology on the subject. Emigration, for example, had been spoken of "as a thing the beneficial effects of which, in every case, have an a priori certainty that leaves no room for discussion".(92) Leslie argued that three separate beliefs had grown around the meaning of the word 'emigration': (i) It occurred such that supply and demand factors interacted to establish labour at its most optimal position. (ii) It was beneficial because it took place through the operation of private interests. (iii) Emigration, so it was argued, must raise the rate of wages by distributing the "aggregate wages fund among a smaller number of labourers".(93) Leslie disputed all these meanings, especially the belief that emigration raised the rate of wages. Yet in maintaining that these three meanings were separate, Leslie neglected their inter-linking nature.

He argued that emigration was not a single phenomenon, as economists were apt to believe. To him, emigration was a complex occurrence, which could not be contained in a single all embracing general theory. He attempted to demonstrate his view by listing the number of emigrants from the United Kingdom to North America, Australia and New Zealand over the period 1853-86, thereby showing that there were differences between emigration patterns to various destinations.(94) However, in condemning general approaches to emigration, Leslie overlooked the common underlying factors.

More specifically, Leslie argued that those who emigrated from Ireland could have been supported at home in comfort, if only the country's evils had been eliminated. In this respect he differed from all contemporary economists, for they considered that emigration conferred benefits on the Irish economy.(95) Leslie strongly argued that it was the 'ancient restrictions' on commerce and manufacturing which held back industrial progress and resulted in the loss of capital and labour overseas.(96) He adopted an heretical stance over the effects of emigration on Irish wages and disagreed with the traditional economists who argued that the rise in wages in Ireland was a direct consequence of the emigration in the 1840s and 1850s. Leslie reversed this contention, arguing that if there had been no emigration from Ireland the rise in wages would have been higher, and there would have been more labour and capital for development purposes. Whilst Leslie did not explain the underlying economic assumptions for this position, it is clear that he had a dynamic conception of long-term economic development.(97)

Leslie's inductive studies of wages and prices convinced him of the widening discrepancy between orthodox economic theory and the conditions of the real world, especially with respect to Irish emigration. His approach to the emigration question was markedly different from other economists for his ideas and analysis were rooted in a desire to offer solutions to Ireland's problems and he did not discuss the broader question of empire.

Fawcett's approach was in direct contrast to Leslie's and he devoted considerable attention to the difficult question of why people emigrated to new lands. The prime reason, he thought, was in order to improve their material position. In such a context, economic theory provided an inadequate rationale for labour movements owing to the interaction of two forces, which were inoperative in the earlier days of political economy. Firstly, peace in the world meant that capital was highly mobile and was invested in those countries where the realised rate of profit was sufficiently attractive. Secondly, unlike previous periods, labour was prepared to leave its native country permanently for new lands.

When capital and labour thus remain stationary many economic principles could be enunciated which have now lost their applicability. Then it could be said, with approximate truth, that the rate of wages in each country depended upon the number of its labouring population, compared with the amount of capital which was accumulated in that country. But now this principal has to be modified, for only a portion of the wealth which is, for instance, annually saved in England is retained to assist our own industry; the vast sums of English capital which are annually invested in foreign countries do not immediately produce any augmentation in our own wage fund. Formerly, if the births greatly exceeded the deaths, it could positively be asserted, that there would be an increasing number of labourers competing for employment. Now, however, it may happen, that numbers who are born in this country may never seek employment here, but may be drafted off to far distant labour markets. These considerations show that the principles of Political Economy have to be stated with constantly widening generality.(98)

Thus Fawcett noted that in order to explain labour's desire to emigrate, the principles of political economy had to be expressed with a "constantly widening generality". This is indeed an interesting, probably novel comment, and somewhat surprising coming from Fawcett. Unfortunately, he failed to explicate his meaning for although he appreciated the changing dimensions of the world economy in the latter half of the nineteenth century, he was unable to interpret them in terms of classical political economy or to adapt classical economics to these changed circumstances. However, he did suggest that government could take an active role in emigration schemes, a thought absent in the first edition of the Manual: "If, therefore, distress is caused by low wages, and it is desirable to make wages higher, Government cannot do anything which will with so much certainty attain this object as to encourage emigration in every possible way".(99) Although Fawcett did not explicitly support Mill's position over State-assisted emigration, in contrast to Cairnes he clearly implied that he would favour state intervention in migration questions.(100)

In the third edition of his Manual published in 1869, Fawcett significantly altered his views on the effects of emigration. The previously entitled chapter, "Popular Remedies for Low Wages", was changed to "National Education and other Remedies for Low Wages". Education was now given the major role in the relief of low wages, not emigration which was considered as a short term solution to the problem. To Fawcett, education would effect a great material and spiritual improvement in the population and would lead directly to greater dexterity and more astuteness in the work force, so increasing productivity. He asserted that as a consequence of education ignorance would disappear, crime decrease, and England would maintain her world supremacy. Unquestionably, Fawcett exaggerated the benefits of education, though - as is evident from the passage below - he did not ignore the benefits of emigration:

Emigration might no doubt become a most effectual remedy for low wages. It not only relieves an overburdened labour market, but by our emigration, countries are developed to which England must chiefly look for those supplies of cheap food which are so essential for her material progress. But in the present condition of the country there is a grave peril associated with emigration. Those who leave our shores are naturally the most energetic and intelligent of our labourers; the consequence is that emigration is constantly drawing away from those whom we can least afford to lose, and least likely to become a burden upon our resources. While so large a proportion of the population is deficient in frugality, the advantages resulting from emigration are quickly neutralised by the increase of population which is invariably stimulated by an advance in wages. During the last twenty years emigration on a large scale has been constantly going on from these islands; yet there never was a time when complaints were more frequent as to the unsatisfactory condition of our labourers.(101)

In addition to education, Fawcett offered three other reasons why he rejected emigration as a long term measure for relieving the United Kingdom's excess population. Firstly, he now adhered to the classical "vacuum theory", popularized by the classical economist Nassau Senior, which held that any gaps in the population created by migration only acted as a stimulus to further population growth. Mass emigration decreased the labour supply, increased money wages and so encouraged the working classes to procreate.(102) Secondly, emigration resulted in the most productive labourers leaving Britain's shores.(103) Thirdly, he had now come to accept the proposition that the world would soon be over-populated. This was a reversal of the optimism expressed in the first edition of his _Manual_, in which he outlined the theoretical argument that one day emigration would cease to be a remedy for overpopulation and that the colonies would become as thickly populated as the mother country.(104) However, he thought such an outcome was a remote possibility

This, as a mere theoretical anticipation, cannot be denied but the day when the earth shall become thus densely populated is, we believe, too remote for us to feel any concern about the difficulties which will result from such an occurrence.(105)

By the third edition, however, Fawcett had reversed this position:

It must however be remembered that emigration must, after a time, cease to be a remedy for over-population. Some of the facts already mentioned show that population has, under favourable conditions, such a high rate of geometrical increase, that our colonies might, before a long period has elapsed, become as thickly populated as the mother-country. Emigration would then no longer afford relief.(106)

Not only did Fawcett reject the view that emigration was the most effective remedy for low wages, but he also reversed his position on state-sponsored emigration schemes. He withdrew his support for the Wakefield-Mill argument on government intervention in migration matters, and accepted Cairnes' argument favouring total voluntary emigration.

In Pauperism: Its Causes and its Remedies, Fawcett attacked

J Wilmot-Horton's scheme of emigration when he contended that the sending of paupers to America and the colonies "would not only prove mischievous, but is impracticable".(107) He was most anxious as to who would bear the cost of such state-emigration and accepted Cairnes' argument that the State should not participate in emigration, which should be voluntary.

> A fatal check would at once be given to all attempts to emigrate by voluntary efforts; people who are willing to strive hard to provide their own passage-money would naturally say, why should we do this, when free passages are given to those who have brought indigence upon themselves through their own fault? It may, however, be argued that it is not paupers alone who would be assisted to emigrate, but that the same aid would be given to all applicants. Nothing could be more dangerous than such a policy. It would be offering a bribe to our best labourers and most skilled artisans to leave these shores. The sources of national wealth and power would be seriously impaired; and the country, thus rendered poorer, would have to bear a heavier burden of taxation.(108)

Both of Mill's disciples rejected their master's position, although Fawcett, so far as we are aware, did not engage in discussion on the matter with Mill, whereas Cairnes did.(109) However in contrast to Cairnes, Goldwin Smith and J E T Rogers, Fawcett was not so interested in demonstrating that most emigrants went to the United States and that the empire was insignificant with regard to total emigration. He was not so concerned to create a case for colonial emancipation based upon the economic disutility of empire.(110) Rather, Fawcett concentrated on those measures which could relieve low wages, and in this theoretical context, emigration was discussed. On this matter, he was more theoretical and systematic than Cairnes, the accredited leading defender of classical political economy.(111)

India Although Fawcett spoke frequently and powerfully on Indian affairs in the House of Commons and always lent a sympathetic ear to Indian problems, it is difficult to point to any specific or definite legislative achievements directly attributable to him. As Leslie Stephen says "The effect of his action is to be found less in any specific change than in the whole temper of English public opinion upon Indian questions".(112) Before examining Fawcett's contribution to Indian discussions in the parliamentary sphere, it is pertinent to note those important references to India in his published work.

(i) Published Material. As with Australia, Fawcett utilised India to support and verify the principles of political economy. He stressed that in order to accumulate wealth, there had to be social order. Referring to India, he categorically stated that nothing had retarded Indian industrial progress and the associated exploitation of resources more than the social anarchy which prevailed for many centuries. "If England's rule and England's power can make the people of India see that the rights of private property will be strictly respected, then India will inevitably become a great commercial nation".(113) While law and order were important for economic development, Fawcett argued that the prime determinant of capital accumulation was the rate of profit. This in turn, depended on the extensive co-operation of labour and capital and, as J S Mill had done, he pointed out that Indian poverty and backwardness had been perpetuated by the lack of communications between the villages.(114)

> There cannot be any extensive co-operation of labour between one employment and another, or between one district and another, unless the means of communication are good. Nothing, probably, has more contributed to perpetuate the poverty and backwardness of India than the want of good roads. There, one district can scarcely lend any assistance to another; an interchange of commodities, which would be advantageous to every party, is often prevented by the want of a road.

> During the terrible famine which ravaged the North-West Province, in the year 1860, wheat which was in one district at the famine price of four rupees per maund of 83lbs, was selling in adjoining districts at less than two rupees per maund. As long as such occurrences can take place, India must continue poor, her resources must remain imperfectly developed, and her labour must be comparatively inefficient. A village community virtually isolated from the rest of India cannot now raise that produce for which their land is best adapted, but must cultivate it with a view of supplying themselves with the first necessaries of life. Manchester would, no doubt, annually purchase off India many million pounds' worth of cotton; but cotton will not be produced on any large scale until the people of India feel that if they grow cotton they will be able to exchange it for food, which is in abundance in one district, but cannot be transported a few miles to alleviate the sufferings of a starving population.(115)

Yet, in order for economic development to occur, labour had to be associated with capital; and if this was lacking then loans could be secured. Fawcett outlined how loans could be appropriated either from a country's capital or an increase in savings, and he applied this principle of political economy to India, noting that substantial loans had already been raised for Indian industrial development.(116) Without these loans, railway and irrigation projects would not have been undertaken. Fawcett contended that in estimating the effects on the population of such loans, general economic principles acted as a guideline and he concluded that loans were a means of enriching a country without permanently injuring the labourers.(117)

> Indian railways have been constructed by loans subscribed almost entirely in England. It has been calculated that

11,000,000 l has been paid to the natives of India for the labour upon railways; and, since this amount was imported capital, the labouring population of India derive the same immediate advantage as if 11,000,000 l had been distributed in gratuities amongst them. If then, a loan in any way causes the capital of the country to be increased, the labourers will receive immediate benefit, even if the loan is spent unproductively; on the contrary, the employers will, under the same circumstances, suffer a loss, because wages will rise as a consequence of the capital being increased. India affords a striking example of this; for the large sums of money raised in England, and spent within the last few years upon the public works of India, have caused the wages of labourers in the country to rise in a very marked manner.(118)

Fawcett considered that an alternative means of raising capital, other than loans, was by taxation. He reasoned that in a wealthy country, like the United Kingdom, income tax could be paid out of either income or capital, but in a poor country (India) there were problems with such a method.

In a poor country such as India, an income tax is a more hazardous expedient. India is poor because sufficient capital has not been applied to develop her great resources. The best opinions agree that an income-tax would in India be in part paid out of capital, and therefore its imposition in that country would only be justified by extreme necessity.(119)

However, as a result of English rule and confidence amongst investors, large loans were raised in England and used to develop Indian railways and roads, thus promoting economic development. And yet, the government had to establish credit facilities in India, not so much to encourage capital imports as to bring forth domestic sources of capital.

England cannot confer a greater blessing upon India than by establishing credit in that country, for if by the proper administration of justice the people of India should be made to feel confidence in their fellow men, wealth would be saved, and the vast resources of that country would be developed by capital accumulated by its own people.(120)

With regard to India, Fawcett did not hold to his free-trade beliefs. Since she was a British dependency, the government was responsible for public works programmes since the construction of railways, canals, roads and other works would not be undertaken by private enterprise.(121) Moreover, Fawcett was in favour of retaining the 5% duty imposed on cotton goods imported into India and since he was most aware that this support contradicted his free trade principles, he carefully outlined the case propagated by those who demanded the abolition of the duty, concentrating upon their claim "that as long as the duty is permitted to remain, a national sanction is given on the part of England to protection". On economic grounds he was opposed to the tax:

> The price not simply of those cotton goods which pay the duty is raised, but the duty causes the price of those goods which are made in India to be also raised; consequently the tax takes from the people of India an amount far exceeding that which it yields to the State. The tax therefore, like every other tax which is protective in character, must be, on economic grounds, unhesitatingly condemned.(122)

Fawcett stressed, however, that the matter could not be regarded as simply involving economic considerations, noting that the the most equitable system of taxation which it was possible to devise for one country, could be inapplicable to other countries. In deciding whether the duties on imported cotton goods ought to be repealed, Fawcett claimed that the peculiar and critical position of Indian finances had to be taken into account:

> The great mass of the people of that country are so poor, and live with such extreme frugality, that with the exception of salt there is no article of general consumption which it is possible to tax; and the duty on salt has been strained to its utmost point, being one of the heaviest duties imposed on a first necessary of life.(123)

This situation had been exacerbated by the steady rise in expenditure and the famines. Under these circumstances Fawcet argued that no existing "source of revenue can with prudence be surrendered".(124)

(ii) Parliamentary Questions. In July 1867, Fawcett began his pronouncements on Indian affairs in the House of Commons when he asked whether the expenses of a ball at the Indian office for the Sultan of Turkey were to be charged to India. He established that they were, and - despite Mill urging him not to protest - Fawcett challenged the Secretary of State for India on how he could tax the toiling Indian peasant for such extravagance.(125) The following year, he demanded that the Indian Civil service examination he held in Calcutta, Madras and Bombay, as well as London, arguing that this would give the Indians more chance of obtaining positions.(126)

Throughout his public speeches, Fawcett pointed to Parliament's need to take an interest in Indian affairs and he was appalled by the lack of interest in Indian affairs shown by the members of the House of Commons.

> The people of India have no votes; they cannot bring so much pressure to bear upon Parliament as can be brought by one of our great railway companies; but with some confidence I

believe that I shall not be misinterpreting your wishes if, as your representative, I do whatever can be done by one humble individual to render justice to the defenceless and powerless.(127)

He frequently raised questions concerning Indian finances and government in the House, but his two most important speeches were delivered on the Indian Budget debates in 1872 and 1873.(128) In the 1872 debate, Fawcett rose and moved the following resolution, as an amendment to the motion that the Speaker leave the Chair, to consider the Indian Financial Statement which had been made by Mr Grant Duff:

That this House, considering the statement of the late Lord Mayo that "a feeling of discontent and dissatisfaction exists among every class, both European and native, in our Indian Empire, on account of the increase of taxation which has for years been going on", and that the "continuance of that feeling is a political danger the magnitude of which can hardly be over-estimated", is of opinion that the income tax, which is generally admitted to be unsuited to the people of India, might, during the coming financial year, be dispensed with, and that other taxes exceptionally burdensome to the people of India might be considerably reduced, if the finances of that country were administered with adequate care and economy.(129)

The sole objective of Fawcett's speech was to direct Parliament's attention to India's financial condition, which he believed was "precarious", since the country's revenue was largely inelastic, whereas its expenditure was highly elastic. He carefully considered the sources of revenue, noting that while land tax was the most important source, at least 20% was fixed for ever in pecuniary amounts.(130) The salt tax was the highest it had ever been, and as this was a necessity, the tax was "unjust" and a "burdensome impact on the population".(131) He was not confident in opium revenue as a means of meeting future increases in expenditure, as it was the most "uncertain" of all revenues. Any other forms of revenue - customs duties on stamps and drugs - formed a very small proportion of revenue.(132)

It cannot be too carefully borne in mind that the English revenue is inelastic in an eminent degree, because many articles we can tax are of universal consumption, such as tea, sugar and beer, whereas the great mass of the Indian people are so poor that it is almost impossible, except by the salt duty, to levy any tax on an article of general consumption. A slowly increasing revenue, a rapidly increasing expenditure, administration each year becoming more costly, a determination to embark on a vast and indefinite expenditure on public works, with the ominous fact constantly staring us in the face, that to use Mr Massey's words, "we have used up every source of revenue, and forced up every tax to a maximum".(133)

Furthermore, as there was no Indian representative in Parliament, no checks and balances existed on the expenditure activities of the Secretary of State, the Governor-General, the Governors of Bombay and Madras, and the Lieutenant-Governor of the North-West Province. "India may be neglected, her money may be wasted, her affairs may be mismanaged, it will not affect the interests of the party, it will scarcely raise a ripple on the surface of politics".(134)

The only solution to Indian financial problems was to curb expenditure and to ensure that the nation's finances were managed with care and economy. In the long-run, this could be achieved by making the English aware of the difficulties. However, in the short-term, Fawcett recommended: (1) that the government should cease to guarantee returns on capital for British investors, so that they would not be "insured against the evil consequences of their own mismanagement"; (2) that Military expenditure should be thoroughly investigated; (3) that the expenditure on all public works should be scrutinised. Fawcett was sympathetic to public work programmes, but because of the financial problems he recommended that "no public works should be undertaken, except from any surplus which might be saved out of ordinary revenue".(135) Fawcett stressed that these three measures were short-term and that the more difficult longer term remedy was to change attitudes in England and the system of government administration.

In the 1873 debate on the Indian Budget Fawcett continued his attack on the means of raising revenue in India and the British administration.(136) One of the main contentions of his speech was over the figures and facts presented by the Government and the existence of local taxes and their relation to schemes of decentralisation. The most exhaustive analysis, however, was that relating to local taxation, which had been briefly alluded to in previous budgets. He was appalled at the way in which local taxation had been forced onto the Indians: "we shall not forget that at the present moment local taxation is threatening the Indian people with a far greater amount of hardship and annoyance than it is ever likely to bring upon our own country".(137)

After his 1873 speech, until he was made Post Master General in 1880, Fawcett applied the principles established in his 1872 speech to considerations of Indian finance. He recommended, after the 1874 famine, that to meet similar difficulties in the future, England should secure a regular surplus of revenue in the prosperous seasons, by which debts might be discharged in poor seasons. In June 1875 he protested that the Prince of Wales' visit to India was to be financed by the Indians. The following year, he opposed measures giving pensions to the Indian army.(138) In 1877 he protested at the advocacy of an abolition of Indian cotton duties and between 1878-1879 he sat on a number of committees concerned with Indian affairs which verified his position on the elasticity of expenditure and inelasticity of revenue.(139)

In February, May and October 1879, he published essays on Indian finance in the Nineteenth Century. Once again, these articles highlighted the difficulties of raising revenue in India and the need for expenditure so as to develop resources. He suggested three guidelines for further policy:

1. A reduction in civil administration, which had grown too rapidly since 1858.
2. An increase of natives in the civil service, thus reducing the cost and effecting a political advantage.
3. A reduction of military expenditure.(140)

In 1880, Fawcett accepted the Post Master General's position in Gladstone's government and held office till his death in 1884. During these four years, Fawcett spoke little on Indian affairs, though he certainly retained an interest in the country.

Conclusion

Traditionally historians of economic thought have decried Fawcett's contribution to political economy, at least when compared with the last leading exponent of classical economics, Fawcett's friend and colleague, J E Cairnes. While this position is broadly correct in relation to Cairnes' contribution to the theoretical and methodological aspects of classical political economy, we cannot agree with Professors Hutchison's and Stigler's exclusion of Fawcett from the list of important British economists or with Professor Blaug's view that

> Henry Fawcett (1833-84) was "a man of one book"; his Manual of Political Economy, published in 1863, the year of his election to the professorship at Cambridge, was simply an abridgement of Mill's Principles with some additional material on co-operatives and poor laws. The only points of interest in it are a series of obiter dicta; these are revealing of that blatant discrepancy between theory and observation which had long sapped the vitality of the Ricardo-Mill line.(141)

Rather, we agree with professor O'Brien that

> Fawcett has long been regarded as a regurgitator of J S Mill. This is perhaps a little unfair in that he was alive to some of the differences between experience and the expected theoretical conclusions; and in any case there can be little doubt that by virtue of his position as professor at Cambridge he was in a position to exercise influence.(142)

Furthermore, it is most evident that with regard to the British empire, Fawcett's contribution was more extensive and important than Cairnes', who re-iterated Goldwin Smith's arguments.

NOTES

1. Cairnes came to the study of economics after taking an arts degree at Trinity College, Dublin. In 1856 he took a competetive examination and obtained the Whately professorship. Three years later he was elected to the Professorship of Political Economy and Jurisprudence at Queens College, Galway, and in 1866 was appointed Professor of Political Economy at University College, London, but resigned in 1872 because of ill health. For an outline of his life see Henry Fawcett, "Professor Cairnes", Fortnightly Review, Vol. 11, January-June 1878, pp.149-54.

2. J E Cairnes, The Character and Logical Method of Political Economy, (London, Macmillan, 1875 edition).

3. Ibid, pp.14-16.

4. Ibid, p.21.

5. Ibid, pp.64-6.

6. Ibid, p.118.

7. Ibid, p.75.

8. Ibid, pp.59-60. On this question also see D P O'Brien, The Classical Economists, op.cit, pp.72-3 and N W Senior, An Introductory Lecture on Political Economy, (London, John Murray, 1831), pp.26-7, and Outline of the Science of Political Economy, (London, Allen and Unwin, 1951 Reprint), pp.86-193.

9. Cairnes, Logical Method, op.cit, pp.51-5.

10. Ibid, pp.94-9.

11. M Blaug, Ricardian Economics: A Historical Study, (New Haven, Conn, 1958), pp.215.

12. Cairnes, The Slave Power, (London, Macmillan, 1st ed 1862, 2nd ed 1863). Preface.

13. Ibid.

14. These essays appear in Cairnes, Essays in Political Economy: Theoretical and Applied, (London, Macmillan, 1873).

15. For a general discussion, see M D Bordo, "John E Cairnes on the Effects of the Australian Gold Discoveries, 1851-73: An early Application of the Methodology of Positive Economics", HOPE, 1975, pp.337-359.

16. See Hutchison, Review of Economic Doctrines, op.cit, pp.22-8, Blaug, Ricardian Economics, op.cit, pp.215-6.

17. Cairnes, Some Leading Principles of Political Economy, Newly Expounded, (London, Macmillan, 1874), pp.3, 47, 103, 117-8, 193-7, 200-222.

18. Ibid, pp.388-406, 450-487.

19. See Cairnes, Logical Method, op.cit, pp.149-151.

20. Cairnes, Leading Principles, op.cit, p.157.

21. See Hutchison, Review of Economic Doctrines, op.cit, p.26.

22. W S Jevons, Theory of Political Economy, (London,

Macmillan, ed. by Harret Jevons, 4th edition, 1911), p.xiv.

23.   Cairnes, Leading Principles, op.cit, p.v.

24.   See G M Koot, The English Historical School of Economics 1870-1920: Economic History, Social Reform and Neo-Mercantilism. (Thesis abstract, New York, Stony Brook Library), p.43.

25.   See T W Hutchinson, On Revolution and Progress in Economic Knowledge, (Cambridge, CUP, 1978), p.223, also Blaug, Ricardian Economics, op.cit, p.219.

26.   Cairnes, "Essays Towards a Solution of the Gold Question" in Essays in Political Economy, op.cit, pp.55-76.

27.   For a discussion of Fawcett's views, see p.80.

28.   Cairnes, Essays, op.cit, p.33.

29.   Ibid, p.35.

30.   Ibid, pp.37-8.

31.   Ibid, pp.77-8.

32.   Cairnes, "Colonisation and Colonial Government", reprinted in Essays in Political Economy, op.cit, pp.273-326.

33.   Ibid, pp.280-90.

34.   See Merivale, Lectures on Colonies and Colonization, (London, Cass, 1967 reprint, delivered in 1829-1841), pp.3-136, and Cairnes, "Colonisation and Colonial Government", op.cit, especially pp.274, 282.

35.   Ibid, p.290.

36.   For Wakefield's position, see D Winch, Classical Political Economy and Colonies, op.cit, pp.90-104, and R N Ghosh, Classical Macroeconomics and the Case for Colonies, op.cir, pp.185-227.

37.   See G C Lewis, The Government of Dependencies, op.cit. He was sceptical as to the utility of colonies, whilst Goldwin Smith in Empire, op.cit, believed the empire was 'useless'.

38.   Cairnes, "Colonisation and Colonial Government. pp.311-2.

39.   Ibid, p.312.

40.   Ibid, p.314. See Merivale, "The Utility of Colonies as Fields for Emigration", op.cit, pp.491-6, and the discussion in Ch. 4, pp.46-48.

41.   See pp.86-89.

42.   For a discussion of Rogers' and Smith's views see Ch. 4, pp.48-49 and 59-61.

43.   Cairnes, "Colonisation and Colonial Government", op.cit. Cairnes offered no indication as to how he arrived at the figure of 4,500,000 pounds which he occasionally referred to in the Essay.

44.   On this point see Ch. 2, pp.10-13, and Ch. 4, pp.48-49.

45.   Cairnes, "Colonisation and Colonial Government", op.cit, p.235.

46.   J S Mill was not for completely severing the political ties between the United Kingdom and the Colonies. For their correspondence and disagreement on this question, see D Winch, Classical Political Economy and Colonies, op.cit, pp.158-9.

47.   Cairnes, "Fragments on Ireland", in Political Essays, op.cit, pp.127-98.

48.   Ibid, p.145.

49.   Ibid, p.146.

50.   Ibid, pp.147-8.

51.   Ibid, p.148.

52.   For Mill's position and their disagreements, see D Winch, Classical Political Economy and Colonies, op.cit, pp.135-43, particularly p.141 and Ghosh, Classical Macroeconomics and the Case for Colonies, op.cit, pp.246-62. Also see the brief discussion in Ch. 2, pp.10-13.

53.   See Schumpeter, History of Economic Analysis, op.cit, p.527. Also see Wood, "Henry Fawcett and the British Empire", The Indian Economic and Social History Review, Vol. XVI, No. 4, December 1979, pp.395-414.

54.   For details of Fawcett's life see Leslie Stephen, Life of Henry Fawcett, (London, Smith, Elder & Co, 1885); Winifred Holt, A Beacon for the Blind, (London, Constable, 1915); H Peto, The Late Life of Henry Fawcett, (London, Elliot Stock, 1886) and L L Price, "Henry Fawcett" in Dictionary of Political Economy, ed. by R M Inglis Palgrave, Vol. II, (London, Macmillan, 1900), pp.41-42.

55.   In the election to the Chair of Political Economy, Fawcett beat 4 candidates - J Mahor, J Bichstith, Leonard H Courtney, H D MacLead. He was supported for the position by T E Cliffe Leslie, J S Mill, J E T Rogers and Herman Merivale.

56.   Fawcett adopted an independent attitude on more than one occasion, supporting Moll in the "proposed extension of the suffrage to women; he advocated the inclusion of the agricultural labourers within the range of the Factory Acts; he pressed for the abolition of religious tests in the Universities in 1870 ...". L L Price, "Henry Fawcett", op.cit, pp.41-2. Also H Peto, Henry Fawcett, op.cit, pp.24, 30, 33.

57.   See M G Fawcett, What I Remember, (London, T Fisher, Unwin, 1924), pp.107-8. In a letter, Fawcett proudly stated how he had only been Post Master General for 2 weeks and had established the parcels post, the issue of postal orders, the receipt of small savings in stamps, increased the facilities for life insurance and amenities and reduced the price of telegrams. See H Peto, Henry Fawcett, op.cit, p.33.

58.   In Memoriam: Life and Labours of Rt Hon Henry Fawcett, MP, Post Master General, (London, E W Allan, 1884), p.7.

59.   Stephen, Life of Henry Fawcett, op.cit, p.23. Fawcett developed his interest in India and the British Empire from a very early age and before his blindness, earnestly wanted to visit India and Australia. In a letter to a friend, Mrs Holding, in Australia, he wrote: "Long before you went to Australia, I had eagerly desired to visit that country, for in my mind it must within a few years exercise a most important influence on the future of England. India, too, is the land I much desire to see and know; and it ought to be by anyone who takes part in public life". Ibid, p.41.

60.   Ibid, p.28.

61.   Stephen, Life of Henry Fawcett, op.cit, p.97. He never lost an opportunity of referring to Mill and the value of his general works, not only his Principles. In distributing prizes at Manchester on 1 October 1866 he remarked: "As I was reading Mill's "Liberty", perhaps the greatest work of our greatest writer, as I read his noble, I might

almost say his holy, idea, I thought to myself, if everyone in my country could and would read this work, how infinitely happier would the nation be! How much less desirous should we be to wrangle about petty religious differences! How much less of the energy of the nation would be wasted in contemptible quarrels about creeds and formulas; and how much more powerful should we be as a nation to achieve workers of good, when, as the work would teach us to be, we were formerly bound together by the bonds of a wise toleration". Ibid, p.103.

62.   Fawcett had established communication with Mill before 1860. In 1858 he wrote to Mill "For the last three years your books have been the chief education of my mind. I consequently entertain towards you a sense of gratitude as I can only hope at all adequately to repay by doing what lies in my power to propagate the invaluable truths contained in every page of your writings". Quoted in H Peto, Henry Fawcett, op.cit, pp.12-13.

63.   See M G Fawcett, What I Remember, op.cit, p.60.

64.   Quoted in Holt, A Beacon for the Blind: A Life of Henry Fawcett, op.cit, p.160.

65.   One of his earliest lectures "Spain and England", delivered at Warminster in March 1858, was an attempt to compare the effects of gold discoveries in the Spaniards in America with those of the later finds in California and Australia. The following year (1859) he read a paper on the drain of precious metals to the East, at the British Association at Aberdeen, where he first met J E Cairnes. Cairnes and Fawcett became close friends and Fawcett frequently visited Cairnes at Blackheath when he was ill. See Stephen, Life of Henry Fawcett, p.144 and Holt, A Beacon for the Blind: A Life of Henry Fawcett, op.cit, p.167.

66.   Stephen, Life of Henry Fawcett, op.cit, p116.

67.   H Fawcett, Manual of Political Economy, (London, Macmillan, 1863), Preface. A keen fisherman, Fawcett would have Mill's Principles read to him while fishing. See H Peto, Henry Fawcett, op.cit, p.9.

68.   Quoted in Stephen, Life of Henry Fawcett, op.cit, p.137.

69.   In the preface of this edition (1869) he claimed, p.vi, "I believe it will be found that this edition has been carefully revised that there is scarcely a page in which more improvements have not been introduced".

70.   Fawcett, Manual, (1863) op.cit, p.264.

71.   Stephen, Life of Henry Fawcett, op.cit, p.161.

72.   See the discussion on pp.88-89.

73.   Stephen, Life of Fawcett, op.cit, p.166, and Peto, Henry Fawcett, op.cit, p.33.

74.   Fawcett, Free Trade and Protection, (London, Macmillan, 1878). The book ran six editions, but apart from the inclusion of sections on protective subsidies and fair trade in the various editions, there were no major changes. See, for example, the fourth edition (1881) p.viii. He also rejected Mill's theory of the unearned increment, see Fawcett Manual, sixth edition, pp.286-287.

75.   See Ch. 2, p.10-13.

76. Fawcett, Free Trade and Protection, op.cit, pp.9-10. Also see Ch. 4, pp. , , and pp. of the present chapter.

77. Ibid, p.111.

78. Ibid, p.112.

79. Ibid, p.113.

80. See pp.88-89.

81. Fawcett, Manual, 1863 ed, op.cit, pp.68-73. Also see Ch. 2, pp. for Mill's support of Wakefield's schemes.

82. Fawcett, Manual, op.cit, p.71.

83. Ibid, pp.71-72.

84. Fawcett,Manual, third ed, (1869), op.cit, p.506.

85. For a discussion of Mill's recantation see Pedro Schwartz, The New Political Economy of J S Mill, (London, Weidenfeld and Nicholson, 1968), pp.91-100.

86. Fawcett, Manual, op.cit, p.158.179.

87. Fawcett claimed this for the period, 1840-60. Modern opinion is divided as to whether real wages rose or fell over this period. See R A Church, The Great Victorian Boom, 1850-1873, (London, Macmillan, 1975).

88. Fawcett, Manual, op.cit, p.160

89. Ibid, pp.206-7.

90. For a discussion of Leslie's life and his economics see G M Koot "T E Cliffe Leslie: Irish Social Reform and the Origins of the English Historical School of Economics", HOPE, Vol. 7, No. 3, pp.312-37.

91. Leslie, Land Systems and Industry and the Economy of Ireland, (London, Longmans and Green, 1870), p.360.

92. Ibid, pp.360-365. Also see his Essays in Political and Moral Philosophy, (London, Longmans, Green and Co, 1879), pp.371-74.

93. Leslie, Land Systems, op.cit, pp.85-116.

94. Ibid, p.92.

95. This was particularly true of the colonial reformers. See Winch, Classical Political Economy and the Colonies, op.cit, pp.90-135, and R D C Black, Economic Thought and the Irish Question, 1818-1870, (Cambridge, CUP, 1960).

96. See G M Koot, "Cliffe Leslie", op.cit, pp.322-30.

97. Leslie, Land Systems, op.cit, pp.325-27.

98. Fawcett, Economic Position of the British Labourer, op.cit, p.228.

99. Ibid, p.229.

100. On Mill's support for State assisted emigration see Winch, Classical Political Economy and the Colonies, op.cit, pp.135-143.

101. Fawcett, Manual, 1869, op.cit, p.218.

102. See N W Senior, An Outline of the Science of Political Economy, (London, Library of Economics, 1934 reprint), pp.39-45 for a comprehensive account of the "vacuum theory".

103. In the first edition of his Manual, Fawcett feared that this could happen "... we shall lose through emigration, the elite of our labouring population, the intelligent and enterprising will go forth first and leave this country burdened with the young, the old and the indolent". Fawcett, The Economic Position of the British Labourer,

op.cit, p.240. See also Pauperism: Its Causes and its Remedies, op.cit, pp.134-135.

104. Fawcett, Manual, 1863 edition, op.cit, pp.217-226.

105. Ibid, p.160.

106. Fawcett, Manual, 1869 edition, op.cit, p.135.

107. Fawcett, Pauperism: Its Causes and its Remedies, op.cit, p.103. On Wilmot-Horton's scheme, see, Ghosh, Classical Macroeconomics and the Case for Colonies, op.cit, pp.132-161.

108. Ibid, p.59.

109. See Winch, Classical Political Economy and Colonies, op.cit, pp.158-9.

110. See, for example, Ch. 4, pp.45-48 and pp.57-61.

111. On Cairnes as the defender of classical political economy, see pp.71-73.

112. Stephen, Life of Henry Fawcett, op.cit, p.341.

113. Fawcett, Manual, 1863 ed, op.cit, p.195.

114. Ibid, p.72.

115. Ibid, p.72.

116. Ibid, p.35.

117. Ibid, pp.41-45.

118. Ibid, p.42.

119. Ibid, pp.44-45.

120. Ibid, p.428.

121. Fawcett, State Socialism and the Nationalisation of Land, (London, Macmillan, 1883), p.12.

122. Fawcett, Free Trade and Protection, op.cit, p.171.

123. Ibid, p.171.

124. Ibid, p.172. In line with many of his contemporaries, Fawcett included in the fifth edition of his Manual, (1876) a chapter on the depreciation of silver. The issue is too complex to treat in this study, but it may be noted that he concentrated upon the reasons why the demand for silver had fallen in India. Fawcett, Manual, (1876) Chapter XVI, "The Depreciation in the Value of Silver", pp.495-513.

125. See Holt, Henry Fawcett: A Beacon for the Blind, op.cit, p.128. Stephen, Life of Henry Fawcett, op.cit, p.343.

126. Ibid, p.345.

127. Quoted in Stephen, Life of Henry Fawcett, op.cit, p.347; from a speech at Brighton, 15 January 1872. Also see Fawcett, Essays and Lectures where he asserted that "Indian questions do not excite so much interest in the House of Commons as a squabble about the cost of a road through St James' Park", pp.312-313.

128. These were published as Speech on Indian Finance, (London, W Tweedie, 1872) and Speeches on Some Current Political Questions, (London, Macmillan, 1873), Ch.2, pp.47-106.

129. Fawcett, Speech on Indian Finance, op.cit, p.3.

130. See Fawcett, State Socialism and the Nationalisation of Land, (London, Macmillan, 1883), p.5.

131. Fawcett, Speech on Indian Finance, op.cit, p.6.

132. Ibid, p.6.

133. Ibid, p.8.

134. Ibid, p.17.

135. Ibid, pp.21-24.

136. Fawcett, Speeches on Some Current Political Questions, op.cit, pp.47-106.

137. Ibid, p.69. Also see pp.49, 74-76.

138. L Stephen, Life of Henry Fawcett, op.cit, pp.361-365.

139. Ibid, pp.390-94. These committees included the Public Works and East Indian Railway committee.

140. See Fawcett, "Financial Condition of India", Nineteenth Century, vol.V, Feb. 1879, pp.193-218; "The Proposed Loans of India", Ibid, May 1879, pp.872-90.

141. Blaug, Ricardian Economics, op.cit, p.214.

142. D P O'Brien, The Classical Economists, op.cit, p.5. Also see Wood, "Henry Fawcett and the British Empire, op.cit.

SECTION THREE

MAINSTREAM ECONOMICS, 1870-1914

Chapter 6

ECONOMIC ORTHODOXY : W S JEVONS, HENRY SIDGWICK
AND ALFRED MARSHALL

W S JEVONS

Introduction

During his brief life of 46 years Jevons made major contributions to
economics, statistics, logic and philosophy. Born in Liverpool in
1835, Jevons' parents were Unitarians who greatly encouraged their
children's education.(1) By 16 he was at University College, London,
studying botany, chemistry and the "mechanisms" of industrial
society.(2) The family's metal business collapsed in the crisis of
1847-48, and when Jevons realised that his education was a drain on
the family's limited capital, he decided to accept a post as an assayer
in the newly established Mint in Sydney, Australia, in 1853.(3) He
remained in Australia till 1859, then resumed his studies at
University College. Four years later he was appointed a tutor at
Owens College, Manchester and in 1866 became the Professor of
Logic, Mental and Moral Philosophy and Political Economy. He
married the daughter of the founder of the Manchester Guardian and
in 1876 moved to a professorship at University College, London.

While in Australia, political economy became Jevons' main
interest, and he seriously studied the classical texts. Subsequently,
he rejected classical authors, and his Theory of Political Economy
commences with a revolutionary challenge to the established
orthodoxy:

When at length a true system of economics comes to be
established, it will be seen that that able but wrong-headed
man, David Ricardo, shunted the car of economic science onto
a wrong line - a line, however, on which it was further urged
towards confusion by his equally able and wrong-headed
admirer, John Stuart Mill.(4)

Jevons' main contribution to theoretical economics is to be
found in The Theory of Political Economy which was a vindication of
abstract methods as well as a challenge to the content of existing
theory.(5) Jevons expressed complete confidence in the proposition

that "value depends entirely on utility".(6) Unquestionably, his great idea that the origin of the objective exchange values of the market was to be found in the subjective valuations of individuals was exceedingly revolutionary. He fashioned the scattered fragments of earlier utility analysis into a comprehensive theory of value, exchange and distribution.(7)

Jevons did not confine his attention to pure theory, and he made important contributions to the fields of monetary, statistical and applied economics. His statistical papers on money, prices and fluctuations which were collected posthumously in Investigations in Currency and Finance, clearly indicate that he was a pioneer in the graphic presentation of economic and financial statistics.(8) In one of these papers, written in 1867, on "A Serious Fall in the Value of Gold Ascertained and Its Social Effects Set Forth", Jevons traced the effect on prices of the increase in the supply of gold. By the use of index numbers, he inductively confirmed Cairnes' conclusion that the inflation of the 1850s and early 1860s had been caused by the Australian and Californian gold discoveries.(9) This paper was professionally acclaimed, yet Jevons achieved a wider measure of popular fame and recognition for The Coal Question, which utilised statistical information to prove the probability of an early exhaustion of Britain's coal resources. In this work Jevons warned his fellow countrymen that the nation's coal deposits were exhaustible and that the cost of coal would rise as the best and most accessible seams were exploited.(10)

Jevons' interest in the application of economic theory was not restricted to the investigation of the relationship among facts for he was extremely interested in the formulation and prescription of policy. His small, but influential volume, The State in Relation to Labour, demonstrates the difficulties to economists in continually supporting the simple doctrine of laissez-faire. On the one hand he thought that

> we can lay down no hard and fast rules, but must treat every case in detail on its merits. Specific experience is our best guide, or even express experiment where possible, but the real difficulty consists in the interpretation of experience. We are reduced to balancing conflicting probabilities of good and evil.(11)

But in the same place he argued that "all the effects of a proposed act must be taken into account". Furthermore, whilst he called himself a "thorough-going advocate of Free Trade", he implied that he did not regard this doctrine as inconsistent with those measures of intervention at home which he was prepared to support.(12)

Jevons in Australia

Jevons left his university studies in London and travelled to Sydney to work as an assayer at the Royal Mint where he arrived on 29th June 1854 and remained till April 1859. His main purpose in accepting the appointment was to make money and not to settle permanently.(13)

> I am no doubt generally supposed to have come out here on a money making errand, and it is certainly my intention to pick up here as much of the precious metal as I can conveniently get, but I think it would be very shortsighted policy in me or in any other of my age or older.(14)

Jevons' work in the Royal Mint was thorough and well received, and he found time to tour the goldfields thereby gaining firsthand experience of the crude state of communications in the colonies.(15) But far more important than the impressions of his travels in the new colonies, were his writings and private study. In his five years at the Mint, he made a systematic study of New South Wales' climate, geology, topography, flora, colonial policy and socio-economic conditions.(16) During his stay Jevons' interest shifted more towards the social sciences, and his keen interest in political economy developed. He also wrote general articles on Australian meterology and kept daily observations on climatic conditions for twenty months. He contributed numerous articles on colonial affairs to such papers as the Empire, and Sydney Morning Herald, as well as preparing papers for the Philosophical Society.

Jevons' articles on land and railway policy, published as letters to the editor of the Empire in 1857, were his first contributions to economic discussion.(17) During 1856 a series of papers were presented to the Philosophical Society on the general topic of "rail-roads". On the 10th February 1857 he contributed a lengthy letter to the Empire on the Western Railway Line and the General Policy of Government Railway Extension.(18) As Black has shown, it is clear that Jevons' consideration of the question of the introduction of railways into New South Wales led to his serious study of economics.(19) Throughout his numerous articles, he stressed that in the longterm railways had to be self-financing:

> No government would construct a railway unless convinced that its advantages to the community would be equivalent to its cost; no private company could be found to undertake it without a reasonable prospect of dividends...no railway should ever be undertaken but with the probability of its being self-maintaining, within a reasonable period after its completion.(20)

The question of land values and government policy in the sale of public land was a crucial factor in the economics of railway developments, and Jevons considered these questions in his article "Comparison of the Railway Policy of New South Wales"(21) and in "The Public Lands of New South Wales".(22) In these articles he was extremely critical of the prevailing policies, which involved (i) a high minimum price in the sale of Crown Lands, (ii) projects for the extensive development of railways, irrespective of direct financial return. Specifically, Jevons contended that a high minimum price was wrong in theory, because land was not of a uniform quality. At a practical level, to demand a high minimum price for land at a period when capital was limited was "most injurious".(23) Hence Jevons advocated the abolition of fixed prices on land and recommended that waste lands should be sold at open auction.(24)

During 1856 and 1857 Jevons read numerous economics classics, including the Wealth of Nations, Mill's Principles, Malthus' Essay on Population and Wheatley's Introductory Lectures on Political Economy.(25) As Keynes wrote:

> His long period of solitary thought in Australia, at an age when the powers of pure originality are at their highest, had been abundantly fruitful. For soon after his return, the outlines of his principal contributions to knowledge were firmly fixed in his mind.(26)

Emigration

In contrast to all the economists considered to this point, Jevons was favourably disposed both to large scale emigration from Britain and continued high rates of domestic population growth at home.(27) He believed that whenever there was redundant population, emigration provided a relief from the problems associated with surplus labour and argued that the massive emigration from Britain in the first half of the nineteenth century was an integral part of Britain's growth and of her position as a world power. While not the first economist to view emigration in relation to Britain's economic development, Jevons was one of the earliest to emphasise it as a means of maintaining her leadership in the world.(28)

Like J S Mill, Jevons argued that the more Britain grew at home, the more she required mineral resources and manufacturing skills, and overseas sources of food and raw materials.(29) This directly raised wages in America, Australia and Africa.(30) In concentrating on external aggregate demand, Jevons ignored the possibility that domestic economic growth would conceivably raise wages and deter emigration. He failed to consider or explicate the causal connections between British demand for food and increased wages in the grain producing regions of the world.

Jevons was the first economist to examine the extent and age composition of emigration. His review reveals that 80% were young people, and that over 60% were either married or of marriageable age.(31) He utilised his compilation of population, age and sex statistics to demonstrate the inaccuracies and inapplicability of the Malthusian population doctrine to Britain in the 1860s. Britain's rich coal resources and the manufacturing industries dependent thereon, enabled her to produce and export finished goods to primary producing countries in exchange for their food. This mechanism removed, for the time being, the Malthusian checks to population increase and meant "that our increase of population was rather under than above, the increasing means of subsistence".(32)

Unlike the classicals and economists writing in the 1860s, Jevons heartily approved of a situation whereby the population void created by emigration was rapidly filled by natural increase, rising productivity, or both.(33) He considered that such a situation represented the highest stage of progress and prosperity that a nation could enjoy. In the short-term this was most beneficial to the British economy for the population became accustomed to early marriages, it was easy to acquire a livelihood, people sought rises in their standard of living, and were able to enjoy leisure and luxuries. In the long-term, Jevons felt that the failure of the coal mines would be the only possible check to prosperity. In contrast to Malthus, Jevons contended that coal and not population was the ultimate threat to rising standards of living. Towards the conclusion of another chapter in the Coal Question Jevons considered the long-term effects of British migration. (34) He feared that those countries largely populated by British emigrants would develop an industrial sector which could result in even more competitors for British industry. This fear is significant, for although other economists noted the potential threats of foreign competition, none specifically mentioned the danger to Britain's industrial position from her former colonies or possessions. (35) Unfortunately, Jevons failed to draw any inferences from his comments.

In short, Jevons held that emigration was a consequence of the nation's progress. It provided a relief to overpopulation and led to the development of new lands which provided food as well as other raw materials for England. It resulted in a surge of population increase at home which was most conducive to future economic growth, prosperity and the maintenance of Britain's industrial supremacy.

Colonial Gold Discoveries

Jevons maintained a keen interest in gold mining throughout his life and was concerned over the future viability of the industry. (36) He believed that his experience in Australia qualified him to comment on colonial gold mining activities and claimed that he spoke "with the advantage of having resided in a gold-producing colony, and travelled over nearly all the chief diggings of Australia".(37)

Like Cairnes and Fawcett, he considered that the Australian

and Californian discoveries were the "great counterpoise to the Peruvian and Mexican discoveries of the sixteenth century.(38) He accurately predicted that gold mining would become more like the operation of an ordinary industry for in order to exploit the "more difficult deposits, it would have to become capital intensive".(39) Moreover, he felt that the United Kingdom had obtained many advantages from gold mining. In 1868, while writing on the necessity for re-coinage, he considered that the diffusion of "the great quantity of British coin over the world" had assisted the extension of British economic influence.(40) By maintaining her policy of free trade, Britain would not only open more ports and markets to her goods, but could also acquire a virtual ascendancy in the specie trade.

> In Australia, in New Zealand, and probably in South Africa, we hold the most productive gold mines in the world, and of what is produced elsewhere a large part passes direct to London, the monetary centre of the world. We shall, therefore, become without doubt, the world's coiners.(41)

Free Trade and the Threat to British Industrial Supremecy

Fear of foreign competition accelerated within Britain towards the close of the nineteenth century. In a manner akin to Giffen and Marshall, Jevons was well aware of foreign competition when writing in the 1860s, although, like them, he did not abandon his faith in free trade. Jevons believed that as applied to domestic and international commercial policy, free trade was an unquestioned and almost unquestionable article of faith:

> Freedom of trade may be regarded as a fundamental axiom of political economy; and though even axioms may be mistaken, and any different views concerning them must not be prohibited, yet we need not be frightened into questioning our own axioms. We may welcome bona fide investigation into the state of trade, and the causes of the present depression, but we can no more expect to have our opinions on free trade altered by such an investigation, than the Mathematical Society would expect to have axioms of Euclid disproved during the investigation of a complex problem.(42)

Jevons' statement is confusing and, surprisingly, hesitant. If axioms may be mistaken (and non-axiomatic) then it is possible that this may also be true of free trade. Of course one may not expect to have axioms disproved, as they are given. Presumably Jevons simply meant that supposed axioms may turn out otherwise on investigation.

Jevons undertook extensive statistical studies on British trade which revealed that Britain's industrial competitiveness was of limited duration, since it rested upon finite coal supplies. Specifically, he foresaw the incalculable economic potential of the United States, and that "at least a sound system of metallurgical industry will grow up on the banks of the Ohio, capable of almost indefinite expansion".(43) He argued that industrial expansion and the increasing population would exhaust the coal deposits in a "few generations". The persistent pursuit of free trade would hasten Britain's eventual decline; yet, he would not abandon the belief, as it was a "doctrine of political economy".(44) In common with Cairnes, Fawcett and Rogers, he felt that trade policies of the colonies would, to a considerable extent, determine the future of the United Kingdom's industrial system: "and should the tendency of all our colonies towards protection increase, the progress of trade may indeed be vastly retarded".(45) Jevons noted that some British colonies (e.g., New South Wales) had large coal deposits and the rate of utilisation of these coal fields would depend on whether they introduced protective measures. If they did, trade would be checked, and the United Kingdom would have great difficulty in obtaining raw materials. Although Jevons did not elaborate the mechanisms by which trade would be retarded, one can assume he thought protection would make it more difficult for British manufacturers to acquire raw materials for their factories.

It is difficult to specify exactly what Jevons envisaged between the mother country and the colonies as regards their future trading relationships, though it would appear that he valued the inter-relationships between the colonial and British economies. His time horizon was a long one, sufficient to include the eventual exhaustion of Britain's coal supplies. Yet there was no necessary reason why Britain should specifically be dependent on the colonies for coal. To say protection may reduce the total volume of trade is one thing; to say it will cut-off specific sources of particular materials is quite another.

Conclusion

Jevons was extremely proud of the extent of the British empire, and the nation's contribution to civilisation:

> Our empire and race already comprise a fifth of the world's population; and by our plantation of new States, by our guardianship of the seas, by our penetrating commerce, by the example of our just laws and firm constitution, and above all by the dissemination of our new arts, we stimulate the progress of mankind in a degree not to be measured. If we lavishly and boldly push forward in the creation of our riches, both material and intellectual, it is hard to over-estimate the pitch of beneficial influence to which we may attain in the present. But the maintenance of such a position is physically impossible. We have to make the momentous choice between brief but true greatness and longer continued mediocrity. (46).

Jevon's pride in British achievements stemmed from his view of progress, which was the foundation of his "whole philosophical system".(47) To Jevons, progress alone constituted all human happiness. He felt that an English emigrant would realise his highest potential in a British colony, and he advised his brother Herbert (whose farm had collapsed in Minnesota) to emigrate to an English colony.(48) He believed that life in either New Zealand or Australia would be more "luxurious" compared with Minnesota and in a letter to Herbert, Jevons claimed that if he was to be an emigrant again, he would settle in an English colony, like New Zealand.

Although Jevons referred to J E Cairnes' lecture on "Colonies and Colonisation" as "admirable" he did not pursue Cairnes' argument on the cost of colonies or the need for separation.(49) Rather, Jevons asserted that it was impossible to overvalue the Anglo-Saxon spirit of colonisation because of the trade colonies performed with the United Kingdom, their internal happiness and the benefits they promised to the future of the world. Moreover, Jevons foresaw the potential benefits of the colonial connections and he accurately predicted that imperial matters would become of increasing concern to British statesmen.

HENRY SIDGWICK

Introduction

Henry Sidgwick was the last major English moral philosopher to make noteworthy contributions to political economy. Marshall claimed him as his "spiritual father and mother".(50) Sidgwick's name is not associated with any particular theory or policy, but through his teaching and writings he exerted considerable influence on his generation of economists. After a brilliant school career, he went to Cambridge, where he obtained a distinction in classics and mathematics.(51) In 1859, at the young age of 21, he was elected to a fellowship in classics at Trinity College, but he subsequently exchanged the post for a lectureship in moral sciences.

J N Keynes described Sidgwick as the "most intellectually gifted man" he knew, and Sidgwick's publications in philosophy, politics and economics were widely acclaimed.(52) In 1883, he published his Principles of Economics in which he examined Mill's political economy, in addition to tracing the "emergent marginalism" of Jevons and Marshall.(53) Sidgwick's Principles corrected and clarified Mill's analysis of the distinction between movements along a demand schedule and shifts from one demand schedule to another. As Myint has shown, Sidgwick contributed some important pioneering distinctions and, clarifications for the systematic analysis of economic policies.(54) The third book of the Principles was a classic discussion of the "perennial problems of the role of the state in economic life".(55) Moreover, he carefully distinguished between the science and the art of political economy: "The first gives information as to what happens without pronouncing whether it is good or bad; the second judges that what happens or would happen under certain conditions is the best thing that could happen".(56) In brief, he refused to accept J E Cairnes' extreme position that economics had no special relevance to normative issues. Sidgwick was anxious to dissociate political economy from the laissez-faire doctrines, and suggested various conditions under which state interference in the production process could become desirable, recommending like Jevons, that each case be considered on its merits.

Sidgwick wrote on political economy after extensive work in classics and moral philosophy and, like Mill and Marshall, felt a "duty to study political economy". While his ideas developed slowly, he found that "political economy is what I really enjoy as an intellectual exercise. It is just the right stage of scientific progress, and there are not too many facts to be got up".(57) However, after the publication of his Principles, he increasingly turned his attention to political theory and topical issues, publishing his superb Elements of Politics in 1897.

Emigration, Colonisation and Imperial Expansion

In Chapter 18 on "Principles of External Policy" in Elements of Politics, Sidgwick considered a range of issues associated with the theoretical and practical aspects of emigration.(58) At a theoretical level, he believed that one had to clearly distinguish, and treat separately, questions of emigration and colonisation, although the two questions were inter-twined in practice, especially in the discussions of large ambitious schemes of state-directed colonisation. He accepted the Malthusian view of emigration, rejecting the contention that an increase in emigration would lead to a fall in domestic population since "general reasoning and experience combine to show that emigration has a stimulating effect on a population in a country that has long been settled: and that, accordingly, every increase in the numbers of emigrants tends to cause a certain subsequent increase which would not otherwise have taken place, in the population of the country from which they emigrate".(59)

In contrast to J S Mill, Sidgwick did not favour government sponsored emigration to the empire and elsewhere, noting that even if the cost of voyages to America or Australia were to be "freely defrayed" by the English government the aggregate number of persons of English origin inhabiting the two countries taken together would still increase at a materially greater rate. Moreover, he argued that State aid to emigration could not be safely recommended as a relief for distress in "congested districts", where the population was too large for the field of employment, except when the cause of such congestion was temporary. Sidgwick perceptively maintained that government would not undertake regular expenditure outlays for emigration unless this brought some substantial returns to the state, other than relieving the pressure of population. There could be some advantages from an organized scheme in the form of extended trade, since initially new emigrants were more likely than old migrants to have tastes which the "producers of their original country would be specially qualified to supply". In alluding to the transitory nature of the new emigrants' preference for their home products Sidgwick, like Marshall, believed that "this advantage will be too uncertain and precarious to justify expenditure for which it is the main return".(60) To Sidgwick, government intervention in emigration matters should be limited to the collection of information, the prevention of deception by emigration agents and the regulation of migrant services.

Sidgwick contended that the question of free immigration and emigration had occupied a smaller place in modern political discussion than the question of free trade. He regretted this, for "freedom of immigration is a recognised feature of the ideal which orthodox political economists have commonly formed of international relations".(61) He maintained that for all the advantages of free trade to be reaped, it was essential that labour should move with "perfect ease" within national boundaries and from country to country where it was in highest demand. While the ideal was the free movement of goods and labor, Sidgwick contended that it was not really in the interest of humanity at large for three reasons: (i) the existence of national and patriotic sentiments which were indispensable to social well-being. (ii) the government's task of promoting moral and intellectual culture would be rendered hopeless by a stream of alien immigrants with diverse social habits and religious traditions. (iii) as a country's institutions reflected the people in that country, a large intermixture of immigrants brought-up under different institutions could introduce corruption and disorder into a previously well-ordered nation.(62)

He observed that during the period of late nineteenth century expansion, the extension of a nation's land area through conquest was almost always accompanied by some immigration of the members of the victorious state to the new territory. However, Sidgwick felt that if the conquered area was densely populated, immigration was unlikely to be considerable. Like Hobson in his classic work, Imperialism, Sidgwick pointed out that conquered regions were often highly unsuitable for colonisation and immigration.(63)

"Given the present state of the world", Sidgwick argued, the founding of a new colony, adapted to the large scale reception of European migrants, was "not a very probable event". Nevertheless, he recognised that the promotion of settlements in unoccupied land remained of "some practical importance", and considered that the government had three principal functions: (i) the disposal of land available for settlement; (ii) the "encouragement", if required, of immigration; (iii) the management of the relations between settlers and aborigines. The first two functions were closely connected, as the land available for settlement normally supplied the chief incentive for migration. Whether either of these methods was adopted would depend on several considerations including

> the distance of the region of immigration from the native home of the settlers whom it is designed to attract, the quality and extent of its natural resources, the amount of labour and capital required to turn them to most profitable account, and last, but not least, the probability of obtaining an adequate supply of immigrants without special encouragement.(64)

By way of illustration, Sidgwick considered two situations. Firstly, where emigration into unoccupied districts was mainly continental, for example, to the United States, so that new settlements were continuously connected by older ones with fully peopled territory. In such a case, government assistance to meet part of the transportation cost of emigrants was obviously "needed less". Secondly, if special attraction was required to quicken and amplify the stream of migrants, the government had to consider whether cheapening transport or cheapening land was the more appropriate policy. He considered the former would be more effectual if the region to be colonised offered special facilities for producing products for the world's markets, since this would provide a large scale capital investment. By contrast, where the land offered no special facilities for production for the outside market, the prosperous development of its resources would probably depend on attracting settlers who would cultivate the land largely with a view to subsistence for themselves and their families. In this case, Sidgwick considered that the most suitable encouragement to immigration would be to offer the land to settlers at a low, nominal price.(65)

Advantages and Disadvantages of Expansion

Sidgwick believed that towards the end of the nineteenth century, there was general agreement that the well-being of the "uncivilized new-comers should be earnestly and systematically kept in view". People also felt that the aborigines should be adequately compensated for any loss resulting from the absorption of their territory by other powers. To Sidgwick, this question assumed different forms as between (i) colonies of settlement where the manual labour is supplied by the civilized race; and (ii) colonies in which it can supply only capital and labour of a superior kind. In the former case, Sidgwick argued that the problems would only be transient, for there was the collision of races and destruction of the aborigine's economic life.

He argued that ultimately "the problem of how to deal with the natives will sink into a part of the general question of dealing with the incapable and recalcitrant elements found in all civilized communities".(66) In the second case the government's difficulties were intellectual and moral and he listed six factors of prime importance in European nations' attempts to govern subject races:

(1)   The claim of a civilised State to supreme control over territory inhabited by uncivilised tribes, should not carry with it any obligation to interfere with the laws and customs of the aborigines, even when these were opposed to civilised morality.

(2)   In regulating the relations between aborigines and settlers, the government had to prevent the interests of the former being damaged through the occupation of the land by the latter. He stressed that natives should never be deprived of any definite property rights without full compensation.

(3)   He felt that restrictions on the freedom on intercourse and exchange between aborigines and settlers may be necessary as a temporary measure, and cited firearms and liquor as examples to support his view.

(4)   The protection of the levies and property of settlers, required the "proper" execution of punishment for crimes. Justice had to be administered so as to "impress the intellect of the aborigines" with the relationship between offence and punishment.

(5)   Extensive education had to be given to the inferior races, so as to make them able to share the life of civilised mankind.

(6)   Slavery and internal wars had to be abolished.(67)

The above six factors reveal Sidgwick's keen appreciation of the numerous problems associated with governing native races. However, he did not confine his discussion to the problems of governing subject races, noting that there were difficult questions associated with the emerging self-governing settlements, such as Australia and Canada.(68) Arguing in a similar vein to Cairnes, Fawcett and Rogers, Sidgwick advocated colonial self-government and was opposed to imperial federation schemes, believing that an imperial parliament would not successfully legislate for the colonies as the mass of the parliamentarians would be ignorant of colonial needs.(69) Furthermore, colonial representatives would become absorbed in the mother-country's political movements and neglect their constituencies. Consequently, Sidgwick recommended that the nature and form of colonial self-government should vary "with the degree of development of the colony, its situation and external relations, and other circumstances". (70) It also depended on the "conception" formed of the "desirable destiny" of the colony, and he argued that if the connection was designed to be permanent, the colony should not have the power to tax or to enact its own external trade policy without the mother country's consent. When colonies had reached a certain "pitch of population and wealth", and enjoyed considerable degrees of self-government, but the mother country retained control of the country's foreign affairs, friction and discontent had to be avoided. In such situations, a department had to be organized by the central government to both avoid and resolve any difficulties:

the head of the department should be advised by a council carefully selected from persons who have empirical knowledge of the different colonies: and the self-governing colonies should be encouraged to use any convenient channel for making their needs and wishes known to the central government.(71)

In a manner akin to Cunningham and Hobson, Sidgwick was acutely aware of the difficulties confronting British settlers in dealing with "less civilised societies" and thought that for the mother country to impose on the colonists the task of dealing unaided with these "aborigines" was to invite bloodshed. Consequently, he thought that Britain had to "retain sufficient control over the colony to enable it to interfere effectually" to avoid any confrontation.(72)

Sidgwick also reviewed the military advantages and disadvantages associated with the conquering of large tracts of land which contained 'inferior' peoples. On the one hand, it meant that there was an increased resource base, and hence enlarged strength in case of war which enabled the state to maintain larger armaments. Yet he thought that these advantages could be more than outweighed by the conquest itself and the increased difficulty of defence, if the conquest was in a distant or otherwise inconveniently located region e.g., England was weakened in formidable conflicts by her possession of India. However, he proposed, much like Rogers and Marshall, that there were sentimental satisfactions derived from the empire and its extension, although it was difficult to weigh these against the material sacrifices and risks.(73) To him, sentimental satisfaction embraced the justifiable pride which the cultivated members of a civilised community felt in the beneficent exercise of dominion, and in the performance by their nation of the noble task of spreading the highest kind of civilisation.

In common with other economists, Sidgwick was proud of the various developments within the self-governing colonies and he was particularly pleased at the Australian federation movement, claiming that it was one of the best hopes for world peace and progress.(74) Sharing the dilemmas of numerous British intellectuals, Sidgwick was unsure whether or not to approve the outbreak of the Boer War, which he feared would end in disaster for England.(75) He believed that the war was unjustifiable on "any principle of International right, and on the whole indefensible on grounds of policy".(76) Nevertheless, he echoed late nineteenth century opinion, and considered that the brightest aspect of the war was the "force and genuineness of the Imperial sentiment in the colonies".(77)

Conclusion

The foregoing account reveals how the discussion on emigration, the beneficial and adverse effects of imperial expansion and government's function in ruling native races involved matters ranging far beyond the conventional boundaries of political economy. Writers such as Sidgwick, who felt themselves to be qualified in geo-political matters considered such issues freely and systematically. Sidgwick's brief though incisive discussion on emigration reflected the classicals' influence, although he was most aware of and interested in the events of his time and European powers' conquest of sparsely populated regions.

Specifically, he was concerned at the form of government applicable to the subjected races and his Elements of Politics deliberated upon such matters. Whilst Sidgwick was not necessarily the only economist to consider such wider issues of statesmanship, for J S Mill, Cunningham and Hobson did also, his discussion of the role of government in the treatment of indigeneous peoples was unique, the product of his interest and expertise in politics.(78)

ALFRED MARSHALL

Introduction

Marshall began his economic studies in 1867 after a mathematical training and the awakening of an interest in metaphysical and ethical problems, that is at a time when Mill was still alive and before Jevons, Menger and Walras had published their major treatises.(79) However, Marshall's first substantial contributions to economic theory were not published until a few years after those of Jevons. His two papers, the Pure Theory of Foreign Trade and the Pure Theory of Domestic Values, were published in 1879, as was the Elements of Economics of Industry, in which he had collaborated with Mrs Marshall.(80) His most important work, the Principles of Economics, appeared in 1890 and ran into eight editions during his lifetime, the last being in 1920.

Marshall was unquestionably the key figure in the development and professionalisation of British theoretical economics between 1880 and 1914.(81) He, above all other contributors, placed economics on a new and firmer basis and his Principles became the standard text of British economists: "It was simultaneously an original contribution to knowledge, pointing the way for future research and a broad exposition of the problems that were, and to some extent still are, of interest to economists".(82)

Marshall was attracted to the study of economics by an interest in practical ethics. He was anxious to establish how men's lives could be improved, as well as the material limitations to human development.(83) Towards the close of his life, he reflected that the greater part of his study had been devoted to the problems of poverty, "And that very little of my work has been devoted to any inquiry which does not bear on that".(84) A great many of Marshall's writings from the Future of the Working Classes in 1873 to the Industrial Remuneration Conference address in 1885, stress the importance of a citizen's social duty.(85) In his paper, the Future of the Working Classes, Marshall emphasised the duty which parents owe to their children and which society owes to its citizens.(86) As an educator Marshall was most concerned to impart to others his deep concern for those less fortunate in society. His inaugural lecture in 1885 was a call to Cambridge men to study economics, so that they would be equipped to enter the world "with cool heads but warm hearts" to grapple with the social suffering around them.(87) He believed that by increasing the number of "sympathetic students, who have studied working class problems in a scientific spirit", it would be possible to prevent "unscrupulous and ambitious men" from assuming the leadership of the working classes.(88) In the same year he told the participants at the Industrial Remuneration Conference that no-one could lay his head "on his pillow in peace with himself, who is not giving of his time and his substance to diminish the number of the outcasts of society, and to increase the number of those who can earn a reasonable income and having the opportunity to living if they will, a noble life".(89)

To Marshall, economics involved the "study of mankind in the ordinary business of life". It treated "some of the laws according to which the well-being of man is affected by the physical, intellectual, ethical and social conditions by which he is surrounded".(90) Whilst economics did not simply deal with "narrow economic man", it was nevertheless concerned with those activities in which motives were more deliberate and regular in their operation, and were capable of quantification.(91) In order to assist the development of quantitative analysis, Marshall introduced tools to assist both empirical and theoretical investigations.(92) Although Marshall utilised and developed such concepts as consumer surplus and elasticities, he did not necessarily believe that economics should be confined to questions which were amenable to scientific treatment. He was particularly conscious of distinguishing between positive matters of economic science and normative matters of economic policy.(93) The economist had to separate out "what courses will follow from a proposed course of action and what must be decided by moral judgments". Nevertheless, he was at liberty to express his own personal opinions, although his "special science could give him no commission to do so". Political economy did not possess the power of "giving direct and complete answers on points involving questions of right and wrong".(94)

Although in his Principles Marshall amalgamated Ricardo and Mill with marginalism and empirical observation - hence extending theoretical economic analysis - he did not confine himself to the pursuit of theory. He was not simply a mathematical economist and his works reflect the influence of the theories of social evolution associated with Darwin and Spencer.(95) As a young man, he had been attracted to the writings of German historical thinkers such as

Hegel, Roscher, Marx and Lassalle. Through their writings, Marshall recognised the relationship of institutions and policies to a particular state and stage of a society's development. His early work contained a good deal of historical content and interpretation and early in his career a synthesis of analysis and history seemed to have been his objective.(96) However the historical passages of the Principles were "brusquely assailed" by William Cunningham in 1892. Consequently Marshall broke his general rule of not replying to criticism in the same issue of the Economic Journal. It is possible that Cunningham's criticism curtailed Marshall's plans to publish more historical work.(97)

Although he was not as critical of classical orthodoxy as the economic historians, Marshall nevertheless attacked the "older generation of economists concept of economic man", claiming that they had been guilty of treating man as a "constant entity". He was concerned with man "as he is" not with an "abstract man", but one of "flesh and blood".(98) As Winch argues, the emergence of biological sciences, coupled with the influence of ethico-historical thinkers, resulted in the new generation of economists being more aware of the diversity and pliability of human nature and social institutions.(99)

Marshall emphasised the continuity of economic doctrine, and he wanted to reconcile the divergent views in the discipline and eliminate unnecessary controversy.(100) Indeed, his moderation on methodological questions and use of history and statistics pacified those who had asserted that economics was an excessively abstract and deductive science. Schumpeter claimed that Marshall's knowledge of history and extensive compilation of the "facts" of contemporary life was "one of the reasons why no institutionalist opposition rose against him in England".(101) However, Marshall was considered an "orthodox economist" and the founding of the London School of Economics was, in itself, an attack on Marshallian economics.(102) Nevertheless, it is incorrect to view Marshall simply as a "deductive economist", for his published work and notes contained strands of inductive methodology, and applied economics. Moreover, his opinions and analysis of the British empire combined all these elements.

Economics and the Empire

Marshall's published writings - apart from a section of his "Memorandum on the Fiscal Policy of International Trade" - do not contain a fully fledged discussion of imperial issues.(103) In contrast to Sidgwick, who did not specify the difference between professional pronouncements and private expressions of opinion on matters transcending the professional's "proper" domain, Marshall, generally speaking, felt that imperial topics were outside the bounds of the professional economist, and he scribbled on a note written in December 1907 that the question of imperialism was "rather beyond my province but important".(104) In the fourth edition of the Principles (1898) he offered a brief explanation why he did not consider imperialism in his published writings:

> But though largely directed by practical needs, economics avoids as far as possible the discussion of those exigencies of party organisation, and those diplomacies of home and foreign politics of which the statesman is bound to take account in deciding what measure that he can propose will bring him nearest to the end that he desires to secure for his country. It aims indeed at helping him to determine not only what that end should be, but also what are the best methods of a broad policy devoted to that end. But it shuns many political issues which the practical man cannot ignore; and it is therefore a science, pure and applied, rather than a science and an art. And it is better described as Social Economics, or as Economics simply, than as Political Economy.(105)

Nevertheless, throughout his publications there are occasional economic thoughts and perspectives pertaining to the British empire. Like other late Victorian thinkers, he devoted his attention to the self-governing colonies and India.(106) In his brief references to the empire, he concentrated on the self-governing colonies as did Ashley and Hewins. Like Rogers, Smith, Nicholson and Cunningham, he appreciated the vastness and complexity of the empire, although he did not specify its constituent parts as did Giffen and Hobson.(107) Marshall frequently employed the "mother-daughter" metaphor. The concept of the United Kingdom as the "mother" of recent settlements had been widely discussed in the years before the American War of Independence and was occasionally referred to in the early Victorian age. Later, as the areas of British settlement emerged as viable self-governing nations, the "mother-daughter" notion became more appealing to British commentators.(108) Marshall argued that the United States was England's first great colony and had now become the colonies' eldest sister, and India, her greatest dependency.(109)

The Self-Governing Colonies Marshall was most aware of Wakefield's scheme of systematic colonisation, although he did not evaluate the implementation of Wakefield's proposals.(110) He believed, much like List, that colonies established by strong European races in a temperate and stimulating climate, such as North America, always flourished.(111) Among the self-governing colonies, he was particularly interested in Australia.(112) Like New Zealand and America, Australia was well endowed with an "alert" population and abundant natural resources.(113) Unfortunately Australia was a great distance from the prime markets for her products - the United Kingdom and Europe - and was also beset by geographical problems, such as a small and uncertain rainfall.

In the fourth edition of his Principles (1898) Marshall included a brief section on Australia, in which he argued that the Australian experiences demonstrated less signs of "rigor" than her "elder sister", the United States.(114) The Australian rate of population increase was no doubt an important factor, and the considerable distance deterred migrants who preferred America. However, in the long term he felt that Australia (like Canada) had one distinct advantage over America, namely, a greater homogeneity of race. Consequently, the development of a social and economic institutional infra-structure could proceed "more easily, and perhaps ultimately even faster than would be possible if they had to be adjusted to all the capacities, the temperaments, the tastes, and the wants of peoples who have little affinity with one another".(115)

Marshall was also extremely interested in the "social advances" in Australia and he asserted that, partly under English influence, she was leading the way in the "great endeavour" of uplifting the labouring population to a higher level of culture and physical enjoyment.(116) Often labour had left Britain in the hope of freedom, "driven forth from oppression, rather than allured by the promise of larger opportunities".(117) Although the United States received a large portion of the "most important energy that Europe sends forth", the colonies also attracted people who were "resentful of old habits and traditions".(118) In his rough notes, Marshall balanced this view of emigration, by pointing out the attractions open to emigrants in new lands, such as higher money wages, better climate, greater real purchasing power and numerous job vacancies.(119)

Between 1905 and 1910 Marshall jotted down in rough form a range of theoretical and practical thoughts on migration questions. He seemed pre-occupied with the association between emigration patterns and a nation's prosperity. Throughout these workings and odd thoughts it is clear that he anticipated the relationship between fluctuations in economic activity and the volume of migration which is now associated with the work of Brinley Thomas. There is, however, nothing to suggest that he was aware of Merivale's fascinating views on this matter or of Sidgwick's broader discussion of the topic.(120)

Marshall argued that when the United States economy grew rapidly the employers increased their efforts to secure greater supplies of labour and introduced labour-saving devices, which further stimulated the economy. However, whenever there was a downturn in the domestic economy, the employers reversed these activities and intake of migrants was reduced.(121) He also devoted considerable attention to the relationship between tariffs and prosperity, concluding that when a high tariff existed, and increased general prosperity, it attracted labour and capital, and vice versa.(122)

Marshall was especially interested in the costs and benefits of migration, both to the country of origin and the emigrant nation. Unfortunately his series of notes, interspersed with figures and ideas, is unclear and too incomplete to reproduce.(123) Nevertheless, it is evident that he was contemplating a cost-benefit analysis of migration, based on the measurement of standard income received by a man (25 shillings) in Britain, and his family expenditure pattern between himself, his wife and their 2 children in one year. He also attempted to calculate how much the same man could earn and spend in America and Australia over a period of forty years.

He evaluated Malthusian population theory and fully appreciated Malthus' position on the issue of emigration. Moreover, he agreed with Malthus' basic proposition that population would outstrip food supply, but claimed that if population growth is "checked for England earlier than for other countries, she cannot hold her 11 million square miles .... that are strongly desired by Germany and others".(124) Whilst he adequately represented Malthus' position on the effect of emigration on domestic population growth, his thoughts vacillated on the issue, and it is impossible to say whether he rejected or accepted Malthus' statements.(125)

Imperial Trade, Capital and the Self-Governing Colonies Marshall did not specifically discuss the issue of whether trade followed the flag, but considered imperial trade in relation to total British trade. In the tradition of classical political economy, he held that the colonies were a market for British products as well as a source of raw materials. In discussing colonial demand for British products Marshall argued that new immigrants wanted, and could often afford clothing and other goods not produced in the colony, from the mother country. He attempted to verify his assertions by referring to the overseas trade statistics, which revealed an extraordinary increase in clothing exports.

> A great part of her colonial trade has always consisted of articles of food, clothing etc., which her sons and daughters want to have after the fashion of the old home; and nearly the same may be said for the personal consumption of British residents in India. This suggests one cause of the commonly observed fact that "trade follows the flag".(126)

Marshall also noted that there were other factors assisting trade between England and her colonies, such as the frequent sailing and mailing services to and from the colonies and financial connections, particularly the ability of the English merchants to supply their shopkeepers with goods on credit. Also, British manufacturers were able to meet the demands of growth industries in the colonies. Although these factors were no doubt operative, they were surely also applicable to Britain's trade with other nations. Marshall must have been aware of this, especially when he argued that the ties of custom and sentiment weakened over time. He believed that as the native population increased in new lands the number of people with direct memory of a British home decreased.(127)

Marshall reasoned that the pattern of growth and development in other countries meant that there were continual changes in the demand for British goods. This was particularly applicable to those members of the empire who had become world leaders in industries in which they had special advantages, e.g. Western Australia and the Transvaal. He noted that such a region "may be quicker than almost any industrial centre of the western world in adopting electrical appliances for saving labour in transport and milling... it may prefer to import the greater part of its clothing ready made".(128) Marshall's notes concerning the evolution of foreign demand in general, not only colonial demand, are interesting in relation to the actual patterns of trade and the modern economic historians' discussions as to the nature and causes of the 'retardation' in British trade per se toward the close of the nineteenth century. Kindleberger argues that British exporters tended to seek new markets for the same goods rather than adapting their exports to changing patterns within given markets.(129)

The empire has frequently been treated by economic historians as coming at the end of the line as regards British exports, with the colonies as dumping grounds for goods that manufacturers could not sell elsewhere. Marshall's analysis does not suggest this explanation, though the two views are not incompatible. With Marshall, there is more stress on the interlocking nature of colonial developments and British progress. On the other hand, his suggestion that the colonies could adapt technology more quickly than the mother country places them in the category of "late comers" to economic development.

Marshall stressed that the empire was a field for the investment of British capital, though he argued there were numerous advantages from investing in the home country, such as sentimental attachments, ease of communication, and the fact that income drawn from investments was obtained with less trouble and cost.(130) He also noted the long-term inverse movement of British home and foreign investment, but did not pursue this matter.(131) However, he did accept that the colonies were regions where British capital could be invested: "Capital is abundant in England; and she has few openings in which it can be made to yield a high return. Her colonies are thirsty for capital; and they have vast openings in which it can be made to yield a very high return".(132) He did not explain why the yields on home investments were less than on colonial investments. In a more general context, however, he did remark that most overseas investments went to the United States, and frequently into railways.(133)

The investment in railways by overseas countries constituted part of a transport revolution which also included dramatic changes in ocean shipping speeds and costs. Among late nineteenth century economists none was more aware of this phenomenon than Marshall.(134) However, he did not integrate the effects of capital investments overseas into an analysis of the British balance of payments in the period.

Marshall noted that in spite of the rise of Germany and the United States as strong industrial nations, Britain still supplied her colonies with the greatest proportion of their capital.(135) Moreover, he argued that the colonies, like the non-colonial countries, traded with England because they were intricately linked with and dependent upon the British market. The crucial element in this pattern was Britain's willingness to accept goods on credit at a distant date.

> But after all the chief cause of the modern prosperity of new countries lies in the markets that the old world offers, not for goods delivered on the spot, but for the promise to deliver goods at a distant date. A handful of colonists having assumed rights of perpetual prosperity in vast tracts of rich land, are anxious to reap in their own generation its future fruits; and as they cannot do this directly, they do it indirectly, by selling in return for the ready goods of the old world promises to pay much larger quantities of the goods that their own soil will produce in future generations. In one form or another they mortgage their prosperity to the old world at a very high rate of interest. Englishmen and others who have accumulated the means of present enjoyment hasten to barter them for large promises in the future than they can get at home; a vast stream of capital flows to the new country and its arrival there raises the rate of wages very high. The new capital filters but slowly towards the outlying districts; it is scarce there, and so many persons are eager to have it, that it has often commanded for a long time two per cent a month, from which it has fallen by gradual stages down to six, or even five per cent a year.(136)

High rates of interest were a temporary feature of the British colonies, a fact which Marshall seems to have appreciated as early as 1879.(137) His work reveals a keen awareness of the role of credit in international trade, though he did not elaborate his ideas with respect to its importance to colonial development. However, in arguing that capital flows led to an increase in wage rates in the colonies, he implied a central role for aggregate demand in colonial economic growth. Furthermore, he was the only economist to realise that investment was largely portfolio, rather than direct; investment in the colonies as elsewhere abroad, was primarily in securities which yielded a fixed rate of return.(138)

India Few of Marshall's published works refer to India, but his letters and notes reveal his keen interest and strong opinions on Indian trade policy and developmental questions.(139) He was proud that Britain had imposed peace upon the Indian subcontinent and abolished anarchy and internal warfare. Prior to British rule India had suffered from a disunity and a scarcity of transport. He felt that the rapid "recent rise of her industries is a source of just pride to her, and of gladness to Britain".(140)

Although he was concerned over the state of Indian finance and poverty, in a manner akin to that of Henry Fawcett, he could not "see his way clear" for any significant policy measures to improve the situation.(141) However, he advocated that Indians should concentrate upon technical, industrial pursuits and education, rather than "mere speech-making in politics and law courts" and general philosophising. (142)

> But I do not believe that any device will make India a prosperous nation, until educated Indians are willing to take part in handling things, as educated people in the West do. The notion that it is more dignified to hold a pen and keep accounts than to work in a high grade engineering shop seems to me the root of India's difficulties.(143)

He stressed the role of the industrial entrepreneur in stimulating Indian development, and urged Indians at Cambridge to imitate the Japanese and initiate Western progress.(144) Although Marshall hoped more businessmen and industrial capitalists like the Tata family would emerge, he did not necessarily believe that an industrial revolution, per se, would solve the nation's problems. He did not think that manufacturers were more conducive to prosperity than agriculture, unless they evoked initiative. "A score of Tatas might do more for India than any Government, British or indigenous, can accomplish. To try for manufacturers as in themselves a remedy for India's ills seems to me a fatal error".(145)

Free Trade, Protection, Imperial Preference and the 1903 Fiscal Controversy

As the leading professional economist of the day, Marshall was a somewhat hesitant signatory of the economists' Manifesto opposing Joseph Chamberlain's imperial preference scheme, published in The Times on 15th August, 1903.(146) In the same month he prepared a memorandum on "The Fiscal Problem" for the Chancellor of the Exchequer which was substantially revised - despite Marshall's claims to the contrary - and published in 1908 as the Memorandum on Fiscal Policy of International Trade.(147) The 1908 publication - the origin, revision and subsequent publication of which has not previously been documented - has recently been acclaimed, "one of the finest policy documents ever written by an academic economist", and reveals Marshall's incisive opinions on imperial preference and the key issues involved in any economic and political federation of the empire.(148)

Marshall was acutely aware of foreign competition, and pondered for many years before writing "The Fiscal Problem" in 1903 whether protection was a feasible solution to the problems facing Britain.(149) He had been a firm supporter of free trade policies since 1875, the year he visited the United States with the intention of studying protection at first hand. As a result of that experience, and his detailed investigations, he later remarked, "I settled in my mind the question as to which I had some doubt till I went to America, and decided that if an American, I should unhesitatingly vote for Free Trade".(150) In a similar manner to List, he argued protection was not a universally applicable policy, relevant to all nations at different stages of development and with different political systems from that of the United Kingdom. His American trip convinced him that the infant industry argument had been misused, since it afforded excessive protection to "industries which were already strong enough to do without it".(151)

Although Marshall did not think American industries needed protection in the last quarter of the nineteenth century, and continued to believe that the protection of mature industries was wrong and unwise, it "appears that his theoretical writings had a contrary effect".(152) Marshall's concept of external economies and his stress on the desirability of promoting those industries with increasing returns reinforced the argument for the protection of manufacturers in developing countries. As early as 1879, in the Pure Theory of International Trade, Marshall attempted a restatement of the theory of international trade under "exceptional circumstances of variables costs and tariff".(153) This article had a lasting impact and was the basis for the re-interpretation of international trade theory and the foundation stone for the development of the theory of tariffs by the economics profession around the time of the fiscal controversy.(154) Investigations were increasingly undertaken to establish the conditions under which State intervention with the free operation of international trade was justifiable. As Jha has demonstrated, the articles in the Economic Journal over the period 1890-1915, re-stated the principles of trade, and these led to the more precise formulation of the case for tariffs.(155)

In a similar manner to Jevons, Marshall attempted to treat the theories of domestic and international values as extensions of the general theory of exchange.(156) He also recognised the possibility of using tariffs to promote the national interest under specified situations, like the argument for the protection of infant industries.(157) Orthodox economists accepted this position and through Pigou's work, the possibility of taxing the foreigner by import and export duties, again under specified situations, became a doctrine of the Marshallian school.(158)

Prior to Pigou's publications in international trade, Edgeworth, inspired by Marshall, had attempted two re-statements of the theory of international trade; one on the basis of J S Mill and Henry Sidgwick and the other around Marshall's mathematical and graphical exposition.(159) Utilising Marshallian concepts, Edgeworth developed a pure theory of international trade. On the issue of protection, he reasoned that it could procure economic advantages, only "if there was a government wise enough to discriminate those cases and strong enough to confine itself to them".(160)

Marshall also considerably influenced the 1903 re-statement of the pure theory of international trade attempted by Henry Cunynghame. Cunynghame was Marshall's first student in the pure theory of foreign trade, and in the former's work, Marshall's influence as to the incidence of export and import duties on the producer and consumer is clearly evident.(161) Furthermore, he used Marshall's diagrams and extended his teacher's analysis to construct a balance sheet of the advantages and disadvantages a nation received from export and import taxes.(162) In addition to his analysis of hypothetical conditions in regard to tariff policies, Cunynghame noted certain indirect advantages which could accrue from protection, and argued that a protected country attracted marginal investors and labourers.(163) Like Edgeworth he was concerned to explore the various possibilities of state intervention in foreign trade. However, Edgeworth's analysis attracted more attention than Cunynghame's, for C F Bastable and Achille Loria attacked and expanded Edgeworth's position.(164) The nature and outcome of the controversy are too detailed to treat here, but what is of significance is that Marshall agreed with a number of these theoretical developments. In a letter to The Times in April 1901, reprinted later in the Economic Journal, he agreed with Edgeworth and Bastable that a general tax on imports and exports had the same effect. Whilst he admitted that such duties had advantages over other revenue raising methods, he was concerned that they could distort consumption. Nevertheless, he contended that, in theory, there were three grounds for "frontier taxes": (i) nondifferential import duties on comforts and luxuries, (ii) protective import duties on items for the production of which a country has great latent facilities that are just ripe for development, (iii) special export duties on commodities with which foreigners could not easily dispense.(165)

Marshall's letter to The Times was the result of a new export duty on coal payable from 1901, of which he strongly disapproved. Although he was opposed to the duty, his more general opposition to protectionist policies surfaced in the tariff reform controversy of 1903. Marshall was a signatory of the letter to The Times, drafted by Edgeworth and signed by such leading theoretical economists as E Cannan and A C Pigou. The letter called forth numerous replies and articles, but Marshall only once offered public comment on the economists' Manifesto and even then it was in reply to L L Price's 1903 article on the "Economic Possibility of Imperial Fiscal Reform".(166)

During the controversy Marshall was invited by his Cambridge undergraduate contemporary, T Llewellyn Davis, private secretary to the Chancellor of the Exchequer, to prepare a Memorandum on the fiscal question. Ritchie, the Chancellor of the Exchequer, was a staunch free trader in Balfour's Cabinet and he wanted the "advantage of any unofficial expression" of Marshall's opinions.(167). Whilst Davies stressed that Richie did not want to impose "any fetters on your discretion", Marshall closely followed Davies' recommendations of pursuing the two topics of imperial preferential tariffs and retaliatory duties, and the "endless issues" arising out of these headings. Marshall promised a paper "in a few days", and "half-deliberately addressed" himself to Mr Balfour "who was supposed to be in some doubt on the question of free trade".(168) Marshall's paper "The Fiscal Problem" replied to some of the issues raised by Balfour's Notes on Insular Free Trade, which was an attempt to placate all sides of the fiscal controversy.(169) Marshall became immersed in the issues raised by Davies' letter and completed Part I (imperial preferential tariffs) in early August and Part II (retaliation) towards the end of that month.(170)

However, Marshall did not publish the Memorandum in 1903 because of the "haste with which it was written", its brevity and "its frequent expression almost dogmatically of private opinion".(171) Regrettably, large corrections and additions to the Memorandum were lost by an Italian post-office worker in the late autumn of 1903 and Marshall did not pursue the offers to publish the work. But five years later, in 1908, it was published despite Marshall's reluctance. On June 1st and 2nd 1908 Lloyd George, then Chancellor of the Exchequer, made several statements in his speech in the House of Commons upon the Second Reading of the Finance Bill on the effect of a protective tariff on the German working classes, which were based on Marshall's Memorandum.(172) When Lloyd George was asked the authority for his statements, he acknowledged his source and was anxious to have the whole Memorandum printed and presented to Parliament, so his private secretary, Armitage-Smith sought Marshall's approval. Marshall felt "bound to accede to the Chancellor's request" and broke his rule that a professional economist should "abstain from controversy of all kinds".(173)

Before its publication Marshall made substantial revisions to the original Memorandum, altering both the format and content to produce his 1908 analytical masterpiece. In contrast to the published version, the original paper focused on the two areas suggested by Davies, namely, Preferential Treatment of the Colonies (Part I) and Retaliation (Part 2).(174) Part One formed the first draft of what became Section O of the published Memorandum, the "Possibilities of Closer Relations between England and her Colonies".(175)

In Part One of "The Fiscal Problem", (1903) Marshall systematically considered preferential tariffs between Britain and the colonies. He observed that there were three different ways in which preferential taxes could be established: (i) the imposition of a duty on everything imported into Britain from foreign countries with the exemption of those imports coming from the colonies, (ii) the establishment of comparatively high duties on certain selected articles forwarded to Britain by foreign countries and lower duties on these articles sent by the Colonies, (iii) the free entry of certain articles largely produced in the Colonies and the taxation of such items when they come from foreign countries.

Assuming, for purposes of illustration, a preferential tax with a 10% ad valorem duty, Marshall followed through the consequences on domestic prices and wages. He rebuked those who claimed that the price increase would be offset by increased wages, stating that there was "no economic law which raised wages, on the increased price of food-stuffs".(176) To him, wage increases were the direct result of trade union activity.(177)

Marshall also undertook a detailed and comprehensive analysis of the value of foreign and colonial trade, constructing import tables which demonstrated Britain's trade with foreign countries and the colonies. His tabulations, which were based on Giffen's statistics, showed that: (i) 4/5 of imports came from non-colonial countries, (ii) 2/3 of aggregate sea-borne trade was undertaken with foreign countries and a 1/4 with the colonies.(178)

He was particularly concerned at the problems involved in the operation of imperial preferences and predicted the following unfortunate consequences: a conflict of interests in the colonies between free traders and protectionists, a reduction in colonial revenue, increased prices to the British consumer with the heaviest burden falling on the poorer classes, and the creation of grievances between colonies with colonial economic questions being dominated by political considerations.(179) But the main problem of any preferential arrangement would be "the loss of freedom of movement between various nations and if Britain adopted any form of protection she would be poorer, and less powerful".(180)

It is said that there must be some business tie between the Colonies and the mother country; but are there not business ties already? Are not the Colonies provided with unlimited capital, and are not their loans treated preferentially by being included in the category of trust securities? and are they not almost entirely dependent on us to defend them in times of danger? Had not these practical ties be better relied on? If regard is to be had to sentiment, is not the best of all ties mutual pride?

Has not the pride of England's power and might appealed to the Colonies of late? and will it not continue to do so? Let it be remembered, then, that by altering the system on which we have so long thrived, we shall quite possibly make the country poorer; if we make it poorer, we shall make it less powerful; and if we make it less powerful, we shall weaken the tie.

If, however, the existing practical ties, together with the sentimental one, are deemed to be inadequate for the purpose of holding the Empire together - if there must be "a greater community of national interests and Imperial effort", and if there must be more settled business relations between the Colonies and the mother country, which can only be secured at the expense of the latter - if, in short, political considerations really outweigh economic ones, had it not better be done, in the interests of the tax-payer at home, in the least costly way? Instead of a preferential tariff, under which the taxation on the community must be greater than the benefit to the Imperial Exchequer, and which, therefore, must entail an unnecessary burden, it might be better to resort to the system of direct grants. At any rate, such a system would be all above board, and under it we should all know how we stood, the Imperial Government knowing the exact cost of encouraging the development of Colonial food supplies and of enlarging the Colonial custom for our manufacturers, and the Colonial Governments knowing the exact amount of encouragement and reciprocity which each of them received. Under this system, too, there would result further advantages. In the first place, the price of food-stuffs, whether coming from foreign countries or the Colonies, or supplied at home, would not be raised, except so far as they might be affected by the additional amount of general taxation which would have to be levied in consequence of the new Colonial grants. In the second place, the assistance to the Colonies ought to admit of being meted out with some better regard to equality and fairness, without merely benefiting the Colonial producers; Colonial questions would not be dragged into the arena of economic partisanship; and foreign countries could not take offence at our action.(181)

Prior to its publication in 1908, Marshall re-wrote the entire Memorandum. Unfortunately, the constraints of the present work preclude a detailed consideration of the changes, and the ensuing discussion concentrates on the re-written section pertaining to colonial questions. In his 1908 preface Marshall understated the extent of his revisions, although he emphasized that he had re-written the discussion on colonies.(182) In the published work the bold, dogmatic statements disappear, as do the discussions on the form of preferences, the trade statistics, and the effects of an ad valorem duty. In their place is a highly sophisticated, general analytical approach, which permeates all of the reconstructed Memorandum.

In this remarkable Memorandum Marshall considered the direct effect of import duties both at a theoretical and practical level, and reviewed England's fiscal policy since 1846. Whilst he regarded England's future "with grave anxiety" and conceded the infant industry argument for less developed countries, Marshall firmly and categorically rejected the senile industries argument for the protection of British manufactures. He did not believe that tariffs were responsible for American and German industrial advances and he contended that in the latter country, real wages were lower and increasing at a lesser rate than Britain's, because of high food costs.(183) Nevertheless, he was concerned that Britain's dominance in world technology was being eroded and that British innovators were no longer so active in pioneering new methods. He contended that a protective policy would exacerbate this trend and it was essential that Britain keep "her markets open to the new products of other nations, especially those of "American inventive genius and of German systematic thought and scientific training".(184)

Marshall's most telling argument against the tariff stemmed from his unique analysis of the elasticities of demand for British exports and the supply of British imports.(185) He concluded that in the long-term, the incidence of higher duties could not be passed on to the foreigner, to the advantage of the domestic consumer; whereas in the short-term, this was possible in a limited number of cases. Marshall was opposed to any situation which shifted the tax burden onto those commodities purchased by the lower income groups.(186)

Much as Adam Smith has noted in 1776, Marshall pointed out the dangers and possibilities of political mismanagement. Whilst he conceded that government's moral standards and general efficiency had increased, he was convinced that the value of free trade lay in the fact that it was "not a device, but the absence of a device".

A device contrived to deal with any set of conditions must become obsolete when they change. The simplicity and naturalness of free trade - that is, the absence of any device - may continue to outweigh the series of different small gains which could be obtained by any manipulation of tariffs, however scientific and astute.(187)

In his new section on "The Possibilities of Closer Relations between England and her Colonies", Marshall brilliantly summarized the nature of, and differences between, British and colonial economic development. He pointed out that England was still richer than her colonies, which were "thirsty" for the "abundant English capital". As in 1903, he remained opposed to imperial preferential schemes, but his main case now revolved around the different natures of the British and colonial economies. He recognized that the colonies, since they were new countries, wanted protection for their infant industries, although he thought that there were "better methods of bringing public funds to the aid" of new nations.(188) In contrast, England was the oldest of industrial nations and had no industries which required protection on grounds of youth, or because of the threat of foreign competition.

She (England) still has advantages in competition with other advanced countries due to her cheap capital; to her cheap coal; and to her climate, which is conducive to steady work, and is especially favourable to the finer cotton industries. But her chief remaining advantage lies in that unapproached freedom of movement, that viability that gives her much of the strength, without the cumbersomeness and want of elasticity of a single huge firm extending over the whole land. In the phase which the twentieth century seems to be opening out for her, viability for all things great and small, that may be needed directly or indirectly for the production of fine and complex goods, is essential to her.(189)

Marshall's use of the term "viability" is an unconventional one, but unfortunately he did not elaborate its meaning. However, it is evident from his 1903 paper that he was referring to that "unrestricted freedom of movement" associated with the free interplay of economic forces.(190) Moreover, he still retained his opposition to imperial preference because of the moral and political risks associated with protection and state intervention.

> In particular there is a danger in the fact that in these schemes the gain which either side is invited to expect is greater than the loss which she is to incur; and yet as the scheme includes differential duties which are essentially wasteful, the aggregate material gain must in my belief be less dangerous if they started with the frank statement: "Imperial unity is an ideal worth much material loss; let us consider how best to share this loss among us". As it is, the scheme appears to me likely to breed more disappointment and friction between England and her Colonies than of good will and the true spirit of Imperial unity. And, if approached in a spirit of greed, rather than of self-sacrifice, they are likely to rouse animosity in other lands, and to postpone the day at which it may be possible to work towards a federated Anglo-Saxondom, which seems to be an even higher ideal than Imperial unity.(191)

Nowhere in Marshall's notes and jottings is there a clear explanation of this revised treatment of colonial questions. However, as a close scrutiny of his notes written between 1903 and 1908 will reveal, he was most concerned with "treating adequately, and professionally the complex questions" of fiscal reform, imperial preference, imperial federation and "more general" imperial relationships. In 1904, he offered some "constructive suggestions" on the implications of Anglo-Saxondom, which were really reflections on the distribution of financial burdens between the mother country and the selfgoverning colonies.(192) He suggested that the United Kingdom could charge to an account of a crown colony, all expenses incurred for the development of the colony. Such expenses could be met by loans raised on behalf of the colony, with a quarter of the normal rate of interest, for a specified number of years, say 30. Alternatively, people's properties in the colony could be taxed or the crown could keep, at the time of the declaration of self-government, "a certain part of the soil of the colony" to cover Britain's expense in funding and governing the territory. Whilst Marshall did not detail a precise account of "Anglo-Saxondom", these thoughts reflect at one stage his concern with the financial burden of empire, a concern shared by other economists.(193)

In the following year, 1905, he was anxious that the United Kingdom should defeat protectionist countries in their quests for British colonial markets. He felt that the nation's manufacturing industries ought to be able to achieve this, except in three cases. Firstly, when a colony, for example Australia, produced its own simple products. Secondly in those "modern appliances" designed for large scale agricultural production. Thirdly, in those products which are the "special facility" of other countries, for example German science.(194) Towards the close of the year, he was anxious that imperial trade should be increased and in 1906 he suggested that England and her colonies should agree that a quarter of all import duties levied on things produced within the Empire be devoted to lowering freights between different parts of the empire.(195)

In other words, much like the opponents of tariff reform Marshall wanted greater freedom of trade within the empire, and he did not believe that imperial preference would promote greater intercourse between the member states. He contended that preferences acted in very different ways, with some merely changing the course of trade without affecting values, while others greatly benefited certain interests and injured others.

> A new preferential system may raise or lower the average level of taxes on imports: in the one case it would be a movement towards a protective policy, and in the other towards freedom of trade. Preferential arrangements between Britain and the Dominions are a move towards protection as far as she is concerned and away from it so far as they are concerned: because their present tariffs are highly protectionist and hers are not.(196)

Marshall stressed that preferential duties were not governed as much by their relative sizes or the economic strengths of the several countries concerned, as by the "elasticities of their several industries". Consequently, they did not fall within the scope of any arithmetical calculations, and the subtleties could be "grasped only by and through study of the physical, technical and human factors of the problem; and even then its solution must be partly instinctive and wholly diffident".(197)

Marshall did not confine his attention to the self-governing colonies and reviewed the consequences of the fact that while the self-governing colonies looked after their own interests in their own matters, the United Kingdom had to manage those of the crown colonies and India. Since Britain's crown colonies in Asia raised "ethical rather than economic problems", it was right that they should receive compensation if they were disadvantaged by imperial policy.

Mooveover, in these "Notes" written in 1907, Marshall devoted attention to the question of India and preferential tariffs. In both his original and revised Memorandum Marshall avoided a discussion of India, and his position on the issue of Indian tariffs only becomes evident by referring to his "Notes" and letters. Marshall observed that the clamour for Indian protection was really to protect British interests.(198) However, in his final sentence he referred to India as "the ward of England" and noted that she was "poor, while the colonies were rich; and that India's commercial policy has been generous".(199) He shared the position of other economists, and objected to excessive protection for nascent Indian industries; he reasoned that customs tariffs were expensive and would enrich European capitalists, not the Indians. He argued that industries like leather, paper, and oil-seed already enjoyed high protection because of transportation costs. Moreover, he believed that India's young industries would be stifled by protection and that "India can help her young industries much better by other means".(200) If Britain granted protection to Indian industries she would "abdicate her great place as ruler of India in India's interests".(201) "The more closely schemes for preferences are examined, whether in relation to India or to self-governing colonies, the more futile and dangerous do they seem to me. Their advocates do not win my confidence".(202)

Around the time he was re-writing the section on colonies for the Memorandum in 1908, Marshall read a book by a leading Chamberlainite, Caillard, on Preferential Duties. In his notes on the work, he recorded that if empire free trade could be obtained, it would only benefit England in the short-run, and in the longer-term foreign powers could retaliate with higher duties. Specifically, he rejected the position that the empire could be self-sufficient, claiming that in order to develop the colonies needed far more capital and labour than they possessed. Like Ricardo, he thought that eventually, there would be diminishing returns in agriculture and the empire would be forced to import food.(203)

Finally, it appears that Marshall re-wrote the 1903 paper because he felt it was a personal, not a professional document which was produced for a specific political purpose. This is reflected in the following draft preface, written in September 1903 when Marshall was considering publication of "The Fiscal Problem".

> I have made it my rule to avoid taking part in the discussion of a burning political question, even if it contains a lengthy economic argument. For however clearly a professional economist may distinguish in his own mind those aspects of the question on which his studies directly bear from those on which he has no special knowledge, the distinction is apt to be ignored by partisans on either side. And if he allows himself to be drawn into the heat of the fight he may himself lose sight of

the distinction. He may at least, swerve a little from that straight path, in which the student rejoices to discover and to promulgate a new truth on a new argument that tells against his own conclusion as much as one that tells on his side. He desires to influence the public. The public will not appreciate subtle distinctions, or complex reasoning. A full discussion of the economic bases of the problem will repel them; and be ineffective. He must lighten the discussion; he must ignore many difficulties. Brought into association with experienced controversialists, he is tempted to work for their ends and to some extent for their methods. If he yields to the temptation he may even begin to adjust his light and shade so as to bring into undue prominence those facts and arguments which tell for his conclusions. His advocacy may then become effective; but at some cost of that impartial sincerity which belongs to the student. But every rule has its exceptions. And the political issues which are now chiefly before the public differ from all others of equal importance that have arisen in this country at all events during the last two generations in the extent to which the leaders on either side have formally accepted certain distinctly economic statements.

The economic utterances of the late Colonial Secretary and of the Reform League of which he is President are of a different kind. The Policy which he would have the country pursue may for what I know be wise. But I do not think it is. And I know that some of the economic propositions which he has laid down as a basis of his policy were invalid. Many million copies of these propositions have been circulated among people who have had no scientific training. Economists seem therefore bound to contradict these statements; and that was, so far as I know anything of the matter, the real motive of a public letter which was issued by most of the professional economists in the country in August; but which was much misunderstood.

And there is one further point. An economist is after all a human being, and has his affections and enthusiasms like others. I have a passion for Anglo Saxon ideals. They are chiefly developed in this country and in the United States. If I had to choose either part, I would frankly prefer the former. But I believe that Englishmen have more to learn from arguments as a part - not the whole - of the basis of their positions.

The Economic Notes issued by the Prime Minister are a new precedent: I think a good precedent. No-one, and least of all the academic economist, can fail to be attracted by its charm, or to concur in the greater part of its arguments. But some of them seem open to objection. Taken all together they do not, I think, cover the whole ground; they ignore some vital considerations. The immediate step suggested is small, and might involve no great national risk if it certainly were to be the last step. But it is on a slope which capineuner (sic) and reason alike seem to show, is steeper and more slippery than almost any other in the whole region of economic practice. The hazard is therefore great and the student seems therefore bound to present his own opinions on those academic points raised by the Prime Minister.(204)

Yet despite Marshall's dogmatic opinions stated in "The Fiscal Problem" his techniques and analysis in his 1879 paper and the Memorandum, as well as the "Edgeworth controversy" no doubt influenced A C Pigou's and C F Bickedike's attempts to investigate the theoretical basis for protection, without reference to the British situation. Pigou's work in "Pure Theory and Fiscal Controversy", and in The Riddle of the Tariff, and Protective and Preferential Import Duties, clearly reflects Marshall's influence.(205) Taking his cue from Marshall's 1901 letter to The Times, Pigou also distinguished between the effects of differential and non-differential taxes. Moreover he utilised Marshallian concepts, like the elasticities of supply, production and demand, to analyse the possible effects of differential and non-differential taxes. Bickerdike also utilised Marshallian concepts and diagrams to prove that except in a peculiar case when supply and demand are inelastic on both sides, "a small enough tax" on exports and imports has advantages.(206)

Advantages and Disadvantages of Imperial Conquests

In common with economists like Ashley, Cunningham, Hewins and Nicholson, Marshall was proud that in the Great War, the English speaking peoples in four continents were united in "spirit and truth".(207) This was a direct product of England's ability to raise her children properly and he recommended that in future, Britain's achievements had to be measured in terms of British and colonial developments. He agreed with Goldwin Smith and argued that in the United States, Britain had attained its broadest and fullest development.

Britain's industrial leadership is to be measured by the achievements of Britons in their new homes as well as in their old: it is but carrying into larger affairs the familiar truth that parents, who have brought up a goodly array of noble and vigorous children, have done more for the world than is shown by their own achievement, somewhat narrowed as this may have been by their responsibilities.(208)

Moveover, he contended that it had long been realised that a colony outgrew its parent. This was the result of four factors: the cheapness and availability of land, the bolder, sturdier and more innovative workers who emigrated in preference to remaining at home, the "physiological causes connected with the mixture of races", and the freedom of peoples' new lives.(209)

Since England was the mother country, she had to bear numerous financial costs associated with the governing and defence of the empire. Furthermore, colonies urgently required capital for their development, and because returns were high in the investments in rich natural resources, British industries lost capital. He agreed with Adam Smith and Nicholson that England was poorer by this loss of capital: "but she herself is poorer, and is to some extent less able to maintain her leadership, than she would have been if her territory had been large and rich enough to enable all her labour and capital to be applied within her own limits".(210)

Such a situation was aggravated by the fact that the colonies did not bear their "proper share" of military burdens.(211) Like the 1860 economists and the mid-nineteenth century anti-imperialists, Marshall was opposed to the high defence costs of empire, though he appreciated that the mother country had to assist the colonies. Whilst he considered himself an anti-jingoist and opposed to the high military expenditures in the Boer War, he felt that the War had to continue until Natal and the Cape "had security from Boer armaments".(212) But imperialistic conquests increased military and naval expenditure.

> So long as our foreign policy aims at pushfulness, especially in those directions in which we imitate other nations with least benefit to ourselves - as in Egypt - I think we are bound to increase our expenditure on Army and Navy at an ever increasing rate. If then we go backwards relatively in more production, we court disaster. Were it not for this, I should be fairly contented with our making progress absolutely, even though most other nations were growing faster.(213)

On the other hand, there were benefits associated with the possession of a large empire. Echoing J S Mill's thoughts, Marshall argued that the improvements in land and sea transport meant that Britain was able to obtain food and minerals from the self-governing colonies at relatively low cost, as long as "the paths of the ocean are relatively secure under the protection of a strong fleet".(214) The influx of food into Britain resulted in a "temporary suspension" of the law of diminishing returns which enabled the British government to engage in much needed social reform.(215) Furthermore the cheap land, in association with sea transport and the opening-up of substantial areas of the earth's surface, had resulted in a rapid rise in real wages, which could not be sustained in the long term, for in the long term the law of diminishing returns would operate in the agricultural sector.(216)

Another dilemma with which Marshall felt Britain would be increasingly involved was the complex political relationship between the member states of the empire. In a similar manner to the 1860 economists, he noted that if Britain had retained control of all the self-governing colonies' external relations, numerous problems would not have presented themselves. But when the self-governing colonies established such laws as "the exclusions of the natives of India", Britain was left with "the burdens and responsibilities of empire, without freedom of action". However, if another stance was adopted and it was postulated that the empire's member states' external affairs were imperial and "must be governed by an imperial congress" four results would ensue:

(1) An imperial budget collected by imperial officers in all parts of the empire.

(2) The real possibility that a "militant" minority of British, together with Colonial representatives would declare war against Germany over some Pacific issue. The result would be "extremely dangerous to Britain" and involve "great losses".

(3) The probable abdication of Britain's rule of India, for the colonies would not allow India to be represented. He strongly felt that anti-Indian legislation would be increasingly probable and dangerous.

(4) Generally speaking, it would confirm the rule that children take all services from their parents without making full remuneration, a rule which applied more to countries than individuals.(217)

Conclusion

Marshall's writings on British imperialism reveal his extensive knowledge and interests as well as his concern with the broader dimensions of political economy. In his discussion of imperial preferential proposals, Marshall stressed that such issues did not simply involve strictly economic choices open to the economists. Rather, all important economic policies required political and moral choices. His Memorandum and rough notes and jottings clearly reveal that he supported the collection of reliable statistical information, as well as the establishment of statistical devices in order to measure the costs and benefits of policy actions. Professionally, he felt that an impartial assessment of all the interests involved was essential and, despite his strong feelings against protectionist policies, his Memorandum was such an assessment. Whilst opposed to the economic unification of the empire, Marshall was extremely proud of the "universality" of the English people and their institutions, as well as the Anglo Saxon contribution to world civilisation:

The chivalry which has made many administrators in India, Egypt and elsewhere, devote themselves to the interests of the peoples under their rules is an instance of the way in which British unconventional, elastic methods of administration give scope for free, fine enterprise in the service of the State; and it atones for many shortcomings in fore-thought and organisation.(218)

NOTES

1. For biographical details on Jevons' life see the introduction in R D C Black and R Könekamp (eds), The Papers and Correspondence of W S Jevons, Vol.1, (London, Macmillan, 1972); R D C Black , "W S Jevons and the Economists of his Time", Manchester School of Economics and Social Studies, 30, pp.203-221; T W Hutchison, Review of Economic Doctrines, op.cit, pp.32-38; "W S Jevons", International Encyclopaedia of the Social Sciences, op.cit, Vol.8, pp.254.259.

2. W S Jevons, The Principles of Economics, (London, Macmillan, 1905 ed), p.viii.

3. On Jevons in Australia see pp.102-103.

4. Jevons, The Theory of Political Economy, (London, Macmillan, 1871 1st ed., 4th ed., edited by Harriet Jevons, 1911), pp.ii-iii. In private correspondence Jevons was even more critical of Ricardo and Mill. See Letters and Journals of W Stanley Jevons, (London, Macmillan, 1886), pp.154, 329-334, 342-344, 419.

5. See L Robbins, The Evolution of Modern Economic Theory, (London, Macmillan, 1870), pp.170-73. Jevons' Primer of Political Economy, (London, Macmillan, 1870) Money and the Mechanism of Exchange (London, Kegan Paul, 9th ed. 1890) and the posthumous Principles of Economics, are primarily "elementary textbooks, devoted chiefly to descriptive matter", Robbins, Ibid, p.170.

6. Jevons, Theory of Political Economy, op.cit, p.1. At the end of The Theory of Political Economy he made a celebrated plea against the "Noxious Influence of Authority", as represented by Ricardo, the two Mills, and Henry Fawcett, Ibid, pp.275-277.

7. See R D C Black, "W S Jevons and the Foundation of Modern Economics", HOPE, Vol.4, No.2, 1972, pp.364-78. In 1862, in a paper read to Section F of the British Association, Jevons revealed his belief that the law of Economics could be reduced to a few principles, which could be outlined in mathematical terms and that such principles could be derived from the "great springs of human action - the feelings of pleasure and pain", reprinted as Appendix III of The Theory of Political Economy, p.304.

8. Jevons, Investigations in Currency and Finance, (London, Macmillan, 1884).

9. For Cairnes's ideas see Ch. 5, pp.73-74.

10. Jevons, The Coal Question, (London, Macmillan, 1865, 1st ed., 3rd ed., edited by A W Flux, 1906).

11. Jevons, The State in Relation to Labour, (London, Macmillan, 1882), pp.v-vi.

12. Ibid.

13. For an account of Jevons in Australia see M V White "Jevons in Australia: A Reassessment", ER, Vol.58, March 1982, pp.32-45 and Black's Introduction in Papers and Correspondence of W S Jevons, op.cit, especially pp.29-31.

14. See Letter to his sister Henrietta, in Black (ed.), Papers and Correspondence, Letter 72, Vol.II, op.cit, p.180.

15. He disliked the Australian country town. See Black,

Papers and Correspondence, Vol.II, Letter 95, W S Jevons to Lucy Jevons, 1/1/1857, p.252.

16. Jevons took a keen interest in colonial politics under "responsible government", see Black, Papers and Correspondence, Vol.I, p.31.

17. See Black Papers and Correspondence, Vol.I, Ibid, pp.26-27; Vol.II, pp.235-237.

18. Ibid, Vol.I, p.26.

19. Ibid, p.27.

20. Ibid, Vol.II, letter of W S Jevons to the editor of The Sydney Morning Herald, p.236.

21. Jevons, The Empire, 8/4/1857.

22. Jevons, The Empire, 24/6/1857.

23. Thus, he implicitly disputed Wakefield's position. See Winch, Classical Political Economy and the Colonies, op.cit, pp.77-105.

24. Jevons, "Comparison of Land and Railway Policy of NSW", op.cit. As La Nauze argues, the articles contain some "acute and vigorously worded criticisms", but these are not of "enduring value". They certainly do not compare to Jevons' reflections on the nature of capital, and the question of the subjective influence on value. Also see Letter from W S Jevons to his brother, Herbert in January 1859, Letters and Journals, op.cit, pp.113-119 and 1/6/1860, Ibid, p.151. Also see Black, Papers and Correspondence, Vol.II, op.cit, Letter 128, to Henrietta Jevons, pp.358-63; Hutchison, Review of Economic Doctrines, op.cit, pp.34-35.

25. Black, Papers and Correspondence, op.cit, Vol.I, p.27.

26. J M Keynes, "W S Jevons", JRSS, Vol.XCIX, 1936, p.518. Jevons left Australia to return to his university education in England. Whilst he conceeded that he had gained many advantages from being in "the Antipodes" he felt that his formal education was "checked an irretrievably deferred". See Black, Papers and Correspondence, op.cit, Vol.II, Letter from W S Jevons on 9/7/1858 pp.331-333.

27. See the discussion in Ch.4, pp.45-48 and 57-58, Ch.5, pp.80-86.

28. Jevons, The Coal Question, (London, Macmillan 1906 ed.), Ch.X, "On the Growth and Migration of our Population", pp.202-231.

29. See Ch.2, pp.10-13.

30. Jevons, The Coal Question, op.cit, pp.219.

31. Judged by modern standards, Jevons' conclusions are reasonably accurate. From 1870-80 to 1911-12, the sex ratios were fairly constant at about four females to every six males. In the late 1870s and the 1880s when there was considerable emigration there was approximately 20 children to every 100 adults. The great majority of emigrants were young men and women; after 1875-95, the population 40 and over tended to fall. See S G Checkland, The Rise of Industrial Society in England, (London, Longmans and Green, 1969), Ch.2.

32. Jevons, The Coal Question, op.cit, pp.220-1.

33. See Ch.4, pp.45-48 and 57-58, and Ch.5, pp.80-86.

34. Jevons, The Coal Question, op.cit, pp.220-38.

35. It is just possible that Jevons' awareness of the colonies as potential industrial nations was a direct consequence of his Australian experiences. See R D C Black and R Könekamp (eds), Papers and Correspondence of W S Jevons, op.cit, Vol.I, pp.107-237 and R D C Black (ed) Vol.II, (London, Macmillan, 1973), pp.108-209.

36. Jevons, Investigations in Currency and Finance, op.cit.

37. Jevons, Money, op.cit, p.66.

38. Jevons, Investigations in Currency and Finance, op.cit, p.71.

39. Jevons, Money, op.cit, p.147.

40. Jevons, "On the Conditions of the Metallic Currency of the United Kingdom", op.cit, p.429.

41. Ibid, pp.429-430.

42. Jevons, Methods of Social Reform, (London, Macmillan, 1883) pp.181-182.

43. Jevons, The Coal Question, op.cit, p.428.

44. Ibid, pp.215, 247-9, 238-39.

45. Ibid, pp.430-31. In 1857, Jevons thought that protectionism was a passing phase in the Australian colonies. See Black, Papers and Correspondence, op.cit, Vol.I, Letter 102 on 28/3/1857, p.28, "People need not, for the future occupy themselves, except for amusement, with any article headed "Protection"."

46. Ibid, pp.459-60.

47. Black, Papers and Correspondence, op.cit, Vol.II, pp.179-83, Letter 72 to Henrietta Jevons, 9/9/1855.

48. Ibid, Vol.II, Letter 143, W S Jevons to Herbert, 27/1/1860, p,p.404-408.

49. Jevons, The Coal Question, op.cit, p.421. For Cairnes' view see Ch.5, pp.74-76.

50. Quoted in Hutchison, Review of Economic Doctrines, op.cit, p.51.

51. For biographical details see J N Keynes, "Henry Sidgwick", EJ, Vol.10, 1900, pp.585-91; Arthur Sidgwick and Eleanor Sidgwick, Henry Sidgwick: A Memoir (London, Macmillan, 1906) and L Stephen, "Henry Sidgwick", Mind, Vol.10, N.S. January 1901.

52. See J N Keynes, "Henry Sidgwick", op.cit, pp.585-91.

53. See Bernard Corry, "Henry Sidgwick", in International Encyclopaedia of the Social Sciences, Vol.14, p,p.235.

54. H Myint, Theories of Welfare Economics, (London, Longmans, 1948).

55. Hutchison, Review of Economic Doctrines, op.cit, p.52.

56. H Sidgwick, Principles of Economics, (London, Macmillan, 1883, 1901 reprint) p.36.

57. Sidgwick, A Memoir, op.cit, (1865) p.131.

58. Sidgwick, Elements of Politics, (London, Macmillan, 1897) pp.289-327.

59. Ibid, p.316.

60. Ibid, p.317.

61. Ibid, p.307.

62. Ibid, p.308.

63. Ibid, pp.309-11.

64. Ibid, p.320.

65. Ibid, p.320.

66. Ibid, p.322.

67. Ibid, pp.324-27.

68. See Chapter XXVII, "Control of the People Over Government", Ibid, pp.545-50.

69. Ibid, p.547.

70. Ibid, p.548.

71. Ibid, p.549.

72. Ibid, p.550.

73. Ibid, pp.311-312.

74. See Sidgwick's letter to Lord Tennyson, then Governor of South Australia, 28/6/1897 in Henry Sidgwick: A Memoir, op.cit, pp.574-76.

75. For a general discussion of British attitudes to the Boer War see B Porter, A Short History of British Imperialism, (London, Longmans, 1975) pp.136-7, 177-9, 193, 203-207.

76. Sidgwick's letter to H G Dakyns, 3/2/1900 , in Henry Sidgwick: A Memoir, op.cit, p.580; also a letter to Lord Tennyson 25/12/1899, ibid, pp.576-578.

77. Ibid, pp.577-578. Also see Porter, A Short History of British Imperialism, op.cit.

78. See Ch.3, pp.10-13, Ch.8, pp.201-204 and Ch.10, pp.250-255.

79. For details of Marshall's life see J M Keynes, "Alfred Marshall 1842-1924", EJ, Vol.34, September 1924, pp.311-72. On Marshall's early life see J K Whittaker (ed), The Early Writings of Alfred Marshall 1867-1890, (Chanton, Macmillan, 1975).

80. A Marshall, The Pure Theory of International Trade, (London, LSE, Reprint 1930 (1879)); A Marshall and Mary Paley Marshall, The Economics of Industry, (London, Macmillan, 1879).

81. See John Maloney, "Marshall, Cunningham and the Emerging Economics Profession", EHR, 1976, pp.440-451.

82. D Winch, Economics and Policy: A Historical Study, (London, Hodder and Stoughton, 1969), p.23.

83. See his notes on "The Future of Mankind", (4/11/1920) and "On Progress", (27/2/1908) in Big Red Box, No.2, Marshall Papers, Marshall Library, Cambridge.

84. J M Keynes (ed), Official Papers by Alfred Marshall, (London, Macmillan, 1926), p.205. Also see his notes on "Realisable Social Needs", (8/8/1920), and "Equality is Desirable", (1/1/1922) in Big Red Box, No.2, Marshall Papers.

85. Ibid, "Notes" written on 10/3/1922.

86. A Marshall, "The Future of the Working Classes" in A C Pigou, Memorials of Alfred Marshall, (London, Macmillan, 1925), pp.101-118, especially p.117.

87. Ibid, p.174.

88. Marshall, "Economic Teaching at the University in Relation to Public Well-Being", Charity Organisation Review, 1903, pp.37-8. Also see Winch, Economics and Policy, op.cit, p.34; Notes on "The Duties of the Logicans of System-maker to the Metaphysician and to the practical Man of Science", Mss.Box 11,

Marshall Papers.

89. Marshall, "Address to the Industrial Remuneration Conference", 1885, p.183.

90. Ibid; also see Mss.Box 5 (18) and his rough notes on "Art and Science" in Large Red Box, Bundles 2-5, Marshall Papers; for a second statement on the limitations of the law of political economy see his letters to The Beehive, 18/4/1874 and 6/5/1874. The letters were replies to criticism of ecnomics by a Mr Holmes. Also in the Marshall Papers, Mss.Box 9 (2).

91. Marshall, Principles of Economics, (London, Macmillan, 1920 ed), pp.15, 26-7; also see Winch, Economics and Policy, op.cit, p.38 and T Hutchison, Review of Economic Doctrines, op.cit, pp.62-94. Marshall felt that he was also protesting at the concept of "economic man", a notion due to the "baneful influence of J S Mill". See Letter from Alfred Marshall to J N Keynes, 30/1/1902 in Keynes Letters, (125), Marshall Papers.

92. See G F Shove, "The Place of Marshall's 'Principles' in the Development of Economic Theory", EJ, December 1942, pp.294-329.

93. Marshall, Memorials, op.cit, p.165; "On Method", Mss.Box 9 (2); "Art or Science" in Large Red Box, Bundles 2-5, Marshall Papers.

94. Marshall, "Notes on Method" in Mss.Box 9 (2), Marshall Papers.

95. See R H Coase, "Marshall on Method", op.cit; Talcott Parsons, "Wants and Activities in Marshall" QJE, Vol.XLVI, November 1931, pp.101-140; "Economics and Sociology: Marshall in Relation to the Thought of his Time", QJE, Vol.XLVI, February 1932, pp.316-347; John K Whittaker, "Some Neglected Aspects of Alfred Marshall's Economic and Social Thought", HOPE, Vol.9, Summer 1977, pp.161-197. For an account of his views on "evolution" see notes written on 5/4/1923 in Large Red Box, No.1 (3), Marshall Papers.

96. See T W Hutchison, Review of Ecnomic Doctrines, op.cit, p.69; Hutchison's view is confirmed by Marshall's notes on "The History of Economic Theory", and "Notes on the Ecnomic History of the Middle Ages, Greece, Rome and the East", in Mss.5 (6-10), Marshall Papers. He was particularly absorbed in Quesnay's Tableau Economique, see Mss.Box 5 (6-7).

97. See J M Keynes, "Alfred Marshall", op.cit, p.354.

98. Marshall, Principles, op.cit, Book 1, Ch.5, fn.9. Also see Notes on "Art and Science", Large Red Box, Bundles 2-5, Marshall Papers.

99. Winch, Economics and Policy, op.cit, p.32.

100. See "On Method", Mss.Box 9 (2), Marshall Papers.

101. J Schumpeter, Ten Great Economists, (London, Galaxy ed, 1965), p.94; History of Ecnomic Analysis, op.cit, p.822.

102. See A W Coats, "Alfred Marshall and the Early Development of the LSE: Some Unpublished Letters", Economica, Vol.36, Nov.1967, pp.408-17.

103. See Section 3, pp.121-132.

104. See Notes on "Imperialism and Centralisation", 27/12/1907 in Large Red Box, Mss.2, Marshall Papers.

105. Marshall, Principles, (1898 ed), Book 1, Ch.VII, 54, p.117.

106. See Bodelsen, Studies in Mid-Victorian Imperialism, op.cit, pp.5-86.

107. See, for example, Ch.4, pp.45-48, Ch.7, pp.150-152 and Ch.8, pp.195-197.

108. See R L Schulyer, The Fall of the Old Colonial System: A Study in British Free Trade 1770-1879, (New York, OUP, 1945), pp.302-8 and Bodelsen, Studies in Mid-Victorian Imperialism, op.cit, pp.5-86.

109. Marshall, Industry and Trade, op.cit, p.105; Memorials, op.cit, p.343. Also see Notes in Two Miscellaneous Open Boxes, Mss.Box 2, Bundles 1 and 2, Marshall Papers.

110. Marshall, The Elements of the Economics of Industry, (London, Macmillan, 1892), Book VI, Ch.X, 53, pp.322-329.

111. Marshall, Industry and Trade, op.cit, p.142. See Marshall's letters to his Mother, Rebecca, written from America during 1875, Letters Nos. 3 (66) to 3 (76), Mss.Box 3, Marshall Papers.

112. It is difficult to explain this interest. Perhaps it was due to the fact that his uncle farmed most successfully in Australia.

113. Marshall, Industry and Trade, op.cit, pp.159-87. Whilst his published work primarily refers to Australia, he read widely all kinds of literature on New Zealand. See Letter from Alfred Marshall to J N Keynes, 28/3/1900 in Keynes Letters 1 (117), Marshall Papers.

114. Marshall, Principles, op.cit, 4th edition, 1898, Book 1, Ch.III, 8, esp. p.50. In the first and subsequent two editions, this section was called "The Influence of the American and German Experience on England". In the 4th edition, this became "The Influence of the American, Australian and German Experiences on England". He retained this section in the fifth edition, but dropped it in the sixth.

115. Ibid, p.50.

116. Marshall, Principles, op.cit, 9th ed, pp.160-181.

117. Marshall, Industry and Trade, op.cit, p.143.

118. Marshall, "Some Features of American Industry", Box Mss.6 (7), pp.6-7, Marshall Papers.

119. Marshall, "Migration and Prosperity", Two Miscellaneous Open Boxes, Mss.Box 2, 14/3/1905, Marshall Papers.

120. See B Thomas, Migration and Economic Growth, (Cambridge, CUP, first ed. 1954, second ed. 1973).

121. Marshall, "Notes on Migration and Fluctuations:, Misc. Open Boxesd, Mss.Box 2, 30/10/1905, Marshall Papers.

122. Marshall, "Tariffs and Migration", Ibid, 18/9/1903.

123. Marshall, "Immigration Bundle", in Large Brown Box, Mss.Box 2.

124. Marshall, "Notes", 27/10/1905, Ibid.

125. For a discussion of Malthus' views see Ghosh, Classical Macroeconomics and the Case for Colonies, op.cit, pp.113-128.

126. A Marshall, Money, Credit and Commerce, (London, Macmillan, 1923), p.123. Although this was published in 1923, it was written in 1875. See Keynes, Alfred Marshall, op.cit, p.327.

127. Marshall, Money, Credit and Commerce, op.cit, pp.123-5.

128. Ibid, p.125. Also see Marshall, "Notes on Migration and

Fluctuations", Misc. Open Boxes, Mss.Box 2, 30/10/1905, Marshall Papers.

129. See C P Kindleberger, "Foreign Trade and Economic Growth: Lessons from Britain and France 1950 and 1913", EHR, Vol.XIV, 1961-2, pp.289-305.

130. Marshall, Money, Credit and Commerce, op.cit, p.9; Industry and Trade, op.cit, p.104.

131. On the movements of home and foreign investments see A K Cairncross, Home and Foreign Investment, (Cambridge, CUP, 1953).

132. Marshall, Memorials, op.cit, pp.415-16. Although Marshall argued capital was abundant in England, he did not believe that there could be general over production. See Principles, op.cit, p.524.

133. This was the case for most of the period, 1860-1914. The United States was the single most important source of new security issues in the British capital market over the period 1860-1914. See S B Saul, Studies in British Overseas Trade, op.cit, p.66.

134. A Marshall, Money, Credit and Commerce, op.cit, pp.8-12, 123-8.

135. Ibid, pp.122-5. Marshall correctly anticipated the trend of colonial borrowing.

136. Alfred and Mary Paley Marshall, Economics of Industry, (London, Macmillan, 1879), p.343. Also see Mss.Box 6 (12) and Mss.Box 7 (1), Marshall Papers.

137. Marshall, Economics of Industry, op.cit, Ch.XII, Bk.Vi, Sec.I, p.343.

138. Ibid, p.344.

139. For a discussion of Marshall and the question of protection for Indian industries, see p.178; also see Large Red Box 1 (4) "India", Marshall Papers.

140. Marshall, Industry and Trade, op.cit, pp.23-25.

141. For a discussion of Fawcett's views see Wood, "Henry Fawcett and the British Empire", Indian Journal of Economic and Social History, op.cit. Also see Ch.5, pp.86-92.

142. See Letter from Marshall to B Mukherjee, 22/10/1910 in Memorials, op.cit, pp.471-473; also his "Notes", 25/7/1899, Large Red Box, 1 (4), Marshall Papers.

143. See Marshall's letters to Manohar Lal, 28/1/1909 in Memorials, op.cit, p.457.

144. See Marshall's letter to B Mukherjee, 22/10/1910, op.cit, p.472. He made long copies of his Indian students' answers to economic questions, perhaps because of the different perspective they brought to the subject. See Large Brown Box, Mss.Box 5 (5), Marshall Papers.

145. See Marshall's letter to Manohar Lal, 22/2/1911, Memorials, op.cit, p.458.

146. Marshall regretted signing the Manifesto, claiming that the professional economist should abstain from controversy. See A W Coats, "Political Economy and the Tariff Reform Campaign of 1903", op.cit, pp.213, 220-221.

147. After an extensive search among the Public Records

Office Treasury papers over a number of years, I have been able to identify - with the patient assistance of G L Beech of the Search Department - Marshall's original 1903 Memorandum. This is entitled simply "The Fiscal Problem" (TI/990B/14949). Although it is dated at the Treasury, 25 August 1903 it is not immediately obvious that this memorandum is the original on which the 1908 White Paper was based; the sections are numbered quite differently, and the two parts are respectively entitled "Preferential Treatment of the Colonies" and "Retaliation", in contrast to the White Paper's "The Direct Effects of Import Duties", and England's Fiscal Policy considered with reference to the Economic Changes of the last Sixty Years". No subsections of this memorandum correspond obviously to those of the White Paper, and there are no notes or minutes on the same file which might establish a connection between the Memorandum and the White Paper. However, the papers, correspondence and records in the Marshall Papers, confirm it is the 1903 paper, which was the basis of the 1908 Memorandum. See Wood, "Alfred Marshall and the Tariff Reform Campaign of 1903", JLE, Vol.22 (2), Oct 1980, pp.481-495.

148. See T W Hutchison, On Revolution and Progress in Economic Knowledge, (Cambridge, CUP, 1978), p.114. D Winch and D P O'Brien also consider Marshall's Memorandum to be one of the outstanding policy documents of Neo-Classical economics. See the "Report of Discussion" at History of Economic Thought Conference, Nottingham, September 1977 in History of Economic Thought Newsletter, Autumn 1977, No.19, pp.7-8. For a reprint of the 1908 Memorandum see J M Keynes Official Papers of Alfred Marshall, op.cit, pp.367-420.

149. For a discussion of Marshall's opinions, see T W Hutchison, "Economists and Economic Policy in Britain After 1870", HOPE, Vol.1, No.2, Fall 1969, pp.231-55; Winch, Economics and Policy, op.cit, pp.61-64. Also see Mss.Box 6 (12), Mss.Box 7 (1) and (2), Mss.Box 10 (1-6) and Mss.Box 11 (1); Large Brown Box (24) and Two Miscellaneous Open Boxes, Mss.Box 1 and 2 for his thorough and detailed empirical and theoretical investigations into the issue of protection, Marshall Papers.

150. Marshall, "Some Aspects of Competition", (1890), reprinted in Memorials, op.cit, pp.256-91, especially p.263; also see his letters to his mother, Rebecca Marshall, op.cit, and Mss.Box 6 (7), "Some Features of American Industry", Marshall Papers.

151. See Mss.Box 10 (1), Marshall Papers.

152. N, Jha, The Age of Marshall, (Patna, Novelty, 1963), p.31.

153. Marshall, The Pure Theory of International Trade, (London, London School, reprint, 1930 (1879)). Jha claims in The Age of Marshall, op.cit, that this led to Edgeworth's re-statement of the theory, pp.34-6. Marshall worked on the theory of international trade till his death in 1924. The Marshall Papers, contain a wealth of unexplored material on his thoughts and ideas on international trade, which he believed was in need of theoretical advances which "could be expressed with great facility by means of diagrams", Mss.Box 7 (1), Marshall Papers.

154. As Winch notes in Economics and Policy, op.cit, it is "a strange fact that the most telling arguments in favour of tariffs have been advanced by economists who have favoured free trade as a general rule", p.60.

155. Jha, The Age of Marshall, op.cit, pp.29-85. Also see Mss.Box 6 (12), 6 (17); Box 11; Large Red Box 1 and 2.

156. Bastable, Theory of International Trade, (London, Macmillan, 1904, 4th ed). Ch.1, pp.1-21; also see Large Red Box 2, Marshall Papers.

157. See Misc. Mss.Box 2, Tied Bundle "Protection", Marshall Papers.

158. A Pigou, A Study in Public Finance, (London, Macmillan, 1928), pp.195-217.

159. Edgeworth, "The Theory of International Trade", EJ, Vol.4, 1894, pp.35-49.

160. Ibid, p.48.

161. H Cunynghame, "The Effects of Export and Import Duties Examined by the Graphic Method", EJ, Vol.13, September 1903, pp.313-323. Also see, Cunynghame's letter to Marshall, 4/10/1888, Marshall Letters 1 (10). On Cunynghame's life see J M Keynes, "Sir Henry Cunynghame", EJ, Vol.45, 1935, pp.398-401.

162. Cunynghame, "The Effects of Export and Import Duties", p.322. Also see Mss.Box 6 (17), Marshall Papers.

163. Cunynghame, Geometrical Political Economy, (Oxford, Clarendon, 1904), p.97. Marshall was pursuing this idea some years before Cunynghame's publication. See Mss.Box 7 (1), Mss.Box 10 (1), Marshall Papers.

164. See Jha, The Age of Marshall, op.cit, pp.41-45.

165. Marshall, "An Export Duty on Coal", Letter to The Times, 19/4/1901 and EJ, June 1901, pp.265-268.

166. For an account of Price's views see L L Price, "Economic Possibilities of Imperial Fiscal Reform", EJ, Vol.13, December 1903, pp.486-504. Also see L L Price, "Free Trade and Protection", EJ, September 1902, pp.305-319; "The Economic Prejudice Against Tariff Reform", Fortnightly Review, November; "Free Trade and Fiscal Policy, EJ, September 1904, pp.372-387.

167. See Letter from T Llewellyn Davies to Marshall, 2/7/1903 in Large Brown Box (24). This and subsequent letters were mis-catalogued and rediscovered by the author, who acknowledges the generous assistance rendered by Mr Finkel and the librarians at the Marshall Library, Cambridge. Also see Marshall's Letter to Mr Clark, 22/11/1908, Ibid.

168. See Marshall's reply to Davies, 14/7/1903, Ibid, and Marshall's letter to Sir F Macmillan 24/11/1908 in Marshall Letters, Mss.Box 4 (40), and his Notes, on 23/9/1903, Large Brown Box (24).

169. Keynes' "Obituary to A J Balfour", EJ, June 1930, pp.336.338 mentions that Marshall was quite excited about Balfour's Notes on Insular Free Trade. Keynes' comment is confirmed by Marshall's jottings on 23/9/1903 in Large Brown Box (24), Marshall Papers.

170. See Letters from Davies to Marshall, 13/8/1903; and

25/8/1903, Ibid.

171. Marshall Official Papers, op.cit, p.368. Also see Marshall's letter to Sir F Macmillan, 24/11/1908, Marshall Letters, 4 (40); Marshall to S Armitage-Smith, 20/6/1908, Large Brown Box (24); Marshall to Mr Clarke, 22/11/1908, Ibid.

172. See Hansard, Vol.C.XXXIX, Nos. 10, 11, 1/6/1908; 2/6/1908. Also S Armitage-Smith's letter to Marshall, 20/6/1908.

173. See Marshall's reply to S Armitage-Smith, 27/6/1908, op.cit. At this time, Marshall had been working on a larger volume on National Industries and International Trade, in which he was attempting to treat in greater detail issues raised in the Memorandum. See his notes in Box Mss.2 (6) and Two Miscellaneous Open Boxes, "Protection Bundle", Marshall Papers.

174. See Letter from T Llewellyn Davies to Marshall, 2/7/1903, op.cit.

175. See Memorandum, op.cit, pp.415-420.

176. Marshall, "The Fiscal Problem", PRO, No.TI/9990B/14949, 1903, p.6.

177. Ibid, p.7.

178. Ibid, p.10. Also see R Giffen, "The Relative Growth of the Component Parts of the Empire", Journal of the Royal Colonial Institute, No.6 Series 2, February 1898, pp.1-21.

179. Marshall, "The Fiscal Problem", op.cit, pp.10-19.

180. Ibid, p.11.

181. Ibid, pp.20-21.

182. See Memorandum, op.cit, pp.367-368.

183. Ibid, pp.378-380, 397-399. Also see Mss Box.11 (5), Marshall Papers.

184. Ibid, p.409. Also see Marshall on "The Industrial Revolution", Large Red Box, No.1 (13), Marshall Papers.

185. Marshall, Memorandum, op.cit, pp.399-401.

186. Ibid, pp.409-10. For a similar view see Winch, Economics and Policy, op.cit, p.62. Marshall's concern for the consumer permeates his notes and jottings on "Protection", see Two Miscellaneous Open Boxes, Mss Box.1 (16), Mss Box.11 (5) and Large Red Box, Bundle "Protection", Marshall Papers.

187. Marshall, Memorandum, op.cit, p.394.

188. Ibid, pp.415-18.

189. Ibid, p.419.

190. See pp.171-172.

191. Marshall, Memorandum, op.cit, p.420.

192. See Marshall's "Notes" of 22/5/1904 in Two Miscellaneous Open Boxes, Box 1.

193. See, for example, Ch.4, pp.45-50; Ch.5, pp.74-76.

194. See Marshall's "Notes", 13/3/1905.

195. Marshall "Notes", 30/8/1906.

196. Marshall "Notes", 28/9/1907, p.120.

197. Ibid, p.126.

198. See Marshall's letter to Manohar Lal, 22/2/1911 in Pigou (ed), Memorials of Alfred Marshall, op.cit, p.458.

199. Marshall, Memorandum, op.cit, p.420.

200. See Marshall's letter to B Mukherjee 22/10/1910, Memorials, op.cit, p.472.

201. Marshall, "Notes", 28/9/1907, op.cit, p.137.

202. See Marshall's letter to B Mukherjee, 22/10/1910 in Memorials, op.cit, p.473.

203. Marshall, "Notes on Caillard's Book on Preferential Duties", 19/7/1908, Miscellaneous Mss Box.2, op.cit.

204. Marshall, "Preface", 23/9/1903, Marshall Papers. In the above quotation the word "capineuner" appears. This is possibly and anglicization of the German kapieren.

205. A C Pigou, The Riddle of the Tariff, (London, Johnson, 1903); Protective and Preferential Import Duties, (London, Macmillan, 1906).

206. Jha, The Age of Marshall, op.cit, p.47. Also see Mss Box.6 (12) and Mss Box. 7 (1); Miscellaneous Box 1, Bundle "Protection", Marshall Papers.

207. Marshall, Industry and Trade, 1932 ed, op.cit, pp.104-6.

208. Ibid, p.104. Also see G Smith, The Schism of the Anglo Saxon Race, (New York, New coy, 1887).

209. Marshall, Industry and Trade, op.cit, pp.104-105; also see Principles, 8th ed, 1920, p.197 and "Notes on the Migration of Labour", 1910 in Large Red Box, Mss Box.1, Marshall Papers.

210. Ibid, pp.104-5. For Marshall's "Notes on Adam Smith" see Mss Box.6 (3), Marshall Papers.

211. See Marshall's letter to F W Pethick Lawrence 12/1/1904 in Pigou (ed) Memorials, op.cit, p.454.

212. Marshall to Dr N G Pearson, Prime Minister of Holland, 3/4/1900 in Pigou (ed), Memorials, op.cit, pp.410-412. Also see his letter to Mr Bosanquet 2/10/1902, Ibid, pp.444-445.

213. Marshall's letter to Edward Caird, Master of Balliol College, 5/12/1897, in Pigou (ed), Memorials, op.cit, pp.399-401.

214. Marshall, Industry and Trade, op.cit, p.105. Also see Ch.2, pp.14-15.

215. See Marshall's "Notes on the Future of Mankind", 4/11/1920, Large Red Box, Mss.1 (3), Marshall Papers.

216. Marshall Industry and Trade, op.cit, p.105. Also see "Notes on Capital", 25/2/1910, 10/4/1910 in Large Red Box, Mss Box.1, Marshall Papers.

217. Marshall, "Imperialism and Centralisation", 27/12/1907, Large Red Box, Mss Box.2, Marshall Papers.

218. Marshall, "Social Possibility of Economic Thinking", in Pigou (ed), Memorials, op.cit, p.343.

Chapter 7

THE CLASSICAL TRADITION : J S NICHOLSON AND THE REHABILITATION OF ADAM SMITH; SIR ROBERT GIFFEN, MASTER STATISTICIAN

J S NICHOLSON

Introduction

J S Nicholson occupied the Chair of Political Economy and Mercantile Law in his native city, Edinburgh, for some forty-five years (1880-1925), approximately twice the length of time Alfred Marshall was Professor at Cambridge.(1) Nicholson was at Cambridge when Marshall held his first teaching appointment in economics, and he generally accepted his teacher's ideas and views, although he later rejected Marshallian economics.(2) After Cambridge, Nicholson completed his formal education in Heidelberg, after which he accepted the Edinburgh professorship.

As a professor in Edinburgh, Nicholson attempted to provide an alternative theory to Marshall, and he emphasised production rather than consumption. However, Nicholson was not solely interested in providing a different position to Marshall, as he hoped to rehabilitate Adam Smith's political economy, since Smith's works "were intelligible and familiar to the common people, and they supplied the ideas for practical statesmen".(3) Furthermore, Smith's ideas were still relevant to the contemporary world, particularly the problems of the British empire: "No other writer has approached him in the breadth of view and in the appreciation of different elements involved in the economics of imperialism".(4)

The dominant characteristic forming Nicholson's ideas and writings was his attitude to his fellow Scotsman, Adam Smith.(5) He continuously defended Smith's writings, or at least his interpretations of them and in "The Reaction in Favour of Classical Political Economy" he maintained that "orthodox, or classical, political economy, so far from being dead, is in full vigour, and that there is every sign of a marked reaction in favour of its principles".(6)

Although Nicholson's writings were primarily devoted to financial, banking and currency questions, such as war inflation and the bi-metallism controversy, he attempted to reconcile the historical, mathematical and statistical approaches to economics in his three volume Principles of Political Economy, which appeared between 1893 and 1901.(7) His reverence for Adam Smith meant that he never referred to his subject as 'economics' but as political economy and the arrangement of the Principles, with the theory of exchange after distribution, followed Smith and J S Mill rather than Marshall who had reversed the order. Despite wanting to reconcile the three branches of economics, Nicholson virtually ignored mathematical and graphical approaches and evaded their use.(8) In the first volume of the Principles, . Nicholson observed that the marginal utility school's identification of production with satisfaction, which derived from utility, was a reversion to the classicals' "economic man". He rejected the theory's dependence upon psychological motivation, since it was immeasurable".(9)

The Principles clearly reflect his preferred methodology, and the economic treatise contained large blocks of historical, descriptive and statistical material. From these, he drew his economic principles, which were relative to a stage of production. Like T E Cliffe Leslie and J S Mill, Nicholson's economics emphasised the impact of custom and habit upon the economic mechanisms of the past and present. He asserted that there were two methods available for economists - "deductive, a priori, abstract, hypothetical, mathematical, analytical, etc" and "inductive, positive, a posteriori, historical, comparative etc".(10) Nicholson's writings are dominated by an inductive approach to economic, social and political problems. Generally speaking, his economic discussions centred around practical problems, rather than pure theory. He reasoned that the solution to the methodological crisis in economics in the latter decades of the nineteenth century was neither to fully accept the new historical or mathematical methods, nor to repudiate all economic theory. Rather, he hoped to return economics to "the best tradition of classical British economics".(11) In reality, Nicholson demanded a return to Adam Smith's economics; he did not hold other classical economists - Ricardo, Malthus and J S Mill - in high esteem. "Whatever opinion is held concerning the theoretical value of Ricardo's doctrine of Rent, it must, I think, be admitted that it is too abstract to be of practical utility".(12)

He was critical of the lack of "historical knowledge" in Mill's work, whereas "a large part of the Wealth of Nations is history of the highest order".(13) Whilst Nicholson claimed that he had availed himself of "the authority of the older masters to include a much greater amount of history than is usual in a statement of principles", he really demanded a return to Adam Smith's economics, since Smith had combined the historical method with judicious use of deduction.(14)

He argued that "at least two-thirds of the Wealth of Nations is history, and it is history of the first rank, and it is so because it is history that is introduction for the illustration, configuration, or qualification, as the case may be of principles".(15)

He claimed that Smith's chapter on "Colonial Policy" in the Wealth of Nations, was one of "the best examples of the historical method". Although Smith was of general relevance to all branches of economic inquiry, Nicholson firmly and frequently stressed that in imperial considerations, Smith was extremely useful.

> We cannot, of course, expect to find in Adam Smith, cut-and-dried answers to our present problems. "Conditions have changed", although, as it happens, the problems of greatest moment at the present time are those which in his day were also of supreme importance, namely problems of empire.(16)

Evolution of Empire

Nicholson's historical approach is amply demonstrated by reference to his discussion on the evolution of the British empire. He commenced his writings on imperial questions during the most rapid expansion of the British empire, though he concentrated on the long-term evolution of the empire, rather than the era of "new imperialism".(17) Like Cunningham, he carefully surveyed the activities of individuals, charter companies, religious organisations and governments in conquest of empire, noting that many of the great charter-trading companies had either died a natural death or lost their charters through abuses. The territories which they had opened up often became "great dependencies and colonies of the British Empire".(18) Every government, he claimed, had been and still was, consciously or unconsciously interested in supporting trading companies "in the acquisition of territory and the expulsion of other foreign powers".(19)

Throughout his many publications, Nicholson referred to the East India Company. Although he applauded the conquest of India as "the suppression of anarchy" and the "extension of liberty", he was - like Adam Smith - highly critical of the East India Company's monopoly power.(20)

> Very great abuses, however, arose from granting to private persons the right of making peace and war in underdeveloped countries, and the strictures of Adam Smith may well be impressed on those who, at the present time, are anxious for the rapid development of Africa. The history of the East India Company is the most striking example, both of the failures and of the success in different ways of this kind of joint-stock enterprise and is one of the best instances of the injurious effect of a monopoly. When the monopoly was strictly maintained the trade with India never prospered; whenever it was relaxed through the attacks of interlopers, as they were called, it increased; and finally, when the monopoly was abandoned the increase in trade was enormous.(21)

Nicholson pointed-out that, initially, the East India Company was supported by the home government, because it was a conquering body. The ensuing conflicts between the Company and other European powers in India, secured the Indian empire.(22) When the East India Company's rule of India was over-taken, people "recognised that the extension of the British empire had been only an extension of British civilisation".(23) Like the classical economists and his contemparies Nicholson was proud of achievements in India, for British rule offered "protection against plagues and famines" and had "broken-down slavery", though in attempting to abolish native customs, had offended natives.(24)

> With regard to the dependencies, of which India may be taken as the most marvellous example which the world has ever seen, for a long period they also were given over to patronage and plunder and to all the methods of exploitation invented by unfettered companies. But with the transfer of the powers and territories of the old East India Company to the crown came the recognition that the primary duty of the British government was to promote the large human interests of the millions of India, and not the narrow, pecuniary interests of a few British adventurers - great spirits though many of them were.(25)

Nicholson noted that in the evolution of the British empire, the nation's foreign policy had not only been guided by commercial ideas. Specifically, he ruled out the idea that British overseas policy had been solely for the purpose of overseas trade. This was not true of any period of British history and "it is specially untrue of the period that has witnessed the formation of the growth of the present German empire".(26) Nicholson re-iterated Smith's argument that throughout the sixteenth, seventeenth and eighteenth centuries, the prime aim of policy was the enhancing of national power.(27) However, Nicholson claimed that over time this power had been used as a means, not an end, for the "British Empire had been extended and is maintained not to increase coercion but to increase liberty".(28)

> Many and varied are the origins of the British Empire, but from the beginning we find not the systematic planting of colonies, or the organised conquest of less developed peoples, but as it were a haphazard sowing of the seeds of future dominion. Everywhere the ruling idea was liberty, and the seeds were blown about where the wind listed. The seeds were planted and grew up into great trees, and the trees grew better than the trees of other nations because they had greater freedom. In the new lands, whether thinly or thickly peopled by the original inhabitants, the new settlers (or invaders) imported from the home country the minimum quantity of the government they found to be necessary.(29)

Nicholson felt that since 1815 there were three factors responsible for the expansion of the empire: technological developments, provision against the incursion of barbarism(30) and the disorders and injustices in Europe.(31) Like Cairnes and Goldwin

Smith, he praised the granting of the powers of self-government to Australia, Canada and New Zealand, and the manner in which their parliamentary government reflected that of the mother country.(32) Nicholson considered that such self-governing colonies were the direct outcome of Britain's free trade policy, and the establishment of colonial self-government had far exceeded the hopes of Adam Smith, especially his desire for a loosening of political power over the colonies.(33)

Apart from briefly discussing German imperial activities, Nicholson offered little analysis or comment on Britain's late nineteenth century expansion, though he argued that because of the activities of the other Western European powers, the growth of empire needed no encouragement and the difficulty was to control the late nineteenth century expansion.(34)

The Self-Governing Colonies

Despite his appreciation of the magnitude and diversity of the British empire, Nicholson concentrated upon the self-governing colonies, though he also wrote a great deal on Indian currency and finance.(35) This preoccupation with the self-governing colonies was consistent with the major works on the empire during the period and with other economists.(36) Nicholson did not undertake a systematic or thorough discussion of the self-governing colonies and his more general writings contain fragments of his ideas. Generally speaking, he implicitly accepted Goldwin Smith's ideas and contended that - measured in terms of profit and loss - Great Britain derived "nothing but loss from the dominance which she assumes over her colonies".(37) Once again, Adam Smith was his mentor and guide in such matters, and he carefully attempted to up-date Smithian notions and arguments with 'facts'.

Labour Nicholson conceded that with an extensive empire, there is a "wider field for the settlement and employment of British stock", although it was not as though British emigrants had gone to the empire. In a more general sense, he noted that every "old country from the beginning of history has felt the need of finding room for an expanding population".(38) Like the 1860 economists he claimed that despite the potential for migration to the empire, most emigrants went to the United States and not the self-governing colonies. Between 1853 and 1898, out of a total of 8,549,569 British and Irish migrants 5,690,712 journeyed to the United States.(39)

Nicholson believed that the question of immigration and emigration was a "most difficult one". Upon this observation, be became favourably disposed to systematic and selected migration, although he never explicitly advocated government intervention in emigration schemes. Towards the close of his life, he argued that the haphazard emigration from the United Kingdom throughout the nineteenth century did not produce "maximum benefit" either in the home country or the empire. Emigration from the United Kingdom had resulted in a mass depopulation of skilled workers, particularly between 1776 and 1826. Moreover, the colonies often accepted people from other lands in preference to the British.(40) In his early works, he stressed that because most emigrants went to the United States, the empire was unimportant as a field for emigrants. However, in later publications he observed that if one wanted a united empire, then it followed that only with government intervention could the flow of emigrants be re-directed to the empire.(41) Nicholson's desire to have more emigrants channelled to the British empire stemmed from his earnest desire to see the United Kingdom remain strong, through its affiliation with the British empire.(42) Nicholson did not discuss the effects of emigration on either British or colonial development. Neither did he take up the issue as to whether or not emigration relieved over-population. Generally speaking, he was sympathetic to Malthus' theory of population, believing that the Essay on Population was "one of the best examples of the inductive method".(43) On the one hand Nicholson considered that a growing population was a source of strength and power; on the other hand he recognised the possibility that food supply could grow at a lesser rate than population.

Capital and Trade   Nicholson rightly claimed that while the British empire was a region for British capital investment, it flowed "at least as readily to the United States as to any of our colonies".(44) He was most aware, much like Marshall, of the geographical spread of British capital throughout the world, believing that it had previously been responsible for the development of numerous new countries, although he did not explain how this capital was utilised for economic development. "The new countries of the world, both in the British Empire and elsewhere, have been largely developed by British capital .... The growth of German manufacturing power has been largely dependent on this external investment of British capital."(45)

Like Adam Smith, Nicholson argued that in general, the export of capital represented a loss to British stocks and, therefore, resulted in a smaller capital fund for internal economic development.(46) Nicholson conceded that there were advantages in the permanent investment of British capital in foreign countries, but

> in general the employment of capital within a country is more advantageous to its people than if it is employed out of the country. The advantage of the employment is not to be measured merely by the profit; we must look to its continuous use and continuous reproduction. And so far what is true of a country is true of an extended empire. Railways, for example, made by British capital in the United States may yield greater profit than similar railways in Canada or South Africa, but the advantage to the empire is very different.(47)

Nicholson did not delineate the advantages which accrued to the empire, but it would seem that he did appreciate that there were gains to the nation's balance of payments from the capital account earnings, for he was convinced that one of the chief causes of the 1873-1884 depression was "the enormous transfer of capital from the old countries such as England to new countries such as Australia for the exploitation of their raw materials and the construction of railways."(48) However, the depression in the 1870s and 1880s was not due to this singular cause but to a combination of factors.(49)

Like other mid- and late nineteenth century economists, Nicholson carefully considered the proposition that "trade followed the flag", contending that two questions had to be distinguished:

> In the first place, it is undoubtedly true that this country depends for the necessaries of existence - for food and raw materials of manufacture - upon supplies drawn from abroad; and it follows, as was admitted by Cobden, that we ought to keep the supremacy of the sea. But in the second place it is by no means so true that this extension of foreign trade has been due mainly to the extension of empire, and that this extension of empire has increased the security of our foreign trade. A few significant facts will show that if, to some extent, trade follows the flag, to a much greater extent trade pays no regard to flags. Our aggregate trade with foreign countries (including exports of British produce and imports) is nearly three times as great as with our colonies and dependencies; our imports from the United States are greater than the whole of the imports from all the British dominions.(50)

Predictably, Nicholson agreed with Adam Smith, who - so Nicholson claimed - argued that foreign trade meant capital was employed outside a country and was therefore, less advantageous than home trade.(51) Under certain conditions, however, there could be gains if "there is generally a surplus of capital that cannot be employed in home trade. On Adam Smith's principle, trade within the empire, other things being equal, is more advantageous than external trade".(52)

And yet, he dismissed the view that at present trade with the empire was more secure, if only because of the extent of the empire and the absence of co-ordination between its members. As a consequence of his survey of the lack of advantages from colonial trade, migration and capital invested therein, Nicholson - like Smith - felt forced to conclude

> that as regards national, as distinguished from a share in cosmopolitan advantage, whether we look to military and naval power, or to the employment of our labour and capital, we have not an empire but the prospect of an empire.(53)

Colonial Protectionism and Intra-Empire Free Trade

Nicholson felt that even if there were substantial advantages accruing to labour, capital and free trade from the empire, they would be negated because of protectionism in the colonies, who wanted to become complex industrial nations.(54) He reviewed Adam Smith's ideas and the history of free trade since 1776, observing that between the repeal of the corn laws (1846) and the outbreak of World War I (1914) free trade policy and non-interference with the foreign trade of other nations was carried to "the height of its development".(55) Generally speaking, he wholly endorsed Adam Smith's views on free trade, claiming - like Marshall - that tariffs forced the costs to rise for domestic producers and increased the cost of living.(56) He highlighted how such economists as Smith, Marshall and Sidgwick had pointed to the exceptions to free trade but claimed that "free trade, like honesty still remains the best policy".(57) Throughout many publications, he devoted considerable discussion to Smith's free trade beliefs, stressing that Smith had allowed numerous exceptions to free trade - defence, protection of infant industries, support of revenue tariffs, and support for countervailing duties upon foreign bounties and taxes.(58) According to Nicholson, Smith rejected all these exceptions, save protection for defence, on the grounds that protection created monopolies, encouraged corruption and fostered administrative chaos.

Perhaps Nicholson's most incisive comments on Adam Smith's free trade beliefs were contained in his preface to List's National System of Political Economy. Nicholson's interest in List was highlighted in the 1903 fiscal debate. Nicholson contended that List had treated Adam Smith most "unfairly", was poor on "facts" and had exaggerated the benefits which England derived from the Navigation Acts.(59) On the other hand, he claimed that List was "of good service" with his distinction between present and future advantages from the national standpoint, particularly his notion that protection involved short-run costs in order to produce long-term benefits. He proposed that List was most useful to contemporary English politicians asking "Is the Empire capable of closer and more effective commercial and political union?"(60) However, he felt "List's work would have gained in power and in popularity if instead of attacking Adam Smith for opinions which were only held by his extreme successors he had emphasised his points of agreement with the original author".(61)

In his edition of the Wealth of Nations as well as his Project of Empire, Nicholson attacked List's view that Smith was an advocate of cosmopolitan economics, claiming that he was an English patriot, even an Imperialist. Nicholson went so far as to suggest that Smith wanted free trade, not so much for the world's benefit, but as a means whereby the British empire could be developed through imperial free trade.(62) Nicholson, like so many of his late nineteenth century contemporaries, qualified the simple doctrines of "orthodox free trade".(63) He carefully specified the two assumptions of free trade: (i) If, through foreign competition, labour and capital are displaced, they will find employment in the home country equally advantageous to themselves and on the whole more advantageous to the country and (ii) within any country, productive forces have perfect freedom of movement, and may be directed to any employment as profit or advantage directs. He believed that these two assumptions had to be either reinterpreted in the same form or modified in the light of recent experience. Nicholson stated that capital was now less nationalistic and more cosmopolitan than it had ever been; hence, "…. if by foreign imports, the capital of any industry is displaced, it may be sent abroad".(64) Moreover, he felt that the same tendencies were true of labour - though to a lesser extent. Thinking along similar lines to Ashley, Cunningham and Hewins, Nicholson held that so long as national divisions existed, the case for protection was unassailable in a number of exceptional and well-defined cases.(65) However, the sole exception Nicholson mentioned was the infant industry assistance.

During the period of late nineteenth century imperial expansion Nicholson advocated free trade as the "wisest policy" for the British empire. Colonial tariff barriers should be eliminated and an internal free trade area created, since their abolition would permit the scale of production to grow, and this would produce beneficial effects via employment, wages, profits and national security. Such a policy would preserve Britain's economic position in the world, for capital and labour would not be forced to other nations.(66)

Nicholson, like his contemporaries, thought that the realisation of intra-imperial free trade would be a lengthy and complicated process as the colonies had established a complex tariff system. which would be difficult to dismantle. If, for example, customs duties were altered, the United Kingdom and the colonies would "suffer certain revenue inconsistencies", although he contended that revenue could be raised in other ways, which he did not specify.(67) However, in numerous publications he considered how internal free trade could be achieved. Above all, he believed that the freedom of trade had to be restored gradually, and noted that this could perhaps be achieved by imperial preference:

> If the ideal of internal free trade is accepted it might no doubt be approached by the method of preferences if they take the form of a gradual and continuous reduction in the duties imposed on British goods being only used as a temporary method of adjustment.(68)

Although Nicholson's suggestion of utilizing imperial preference as a means to establish intra-imperial free trade was cautious, it represents a marked change from his position in 1903 when he firmly opposed any form of imperial preference and signed the Professors' manifesto issued during the fiscal controversy. Moreover, when the leader of the tariff-reform movement, Joseph Chamberlain, listed

Nicholson amongst his supporters, he outrightly rejected Chamberlain's interpretation of his writings and stressed his disapproval of the imperial preference proposals.(69) However, by 1909, when his Project of Empire was published, Nicholson earnestly wanted free trade to be established within the empire and reluctantly accepted that external protection was the means whereby this could be achieved. His justification of internal free trade and external protection was supposedly based upon the "pattern of recent history", for he noted that throughout history, confederations had been opposed to free trade.(70) He contended that national progress was associated with the development of intra-national free trade and external protection, citing Australia, Canada, Germany and the United States as recent examples of this pattern.

> This uniformity in experience in the adoption of internal free trade offers a very remarkable contrast with the general adoption of the opposite policy in external relations ... This striking difference suggests that the policy of free trade cannot rest on a few simple dogmas universally applicable, but must be supported by different reasons in different circumstances.(71)

At the centre of Nicholson's concern over the establishment of intra-imperial free trade was his burning desire to secure the necessary military and naval defence of the United Kingdom, for he considered it was the first duty of any empire to protect its mother.

> If, little by little, colonial statesmen would follow the example set by the great British financiers of this century, and reduce and abolish their duties, it would be easy to establish a fiscal union. Such a union would bind far more closely than a nominal association for defence. It would naturally lead to the creation of other commercial ties, and silently and insensibly would weld together the fragments of our so-called empire.(72)

In this context he considered the concept of a "customs union" which, he thought, would strengthen and promote the ability of the empire to defend itself against foreign aggression arguing that in a customs union there could be provision of the revenue yield to be used for imperial defence. He proudly claimed that a customs union for the entire British empire would be one of "the most powerful instruments that ever existed", especially if it was utilised for commercial agreements or retaliation measures.(73) However, he wanted to witness the establishment of internal free trade and he constantly argued that it was up to the colonial statesmen to reduce their duties against British products.(74)

> The ideal of internal free trade would be attained if the colonies were to carry their preferences to the extreme of reducing the duties on the products of the rest of the empire to zero; although the United Kingdom retained its free trade system and the colonies each its own protective system against the rest of the

world.(75)

There are obvious similarities between the ends sought by Nicholson in imperial policy and those of Ashley, Cunningham and Hewins.(76) They all appreciated that the United Kingdom required reliable raw materials and food supplies, and markets for her produce; and, like them, Nicholson believed that these could be found in the empire. Like Ashley, Nicholson argued that a large market was required for large scale mass production. In common with Cunningham, he reasoned that a strong navy was essential for imperial defence. The prime area of disagreement was over the question of free trade or protection. In contrast to Ashley, Cunningham and Hewins, Nicholson demanded free trade within the empire. His proposals for internal intra-empire free trade were privately opposed by Hewins, who believed that any notion of imperial free trade was most unlikely to appeal to the constituent states of the empire.(77)

> It would involve the sacrifice on the part of the Dominions of just those autonomous powers it is one of the main objects of British imperial policy to safeguard. Secondly, it is impossible to bring about within the British empire the assimilation of internal economic conditions which the organisation of an imperial Exchequer would involve.(78)

Nicholson hoped for the evolution of a great, non-exploitive empire, with internal free trade, mingled with a common external tariff barrier. In such an arrangement, British resources would reap the advantages enjoyed by the home trade, but on an imperial scale. The empire, which was to be a large free market (an essential condition for large-scale mass production) would also provide a steadier and more reliable source of raw materials for the United Kingdom. As for the colonies, they would have an expansive market for their products and an adequate source of capital and labour. Nicholson believed that if the creation of an internal, free-trading empire meant there would be external tariff barriers, then it was "worth the risk", because such matters had to be dealt with historically and empirically, rather than dogmatically and categorically. He was insistent, however, that "any attempt to confine the trade of the empire to the limits of the empire, was to abandon for the empire the real advantages of foreign trade".(79) Any check to the United Kingdom's trade would weaken the empire. Furthermore the "greater the extension of the commerce of the British empire so much the greater would be its moral and political influence in promoting the general advance of civilisation".(80)

Imperial Federation and "A Project of Empire"

Nicholson drew heavily upon Adam Smith's ideas - or at least his own specific interpretation of them - in demanding reform in the administrative, economic and political relationships between Britain and her colonies. In Nicholson's opinion, Smith had formulated the most thorough scheme for British imperial union and while he was disappointed that Smith's plan had not been realised, he believed that it would not long be deferred. To Nicholson, Adam Smith was an imperialist who proposed a great federated empire for the purpose of common defence and joint political power. It was his contention that Smith's "dream" was the establishment of perfect free trade within the bounds of the British empire:

> But he did propose to establish the ideal empire by a complicated system of checks on the commerce of other nations. He sought to carry out his scheme by binding together into an organic whole the scattered members of our possessions. He proposed to make the colonies contribute to the 'imperial revenue', and in return to allow them to send representatives to the British Parliament or States-General of the empire.(81)

To Nicholson, Smith was the only commentator to propose a "thorough scheme of imperial federation", based on imperial taxation throughout the empire, and representation in proportion to taxation.(82) Nicholson claimed that, politically and economically, Smith's ideas were rooted in English history. Politically, the British constitution had allowed representation from those areas under its domain. Economically, the empire was one immense internal market. He cited two of Smith's "lost ideas": (1) Only the surplus of a nation's capital could be exploited to the advantage of a nation, and home demand had to be initially satisfied. (2) Capital was highly mobile, and one only had foreign trade by sending capital out of a country.(83)

But was Nicholson correct in claiming that Adam Smith demanded an imperial federation as a solution to the problems of the empire? The idea of an imperial federation had been widely discussed around the time of the American revolution when it was primarily viewed as a means of solving the problem of 'taxation without representation'. It was in relation to the "present disturbances" that Adam Smith considered the possibility of an imperial parliament; he declared that the old colonial system had caused the nation great losses and that such a situation could be remedied in either of two ways: separation or federation of political powers.(84) Smith examined both solutions, but devoted far more attention to imperial reform since he thought it essential to demonstrate the form of organisation which could remedy the problems of empire. As an alternative to complete separation, Smith held that it was possible to let the colonies assume a proportionate share of the cost of imperial government, especially defence expenditure by imposing direct taxation on all its members and he advocated colonial representation in parliament in proportion to taxation.(85)

These thoughts, coupled with Smith's defence of the Navigation Acts and his comments on a "project of empire", led such commentators as W A S Hewins, John Rae, William Cunningham and

C R Fay to claim that Smith was as imperialist, par excellence.(86) However, as Knorr argues, they all overlooked Smith's alternative to imperial federation - the desire to see complete sovereignty in the entire empire.(87) Recently, Winch has discussed the historical context in which Smith proposed his scheme of imperial federation, arguing, correctly in our opinion, that

> while Smith devoted a good deal of effort to showing just how this ambitious economic scheme might be implemented, the exercise can be interpreted as marking out the economic boundaries for an acceptable solution rather than as a piece of straightforward advocacy. In other words, he was setting out the stringent conditions that would have to be met if empire was to be made tolerable, without necessarily endorsing imperial union as a practicable solution.(88)

Over a thirty year period, Nicholson's views on imperial federation underwent significant modifications, although he tended to understate his changes in attitude and ideas, remarking that in the final chapter of A Project of Empire (1909) he had

> ... given my own opinions on the ultimate aims of imperial union and on the methods by which the ideal may be approached. These opinions are in some respects different from those expressed in the chapter on Colonies and Dependencies in my Principles of Political Economy. The difference is in the main one of emphasis and the change in emphasis is due to the change in conditions. Now that imperial organisation for defence has become a necessity, imperial union for other purposes may be an advantage.(89)

Yet. the difference in his position is not simply one of emphasis, for in 1902 he was opposed to formal organisation in the empire, whereas in 1909 he advocated the establishment of an imperial parliament and suggested the formation of a customs union. In the Principles Nicholson stressed the evolution of the self-governing colonies and the loosening of commercial and political bonds between the mother country and the colonies. Furthermore, he was opposed to any plans for imperial federation, based upon colonial taxation.

> The idea that the colonies should help to "manage" the empire, and should "pay" for the privilege may possibly appear to be good economy, but it seems bad in policy and false to history.(90)

On the other hand, he maintained that the celebrations at the end of Victoria's reign (1897) revealed an extremely deep loyalty to the Crown and he argued that the dissatisfaction which was occasionally expressed with the present state of the management of the empire and the aspirations for closer union did not rest upon any solid basis of "discontent or any idea of economic advantage". Rather, they were founded on a "doctrinaire or philosophical notion that the union of the parts of the empire ought to be more formal and the constitution more logical".(91) Yet, he expressed two major objections to schemes aimed at formal organisation. Firstly, he contended that the "whole constitution" of the British empire was full of anomalies, simply because it grew over many centuries, and was not specifically created. His second (and greater) objection concerned the notion of "tightening the ties of union" and he argued that the method of estimating the advantages and privileges in terms of money was altogether "inapplicable and fallacious".(92)

However, by 1909 Nicholson demanded a more formal organisation between the self-governing colonies and the mother country. At the heart of his enthusiasm for the political unification of the empire was his strong desire to secure the defence of the United Kingdom and retain her supremacy of the seas.

> If our empire is to be preserved under modern conditions, the power of the sea must be upheld, not merely by the United Kingdom but by the united empire. That is the first essential prerequisite and if this is attained the way is prepared for a closer union for other political and social requirements.(93)

He believed that British command of the sea could only be retained with the effective aid of the colonies. In an informal situation, any financial contribution for defence from the colonies had to be voluntary, in proportion to their wealth and population and had to increase with economic progress.(94) However, because imperial defence was such a pressing problem, Britain could no longer attempt to defend the whole empire, and the colonies had to be enticed to join a formal organisation.

To Nicholson the most compelling problem of his time was whether or not the potentialities of the empire could be turned into actualities; he thought the the United Kingdom had not an empire "but the project of an empire".(95) Consequently, in the final section of A Project of Empire he considered the 'difficult topic' of the "Fiscal and Commercial Relations of the Empire with Foreign Countries". Again, he invokes the wisdom and authority of Smith, claiming he had "certainly approved of a customs union for the whole empire".(96) Nicholson stressed that Smith wanted the union "monopoly practices".

> If, then, a customs union could be adopted by the British Empire with a provision for the assignment of a certain proportion of the yield for imperial purposes, especially defence, it would be absurd to object merely on the grounds of the difficulty of imposing equivalent excises. Internal free trade throughout the empire, though possible without any customs union, would be promoted and strengthened thereby, and the benefits of real commercial union are too great to be cast aside on account of a literal interpretation of free trade, which is as little defensible as the literal interpretation of a scriptural text badly translated from

the original.(97)

However, he was concerned that the adopted system be kept as simple as possible, thus reducing the likelihood of corruption and monopoly as well as ensuring the maximum revenue contribution. Moreover, he visualised the customs union for the empire as becoming "the most powerful instrument that ever existed". To Nicholson's neo-mercantilist beliefs, it was a potential weapon for retaliation in trade wars and use in commercial agreements but he stipulated that only once the idea of imperial union was accepted, could a customs union be formed. In itself, it would promote imperial union and "might aid in the adoption of internal free trade".(98) In concluding his book, Nicholson outlined what he envisaged was involved in a "project of empire".

> In parting, let us look at the main objects from detail; imperial defence, to which every nation or dominion or commonwealth or dependency or possession contributes its share, a system of representation by which every responsible constituent of the empire has a voice in the control of the concerns of the whole; an immense internal market for every part of the produce of all the constituents; a customs union and a common policy in commercial relations with other countries; a policy adverse to every kind of monopoly, and favourable to everything that increases the revenue and the prosperity of the great body of the people throughout the empire.(99)

Generally speaking, he was optimistic that imperial federation would soon be realised.(100) He had not been dismayed at the failure of the imperial federation league and similar societies in the 1890s; nor was he in complete sympathy with those of its members who wanted to use federation to establish permanent preferential trading arrangements with the empire.(101) In 1896 Nicholson held that Smith's scheme for an imperial parliament was not yet within the range of British politics, but by 1915 he thought it was "just beginning to be so".(102) Yet Nicholson was completely wrong in believing that imperial federation would soon be achieved. The imperial conferences which began in 1887, generally reveal that the colonies were opposed to any scheme or project of political unification. This was most evident in the colonial conference of 1911, the climax of which was the decisive defeat of a plan for imperial federation, formally proposed by Sir Joseph Ward, the Prime Minister of New Zealand. His conception of the functions of an imperial parliament was similar to Nicholson's. Ward submitted a scheme for the establishment of an imperial parliament of defence with jurisdiction over the declaration of war and peace, with allotments for the costs of maintaining the imperial forces. Neither the mother country nor the colonies were prepared to make the sacrifice of autonomy demanded by the scheme.(103) Nicholson's aspirations and plans for the political re-organisation of the empire ignored the nationalism and the ambitions of the new independent self-governing colonies.

Conclusion

Nicholson's efforts to rehabilitate and bring to the forefront of imperial discussion Adam Smith's ideas, coupled with a blind reverence of Smith's theories, led to an extreme interpretation of his master. This single-minded interpretation of Smith, meant that Nicholson missed the subtleness and complexity of Smith's ideas, particularly in regard to his views on imperial federation.

SIR R GIFFEN

Introduction

Sir Robert Giffen's statistical work was widely praised and utilised by numerous commentators and professional economists, among whom he enjoyed considerable stature. Even J E T Rogers, who rarely praised fellow economists, remarked

> I know of no better work on statistics than Mr Giffen's second volume of essays, particularly those on the volume and character of English trade. I do not say that my friend has exhausted the whole elements of the question, but he has mastered those which he has selected with consummate skill.(104)

Giffen's career was remarkable; he was born in the small Lanarkshire village of Strathaven, where he received his formal education.(105) He left school at 13 and spent seven years working in a Glasgow solicitor's office, although he managed to attend lectures at the University. After contributing anonymous articles and poems to various local newspapers, he became a full-time journalist, eventually joining the London Globe, which was a semi-official organ of Lord Palmerstone's administration. He moved to the Fortnightly Review, and in 1868 became a sub-editor of the Economist, then under the editorship of Walter Bagehot. In 1871 he assisted the Government's Report on Local Taxation, and five years later he was appointed the chief of the Statistical section and controller of corn returns at the Board of Trade. When he accepted this position in the civil service he obtained permission to publish his views on economic matters in the nation's leading journals and newspapers. In 1897, two years after he received a KCB for his service to government, he became the first head of the newly created Labour Department.

Giffen's reputation rests on his work in official statistics, and he was largely responsible for the first attempts to collect figures relating to the wages of manual labourers. He was also the editor of the Royal Statistical Society Journal from 1876 to 1891, and president of the Society from 1882 to 1884. He was influential in assisting the establishment of the Royal Economic Society in 1890, and subsequently wrote the financial section in the Economic Journal.

In 1887, Foxwell claimed that classical political economy's unpopularity was due to the contradictions between orthodox economic theory and the actual experiences of society.(106) Giffen, among others, attempted to remedy this situation by statistically verifying the tenets of classical economics. Associating himself with Leone Levi and A L Bowley, Giffen detailed the progress of the English working class, and stressed the positive aspects of industrialisation.(107) Giffen's statistical work was constructed in order to illustrate the orthodox principles of classical political economy.(108)

Giffen believed that abstract and hypothetical truths or deductive political economy were of little practical utility for "in the real world questions must be dealt with; and in the measurement of tendencies or forces statistics are absolutely essential".(109) He was a firm supporter of Malthus' statistical investigations, and defended him against many critics. To him, Malthus' work was essentially statistical and deductive: "its facts and deductions are derived from the study of statistics of population during the previous century; many of them of an imperfect sort, but still for the most part sufficient to enable an acute reasoner like Malthus to draw out important deductions".(110)

As a journalist and civil servant, Giffen demanded a political economy which was useful in solving contemporary problems. Through his extensive collection and tabulation of statistics, he aimed to provide reliable data for the interpretation of economic phenomena, present and past. In his presidential address to the London Statistical Society, he dealt with the condition of the working classes since G C Porter's 1833 study. He set out to prove that the working classes had received their share of the United Kingdom's prosperity.(111) He utilised index numbers which were based on Jevons' pioneering work and argued that real wages had risen between 50% and 100% in the period 1833 to 1883. Giffen's main intention with this study and many others was to appreciate the complexities of contemporary conditions and decide upon the appropriate policy to pursue.

Statistics and the Empire

Size and Population Giffen undertook a comprehensive survey of the key features of the British Empire - exports, imports, population and area - and his statistical studies were widely utilised and cited, notably by J A Hobson in Imperialism.(112) In his discussion of "Area and Population Statistics", he constructed a table showing the empire's population and area. It was based on the 1890-1896 census, which revealed the number of people per square mile throughout the British empire.(113) However, it was his more influential and widely quoted paper, "The Relative Growth of the Component Parts of the British Empire", read before a meeting of the Royal Colonial Institute, in which Giffen carefully specified the growth of the empire since 1871.(114)

Giffen had always been most concerned with the "fantastic" rates of population increase in the "subject races" (eg India, Africa) and amongst the American and English speaking colonists.(115) Moreover, he was worried at the increased dependency of the European nations upon the foreign supplies of food and the lack of availability of new lands to which their populations could spread. From his statistical survey, he argued that the power of the United Kingdom's surplus population to resort to new lands was being lost. He believed that the European nations had "been saved from starvation" by the outlets afforded by the "new countries" in North America and Australasia. While these new lands had "attracted the modest and poorest labour from the old countries of Europe", they had greatly advanced their material positions and contributed to the high rates of growth in the settled regions.(116)

Giffen believed that Britain had been more fortunate than her European neighbours in relieving the nation of surplus population, because of the size of her empire.(117) However, Giffen was anxious at the rate of population increase among the member countries of the empire, claiming "it would be a serious matter if the Empire were to be increasing beyond the force of the race by which it is held together". However Giffen correctly pointed out that merely to review population growth was to give a biased view:

> On the other hand, however, has to be reckoned the enormous growth of the governing race in resources. The increase of revenue and of business, apart from annexations, is most remarkable, in reality, in the English portions of the Empire; and if we were to go more into detail, and include such elements as the growth of the shipping fleet of the Empire, this relative growth of the English portions of the Empire would be still more remarkable.(118)

Nevertheless he claimed that India's population growth was "one of the most formidable problems which have to be dealt with by our imperial government, and for the knowledge of which we are mainly indebted to Statistics".(119) He contended that the "Roman peace" which England established in India removed many former "obstacles" to population growth, namely the Malthusian "natural checks" like war and disease. Consequently, India's population was growing extremely rapidly and was pressing on the means of subsistence.(120)

> In that country (India) the population has increased at the rate of rather more than 10 percent in ten years, which upon the population of India at the present time would add to that country some 30 millions of people in ten years. At the same time, according to the acreage statistics of the Government of India itself, there are no more than about 100 million acres of land to be taken up, and in a very few years the whole of this acreage must be absorbed, while it is doubtful whether in reality so large an acreage is really available. Unless, therefore, in India a very

great improvement takes place quickly in the capacity of the people for agriculture, the question of an insufficiency of food, which has really been intimated from time to time by the great famines which take place, will become one of chronic importance.(121)

Giffen reckoned that the greater proportion of fertile soil had already been appropriated in India, and that there were no signs that more land was being brought under cultivation. He felt that unless "the character of the people changed", there would be widespread famine.(122) It is unclear just what he meant by this change in attitude, although it would appear he was more concerned with the "release of native energy and enterprise" than with the Malthusian view of "moral restraint". On the other hand, if there was a release of native energy it could pose problems for imperial government since it would "bring with it a rise in the scale of living, tending to make the masses discontented instead of submissive to their lot".(123)

Giffen's discussion of India and imperial population problems stemmed directly from his statistical work and admiration of Malthus' basic proposition, that population tended to increase at such a rate that it tended to outstrip the means of subsistence.

> ... owing to various causes the means of subsistence have increased faster than the population, even when increasing at a Malthusian rate, is no disproof surely of the teaching of Malthus ... Until the present time, however, the experience since Malthus is almost uniform as to the tendency of the race to increase when there is an abundance of food and wealth.(124)

Giffen was not interested in pursuing theoretical aspects of Malthus' work. To Malthus, he owed his statistical interest in population, food supply and land area and he claimed that the problems of population growth and food availability were discernable from statistics "from which we learn everything".(125)

In addition to measuring the size and rates of increase of population and land area, Giffen estimated the total revenue of the empire as well as its exports and imports. He disaggregated these general figures to review the relative rates of growth within the empire, and divided the empire into the "subject areas" (eg, India, Hong Kong, Malta) and the "self-governing" colonies (eg, Australia, Canada). On reviewing the rates of population increase and the trend in revenue, exports and imports, Giffen concluded that the colonies were developing at a greater rate than the mother country.

> The Colonies progress at a greater rate than the Mother Country, as their increase of population is greater, this increase being specially manifest in Australasia; but the growth in the United Kingdom in amount is still much the largest, and, in such a matter as the increase or reduction of debt, the comparison is

rather to the advantage of the Mother Country, though there need be no question of the necessity and usefulness of the borrowing itself.(126)

However, of much greater significance and importance than the growth in population of the subject races were changes external to the empire. Giffen contended that in 1800, and even up to 1875, England had no rivals in the "business of colonising or of an overseas empire". By 1900, France, Germany, Russia and America held overseas empires. However, they posed little threat to the British empire, since she was the largest in population and resources.(127)

Nevertheless, he was anxious about the growth of the German empire, and the acclaimed increase in German overseas population. He argued that the so-called European increase in population outside of Germany, was a blend of the English and German. Thankfully, the English were the more predominant in the blood.

> Germany, for instance, by acquiring a territory of its own suitable for colonisation, may increase at a greater rate than in the past while the diversion of German emigration from the English colonies and the United States may diminish the rate of increase in those regions. But there is hardly time now for such a diversion to make a great difference in the eventual result. A material diversion of German emigration is hardly possible very soon, on account of the greater alternatives of existing settlements as compared with settlements that are wholly new, as we see in regard to the United States; which continues to be the main field for emigration just because there is more partly settled country than in any other quarter.(128)

Trade and Finance In addition to establishing the growth in the empire's population, Giffen contended that statistics were of crucial importance in discussing the question as to whether or not, "trade followed the flag". Associating himself with many other late nineteenth century commentators, Giffen was generally sceptical that trade with the empire was a direct consequence of British political control, considering that other more economic causes were primarily responsible. Specifically, he argued that the colonies produced commodities in which they had a virtual monopoly eg, Australian wool, Indian jute and opium, and West Indian sugar. Giffen concentrated on the import side of the visible balance of trade although he did not ignore questions concerning the share of British exports going to the empire. Consequently, he asserted that trade with the empire was the result of the United Kingdom's inability to supply her own requirements, and the fact that the colonies demanded British produce for their development purposes.

> The countries being able to export articles of this sort were in a position to be purchasers of such goods as they require, and which Great Britain happened to be able to dispose of. Hence

trade arises, but the cause of its arising is not the flag, it is some entirely different cause.(129)

In discussing the general types and forms of finance, Giffen noted that the British empire exhibited two different kinds, and asserted that India and Australasia (Australia and New Zealand), presented "great contrasts to each other in matters of finance".(130) India, in 1896-7, contained a population of approximately 300 million and the government received a revenue of approximately 62 million pounds. Expenditure of local authorities was small, and over half the revenue obtained by the government was "not taxation in the proper sense of the word", since it was in the form of land payments. In the same way as Fawcett argued, Giffen concluded that "all the items, both of revenue and expenditure, clearly manifest the economic weakness of the great dependency of India".(131) In striking contrast to India, Australia and New Zealand contained a population, in 1896-7, of approximately 4 million and government collected almost 30 million pounds in revenue, due to the magnitude of the natural resources and the populations' energy.(132)

Generally speaking, Giffen was optimistic concerning the empire's future. Nevertheless, he considered Indian population problems a "dilemma" for the British, and apart from recommending a change in the "character of the peoples", he offered no solution to "this difficulty". While the rate of population growth was still too high in the United Kingdom, there was considerable potential for overseas migration. Based on the extent of British territory throughout the world, and the proportion of it which was fertile, the British empire contained far more room for population increase than any other nation or empire.

Free Trade, Preference and the Empire

Sir Robert Giffen was one of the most outspoken commentators who denied that British supremacy was threatened by the combined forces of other industrial nations, and their tariffs, although he did come to recommend a modicum of preferential duties. In common with other free traders he attempted to justify his defence of free trade by utilising statistical evidence to disprove that protective retaliation by the British government would be an effective defence against foreign competition.(133) A solid defender of free trade policy since 1882 he inevitably became involved in the fiscal controversy in 1903. Like another statistician A L Bowley, Giffen defended the utility of free trade with statistical reckoning and made extensive use of statistics to demonstrate the satisfactory progress of Britain's economic growth, the standard of living of the nation and the continuing viability of free trade.(134)

In "The Use of Import and Export Statistics", published in 1882, Giffen produced an argument against protection.(135) Throughout the 100 page essay, he pointed out that there was a general failure of commentators and the public at large to appreciate the complexity of trade statistics. To simply demonstrate a balance of payments deficit was not a sufficient claim for protection, as invisible earnings could satisfactorily reduce this deficit. He attacked the protectionists, claiming they had to prove that the State should interfere with the nation's trade.

> The protectionists do not make clear to themselves what they wish to prove. They show, for instance, that the United States is prosperous; but that is not what they have to prove. What they have to prove is that it is more prosperous than it would have been under a free trade regime, a statement in which statistics cannot help them.(136)

In seeking to answer which regime "favoured the general prosperity of the people", Giffen echoed the classical economists' view that the nation's moral and political situation had to be taken into consideration. On the other hand, however, Giffen claimed that statistical studies clearly demonstrated the United Kingdom's high rate of economic growth. He wanted the status quo of free trade maintained, arguing that the superiority of a protective system could not be demonstrated with statistics.(137)

Throughout the 1880s Giffen pioneered numerous studies of the United Kingdom's trading position and noted the future prospects for trade. During the depression of trade and industry in the 1880s, he denied that the nation's rate of economic growth was declining relative to other countries and discussed the view that it was a result of foreign competition, a position widely accepted at the time.(138)

> The assumption that foreign manufacturing has largely increased by means of protection is one of those wild assumptions which constantly crop up in a certain species of political and party literature, but for which it is never possible to find a scintilla of evidence, and which are entirely opposed to broad facts regarding which there can be no dispute.(139)

However, Giffen conceded that his statistical studies revealed a relative decline in the textile, iron and steel and ship building industries. The solution was not to protect British industry, but to increase the nation's domestic productivity and to "encourage those industries which have a comparative advantage".(140) In 1898 Giffen compared the performance of free trade New South Wales with protectionist Victoria, in order to demonstrate that tariffs were incapable of creating specified heavy industries in the absence of a home market.(141) He emphasised Mill's comparative advantage argument and extended Adam Smith's ideas on the extent of the market to demonstrate that small domestic populations in new countries (like Australia) had to restrict manufacturing to the essentials of life which could easily be produced in small scale enterprises. On the other hand, large scale manufacturing industry depended for its success on extending its markets through export sales.

Thinking along similar lines to Cairnes, Fawcett and Rogers, Giffen attempted to refute Mill's argument for the protection of infant industries but, in contrast to them, he noted that there were certain minimum economic scales of operation for various industries which were statistically determined, and if this production could not be domestically consumed, the industries could not be developed.(142) To Giffen, the actual experience of protectionist Victoria and free trade New South Wales conclusively proved that tariffs in a new country would only induce small scale, and not large scale, industries. While this may have been the situation in the Australian colonies towards the end of the nineteenth century, Giffen's thesis had been resoundingly refuted by the early twentieth century experience.(143) In 1898 he prophesied that the advantages of free trade were so great that in "a generation or so", protectionist politicians would vanish: "the breed, I am confident, is very nearly extinct, because the modern atmosphere and conditions, not theory, are making the policy next to impossible".(144)

However, two years later in 1900, Giffen was again attempting to undermine the tariff reformers' arguments with his study of Britain's export performance, as well as that of her industrial rivals. Upon this basis, he claimed there was little, if any, cause for concern.

> I am disposed to hold that the conditions of prosperity in this country are generally stable. It was a mistake to fix attention on specific industries as necessary to a particular commodity... What was needed was a great variety of population, great industrial and commercial capacity and large capital. If the latter are assured, any specific trades are not essential. The community ought in fact to follow the times and to be continually changing... the indispensable industry of one period may sink to quite a secondary place at a later date and perhaps altogether disappear.(145)

On the other hand, he recognised the growing agitation for reform in the political and economic relationships between the mother country and her colonies. Twelve months before Chamberlain launched his campaign for imperial preference Giffen carefully considered the case for a customs union and preferential arrangements throughout the empire.(146) Moreover, in "The Dream of a British Zollverein", he endorsed the movement for imperial federation among the self-governing nations of the empire, noting that this could be achieved by political changes, assisted by commercial arrangements.(147)

He discussed the view supported by Ashley, Cunningham and Hewins, that political union always followed commercial federation, arguing that the one example - the German zollverein - was insufficient to prove that financial union always facilitated a closer union of a political kind. After stating the essential aspects of a zollverein (unified commercial laws, identical money, single customs barrier against the rest of the world) Giffen outlined four difficulties which could render it unsuitable for the British empire - the extensive distances between the constituent parts of the empire; the variety of races, businesses and tariffs; the problems of revenue raising and allocation; and the uncertain political status of protectorates eg, West Africa.(148) In order for political unification to be achieved, the colonies had to recognise the immense aid which Britain's free trade policy conferred on the empire: "If the United Kingdom is for Free Trade, surely it is a great mistake for self-governing colonies, having only a fifth of the population of the United Kingdom, to try to force the mother country into their way, and drag the rest of the Empire with them".(149) While Giffen did not expand his ideas, he suggested four guidelines to assist the commercial union of the empire which could be established by a "Council of Empire": the formation of postal, telegraph and communications unions, independent of other nations; consideration be given to monetary union; the enactment of identical legislation on subjects of commercial law - bills of exchange, marine insurance, shipping laws, bankruptcy and copyrights; a common negotiation of all commercial treaties.(150)

At the outbreak of the fiscal controversy in May 1903, Giffen did not pursue his ideas on commercial union. Rather, he was concerned to point out the extreme difficulty of reconciling in both economic and political terms, free trade doctrine with imperial unity. A few days after Chamberlain's Birmingham speech, which formally launched the movement for imperial preference, Giffen wrote a "remarkable" letter to the Times, which Amery claims "reveals more clearly than any other contemporary document" this difficulty.(151)

The main object of Mr Chamberlain's speech, as I read it, was to show that a new stage has been reached; that a practical issue has now been raised by Canada on which a decision must be taken; and that this decision can no longer be arrived at on grounds of economic policy alone, but for political considerations regard must be had to the wishes and desires of the colonies, however much we may disagree with them economically. Mr Chamberlain himself is not in disagreement. Evidently he regards it as possible to bind the Empire together by a system of mutual trade preferences given by the mother country and the colonies to each other as compared with the treatment they give to foreign countries. But if we do not agree with him on this point, and I for one do not agree, the question still remains whether it may not be expedient politically to assent to the wishes of some of our colonies at least and follow their method of binding the Empire together, for political reasons, though we may dissent from their economic arguments. In other words, the question now before the country is more political than economic; and it is most important that the nature and gravity of the political issues should be fully understood.

What is really in question, as between the British Empire and foreign countries, is the assertion of the unity of the British Empire itself. Canada may be right or wrong economically in giving a preference to the mother country as compared with foreign countries in its import duties; but for foreign countries to object is surely a claim on their part to intervene in the internal affairs of the British Empire, which the whole Empire must resent...

The argument may be carried a step further. If we are bound to take up the quarrel of Canada this is a good reason for our considering the possibility of helping Canada in the way it would like to be helped, although that way may not commend itself on its own merits to the judgement of people in England. A sympathetic Government is entitled to ask Canada to look at the question of remedies from the point of view of England as well as its own; but the case is not one for a non possumsus on either side...

The practical point, let me repeat, is that we have now a case where something must be done or the Empire itself will be in danger. It is hardly to the point to show, when the colonies are so much concerned, that a particular course is against the settled fiscal policy of the mother country. I have no fear myself that any serious infraction of free trade policy is probable; but, at whatever risks, the issues before the country must be faced. And there is less risk to the cause of free trade in an open discussion with the colonies than in a blind refusal to discuss the matter at all.(152)

Furthermore, at the commencement of the controversy, Giffen also reiterated his 1882 case against protection, noting that the balance of payments could be kept at equilibrium with the earnings from invisibles, thus offsetting the deficit on the balance of trade. He asserted that the free trader's case "appears to be complete both theoretically and experimentally".(153) However, during the controversy he cautiously endorsed imperial preferential arrangements although he did not necessarily reverse his earlier opposition to the scheme - a position, which at first glance, may seem inconsistent.

In 1887, a South African, Holmeyer, proposed a preferential tariff of 2 per cent between Britain and the self-governing colonies, which would yield 7 million pound per year for an imperial defence fund. Hicks Beach, then at the Board of Trade, requested Giffen, his permanent secretary, to outline the economic objections to the scheme.(154) In "Commercial Union between the United Kingdom and the Colonies", Giffen argued that a 2 per cent tariff on foreign materials would reduce profits and wages, with the greater part of the reduction falling on wages.(155) According to his statistics, money wages would fall by 4 or 5 per cent, whilst real wages would be reduced by a further 5 per cent because of the 2 per cent preferential tariff on foreign food. He concluded that "no one in England dare propose differentiated duties on food and raw materials... The proposals are not seriously within the range of practical discussions".(156) In his private correspondence with Chamberlain in 1902, he set little value upon the adoption of preference by the colonies, and was consistently opposed to reciprocity by the United Kingdom. He attended the Colonial Conference of 1902 as a member of Gerald Balfour's (then President of the Board of Trade) delegation, which also included Sir Francis Hopwood, the Permanent Under-Secretary and Sir Alfred Bateman, a supporter of economic orthodoxy.(157) Although Giffen opposed preferences on economic grounds, the Colonial Conference made him acutely aware of the colonies' political case for preference.

In "Imperial Policy and Free Trade", published the year after the Conference (1903), Giffen stated, that "even if we disapprove economically, we may have to assent for political reasons to colonial policy".(158) He felt that for the sake of imperial unity, Britain might have to depart from her free trade policy. He extended his 1902 article on the "Dream of a British Zollverein" and stressed that already a third of colonial imports came from the United Kingdom and other colonies. Furthermore, colonial imports often came from nations against which Britain could not compete for certain specialised products eg, Indian imports from China, Japan and Thailand.(159)

However, since May 1902, the political considerations for preference had become paramount and the "crisis is upon us".(160) He surveyed the recent history of preference with the colonies and noted that British politicians had encouraged mutual preferences at the various colonial conferences, while the case for free trade was neglected. Consequently, the colonies had been misled, and now they had genuine grievances. This was particularly so with Canada, who had given the mother country an effective preference compared with other nations and suffered from Germany, who refused her "most favoured nation treatment".(161) Giffen believed that Canada's experience highlighted the need for common agreements and negotiations with foreign countries to be made for the whole empire. In order to achieve this, a permanent commercial council of the empire, along the form outlined in his 1902 article, was required.

> For these political reasons, then, I should as a free trader, contemplate with equanimity a good understanding with our self-governing colonies as to the internal trade arrangements of the Empire, even if it should include a tincture of those preferential arrangements to which the colonies appear so much attached. It is vain to expect that we are to have all our own way. We must give as well as take if we are to succeed in the main object of Imperial union. We must do our best before the final arrangements are settled to bring the colonies to our mind, and to minimise the deviation from free trade methods to which

we may have to consent for the sake of Imperial union; but there must be no absolute refusal to discuss the matter - no determination to insist that the Empire is to be united on an ideal and symmetrical free trade basis or not be united at all. The nearer to free trade the arrangement approaches, the more likely it will be to have permanent success; but a partial departure is not to be rejected, however little, when great objects in the political sphere are to be attained.(162)

Giffen supported political union because of the increased dangers both to the empire and to British industries which were "indispensable to national existence". He wanted to guard the "special interests" of the empire against the concerted attacks of either foreign governments of foreign trusts.(163)

Once he adopted this position, Giffen never shifted from it during the last seven years of his life. However, he did not wholly endorse Chamberlain's programme and he occasionally challenged the leader's use of statistics. Chamberlain took criticism of his statistics seriously, and he asked Hewins to provide him with a weekly account of his opponent's speeches accompanied by suggested replies.(164) Hewins earnestly requested Chamberlain to have his statistics checked by professional statisticians, but his suggestions were never adopted.(165) In October 1903 the problems associated with statistical interpretation became known to the general public with an interesting exchange of letters between Chamberlain and Giffen, who had written to the Times challenging some of the figures used by Chamberlain in a speech made in Glasgow.(166) In reply, Chamberlain, who had cited the increase of manufacturing imports between 1872 and 1902 as evidence of Britain's growing industrial weakness, produced the official source of his figures.(167) Subsequently, Giffen argued that due to the method of presentation, Chamberlain's figure was subject to an error of approximately 70 percent.(168) This was a devastating conclusion, to which Chamberlain evidently had no reply.

To Giffen, imperial preference was an incorrect course economically, though it sometimes proved politically expedient. He never fully endorsed Chamberlain's tariff reform campaign and consistently called for the proper and more systematic use of statistics. Whilst he wanted to maintain free trade, he was prepared to accept a 'tincture' of preferential duties for the sake of imperial unity.

Conclusion

It is difficult to envisage in our documented age, how little statistical information was available to Government departments, economists and commentators in the closing decades of the nineteenth century and at the time of the fiscal controversy. Apart from export and import figures which were known from the customs returns, there was little reliable data on production, investment, employment, capital flows and consumption. Through his activities at the Board of Trade, Labour Department and his numerous publications, Giffen popularised the collection and use of statistics. In his inquiries he established the growth of the empire's population and area in the period 1870-1897, as well as the magnitude and extent of wealth and poverty throughout the empire. By his brief, though pioneering study of expenditure on food and drink, housing and education throughout the empire, Giffen established that there was a "fantastic gulf" between the United Kingdom and the subject races.(169) Perplexed as how to eliminate this vast poverty, he mentioned that Britain could grant sums of money to assist the growth of "industrial forces" among the subjected races, which in turn would provide the basis for education expenditure, thus uplifting the population and increasing their ability to manage the nation's financial affairs.(170)

Essentially a pragmatist, Giffen was prepared to accept imperial preferential proposals on political grounds, though he never deviated from his belief in the economic arguments for free trade and his last public utterance was on the benefits of unhindered trade.(171) While he applied his commonsense to economic and political problems, rather than complex economic theory, his unusual powers of accurate generalisations from voluminous and complex evidence produced a coherence in his arguments and he was respected in fields of applied and theoretical arguments. He devoted little attention to the mathematical analysis of statistical data and was acutely aware of the limitations commonly inherent in quantitative material. Moreover, in discussing imperial questions, he focused on aggregate aspects of the British and colonial economies.

NOTES

1. For biographical sketches, see the obituary notices by W R Scott and Henry Higgs in Economic Journal, Vol.37, (September 1927), pp.495-502 and Journal of the Royal Statistical Society, XC, (Part IV, 1927), pp.811-13. For a short analysis of Nicholson's economic writings see L L F R Price, A Short History of Political Economy in England, (15th ed, London, Methuen & Co Ltd, 1937). No systematic study of Nicholson exists, but there is an excellent discussion of his economic analysis of trade unions by A Petridis in The Economic Analysis of Trade Unions by British Economists 1870-1930, (Duke University, Dissertation Abstract, 1974), Ch.IV.

2. See J S Nicholson, "The Reaction in Favour of Classical Political Economy", B A Report, JRSS, December 1893, pp.627-639.

3. Nicholson, "The Economics of Imperialism", EJ, Vol.20, June 1910, pp.155-6.

4. Nicholson, A Project of Empire, (London, Macmillan, 1909), p.x.

5. For a similar view see Scott, J S Nicholson, op.cit, p.497 who writes "Nicholson's life and work may perhaps be best described as that of a lineal successor of Adam Smith, and if one desires to be

more precise, it is necessary to add Adam Smith as Nicholson conceived him". Also see G M Koot, The English Historical School of Economics 1870-1920, (Unpublished PdD thesis, Stony Brook, New York 1972) pp.269-274; Petridis, The Economic Analysis of Trade Unionists by British Economists, op.cit, p.84.

6. Nicholson, "The Reaction in Favour of Classical Political Economy", op.cit, p.628. In all his major published works, Nicholson repeatedly cites Adam Smith.

7. Nicholson, Principles of Political Economy, (3 Vols, London, A and C Black, Vol.I, 1893, Vol.II, 1897, Vol.III, 1901).

8. Petridis, The Economic Analysis of Trade Unionists by British Economists, op.cit, p.86.

9. Nicholson, Principles, Vol.I, op.cit, pp.v-vi, 4, 16-21, 23-31, 59-60, 229-31, 267-69. Also see Vol.III, op.cit, pp.iii-iv.

10. Nicholson, Elements of Political Economy, (London, A and C Black, 2nd Edition, 1909), pp.13-14.

11. Koot, The English Historical School of Economics, op.cit, p.272.

12. Nicholson, Principles, Vol.I, op.cit, p.417. Also see Elements of Political Economy, op.cit, and The Revival of Marxism, (London, John Murray, 1921).

13. Nicholson, Principles, Vol.I, op.cit, p.vi.

14. Ibid, p.vi. For Nicholson's views on the appeal to the authority of earlier economists for support in the 1903 tariff debate see his "The Use and Abuse of Authority in Economics", EJ, Vol.13, December 1903, pp.554-566.

15. Nicholson, "The Reaction in Favour of Classical Political Economy", op.cit, p.628.

16. Nicholson, A Project of Empire, op.cit, p.260.

17. For a statistical account of the period 1870-1900, see M B Brown, The Economics of Imperialism, London, Penguin, 1974, pp.185-186. Ch.3, Table 1, p.19.

18. Nicholson, Principles, Vol.I, op.cit, p.251. For Cunningham's views see Ch. 8, pp.195-197.

19. Ibid, p.206.

20. Nicholson, The Neutrality of the United States in Relation to the British and German Empires, (London, Macmillan, 1915).

21. Nicholson, Principles, Vol.I, op.cit, p.133.

22. Ibid, pp.133-134, 258-261.

23. Ibid, p.264.

24. Ibid, p.264.

25. Nicholson, Principles, Vol.III, op.cit, p.419.

26. Nicholson, Neutrality, op.cit, p.14.

27. Ibid, pp.15-16, 24-27.

28. Ibid, p.27.

29. Ibid, p.33.

30. Ibid, pp.34-5.

31. Nicholson, Principles, Vol.III, op.cit, pp.416-419. He stressed that the original foundation of what became the self-governing colonies was not due to surplus capital or labour, but to the existence of slaves and criminals.

32.   Ibid, pp.416-419. Also see Ch.4, pp.44-50 and Ch.5, pp.74-76.

33.   Nicholson, Neutrality, op.cit, p.19.

34.   Ibid, p.14. However, Nicholson believed that "Zanzibar ... although the Sultan still has some minimal or delegated power, is, to all intents and purposes, as much as part of the British empire as India", (Strike and Social Problems, London, A & C Black, 1896), p.208.

35.   Nicholson's writings on Indian currency and finance were associated with the bi-metallism controversy and, due to constraints of this study cannot be discussed.

36.   For evidence of this, see, for example, H E Egerton, A Short History of British Colonial Policy, (Oxford, Clarendon, 1903); J A Froude, Oceana, (London, Longmans, Green & Co, 1886); H George, Statistical Account of the British Empire, (London, Methuen, 1904); J Seeley, The Expansion of England, (London, Macmillan, 1914 ed).

37.   Nicholson, Neutrality, op.cit, p.16.

38.   Nicholson, Project of Empire, op.cit, p.233.

39.   Although Nicholson did not cite a source for his figures, generally speaking, they tally with contemporary listings. See W F Willcox, International Migrations, (New York, National Bureau of Economic Research, 1929), Vol.I, pp.627-8, 636-7. Also see Table 3, Ch.3, pp.21-22.

40.   Nicholson, A Project of Empire, op.cit, p.233-234.

41.   Nicholson, Principles, Vol.III, op.cit, p.422.

42.   See the discussion on pp.158-160.

43.   Nicholson, Principles, Vol.I, op.cit, p.175. See Chapter XI, "The Principles of Population", Ibid, pp.175-196 for a discussion of the Malthusian theory.

44.   Nicholson, Principles, Vol.III, op.cit, p.422.

45.   Nicholson, War Finance, op.cit, p.198. For Marshall's views see Ch.6, pp.118-120.

46.   See A I Bloomfield "Adam Smith and the Theory of International Trade" in A Skinner and T Wilson, Essays on Adam Smith, (Oxford, OUP 1975), pp.4550481, and D Winch, Classical Political Economy and Colonies, (London, G Bell, 1965), pp.6-24.

47.   Nicholson, Project of Empire, op.cit, pp.235.

48.   See Nicholson's introduction to The Wealth of Nations, op.cit, p.26.

49.   For an account of this period see S B Saul, The Myth of the Great Depression, (London, Macmillan, 1969).

50.   Nicholson, Principles, Vol.III, op.cit, p.421.

51.   Nicholson, Project of Empire, op.cit, p.235.

52.   Ibid, p.235, and Principles, Vol.III, op.cit, p.422.

53.   Nicholson, Project of Empire, op.cit, p.236. For Adam Smith's position see Winch, Classical Political Economy and the Colonies, op.cit, pp.6-24.

54.   See Nicholson's introduction to F List, National Systems of Political Economy, (London, Longmans, Green, 1904), p.xx.

55.   Nicholson, Neutrality. op.cit, pp.19-20.

56.   Nicholson, "Tariffs and International Commerce", in A.S. White (ed), Britainia Confederation, (London, George Phillip, 1892),

pp.93-122, especially pp.111-112.

57. Ibid, p.118

58. Nicholson, Principles, Vol.II, op.cit, pp.322-27; Preface to Wealth of Nations, op.cit, Project of Empire, op.cit, pp.xii-xvi, 5-6, 36-69, 232035.

59. Nicholson (ed.), National Systems of Political Economy, op.cit, pp.xii-xvii.

60. Ibid, p.xvii.

61. Ibid, p.xxvii.

62. Nicholson (ed.), Wealth of Nations, op.cit, Preface; Project of Empire, op.cit, pp.xii-xvi, 5-6,39-60, 79-81, 93-6, 232-35; Principles, op.cit, Vol.II, pp.322-27.

63. On this general point see N Jha, The Age of Marshall, (Patna, Novelty, 1963), pp.42-44.

64. J S Nicholson, "The Economics of Imperialism", EJ, Vol.20, June 1910, pp.155-72, especially pp.155-56.

65. See, for example, Ch.8, pp.185-188; Ch.9, pp.220-226.

66. Nicholson, Principles, Vol.II, op.cit, pp.322-37.

67. Nicholson, Project, op.cit, pp.247-8. Also see C A Bodelsen, Studies in Mid Victorian Imperialism, (Copenhagen, Glydendalen, 1924).

68. Nicholson, Project, op.cit, p.258.

69. See Nicholson's letter to The Times, 3.10.1903, and A W Coats, "Political Economy and the Tariff Reform Campaign of 1903", JLE, Vol.II, April 1968, pp.181-229, esp. p.228. Also see the discussion in Ch.3, pp.25-35.

70. Nicholson, Project for Empire, op.cit, p.48; The Economics of Imperialism", op.cit, pp.166-68.

71. Ibid, p.162.

72. Nicholson, Tariffs and International Commerce, op.cit, p.121.

73. Nicholson, A Project of Empire, op.cit, p.246.

74. Nicholson in A E White, Britannia Confederation, (London, George Phillips and Co, 1892), pp.121-2.

75. See Nicholson's introduction to F List's National System of Political Economy, (London, Longmans Green and Co, 1904), p.xviv.

76. See, for example, Ch.8, pp.191-192 and 197-201; Ch.9, pp.223-230.

77. Hewins privately attacked Nicholson's position, see his notes in Hewins Papers, Box Mss. 161 and 162. Shieffield University Library, Sheffield.

78. Hewins Papers, Box Mss. 162, p.65.

79. Nicholson, Project of Empire, op.cit, p.266.

80. Ibid, p.268.

81. Nicholson, (ed.), Wealth of Nations, op.cit, p.31.

82. Nicholson, Principles, Vol.III, op.cit, p.423; Introduction to List's National System of Political Economy, op.cit, p.xvii.

83. Nicholson, Project of Empire, op.cit, p.xiii. He argued that "These lost ideas have again been forced on the public attention by two significant facts; first, the enormous investments of British capital in foreign states; and secondly, the increasing tendency in recent years in the commercial policy of other nations towards the protection of native industries". Ibid, p.xiii.

84. A Smith, Wealth of Nations, op.cit, pp.207-14, 583-7. For a discussion of the context of Smith's writings see D Winch, Adam Smith's Politics: An Essay in Historiographic Revision, (London, CUP, 1978), Ch.7, "The Present Disturbances", pp.146-63 and Classical Political Economy and the Colonies, op.cit, pp.14-17. Also see A S Skinner, "Adam Smith and the American Economic Community", JHI, Vol.37, 1976, pp.59-78; E A Benians, "Adam Smith's Project of an Empire", Cambridge Historical Journal, I, 1925, pp.249-83; D A F Veal, "Adam Smith on Imperial Union", Empire Review, Vol.29, No.180, January 1916, pp.537-40; D Stevens, "Adam Smith and the Colonial Disturbances", in A Skinner and T Wilson, Essays on Adam Smith, op.cit, pp.202-17; R Köebner, Empire, op.cit, pp.226-37, 357-8.

85. Smith, Wealth of Nations, op.cit, p.587.

86. W A S Hewins, "The Fiscal Policy of the Empire", The Times, 5.6.1903, p.4; John Rae, Life of Adam Smith, (London, macmillan, 1895), p.281; W Cunningham, Richard Cobden and Adam Smith, (London, Tariff Reform League, 1904), pp.21-38; (London, Longmans Green & Co, 1928), p.3, claimed that Smith "was a Scotsman, with the national sense and original humour of Scotland at its best. This Scotsman was in policy a "liberal imperialist". He was "eager" to see the project of empire turned into reality - this was because he hated tyranny and was disgusted by shams".

87. Klaus E Knorr, British Colonial Theories 1570-1850, (London, Cass, 1963), pp.187-95.

88. Winch, Adam Smith's Politics, op.cit, p.154. Also see Classical Political Economy and the Colonies, op.cit, p.16.

89. Nicholson, Project of Empire, op.cit, p.xv.

90. Nicholson, Principles, Vol.III, op.cit, p.424.

91. Ibid, pp.424-5.

92. Ibid, p.425.

93. Nicholson, A Project of Empire, op.cit, p.238.

94. Ibid, p.238.

95. Ibid, p.236.

96. Ibid, pp.260-71.

97. Ibid, p.264.

98. Ibid, p.270.

99. Ibid, p.270.

100. These hopes were increased during the war when he contended that such a situation would force imperial unification upon the empire. See Nicholson, The Neutrality of the United States in Relation to the British and German Empires, op.cit, pp.15-18. Also see his introduction to List's The National System of Political Economy, op.cit, p.xiv.

101. In the years leading up to the Great War 'new prophets' stepped forward with schemes aimed at preventing the disintegration of the empire. In such a context Lord Milner's 'kindergarten' developed. Milner had worked in South Africa for a united country which was loyal to the British empire. After the creation of the union of South Africa in 1909, there was a renewed effort to utilise similar forms for the union of the Empire. The 'round table' movement sought

to establish an imperial government responsible to all the self-governing colonies as well as to the United Kingdom; a government having control over matters of common interest to the independent members. See W Nimmocks, Milner's Young Men, (London, Hodder and Stoughton, 1970), Introduction.

102. Nicholson, Strikes and Social Problems, op.cit, pp.186-7.

103. See C E Carrington, The British Overseas, (Cambridge, CUP, 1950), pp,852-4; J A Williamson, A Short History of British Expansion, (London, Macmillan, 1942), p,p.624-5.

104. J E T Rogers, The Relation of Economic Science to Social and Political Action, op.cit, p.41.

105. On Giffen's life see F Y Edgeworth, "Sir Robert Giffen", EJ, Vol.20, January 1910, pp.318-21; L L Price, A Short History of Political Economy in England, (15th ed., London, Methuen, 1937), pp.244-48; K J Perry, "Sir R Giffen" in International Encyclopaedia of the Social Sciences, (London, Macmillan, 1968), Vol.6, pp.181-182.

106. H S Foxwell, "The Economic Movement in Britain", QJE, 1887, pp.84-103.

107. G M Koot, The English Historical School of Economics 1870-1920, op.cit, pp.150-8.

108. E Y Edgeworth, "Sir Robert Giffen", op.cit, pp.318-21.

109. Giffen, Economic Inquiries and Studies, (London, Macmillan, 1904), I, p.380; also see "Utility of Common Statistics" in Essays in Finance, (2nd Series, London, George Bell, 1890).

110. Giffen, Statistics, (ed. by H Higgs, London, Macmillan 1913), p.41.

111. Giffen, The Progress of the German Working Class in the Last Quarter of the Nineteenth Century, (London, G Bell and Sons, 1884).

112. See, for example, Ch.10, p.246.

113. Giffen, Statistics, op.cit, p.31. Also see pp.15-44.

114. Giffen, "Relative Growth of the Component Parts of the Empire", (1903), reprinted in Economic Inquiries and Studies, (London, G Bell and Sons, 1904), Vol.II, pp.222-241. Also see Ch.XXIV, "The Wealth of the Empire and How it Should be Used", (1903), Ibid, pp.363-386.

115. Giffen, Essays, (2nd Series), op.cit, pp.293-96, 319; Statistics, op.cit, pp.360-65; "Relative Growth of Empire", op.cit.

116. Giffen, Statistics, op.cit, pp.339-340. He noted that "the people of Europe have outgrown their narrow limits and have become the peoples and powers of the world. It would be out of place here to discuss all the consequences of these widely extended imperial relations. They are, however, most directly connected with the predominance of the European races in the world, which has developed so greatly during the last hundred years, and which is still developing so fast". Ibid, p.330.

117. Ibid, p.34.

118. Giffen, "The Relative Growth of the Empire", op.cit, p.234.

119. Giffen, Essays, (2nd series), op.cit, p.293. Also see "Relative Growthof the Empire", op.cit.

120. Giffen, Essays, op.cit, pp.293-4; Statistics, op.cit, pp.35-36.

121. Ibid, p.127.

122. Ibid, p.127, Essays, op.cit, pp.294-6.

123. Ibid, p.295.

124. Ibid, p.294.

125. Ibid, p.294.

126. Giffen, "Relative Growth of the Empire", op.cit, p.228.

127. Ibid, p.235.

128. Giffen, Statistics, op.cit, pp.326-7.

129. Giffen, Statistics, op.cit, p.98. Also see pp.96-100. In his classic work, Imperialism, op.cit, J A Hobson relied heavily on Giffen's statistical work and claimed that trade did not necessarily follow the flag. See Ibid, Ch.II, "The Commercial Value of Imperialism", pp.30-45.

130. Giffen, Statistics, op.cit, p.267.

131. Ibid, p.268. For a discussion of Fawcett and India, see Ch.5, pp.86-92.

132. Giffen, Statistics, op.cit, p.268.

133. For brief notes on Giffen's position see Koot, English Historical School of Economics, op.cit, p.150 and N Jha, The Age of Marshall, (Patna, Novelty, 1963), pp.62-64.

134. See A L Bowley, England's Foreign Trade in the Nineteenth Century, (London, Swan Sonnenschein, 1905).

135. Giffen, "The Use of Import and Export Statistics", (1882), reproduced in Economic Inquiries and Studies, (London, Macmillan, 1904), Vol.I, pp.344-350. For an earlier statement of Giffen's free trade beliefs see his anonymous article, The New Protection Cry, (London, Imperial, 1879)

136. Ibid, p.50.

137. Giffen, "The Use of Import and Export Statistics", op.cit, p.344.

138. Giffen, The Recent Rate of Material Progress in England, (London, George Bell, 1887). Also see the various articles on foreign trade in both editions of his Essays.

139. Giffen, The Recent Rate of Material Progress, op.cit, p.26.

140. Giffen, The Growth of Capital, (New York, A Kelly, 1970-1887 reprint) p.113.

141. Giffen, "Protection of Manufactures in new Countries", (1898), Reprinted in Economic Inquiries, op.cit, II, pp.159-60.

142. Ibid, pp.159-165. Also see Ch.4, pp.58-60 and Ch.5, pp.73-76.

143. See C B Schedvin, Australia and the Great Depression: A Study of Economic Development and Policy in the 1920s and 1930s, (Sydney, SUP, 1970).

144. Giffen, "Protection and Manufactures in New Countries", op.cit, p.159.

145. Giffen, "Our Trade Prosperity and Outlook", EJ, Vol.10, 1900, pp.295-309.

146. For an outline of the fiscal controversy see Ch.3 pp.25-31.

147. Giffen, "The Dream of a British Zollverein" in Economic Inquiries, op.cit, Vol.II, p,p.387-404.

148. Ibid, pp.391-94.

149. Giffen, "The Dream of a British Zollverein" op.cit, p.400.

150. Giffen wanted a unified mechant navy: "If we are to be a

united Empire, the whole body should be knit together by lines of steamers under the Imperial Flag which omit no part of consequence, present or prospect". Ibid, p.400.

151. Amery, Joseph Chamberlain, Vol.5, op.cit, pp.292-294. See Giffen's letter to The Times, 28.5.1903.

152. Ibid.

153. Giffen, Economic Inquiries, op.cit, Vol.I, p.viii; Jha in The Age of Marshall, op.cit, claims Giffen would have been a signatory to the 14 economists' Manifesto on free trade. See p.65.

154. See P Fraser, Joseph Chamberlain. Radicalism and Empire 1868-1914, (London, Cassel, 1966), pp.228-230.

155. Giffen, "Commercial Union betwen the United Kingdom and the Colonies", PRO, Cab 1/2, 9.2.1891.

156. Ibid.

157. Amery, Joseph Chamberlain, Vol. 5, op.cit, pp.44-47.

158. Giffen, "Imperial Policy and Free Trade". The Nineteenth Century and After, Vol.XIX, July 1903, pp.1-11, especially p.7.

159. Ibid, pp.7-9.

160. Ibid, p.9.

161. Ibid, p.10.

162. Ibid, pp.12-13.

163. Ibid, p.14.

164. See Hewins' Diary, Hewins Papers, op.cit, Box Mss 195.

165. Hewins, Apologia, Vol.I, pp.72-73.

166. See Giffen's letter to The Times, 24/10/1903, p.13.

167. Chamberlain to Giffen, The Times, 27/10/1903, p.9.

168. Giffen to Chamberlain, The Times, 29/10/1903, p.6 Also see A W Coats "Political Economy and the Tariff Reform Campaign of 1903", op.cit, pp.206-207 for an account of the interchange. A review of the letters can also be found in Amery, Joseph Chamberlain, Vol.6, op.cit, pp.479-489.

169. Giffen, "The Wealth of the Empire and How it Should be Used, Economic Inquiries, Vol.II, op.cit, pp.363-386, especially pp.370-79.

170. Ibid, p.379.

171. See Edgeworth, "Sir Robert Giffen, op.cit, pp.318-322.

ALTERNATIVES TO ORTHODOX ECONOMICS

Chapter 8

WILLIAM JAMES ASHLEY AND WILLIAM CUNNINGHAM: ENGLISH ECONOMIC HISTORIANS

W J ASHLEY

Introduction

William James Ashley was one of the founders of the study of English economic history. The son of a journeyman hatter, he was the eldest son of a large family. He grew up in the religious and political tradition of dissent, and was educated at dissenting schools, notably St Olaves.(1) In 1877, he made a preliminary attempt at the Brackenbury History Scholarship at Balliol, but was unsuccessful. After extensive coaching the following year from T F Tout and S R Gardiner he won the scholarship and studied constitutional history under Stubbs and graduated in 1881 with a first in history.(2) Thereupon he established himself as a private tutor and began a more serious study of economics and economic history.

Ashley's introduction to economics was through the political economy of the Oxford History School and Arnold Toynbee, with whom he developed a close relationship in his final undergraduate year. Ashley personally requested if he could attend Toynbee's lectures since he was interested in social reform. Toynbee suggested that Ashley write fortnightly essays on economic doctrines as dealt with by the classical political economists.(3) Subsequently, he worked jointly with Toynbee on the evolution of wage theories and after Toynbee's sudden death, Ashley assisted in the preparation of his Lectures on the Industrial Revolution.(4)

Toynbee's "catastrophic" interpretation of the industrial revolution, his unorthodox views of economics, and his reforming zeal exercised a great influence on Ashley; who later remarked that Toynbee was "a sensitive and overwrought scholar who lived a saintly life".(5) To Ashley, Toynbee was the initiator of revolutionary and fertile developments in English political economy. As a history tutor, Ashley was invited to lecture on political economy and in 1890 he told Lujo Brentano, the Liberal German economic historian, that he had first come to the study of political economy through Toynbee, "whom I regard more than any other man as the source of whatever inspiration has come to be in the investigation and study of the subject".(6)

Toynbee encouraged Ashley to study the writings of T E Cliffe Leslie, and in 1882 Ashley bought and thoroughly read his Essays. Through Leslie, Ashley became more interested in the German Historical School, and decided on a close and systematic study of the School's leading writers. As an undergraduate, Ashley had travelled to Germany after Benjamin Jowett, the Master of Balliol College, persuaded him to visit Göttingen.(7) Jowett took a keen interest in Ashley's progress and it is possible that he influenced Ashley's reformist attitudes to English institutions.(8)

A recent study has labelled Ashley the "Socialist of the Chair" and compared him to Gustav Schmoller, the leader of the German Kathedersozialisten.(9) Schumpeter argued that Ashley found "close sympathy with the younger German historical school, and he was greatly influenced by the legal historians".(10) Whilst his Nine Lectures on the Earlier Constitutional History of Canada are in the tradition of the early German historical school, he was most certainly influenced by the older school.(11) Ashley was considerably indebted, as he acknowledged, for many of his beliefs and methodology to Schmoller, who combined the historical progress of the older German historical school with an active role in matters of social reform. Schmoller argued that history exhibited a gradual evolution of the various stages of economic, political and ethical developments, so that such change constituted the "social problem" which accompanied the growth of nation states.(12) Ashley dedicated his inaugural lecture at Toronto, as well as his Surveys to Schmoller, noting that despite numerous differences between them, "I feel that for a dozen years I have received more stimulus and encouragement from your writings than from those of any others".(13)

Ashley's long-term interest in social and economic reform was firmly rooted in the Oxford of T H Green, Benjamin Jowett and Arnold Toynbee. Although Ashley was too young to be directly influenced by Green, when he considered the evolution of Britain's laissez-faire policy Ashley accredited Green with having substituted "freedom of restraint" of the utilitarians with a new and more positive freedom, namely "the power of men to make the best of themselves".(14) Like Toynbee and Jowett, he assigned a larger role for the State in economic and social matters.

During his time in Oxford as an undergraduate and resident tutor, as well as through his Extension Service lecturing in Southampton, Ashley developed his heterodox view of economics. After graduating in history, Ashley intended to construct a new, historical economic theory. By 1893, however, he had reconciled himself to establishing economic history as the major force within economic theory.(15) In his inaugural address as the Professor of Political Economy and Constitutional History at Toronto in 1888, Ashley stressed the importance of inductive or empirical economics.(16) As the first Professor of Economic History at Harvard from 1892 to 1900, he expounded the advantages of a historical approach to economic phenomena. In his introduction to English Economic History and Theory he stated that economic doctrines were relative to their particular environment.(17) His economic history attempted to review the various phases of production to account for the economic theory and institutions produced by each stage.(18) Ashley identified himself closely with W A S Hewins when he undertook a systematic study of the mercantilist writers, emphasising their use of the empirical method.(19) Thinking along similar lines to Cunningham and Hewins, he rejected the notion that there were laws in economics.(20) Nevertheless, he accepted the argument that it was impossible to include the multiplicity of factors which governed men's actions and that it was, therefore, useful to make assumptions which led to generalisations, "sometimes called laws". He was unrelenting in his attacks on Ricardo, and rarely missed an opportunity to proclaim that Ricardian economics should have been banished from England, since it was inapplicable to other epochs and phases.(21) Associating himself with Hewins and Cunningham, Ashley frequently attempted to demonstrate that economic theory was relative and hypothetical and stated that "the old doctrines will be shown to be not untrue, but to have only a relative truth, and to deserve a much less important place than has been assigned to them".(22)

In attempting to formulate policy, economists had to examine recent economic history and the complex features of a modern industrial society.(23) They should "leave to the Cambridge people hair-splitting analysis of abstract doctine".(24) Despite Ashley's criticism of the Cambridge approach, and therefore Marshallian economics, he praised Marshall's Principles and believed it was a most significant work for the further development of economics. However, he believed that economic history was "destined to take a larger place in the future in the circle of our studies".(25)

> The Principles of Economics is a work mostly of its author's reputation, and his position as the doyen of English economists. It casts into the background almost all that has been written in England since John Stuart Mill; it sums up the economic movement of the last forty years, and furnishes the point of departure for a new and fruitful development.(26)

After Ashley relinquished his Harvard professorship he returned to England and became the Professor of Commerce at Birmingham where he wrote on contemporary social and economic subjects, especially tariff and labour questions. He became heavily involved with Unionist politics, and in 1906 joined the Party. In a letter to Brentano in 1913 he described how he had begun to move away from the Liberal Party, claiming it had never "been fundamentally the party of Social Reform".(27) To Ashley, the State had a positive social function and it was important that this be appreciated and understood by legislators and voters.(28) He was appointed a member of the Unionist Social Reform Committee, which had been brought together in 1912 by F E Smith and Sir Arthur Steel-Maitland and he wrote and reported on labour questions, budgetary policy, tariff matters and imperial questions.(29)

England's Commercial Legislation and the American Colonies

In November 1899 Ashley published an article entitled "The Commercial Legislation of England and the American Colonies, 1660-1760", in which he invoked his historical approach and attacked Adam Smith's view that the English Colonial System hindered colonial resource utilisation and reduced colonies' wealth.(30) Ashley aimed to demonstrate that British colonial policy was not disadvantageous but beneficial to the colonies. His approach was to examine various English laws which affected the trade and industry of the American colonies believing that such laws fell into 3 groups: Navigation Laws, Enumeration Laws, Manufacturing Laws. He contended that the Navigation laws, particularly the Act of 1660, were primarily directed at the Dutch. The 1660 Act stipulated that no commodities should be imported into, or exported from, any British plantation in Asia, Africa or America, except in British vessels. The Virginians openly defied the law, and loaded large quantities of tobacco onto Dutch ships. He conceded that, in the short-term, such laws were unfavourable to the pursuit of foreign commerce, but rejected Smith's position that this was the case over the longer term.

> We might be content to share his position (ie Smith's) that, even if the law were economically disadvantageous both to England and the colonies, it was nevertheless wise, on the ground that 'defence is of much more importance than opulence'.(31)

However, Ashley contended that the colonies did benefit by the laws and he cited a mass of historical evidence to support his position. In particular, shipbuilding became the chief industry of New England in less than 20 years after the passage of the Act, for the region had an abundance of cheap, accessible timber, and the restriction on trade with England and colonial vessels stimulated the industry. The expansion of commerce occurred under the protective shield of the British navy and colonial enterprise benefited by the opportunities afforded to it by the naval success of the mother country.

Turning to the Enumeration Laws, Ashley highlighted the 1660 Statute which forbade the exportation of certain enumerated articles - sugar, tobacco, cotton, indigo and dyes - from the colonies to any country, save England. To Ashley, a significant feature in discussing such laws was that statistical records of vital stable articles of New England's trade were never kept during the 1660-1760 period. He conceded that the colonies suffered from the loss of exports to the Portuguese market, but in 1730 Parliament relaxed this measure. Nevertheless, tobacco - the main export item of New England - was re-exported from England to Europe and the import duty was repaid.

Although there were English middlemen, the American planter was not shut out of the market.

Ashley believed that the laws concerning manufacturing were "altogether insignificant" and he examined three cases: 1699 - no woollen yarn or woollen cloth produced in English plantations was to be shipped out of the plantation; 1732 - no hats should be exported to England, Europe or the other colonies; 1750 - no steel furnaces or sheet mills were to be erected in the colony. Ashley's concern was to assess the impact of these laws on the pattern of economic development. Unfortunately, he found the available evidence conflicting, although he was impressed by Benjamin Franklin's (1760) and Adam Smith's (1776) work; the former argued that the colonial inhabitants followed their own self-interest, the latter that the colonies imported very cheaply from the mother country. Ashley found evidence which supported Franklin's and Smith's position, although the 1750 Law remained the "one weak point" of their argument.(32) Generally speaking however, these laws did not inflict great harm on the colonies and the British government encouraged their development. "Because it restricted, it felt bound to encourage; because it encouraged it felt the more justified in restricting".(33) He cited the Molasses Act of 1733, and argued that if it had been enforced, it would have hampered American trade. Consequently, Ashley reached the conclusion that English commercial legislation did not harm the colonies before 1860, and they gained from their connection to the wealth of the United Kingdom.(34)

The significance of Ashley's article was in his systematic approach, the effort to evaluate Adam Smith's position, his balanced discussion of the various issues and his efforts to re-assess mercantilist activities. Moreover, Ashley's contribution is the most detailed discussion of a specific aspect of Smith's work on the value of imperial connections in the period.

The Tariff Problem and the 1903 Fiscal Controversy

Although Ashley did not publicly endorse tariff reform till 1903, his early rejection of orthodox economic theory and historical approach to economic questions meant that he was sceptical of the acclaimed advantages of free trade. As early as 1888, he suggested that free trade policy was "dead", and "young economists" were judging each situation on its merits and no longer accepted laissez-faire policies.(35) Nevertheless, he believed that if a new colony (eg, Australia) wanted the largest possible increase in its wealth, then free trade would be the wisest policy. Towards the close of the nineteenth century, he demonstrated that a policy which was so often assumed by people of the day to be the logical outcome of economic truth, could simply be regarded as a historical phenomenon. Furthermore, free trade's association with one particular party was the "result of changing accidents", and not due to logical necessity.(36)

Two days before Chamberlain launched his tariff reform campaign, on 15 May, he suggested that Ashley write a book on the question.(37) Ashley had little personal contact with Chamberlain, and in reply to the accusation that Chamberlain was responsible for the Tariff Problem, he noted "my book was written entirely on my own motion, and without the slightest inspiration and direction".(38) Whilst he publicly defended Chamberlain, Ashley criticised Chamberlain's ignorance of economic questions within the circle of his supporters.(39) He fully endorsed Chamberlain's proposals and condemned the fourteen economists' manifesto to The Times, disputing the position that "a majority of British economists have signed a pronouncement intended to veto any serious reconsiderations of the commercial policy of this country".(40)

The Tariff Problem became widely regarded as the most sophisticated statement of the anti-free trade case and it ran three editions between 1903 and 1911.(41) There were minor changes in the second edition when Ashley included some observations on British shipping and on England's position for entrepot trade, and in the third edition there is a new introduction. He commenced the book by examing the repeal of the corn laws in 1846, and showed how it represented the triumph of the movement towards political and industrial individualism. However, factory legislation had accompanied the industrial revolution, and the principle of the unrestricted pursuit of individual self-liberty had been totally discredited.(42) Ashley also carefully examined Adam Smith's arguments for free trade, agreeing that initially protection involved an economic loss because consumers had to pay more for the protected commodity. Smith listed exceptions to free trade (eg Navigation Acts) because of his strong nationalistic feelings and the persistent possibility of international conflict.(43) Nevertheless, subsequent commentators on Smith's writings ignored these concessions to free trade doctrines, but J S Mill's defence of protection for infant industries destroyed any claims people made for the universal validity of Smith's teachings.(44)

Ashley carefully examined free trade legislation after 1820, particularly the 1846 repeal of the Corn Laws which he argued was due to the Irish potato famine, the self-interest of manufacturers and the needs of British industrialisation. He claimed that, contrary to popular belief, the farming community had initially experienced adverse consequences of the repeal. Moreover, Ashley attached the Ricardian concept of world specialisation based on the assumptions of the perfect mobility of labour, free trade and competition and maintained that prices had fallen after 1846 not because of free trade, but as a consequence of improvements in land and sea transport which had opened virgin land in the United States and Australia.(45)

In order to explain the recent patterns of trade Ashley insisted, in a manner akin to Giffen, that the "facts of trade" had to be established.(46) He reviewed the value and volume of exports and imports from 1870 to 1900 and echoed Jevons' anxiety at the increasing export of British coal, since in exporting coal Britain was "living upon its capital which could never be replaced".(47) In common with other tariff reformers he stressed that the dwindling condition of British exports was a direct consequence of the increasing competitiveness of overseas manufacturers, who had been expected to remain primary producing nations. However, British capital, machinery and skill had greatly assisted them to become complex industrial nations.(48) Ashley re-iterated the position advocated by the Tariff Reform League that imports had increased into the United Kingdom as a consequence of increased world production, Britain's increasing dependence on food and raw materials and the dumping of industrial products by foreign manufacturers on the British market by foreign trusts.(49)

It was upon the basis of an analysis of trusts that Ashley presented an interesting defence of tariffs for British industry. During his residence in Canada and the United States, Ashley had become acutely aware of the threat posed to British staple industries by the large-scale North American (and German) trusts. Two years before the publication of The Tariff Problem he argued that people had to be "trained" to realise that Britain's commercial position was different and that it was impossible to restore early Victorian relations between England and other countries. Britain, the first industrial nation, had provided the basis for other countries' industrial revolutions:

> The struggle of the future must inevitably be between a number of great nations, more or less equally well-equipped, carrying on production by the same general methods, and each trying to strengthen its industrial and commercial position by the adoption of the most highly developed machinery, and of all the methods suggested by scientific research policy, or experience.(50)

By 1903, Ashley argued that the solution to the decline in Britain's staple industries was to establish a detailed programme of protective tariffs and imperial preferences. These measures, in association with policies to increase the size and efficiency of industries, would lead to increasing returns to scale, guarantee employment and maintain Britain's vital staple industries.(51) Like Cunningham and Hewins, Ashley's support for tariff reform was the outgrowth of a sincere conviction that the political and economic theory of free trade was unsuited to Britain's different stage of production.(52) If foreign competition increased, a movement to unskilled trade would result and the working class would suffer as capitalists devoted themselves "more and more to those industries which flourish on cheap labour".(53) Thinking along similar lines to the popularist Tariff Reformers, he conceded that tariffs would increase the price of bread to the working class, but this would be more than compensated for by the increase of employment opportunities, which would ultimately benefit all Englishmen.(54)

Aligning himself with the tariff reformers, he proposed that Britain's hope for the future lay in closer solidarity with the self-governing colonies. Since Great Britain was an island deficient in some of her resource requirements, she could not always retain the leading place in the world's economic activity and only in the self-governing colonies could Britain find the large and dependable market she required. Moreover, the colonies were willing to give the nation access to those markets in exchange for preference on their foodstuffs.(55)

In his other important, though neglected, 1903 publication - The Adjustment of Wages - Ashley extensively compared the British and American coal and iron industries and concluded that British industrial supremacy had passed away, "never to return".(56) In pig iron, steel and cotton production, the United States had surged ahead of Britain, particularly in the decade 1890-1900. Britain was no longer able to "stand alone" against her industrial competitors and she had to "join forces" with the self-governing colonies:

> The time is passing when we could profitably compare the productive capacity of the insular Great Britain with that of the United States; the time has not yet come when we can compare with the United States the British empire as a Whole.(57)

He re-iterated his Tariff Problem position contending that Britain had to respond affirmatively to the colonial demands for imperial preference if she was to remain a major industrial nation and compete successfully with German and American industries. Moreover, only with tariff reform could the working classes be guaranteed regular and secure employment. Unless the empire could be knit together through imperial preference (and political federation) it would continue its "alarming disintegration".(58)

Tariff Reform 1903-1914

Ashley's Tariff Problem was well received by tariff reformers, and on 26 April, 1904 Chamberlain wrote "I think your book is the best manual we have from the economic point of view".(59) However, some of his specific proposals came under attack, especially his suggestion that if retaliation were adopted, the government would have to adjust duties by executive decree. In such a situation, Ashley suggested the establishment of a Ministry of Trade and Commerce which would be assisted by either local correspondents or delegates advised by various provincial university professors of Commerce.(60) This scheme was attacked on both constitutional and professional grounds; it was believed that professors were not able to tender such advice.(61)

Throughout 1904, Ashley attempted to meet the criticism that tariff reform would increase the price of bread, by agreeing that while in the short-term this would be the case, it would not hold in the long-term. In his defence he contended that List had demonstrated that "the question of the productive powers of a country and their possible development is far more important than that of present values; it might be well worth while to incur a loss for a time in order to secure a more than proportionate future gain".(62)

In The Progress of the German Working Classes in the Last Quarter of a Century, Ashley wanted to "clear the air" of the fiscal controversy with concrete statistical evidence. In his preface, he concisely outlined the allegations made by free traders that since British workers were "better off" than their German counterparts, Britain should not depart from its present policy. He doubted if a legitimate comparison could be made between the two countries, and if it could, the "balance of advantage" would by no means be indisputably in favour of this country. The economic, social and institutional structures of the two nations were so different that it was impossible to give a brief evaluation of which country was more successful or enjoyed a higher standard of living.(63) The main thrust of his argument was that whatever the comparative positions of the two countries, Germany, under a policy of protection, had made great advances in the well-being of its peoples. "That while a protective policy has been in force - whether because or in spite of it - there has been on the whole a great rise in wages and a real advance in comfort on the part of the work people in German industries".(64)

Ashley exhaustively investigated the rates of pay, general working conditions and industrial structure of the steel, coal, and textile industries. he was most impressed at the benefits workers received, the state insurance system, the old-age pension schemes and the evidence which suggested falling food prices and higher bank deposits.(65) As a social reformer he was greatly encouraged by the German experience, where social reform was possible side-by-side with protective tariffs:

This is a great comfort to those of us who are Social Reformers first and Imperialists afterwards; those of us who, in the present crisis of our national fortunes, are such ardent Imperialists that we are ready to risk even the real dangers of tariffs, and to do this just because we are Social Reformers.(66)

In 1904, Ashley and Cunningham became members of the Compatriots Club, a non-partisan body established in March of that year to advance the ideal of a united British empire and to advocate principles of constructive policy on all constitutional, economic, defence and educational questions which would attempt to fulfil that ideal. Through his participation in the Club, Ashley regularly met leading tariff reformers, including Chamberlain, Garvin, Amery, Ridley and Milner.(67) He spoke at Club meetings, and on

19 May 1904 delivered a stimulating lecture on "Political Economy and the Tariff Problem" in which he surveyed the history of economics since Adam Smith, and stressed the relativistic nature of economic policy prescriptions. He repeated his claim that while free trade was Britain's wisest policy in 1846 because of the nation's industrial supremacy, this was no longer the case. Furthermore, other countries - notably Germany - had found it necessary to enact protective tariffs in order to become complex industrial nations. Britain now faced strong competition in her manufactured products, as well as rivals in the field of colonisation. Nevertheless: "Great Britain has its place in the sunshine; it already has its vast nominal empire; with us the question is whether that empire can be maintained and converted into an economic reality".(68) He recognized that a major obstacle to the implementation of imperial preferential proposals was the fear of higher food prices and concluded his lecture with an appeal to all sides in the fiscal controversy to engage in greater observation, more history and theory as well as a demand for better official statistics.(69)

Ashley remained cautious in his endorsement of tariff proposals, and even in 1907 he was concerned that protection would result in superfluous forms of support for various industries. In contrast to Cunningham and Hewins, he was extremely anxious that protection might "open the door to forms of protection that are unnecessary and undesirable" and added that "only a grave sense of the needs of the nation and empire could induce any of us to be ready to face the risk".(70) Initially Ashley had advocated simple preferential arrangements between the mother country and any given colony; a preference would be granted for British manufacturers in a colonial market. However, his position developed and changed over the first decade of the twentieth century, as the introduction to the third edition of this Tariff Problem reveals:

> I am myself more sympathetic towards the plan of a low general tariff, as a basis both for preference and for negotiation, than I was 8 years ago. The fear that thereby certain sweated industries may be undesirably protected has been considerably lessened by recent legislation as to wages boards, and by the tightening up of the fair wages clause in public contracts.(71)

Ashley had been concerned, as was Marshall, about the potential evils of protection.(72) Subsequently, his fears were reduced when he realised there was adequate labour legislation to protect the interest of the working classes. Based on this security, he fully accepted protection as a weapon to guarantee employment. Furthermore, Ashley reviewed the forces contributing to the movement of the empire towards "closer association".(73) He contended that it was other nations' protectionist policies which had inspired the colonies to attempt to establish trade relations within the empire and he proudly noted that the Imperial Conferences were the means of implementing the preferential proposals.(74) He felt that "something like a permanent imperial organisation for trade affairs had been coming into existence". There was a growing need for more information on the colonies, and he argued that the Imperial Intelligence Service, established in 1908, had to be extended:

> With an Empire, however, whose natural resources are still so imperfectly known, it is highly desirable that information as to the present production and demand should be supplemented by the best available scientific opinion as to further possibilities. There should, in short, be an Imperial Scientific Research Centre for economic purposes.(75)

Whilst Ashley was regarded as "the leading academic defender of Chamberlain's scheme, his academic detachment from the political squabbles and individualistic social views meant he was often ignored by the politicians".(76) In Monthly Notes on Tariff Reform, Ashley argued that a system of national insurance depended on tariff reform; his name was added to the Notes - an unusual procedure - and he never repeated his argument.(77) As Semmel contends, his opinions did not fit the type of campaign the Unionist Party was fighting and his view that Chamberlain's industrial supporters acted from self-interest and that the working classes had to safeguard the tariff from selfish abuse, were not suitable for the politicians.(78)

The Political Unification of the Empire

Although the question of imperial federation had been much debated in the 1880s and 1890s, Ashley took little part in the discussions.(79) However, in the first decade of the twentieth century, he was enthusiastic at the prospect of an economic and political union of the United Kingdom with the self-governing colonies. In 1903 he believed that the movement to political federation was most encouraging and argued in a similar manner to Lord Salisbury and a minority of the early proponents of imperial federation in the 1880s, that if a permanent union was to be achieved, it was essential to first establish economic co-operation.(80) Economic pressures would force political union: "the possibility of utilising for English manufacturers the iron ore of Newfoundland or the cotton of West Africa will become something more than a commercial question if the imperial sense continues to grow more acute".(81)

Ashley contended that a closer union between the mother country and the colonies was inevitable, and politically "extremely justifiable", due to the rise of other competitive nations. Britain was becoming increasingly dependent upon trade within the empire, especially imports. He identified closely with some early imperial federationists when he offered no firm guidelines as to how political unification would be implemented, although it is probable that he believed imperial preference was an essential foundation stone. In 1911, he tentatively suggested a "Congress of Chambers of Commerce and Empire", which would be a non-official commercial parliament of the empire. He referred to the 1901 Pacific Cable Board which was a joint effort of the British, Australian, Canadian and New Zealand governments, observing that the more governments co-operated on projects, the greater would be the prospect for political union. Moreover, he suggested that in a political union, the United Kingdom would be forced to enact sound social reform legislation which had already been passed in the self-governing colonies. He was most impressed by the "experience of social reform" - old age pensions, compulsory insurance, minimum wages - in the "daughter" nations.(82)

Until the outbreak of War in 1914, Ashley was pessimistic at the possibilities of success for imperial federation. However, he believed that an outcome of the conflict would be the further consolidation of the empire. It would contribute to the solution of the "great British problem", namely that of allying the self-governing nationalities in a permanent federation:

> A war in which the self-governing Dominions voluntarily take an active part reveals to themselves the strength of their sense of imperial solidarity; the very fighting side-by-side creates a mutual knowledge, mutual understanding and respect, a fund of common memories; and it is out of such a toil that the confederate organisation, appropriate for so unique an Empire as ours, is most likely to spring.(83)

Conclusion

Ashley's discussion of imperial problems left the wider issues of empire and colonies in the background and focused on tariff reform and protection. Nevertheless he claimed that his discussions of the tariff problem in 1903 had commenced from an imperial standpoint.(84) He acknowledged that there were many imperial needs, and political economists had to recognise these: "I look forward with some confidence to the time when the great majority of teachers of political economy in this country will recognise imperial needs, and have the courage to face great dangers for a worthy end".(85) Semmel has argued, correctly in our opinion, that Ashley was not an expansionist, but an imperialist and a patriot.(86) In "Political Economy and the Tariff Problem", Ashley asserted that the attitude which judged "the nation as an indispensable instrument for the ultimate well-being of humanity" was consistent "with a noble idealism".(87) In "The Argument for Preference", he regarded the British empire as "the mightiest of instruments for good" and the "fairest hope of humanity".(88)

He considered his imperialism to be of a "democratic nature", with a genuine concern for social amelioration, and his daughter argues this was the "only kind of imperialism he cared for".(89) However, as we have seen, a strong element in Ashley's imperial arguments was his desire to retain the United Kingdom's dominance in world affairs.(90) He was most aware and fearful of the economic and political consequences of the rise of foreign competitors, particularly the Americans and the Germans. Consequently, he stressed, like Hewins and Cunningham, that it was only in the self-governing colonies that Britain could find the large and dependable markets she required to remain a great power.(91)

W CUNNINGHAM

Introduction

During his long career as an academic and cleric, Cunningham wrote numerous articles and books on a range of economic, historical and ethical subjects. Born in 1849 to a devout Free Church family, Cunningham received his first sermon at six, and later entered Edinburgh University in November 1866 to read an arts course and prepare for the ministry.(92) As a teenager, Cunningham wanted to study medicine and then undertake missionary work in India. While at Edinburgh, he read logic, moral and general philosophy and then decided to undertake the Moral Science Tripos at Caius College, Cambridge. He entered Cambridge in 1869, and two years later was lectured by Marshall on political economy, and Sidgwick on metaphysics and ethics. However, it was the Christian Socialist, F D Maurice, who - together with T H Green and Charles Kingsley - exerted the strongest influence on the young Cunningham.(93)

Cunningham graduated in 1872 and attempted to win a moral science fellowship on the basis of his study of Hegel and a dissertation on the influence of Descartes upon English politics.(94) In this he failed, but soon found work as a lecturer in political economy with the Cambridge University Extension Movement. In his lectures in Leeds, Bradford and Liverpool, he attempted to make economics intelligible to the working classes. His training as a philosopher and historian turned him against the orthodox, deductive approach and in July 1878, he attacked orthodox economic theory, suggesting that it had a limited utility in explaining the economic conditions in contemporary England, and postulated that there were wide discrepancies between the economic theory of wages, population, and rent and the actual circumstances.(95) Furthermore, he argued that classical political economy's assumptions were rooted in the faulty picture of self-interest and he demanded the injection of an ethical dimension into the subject, with a stress on the practical aspects of the discipline.(96) An examiner in the historical Tripos in the same year as his "Political Economy as a Moral Science" appeared, Cunningham noted that there was no suitable textbook in English economic history so he began to compile notes for one. Just before his death in 1919, Cunningham told a correspondent:

> It was rather accidentally that I came to devote myself to economic history. It had a place in the History Course at Cambridge from the first (1878), and as there was no teacher for

the subject, I was asked by the History Board to do my best with it. I had some knowledge of Political Economy and did my best to get up the History. I found a textbook was much needed and managed to write one in 1880.(97)

Two years later, in 1882, The Growth of English Industry and Commerce was published, and grew to three volumes and ran six editions during Cunningham's life-time.(98) Shortly before its publication, Cunningham toured India and claimed that it was the turning point in his career as an economist.(99)

On his return to the United Kingdom, Cunningham continued his teaching in economic history, but after obtaining a position at Trinity he retired from University teaching, and devoted himself to research and supported Maitland's and Lord Acton's successful removal of economic theory from the historical tripos.(100) Cunningham grew increasingly sceptical of the claims of orthodox political economy and in 1885, in Politics and Economics, he attempted an essay on the principles of political economy with a survey of recent legislation. He denied that economic principles were true "for all time and place", arguing that they had to be relative to circumstances, because economic policy was concerned with human conduct.(101) Two years later in Political Economy Treated as an Empirical Science Cunningham reiterated these arguments, stressing that the principles of political economy as found in the United Kingdom were inapplicable to India.(102) In this period, Cunningham had some personal contact with the German historical school, though it was less direct than either Ashley's or Hewins' and he came to the school's ideas through their published works.(103)

Cunningham unhesitatingly accepted the Comtist criticisms of economic theory, contending that economics had to emerge from the study of society and that economic principles had no independent validity.(104) Inevitably, he came into conflict with Alfred Marshall, the economics don at Cambridge.(105) This is not the place to discuss their disagreements; suffice to say, Cunningham began the interchange when he charged that Marshall's Principles, which contained a wide survey of world economic history, was drawn from "two or three badly chosen books".(106) Drawing upon the impressions of, and experience in India, Cunningham claimed that Marshall's mistake had been the assumption that similar motives for economic development had been operative in all historical epochs, which resulted in an abstract universally applicable law of economics. Marshall's reply stated his interest in economic history, and partially defended his discussion in the Principles on the grounds that it was an introduction.(107) Cunningham became increasingly critical of Marshallians, and he attacked Pigou's welfare economics in 1916, declaring that the method of measuring peoples' satisfaction in the abstract for the purposes of formulating a public welfare policy produced a socially inapplicable pure theory.(108) Economics had to be descriptive, practical and based upon inductive research.

In discussing Cunningham's approach to political economy and his wide-ranging views it is impossible to ignore his religious opinions, for he was, above all else, a cleric.(109) As a young undergraduate at Cambridge, Cunningham rejected his father's Free Church and embraced Anglicanism. In 1874 he took orders in the Church of England and became a vicar at St Mary's Cambridge from 1887 to 1908, when he was appointed Archdeacon of Ely. Cunningham's religion, like that of the Christian Socialist F D Maurice, who was also at Caius College, was Christ-centred. He stressed that the Christian had to exercise self-discipline and find salvation through the New Testament. He found the Universal Church of the Middle Ages too restrictive in its discipline and protestantism too anarchic in organisation and theology. By contrast, the Elizabethan period properly combined freedom and authority and in its modern form provided religious ideals and the direction for eternal salvation.(110)

Cunningham accepted Maurice's teaching that the Church was not to direct the State in political or social affairs, or to advocate particular political measures. Nevertheless, it was the explicit duty of the Christian, as an individual citizen, to assist in the wise government of the realm.(111) Christianity had to teach man self-discipline and a moral consciousness capable of participating in politics. Accepting Maurice's position, he argued that because Kingship had a divine origin, and since popular sovereignty had replaced the King, democracy owed its ultimate authority to God.(112)

Although he studied Hegelian and Comtist philosophy, Cunningham argued that T H Green "was master in all that I care about philosophy".(113) He combined his Christ-centred religious beliefs with Green's emphasis upon the duties of democratic citizenship.(114) He asserted that utilitarianism could never act as a justification for government's authority, since all ultimate authority was derived from God and expressed in the democratic process, protected by the Church of England, "the guardian of the British empire".(115)

Empire : Conception, Evolution, Colonisation and Imperialism

Cunningham, like Giffen and Hobson, dealt with the full range of British overseas possessions - the self-governing colonies, the crown colonies, India, military outposts and dependencies, and he elaborated the idea of a mother country and her daughters in a similar manner to Ashley, Marshall and Hewins.(116) The empire was a group of scattered territories which contained the "most varied" resources, populated by "very different races".(117) Furthermore, it was a dynamic, growing entity:

> The British Empire is not a mere machine organised so as to attain high efficiency in one department after another, such as can be recorded by statistical tests, but it is a living growth in which all the various elements are given opportunities to

co-operate for the developments of resources and the progress of mankind. Its life does not consist merely in the play of present day sordid interests, for it has a heritage of experience and achievement in the past and a conscious responsibility for the future.(118)

In the first edition of his Industry and Commerce (1882), Cunningham attempted to measure the growth of the British empire since the end of the seventeenth century. In an appendix, "Note on British Possessions and Dependencies", he constructed two maps which revealed the increase in the empire during the nineteenth century.(119) Although he did not pursue the matter in the subsequent editions, Cunningham did suggest that a variety of causes were responsible for the evolution of the empire - the gradual extension of commerce, the advent of trading companies coupled with the desire to enrich the power and prestige of the mother country and a sense of "moral mission to the world"(120) To Cunningham, Englishmen had been "curiously unwilling" to increase the bounds of their responsibilities and rule.(121) Nevertheless, the self-governing colonies had evolved from convict settlements, trading factories and because of a desire to enrich the mother country. Underlying Britain's acquisition of all overseas territory was the world supremacy of the navy.(122) Cunningham believed that England had preserved her empire, because the English concept of welfare included a deep regard for historical tradition and the recognition that racial differences could not be assimilated into the English model:

> The right and freedom for different nations to preserve their own languages and traditions and sentiments within a single political community has been acknowledged, and this is the basis of English policy in all parts of the world. There is no other great civilised community in modern times which has shown itself ready to take this line.(123)

In the same way as Benjamin Kidd argued, Cunningham claimed that the essential difference between Western peoples and the "savages of the East", was the former's highly developed care for human life. British policy throughout the globe had endeavoured to implement such a policy and gave extensive scope, under its institutions which protected life and property, for the varieties of tradition, sentiment and culture.(124) Britain also preserved and strengthened the empire by diffusing power to those communities willing and able to govern themselves in these areas.(125) He considered it a duty for the United Kingdom, as a powerful and influential nation, to diffuse the heritage of self-government, "which has been built-up in this island", throughout the world.(126)

Cunningham argued that since Burke's impeachment of Warren Hastings, Britain's duty to her colonists and the native races under her domain had been acutely felt and an aim of British rule had been to provide self-government in the white colonies.(127) This aim, in association with the cessation of the economic exploitation of the colonies, had both preserved and enhanced the ideals of British empire.(128) The colonisation movement throughout the nineteenth century further extended British influence in the World. Cunningham accepted Wakefield's definition of colonisation, arguing that the movement involved the formation of new communities in hitherto relatively unoccupied parts of the globe.(129) The tremendous inventions and innovations in rail and shipbuilding had provided reliable, cheap and efficient means of transporting labour and goods to this "new world".(130) Colonisation was the "thread" which took England from isolationism to internationalism. The nineteenth century colonisation of Australia and New Zealand had been conducted in a much more organised manner than the haphazard movement of people to the United States.(131) To Cunningham, Wakefield's colonisation scheme had greatly relieved domestic congestion and developed backward parts of the empire.(132) In this context, Cunningham believed that the empire had always furnished an outlet for England's surplus population although like Hewins and the mercantilists he did not accept that there was overpopulation, and argued that a large and growing population was a source of strength and power.(133)

Cunningham was most aware of the "new imperialistic" movement after 1870, and he argued that in such circumstances, Wakefield's simple scheme of colonisation was inapplicable due to the complex factors involved, particularly the inter-relationship between "civilised and half-civilised" people.(134) "Contact between highly developed peoples, possessed by modern resources and ideas, and primitive races is going on for good and for evil, in all parts of the world".(135) Cunningham considered that the question of making the most of the empire's material resources, as well as giving "fair-play" to the uncivilised or half-civilised peoples of the world, was one of the great problems of his day.(136)

In his historical studies Cunningham detailed the decline of various empires. In <u>An Essay on Western Civilisation in its Economic Aspects</u>, he argued that the Phoenician empire had fallen because of the excessive specialisation in trade. The Roman empire, by contrast, had declined through the lack of an imperial federation, insufficient domestic investment and an unpatriotic citizenry. The Spanish empire collapsed because of "narrow bullionist policies" which fully exploited domestic and colonial resources. The French empire had been rendered impotent by the minute regulations of Colbert. Whereas all these empires had declined, British imperial domination continued and flourished. Britain succeeded in her conquests because she combined freedom and authority, permitted individuals to accumulate wealth and its citizens were welded together by a truly national will.(137)

The Economic and Political Unification of the Empire

During the last decade of the nineteenth century Cunningham's views on free trade underwent significant changes.(138) In his address to the British Association in 1891, Cunningham stated his position on the beneficial effects of the United Kingdom's free trade policy, contending that he did not regret that Britain was the first country to adopt the "cosmopolitan economic science".(139) However, around the beginning of the Tariff Reform debate in 1903 he read another paper to the British Association in which he advocated a bounty on cotton from the colonies and a tax on wheat grown in countries which did not buy British manufactures.(140) By the fifth edition of his Growth of English Industry and Commerce (1910), he had totally rejected the fundamental doctrines of free trade, arguing that the "dream" of international free trade had not been realised.(141)

In common with his contemporaries, Cunningham noted the inter-dependence of the world economy, and Britain's particular dependence on raw materials and food supply.(142) During a lecture tour at Harvard in 1899, when he temporarily replaced Ashley, Cunningham argued that among the world imperial powers, only Britain was "cosmopolitan" in policy. British goods were increasingly excluded from foreign and colonial markets by hostile tariffs. However, he did not advocate that Britain should return to its former protectionist policy, because he felt that by pursing "cosmopolitan imperialism", Britain could extend the free trade region, guarantee world peace and protect uncivilised natives from excessive exploitation.(143)

By the time of the fiscal controversy in 1903, Cunningham had fully endorsed the tariff reform movement. During the campaign he was a loyal member of the Unionist party, a regular participant in the Compatriots Club through which he met the tariff reform leaders, and was the founder of the Cambridge Branch of the Tariff Reform League.(144) He had become very concerned that foreign competition would further erode Britain's world leadership:

During the last fifty years the development of manufacturers in America and Germany has led to an international competition in industry, and England has lost her leading position. The struggle is now so keen that we are bound to attend to our manufacturing and commercial interests; we cannot afford to let things drift. There is a double danger in continuing to pursue the Cobdenite policy today. As our goods are gradually driven from one market after another, we have diminished opportunities of purchasing the food we require for our population, while the reckless optimism, which "laissez-faire" politicians exhibit in the face of serious dangers, is fated to British influence in our colonies or on our neighbours. We cannot retain the respect of any other people if we are too careless or too arrogant, as a nation, to attend to our own business interests.(145)

Cunningham identifies himself closely with Ashley and Hewins when he condemned the fourteen economists' manifesto to the Times, which had rejected Chamberlain's tariff reform proposals.(146) "The professors who protested that there could be no change of circumstances which made it desirable to reconsider the trading policy of the country did much to discredit the scientific character of the doctrine they taught".(147) He considered the manifesto was yet another example of the false authority of economic theory as applied to practical affairs. Numerous economists, for example J S Mill, had already supported economic policies which contradicted laissez-faire principles - protection of infant industries and support for retaliatory tariffs.(148)

In a series of lectures delivered in 1903, Cunningham carefully reviewed Britain's free trade policy, claiming that since she was the first industrial nation, British merchants wanted free access to all nations and demanded an end to the restrictive corn laws as well as the remnants of the mercantile period. Subsequently, the corn laws had been repealed "so that we might be able to crush rival industries in every part of the world by supplying the markets with goods produced on the better and cheaper methods which were practised in England".(149)

Accepting List's position, he argued that free trade was the appropriate policy for Britain to pursue as the world's first and leading industrial nation. However America and Germany were forced to erect tariffs so as to establish themselves as complex industrial nations. The decline of Britain's staple industries and her dependence on foreign supplies of food and raw materials demonstrated that free trade was no "longer the appropriate policy for the nation to follow".(150)

He correctly pointed out that other countries suffered as the result of Britain's free trade policy. For example, India had been forced to submit to free trading practices without being consulted as to the possible effects on her economy.(151) In the early nineteenth century the free importation of British cottons destroyed Indian hand loom weaving on a commercial scale; thereafter the British ban on protective tariffs held back mechanised cotton production and retained the markets for Lancashire.(152) Indian cottons were not protected till 1926, and textile imports from Britain then dropped significantly.(153)

In November 1904, the Guardian printed a manifesto from leading ecclesiastics who denounced the tariff reform campaign as "immoral" since it would lead to corruption in public life, international rivalries and adversely affect the poorer classes.(154) Cunningham, who knew several of the signatories "quite intimately", attacked the manifesto on the grounds that it would reinforce the misguided public opinion that there was no relationship between political life and morality.(155) Cunningham accepted Maurice's teaching that Christian morality had everything to do with practical affairs and economic studies.(156) On the other hand, he believed that it was an impossibility to deduce from fundamental moral principles the course a nation ought to pursue. It was even harder to forecast the inevitable moral effects of any economic change. The economic sphere was not distinct from political realities, and political aims and considerations had to be taken into account.(157)

In the same manner as Chamberlain, Cunningham advocated a policy of economic co-operation throughout the empire, in order that each member would develop to its maximum capability and the British empire would remain a powerful force throughout the world.(158) Arguing in a similar manner to Ashley and Hewins he supported imperial preferential schemes, claiming that the empire was a means by which Britain could secure her essential supplies of raw materials and sell her products.

> Imperial preference is advocated primarily with reference to the future of the Mother Country, as the only suggestion which has yet been made for strengthening our connection with the most important sources of supply, for securing us opportunities for sale, and for increasing the purchasing power of our manufactures.(159)

Cunningham's writings on the form of imperial preference were vaguer than Ashley's though he was much more specific as to its effects. Cunningham merely noted that a tariff would have to be imposed on goods and products from the non-empire parts of the world, which would include the corn-growing regions of Russia, America and the Argentine. He did not consider how high the tariff should be, believing that the essential point of imperial preference was the free entry of imperial corn.(160) He felt that there would be "a few" adverse effects of this policy, but did not specify them. However, he did argue that Britain would gain more than the colonies from such an arrangement: she would secure her food supplies, establish trading connections, and attract colonial buyers to her shores. On their side, the colonies would obtain a better price from England than from rival importers. He boldly asserted, without substantial argument or evidence, that preference would lead to the most efficient utilisation of the empire's resources.(161)

Underlying Cunningham's thoughts and policy prescriptions was his desire to keep the United Kingdom strong and secure. Associating himself with leading tariff reformers such as L S Amery and J J Mackinder, Cunningham confidently asserted that once an ample food supply was secured, Britain would be able to retaliate against other nations through her system of imperial preference by imposing duties on the goods imported into countries which endeavoured to exclude British manufacturers.(162) Cunningham viewed imperial preference both as a political and an economic weapon and consequently stressed that the United Kingdom had to maintain her naval power if she wished to operate a preferential scheme effectively, since trade was performed along extensive sea voyages.(163) Cunningham wanted the colonies to grow in strength and power, so that they could support the mother country in times of economic and military crisis and he believed that the material prosperity of the empire could be most effectively promoted by the mother country offering her technology to the member states.(164) In contrast to the other economists Cunningham argued that the backward parts of the empire offered the greatest hope for ᶠuture markets for British goods, though he did not justify this claim. He did state, however, that in developing these markets, the self-governming colonies could be most helpful to the mother country.(165)

Cunningham agreed with Ashley and argued that only by the economic consolidation of the empire would there be the political unification of the empire.(166) However, he did not indicate how this unification would occur, and unlike Ashley, he devoted little attention to imperial federation schemes, a position common to numerous advocates, such as Burgess, Dumraven, Harrowby and Herby.(167)

Civilisation, Religous Duty and the Empire

Cunningham felt that the most striking contrasts in the economic conditions between various parts of the world were those associated with differences of race.(168) Echoing the <u>Social Darwinism</u> of Kidd and Karl Pearson, he pointed out that there were many important differences between civilised, Western man and half-civilised savage man, who excelled civilised man in his "quickness of foot" and skill-sense perception. But savage man had "no part in the skill and wisdom and strength of character which have been accumulated through the ages".(169) While primitive man was immersed in nature and restricted by his physical surroundings, civilised man was much more responsive to the influences of ideal objects and "has attained the power of creating ideas for himself".(170) To civilised man war was an outrage, but with savages it was a pattern of routine existence. Cunningham agreed with F D Maurice and argued that civilisation depended on the wise utilisation of physical resources, the evolving of enterprise and skill, as well as the guidance of Christian rulers.(171)

Following his former teacher, Maurice, Cunningham sketched the development of spiritual consciousness in man in <u>The Secret of Progress</u>, arguing that the advance of civilisation had increased man's power of giving effect to his will. This had not prevented war because of the extraordinary diversity of mens' wills in other nations.(172) He argued along similar lines to J Seeley and J A Froude that the British had a highly developed "care" for human life, and their concern for humanity was the essential difference between themselves and all primitive peoples.(173)

However, Cunningham did not advocate the immediate occupation of primitive peoples' land by the British and much like the late nineteenth century "radical liberals", (for example, William

Clarke, J A Hobson, Ramsay MacDonald and J M Robertson) argued that because of the warring activities of the uncivilised peoples, and the exploitive activities of Western capitalists, there was a need for effective police action in numerous parts of the globe.(174) The regions occupied by the primitive races were likely to suffer from such activities, until they were brought under the authority of "some power which the white man respected". He considered that there were great difficulties in allowing natives to retain their independence; and the various attempts at the rapid assimilation of backward races to modern habits of thought and action, had often been failures:

> It is wisest to preserve an artificial isolation in order that the necessary modification may take place gradually, and without causing the best elements in native character and traditions to be subverted. Only under the aegis of a strong political power can territorial 'reservations' be allotted to the primitive tribes and proper steps taken for promoting their gradual amelioration.(175)

The British had clearly demonstrated that they could avoid interference with the sentiments of the subjected races, for example, in Quebec in 1759 there had been insistence that English be spoken and in India there was a "scrupulous effort to understand native laws and customs".(176) Despite these successes, Cunningham felt that it was imperative to develop and extend the British sense of "imperial duty". It was a duty to ensure that British subjects enjoyed "fair play, fair order" and realised their maximum potential as human beings. The British had to seek the good which could be obtained in the long-term rule of the empire and not look for short-term gains which increased political and economic power.(177) On this account he parted from radicals, like Clark, Hobson and MacDonald, and urged the British to take up the "white man's burden" and guarantee adequate opportunities for native development. He agreed with the historian W E H Lecky and poet Rudyard Kipling, that Britain had a mission to the empire and to mankind.(178)

> The White Man's Burden is that of protecting the native races from the evil effects of contact with the enterprise of Western Civilisation until they are able to benefit by that contact themselves.(179)

The white man's burden was, in effect, the task of training the native races and of modifying their habits and institutions. If this was achieved then natives would be able to "live a wholesome life among the other peoples of the world", and also "appreciate the best gifts of civilisation". Furthermore, Cunningham believed that by cultivating a strong sense of imperial responsibilities in the British peoples, they may learn to deal more successfully with domestic problems which would "regenerate the national life of the mother country".(180)

To Cunningham the white man's burden was aggravated by modern economic methods, which necessitated an entire change in the economic and social life of subjected peoples, particularly those in the backward nations. There is a close parallel between Cunningham's thoughts on the adverse effects of British imperialism and those of J A Hobson and the members of the South Place Ethical Society, particularly when Cunningham argued that the opening-up of South Africa and India had caused more social disintegration than had occurred during the British industrial revolution.(181) Western man could disintegrate primitive societies, exploit the peoples and eliminate a race's cultural heritage. Nevertheless, in certain regions, for example India, peace had been established:

> The whole region (India) is marked with monuments of the utter chaos and disorder which preceded our rule; and here on the spot one realises as I never did at home, the incalculable good we have conferred by establishing peace.(182)

But on balance, Western civilisation had generally exerted a baneful influence on the races which with it had been brought into contact and neither rational intelligence, nor philanthropic sentiment, could correct these injustices. Re-iterating Maurice's ideas and emphasising his Christian beliefs Cunningham argued that the best ways of "avoiding shame" lay in adopting and implementing the truths embodied in Christian morality.(183) People had to take God's right as absolute and supreme and recognise that there was a common citizenship in each nation and a common humanity. There was little hope for the orderly life of the world while racial and religious differences split mankind into various sections.(184) Cunningham believed "that He rules the world, and He will not give the victory to those who do not acknowledge their responsibility to Him".(185)

Whilst Cunningham argued that the effort to give backward peoples "real opportunities" was "specifically Christian work", a position rejected by Hobson, he was disillusioned by some missionary activities.(186) He devoted considerable attention to the problems confronting the Christian church in India, maintaining that the form of Christianity most likely to succeed was that which presented itself as "compatible with native social instincts".(187) The British government had to finance missionary work, and the Church had to encourage the natives to take an active role in clerical administration. Aligning himself with the Christian churches, Cunningham wanted to see the s read of God's kingdom among the native peoples and the fostering of a "free political life" by the Church. He thought the task was most formidable, because such races, as the Indians and Chinese, which had previously enjoyed a "high civilisation", were unwilling to abandon their racial traditions and modify their habits of life:

> The Hindu and the Chinaman are much less ready to accept new ideas, and much less susceptible to new ideas, and much less

ready to accept new modes at work, than races who have little organisation of their own, and who are willing to take their places as hewers of wood and drawers of water....But unless a people has some power of adapting itself, it must disappear before the march of progress.(188)

Cunningham asserted that the extension of the Church in the empire had frequently resulted in the checking of the nation's spiritual progress because of the "secular forms it assumed". Regrettably, Anglicanism had suffered from its close connection with the English Crown. If only it could become separated from the state, then "the powerful form of Christianity" could protect the natives from the excesses of Westernisation and increase the intellectual and moral qualities of subjected citizens.

Conclusion

Cunningham believed that imperialism was a true system of internationalism under which the great empire would secure peace and order.(189) Although he was concerned to guard the backward parts of the empire against the penetration of Western technology and exploitation, he wanted such regions to develop and become independent communities. In this regard, he was particularly critical of America's imperialistic activities:

> Mr Roosevelt and his supporters have thrown themselves heartily into the task of exercising authority over half-civilised and backward peoples, instead of leaving them to work out their own salvation for themselves, and have thus shown that they believe it is the duty of America to use her power for the good of the people subjected to her rule.(190)

Although Cunningham was sympathetic to Goldwin Smith's and Nicholson's position over the defence costs of the empire, he felt that imperial defence expenditures were justified, if only for the sake of extending British civilisation.(191) He believed that British people had a grave responsibility to spread the distinctive features and advantages of Western civilisation, and that the whole history of Great Britain - her civic pride and integrity - made her especially qualified to "take up the white man's burden among the uncivilised races of mankind". Given that Britain had great power over large areas of land and millions of people, "we are called upon not only to develop the material resources of the countries but to make the most of the people".(192) The empire, to Cunningham, afforded numerous opportunities for the fulfilment of the "human potential", whatever the financial costs, and he recommended that British workers and officials in various territories should acquire greater familiarity with native customs and traditions.(193)

NOTES

1.   For biographical details of Ashley see J H Clapham, "Obituary: Sir William Ashley", Economic Journal, Vol.37, December 1927, pp.678-684 and Anne Ashley, William James Ashley - A Life, (London, P S King and Son Ltd, 1932). Also see Koot The English Historical School of Economics, op.cit, pp.174-201.

2.   Anne Ashley, Ashley, op.cit, pp.1-39.

3.   Ibid, p.22.

4.   See Ashley Papers, Bodleian Library, Oxford, 1890-97, No.232 e641 (2), p.1.

5.   Ashley, Surveys: Historic and Economic, (first published 1900, New York, A M Kelley, 1966), p.428. See pp.429-31.

6.   See letter from Ashley to Brentano, 16/10/1890, in H W McCready, "Sir William James Ashley: Some Unpublished Letters", JEH, Vol.15, 1955, pp.34-43.

7.   Anne Ashley, Ashley, op.cit, p.19.

8.   Ibid, p.55. Also see Bernard Semmel, "Sir William Ashley as 'Socialist of the Chair'", Economica, November 1957, pp.343-353.

9.   Ibid, and Semmel, Imperialism and Social Reform, op.cit, Ch.11, pp.205-215.

10.   Schumpeter History of Economic Analysis, op.cit, pp.822-823.

11.   Ashley, Nine Lectures on the Earlier Constitutional History of Canada, (Toronto, Roswell and Hutchinson, 1889).

12.   Ibid. Schumpeter, History of Economic Analysis, op.cit, pp.803-805, 809-814; Also see Ashley, "Roscher's Programme of 1843", in Surveys, op.cit, p,p.31-37.

13.   Ashley, What is Political Science? (Toronto, Roswell and Hutinson, 1888).

14.   Ashley, The Economic Organisation of England; An Outline History, (London, Longmans, Green & Co, 1926), p.168.

15.   Anne Ashley, Ashley, op.cit, pp.35-38.

16.   Ashley, Nine Lectures on the Earlier Constitutional History of Canada, op.cit.

17.   Ashley, An Introduction to English Economic History and Theory, (London, Longmans, Green, Part I, 1888 Part II, 1893, 1902 edition).

18.   See Koot, English Historical School of Economics, op.cit, pp.186-190.

19.   Ashley, English Economic History and Theory, op.cit, Part 2, pp.379-470.

20.   On Cunningham and Hewins, see pp.193-195, Ch.9, pp.214-220.

21.   Ibid, p.371. Also see pp.3-9.

22.   Anne Ashley, Ashley, op.cit, p.50. Also see pp.193-195 and Ch.9, pp.214-220.

23.   Ashley, "A Survey of the Past History and Present Position of Political Economy", (1907) in R L Smythe (ed.), Essays in Economic Method, (London, Duckworth, 1962), pp.223-35.

24.   Anne Ashley, Ashley, op.cit, p.35.

25.   Ashley, "The Enlargement of Economics", EJ, June 1908, pp.188-189.

26.   Ashley, "The Rehabilitation of Ricardo", op.cit, p.489.

27.   Ashley to Brentano, in McCready, "Some Unpublished Letters", op.cit, p.43. Also Anne Ashley, Ashley, op.cit, pp.111-117, 126-129.

28.   Ashley, "On Social Study", reprinted from The Year Book of Social Progress, (London, 1912).

29.   Anne Ashley, Ashley, op.cit, pp.109-135.

30.   Ashley, "The Commercial Legislation of England and the American Colonies". (1899) in Surveys, op.cit, pp.313-333. See A Smith, Wealth of Nations, op.cit, Bk. 2, p.115; Arthur H Johnson in "Professor Ashley on the Commercial Legislation of England", EJ, Vol.10, March 1900, pp.96-103 maintains that Ashley attempted to prove too much. For Smith's position see the brief discussion in Ch.2, pp.10-13 and the accompanying references.

31.   Ashley, "The Commercial Legislation", op.cit, p.313. For a discussion of Smith and the Mercantilists, see A W Coats, "Adam Smith and the Mercantile System", in Skinner and Wilson (eds) Essays on Adam Smith, op.cit, pp.218-236.

32.   Ashley, "The Commercial Legislation", op.cit, pp.320-327.

33.   Ibid, p.328.

34.   Ibid, pp.332-3.

35.   Ashley, What is Political Science? op.cit, pp.11, 23.

36.   Ashley, "The Canadian Sugar Combine", (1889) in Surveys, op.cit, pp.361-77, especially p.372 and "The Tory Origin of Free Trade", QJE, July 1897, pp.335-9.

37.   Letter from Joseph Chamberlain to W J Ashley, 13/5/1903, cited in A W Coats, "Political Economy and Tariff Reform", op.cit, p.222.

38   shley to John Morely, 9/2/1904 in A W Coats, "Political Economy and Tariff Reform", op.cit, pp.222-223. Also see Ashley's letter to The Times, 11/2/1904.

39.   See Anne Ashley, Ashley, op.cit, pp.134-135; also see the letters between Ashley and Chamberlain, and Ashley and Garvin in J Amery, Joseph Chamberlain, Vol.5, op.cit, pp.289-292.

40.   Ashley, Political Economy and the Tariff Problem, (London, Macmillan, 1905), p.256.

41.   Ashley, The Tariff Problem, (London, P S King, 1st ed. September 1903, 2nd ed. December 1903, 3rd ed. 1911). All references are to the 3rd ed.

42.   Ibid, pp.25-46.

43.   Ibid, pp.25-46.

44.   Ibid, p.25.

45.   Ibid, pp.68-93.

46.   Also see Ashley's Preface to the British Trade Book, (London, John Murray, 1908).

47.   Ashley, The Tariff Problem, op.cit, p.104.

48.   Ibid, pp.74-77.

49.   Ibid, p.70. On the Tariff Reform League see Semmel, Imperialism and Social Reform, op.cit.

50.   Ashley, "Commercial Education" in National Education: A Symposium, (1901), pp.182-194, 184.

51.   Ashley, Tariff Problem, op.cit, pp.119-26, 140-52, 177-92.

52.   Anne Ashley, Ashley, op.cit, p.108.

53.   Ashley, Tariff Problem, op.cit, p.112.

54.   Ibid, pp.169-177, 187-188. Also see B H Brown, The Tarfiff Reform Movement in Great Britain, op.cit.

55.   Anne Ashley, Ashley, op.cit, pp.119-126.

56.   Ashley, The Adjustment of Wages: A Study in the Coal and Iron Industries of Great Britain and America, (London, Longmans, Green and Co, 1903) p.1.

57.   Ibid, p.3.

58.   Ibid, pp.3-12 and The Tariff Problem, op.cit, p,p.x-xiv, 139-60, 196-97.

59.   Quoted in Anne Ashley, Ashley, op.cit, p.127.

60.   Ashley, Tariff Problem, op.cit, pp.133-136.

61.   See Parl. Debate 129, Hansard 4th Series, 1904, 640 and Parl. Debate 130. Hansard 4th Series, 1904, 406-7. Also Coats, "Political Economy and Tariff Reform", op.cit, p.209.

62.   Ashley, The Progress of the German Working Classes in the Last Quarter of a Century, (London, Longmans, Green and Co, 1904), pp.140-141.

63.   Ibid, pp.5-7.

64.   Ibid, p.82.

65.   Ibid, p.81.

66.   Ibid, p.vii.

67.   See Semmel, Imperialism and Social Reform, op.cit, p.193.

68.   Ashley, "Political Economy and the Tariff Problem", op.cit, p.248.

69.   Ibid, pp.260-261. Also see his "The Argument for Preference" EJ, Vol.14, March 1904, pp.1-10.

70.   Ashley, "The Present Position of Political Economy", EJ, Vol.17, December 1907, pp.474-89.

71.   Ashley, The Tariff Problem, op.cit, 1911.

72.   For Marshall's views see Ch.6, pp.121-132, especially p.127.

73.   Ashley, The Adjustment of Wages, op.cit, p.3.

74.   Ashley (ed), British Dominions, (London, Longmans, Green & Co, 1911).

75.   Ibid, p.x.

76.   Semmel, Imperialism and Social Reform, op.cit, pp.209-210.

77.   See Ashley in Monthly Notes on Tariff Reform, Sept, 1907, VII, No.3, p.91.

78.   Semmel, Imperialism and Social Reform, op.cit, pp.209-10.

79.   Ashley, "Political Economy and Tariff Reform", op.cit, pp.248-91; The Adjustment of Wages, op.cit, pp.4-5.

80.   Ibid, p.5. On this point see Bodelsen, Studies in Mid-Victorian Imperialism, op.cit, pp.208-313.

81.   See Ashley (ed), British Dominions, op.cit, p.x.

82.   Ashley, Introduction to The Federalist by Alex Hamilton, (London, J M Dent, 1911), pp.18-19; Commercial Year Book of the Birmingham Chamber of Commerce, op.cit, p.19.

83. Ashley, The War and its Economic Prospects, (London, OUP, 1914), p.15.

84. Ashley, The Tariff Problem, op.cit, 3rd ed, 1911, p.ix.

85. Ashley, "Political Economy and the Tariff Problem", op.cit, p.263.

86. Semmel, Imperialism and Social Reform, op.cit, p.171.

87. Ashley, "Political Economy and the Tariff Problem", op.cit, p.264.

88. Ashley, "The Argument for Preference", op.cit, p.1.

89. Anne Ashley, Ashley, op.cit, p.109.

90. Ashley, The Progress of the German Working Class, op.cit, pp.140-141; The Tariff Problem, op.cit, pp.x-ix, 139-160, 196-197.

91. Ibid, The Progress of the German Working Class, op.cit, pp.140-141.

92. For biographical details of Cunningham see Audrey Cunningham, William Cunningham, Teacher and Priest, (London, Society for Promoting Christian Knowledge, 1950) and H S Foxwell, "Obituary: Archdeacon Cunningham", Economic Journal, XXIX, September 1919, pp.382-90.

93. See p.195.

94. W Cunningham, The Influence of Descartes Upon Metaphysical Sepculation in England, (London, Macmillan, 1876).

95. Cunningham, "Political Economy as a Moral Science", Mind, Vol.III, July 1878, pp.371-80. Also see G M Koot, English Historical School of Economics, op.cit, pp.278-309.

96. Cunningham, "Political Economy as a Moral Science", op.cit, p.380.

97. Quoted in N S B Grass, "The Present Condition of Economic History", QJE, 34, February 1920, p.211n.

98. Cunningham, The Growth of English Industry and Commerce, (Cambridge, CUP, 1882, 1st ed.; 2nd ed, 1892; 3rd ed, 1903; 4th ed, 1907; 5th ed, 1910; 6th ed, 1919).

99. Cunningham, "Unconscious Assumption in Economics", Section F of the British Association for the Advancement of Science, 1905, pp.466-472. Audrey Cunningham, Cunningham, op.cit, pp.38-41. Cunningham's impressions of India are recorded in The Cambridge Review, Vol.III, Nos. 60-64 as a series of letters written during February and March 1882.

100. Audrey Cunningham, William Cunningham, op.cit, pp.63-68.

101. Cunningham, Politics and Economics, (London, Kegan Paul, Trend & Co, 1885), p.4. Also see Christian Opinion on Usury, (Edinburgh, Macmillan, 1884).

102. Cunningham, Political Economy Treated as an Empirical Science, (Cambridge, Macmillan and Bowes, 1887), p.6.

103. He readily admitted that he was accurately described by J N Keynes as a member of the "extreme" German historical school. See Cunningham, "A Plea of Pure Theory", ER, Vol.2, January 1892, pp.25-41.

104. Cunningham "The Comtist - Criticism of Economic Science", Section F, British Association for the Advancement of Science 1889, pp.462-471. Also see "A Letter to the Clergy on the

Subject of Labour Organisations" in The Church and Trade Unions, (London, Sotheran, 1880), p.4.

105. Cunningham, "The Relativity of Economic Doctrine", EJ, Vol.2, March 1892, pp.1-16.

106. Cunningham "The Perversion of Economic History", EJ, September 1892, p.491. For a discussion of their disagreements, see John Maloney, "Marshall, Cunningham and the Emerging Economics Profession", EHR, 1976, pp.450-51.

107. Alfred Marshall, "A Reply" in EJ, September 1892, pp.507-519. Cunningham retained his aversion to Marshall's work in economic history as late as 1919. See Cunningham, Hints on the Study of Economic History, (London, Society for Promoting Christian Knowledge, 1919), p.27. Also see "Perversion of Economic History", The Academy, op.cit, p.288. The Progress of Capitalism in England, (Cambridge, CUP, 1912), pp.14-24. "Why had Roscher so Little Influence in England?" Annuals American Academy of Political and Social Science, 1894, pp.320-21.

108. Cunningham, The Progress of Capitalism in England, op.cit, pp.7-8, 12, 90-91. His rejection of the marginal utility approach found a sympathizer in J S Nicholson whose Principles Cunningham praised as being "the most complete treatise published in English in recent years". See Cunningham, British Citizens and their Responsibility to God, (London, Society for Promoting Christian Knowledge, 1916), p.43.

109. For an account of Cunningham's religious opinions see Koot, English Historical School of Economics, op.cit, pp.278-300.

110. Cunningham, "Religion and the Higher Education at Cambridge", The Nineteenth Century and After, 83, June 1918, p.1235; Christianity and Social Questions, (London, Duckworth, 1910), pp.20, 175-76; Making the Most of Life, (London, Society for Promoting Christian Knowledge, 1920), pp.27-30, 50-55; Christianity and Politics, op.cit, pp.15-25, 30-63.

111. See Audrey Cunningham, Cunningham, op.cit, pp.99-100. hortly before his death Cunningham embarked on a major review of aurice's writings, so as to inter ret Maurice for the public, Ibid, p.120.

112. Cunningham, Making the Most of Life, op.cit, pp.70-78; Christianity and Social Questions, op.cit, p.20; The Secret of Progress, (Cambridge, CUP, 1918), pp.3-4, 160-168.

113. Quoted in Audrey Cunningham, Cunningham, op.cit, p.50.

114. On T H Green see Melvin Richter, The Politics of Conscience: T H Green and His Age, (Cambridge, Mass, UP, 1964). See Cunningham's "The Duties of Citizenship", Cambridge Chronicle Weekly from 3/5/1916 to 7/6/1916.

115. Cunningham, Christianity and Economic Science, op.cit, pp.95-97; Politics and Economics, op.cit, pp.135-155; Christianity and Social Questions, op.cit, pp.48-54.

116. See for example, Ch.6, p.115-121; Ch.10, pp.241-250.

117. Cunningham, The Case Against Free Trade, (London, John Murray, 1911, 3rd ed) p.2.

118. Cunningham, English Influence on the United States, (Cambridge, CUP, 1916), p.157.

119. Cunningham, Industry and Commerce, 1882 ed, Appendix IV, pp.468-471.

120. Ibid, 1910 ed, p.884.

121. Cunningham, Christianity and Social Questions, op.cit, p.43,

122. Cunningham, Industry and Commerce, op.cit, pp.39, 323-27.

123. Ibid, p.882.

124. Ibid, p.883. English Influence on the United States, op.cit, pp.149-52. Also see Benjamin Kidd Social Evolution (London, Macmillan, 1896), pp.227-287.

125. Cunningham, Industry and Commerce, op.cit, p.885-886.

126. Cunningham, Socialism and Christianity, op.cit, p.24.

127. Cunningham, The common Weal: Six Lectures on Political Philosophy, (Cambridge, CUP, 1917), p.74.

128. Ibid, pp.74-76.

129. Cunningham, Industry and Commerce, op.cit, pp.858-862. On Wakefield's definition see Ghosh, Classical Political Economy and the Case for Colonies, op.cit, pp.7-9.

130. Cunningham, Industry and Commerce, op.cit, pp.850-864.

131. Cunningham, Hints on the Study of English Economic History, op.cit, pp.52-54.

132. Cunningham, Socialism and Christianity, op.cit, p.23.

133. Cunningham, The Growth of Industry and commerce, 1882 ed, p.201; 1910 ed, p.884; The Case Against Free Trade, op.cit, pp.1-3; An Essay on Western Civilisation in its Economic Aspects, (Cambridge, CUP, 1900). See Hewins Papers, op.cit, Boxes Mss 60-64, and Ch.9, pp.215; 220-223.

134. Cunningham, The Case Against Free Trade, op.cit, pp.3, 122, 136; English Influence on the United States, op.cit, pp.v-vii.

135. Cunningham, Hints on the Study of English Economic History, op.cit, p.53.

136. Ibid, also see pp.293-298.

137. Cunningham, An Essay on Western Civilisation in its Economic Aspects, op.cit, vol.I, pp.68-70, 175-194; Vol.II, pp.190, 204, 213-215.

138. For an outline of these changes see B. Semmel, Imperialism and Social Reform, op.cit, pp.188-201; G M Koot, English Historical School of Economics, op.cit, pp.297-308.

139. See Cunningham, "Nationalism and Cosmopolitanism in Economics", Section F of the British Association for the Advancement of Science, 1891, pp.723-34.

140. Cunningham, "The Failure of Free Traders to Attain Their Ideals", Section F of the British Association for the Advancement of Science, 1903, pp.759-51.

141. See Audrey Cunningham, Cunningham, op.cit.

142. Cunningham, Modern Civilisation in Some of its Economic Aspects, op.cit, p.29.

143. Cunningham, "English Imperialism" in The Atlantic Monthly, Vol. LXXXIV, July 1899, pp.1-7; "The Prospects of Universal Peace", Ibid, August 1899, pp.236-41; "Good Government of the Empire", Ibid, November 1899, pp.654-60.

144. Audrey Cunningham, Cunningham, op.cit, pp.96-103.

145. Cunningham, Richard Cobden and Adam Smith, op.cit, p.16. He also felt that to survive as a national power, Britain had to strengthen her business connections with the corn growing regions of the world. Cunningham, English Influence on the United States, op.cit, p.1; Case Against Free Trade, op.cit, pp.49-54' Christianity and Social Questions, op.cit, pp.168-9.

146. See Ch.3, pp.25-31 for a brief discussion on the manifesto.

147. Cunningham, The Progress of Capitalism in England, op.cit, p.13. Also see The Wisdom and the Wise, op.cit.

148. Cunnin ham, The Case Against Free Trade, op.cit, pp.72-3, 105, 118-30; Tariff Reform and Political Morality, op.cit, pp.304-5.

149. Cunningham, The Rise and Decline of the Free Trade Movement, (Cambridge, CUP, 1912 ed.). This book was the result of Cunningham's lectures delivered in Cambridge from October to December 1903. See Audrey Cunningham, Cunningham, op.cit, p.102.

150. Ibid, pp.104-122, 137-144.

151. Cunningham, The Case Against Free Trade, op.cit, p.50.

152. W Schlote, British Overseas Trade, op.cit, p.154.

153. Ibid, p.193.

154. See The Guardian, 23/11/1904.

155. Cunningham, Tariff Reform and Political Morality, op.cit, pp.321-22.

156. See Audrey Cunningham, Cunningham, op.cit, pp.98-100.

157. Ibid, pp.325-7. Also see The Common Weal : Six Lectures on Political Philosophy, (Cambridge, CUP, 1917), p.105

158. See Christianity and Social Questions, op.cit, p.90.

159. Cunningham, The Case Against Free Trade, op.cit, 1911 ed, p.53.

160. Ibid, pp.55-61.

161. Cunningham, The Case Against Free Trade, op.cit, pp.49-54, 72, 83.

162. Cunningham, Growth of Industry and Commerce, op.cit, 1910 ed, pp.869-70. On tariff reformers see Cambridge History of the British Empire, Vol.III, pp.401-3, 446-7; Semmel, Imperialism and Social Reform, op.cit, pp.83-97.

163. Cunningham, An Essay on Western Civilisation, op.cit, Vol.1, pp.6-7, 175-94, Vol.2, pp.190-204-225. The Case Against Free Trade, op.cit, p.82; English Influence on the United States, op.cit, pp.138-150.

164. Cunningham, The Case Against Free Trade, op.cit, p.82.

165. Cunningham, Socialism and Christianity, op.cit, p.25.

166. Cunningham, Christianity and Social Questions, op.cit, pp.71, 262.

167. See Cambridge History of the British Empire, op.cit, Vol.III, pp.177-8, and Edwin Burgess, Perils to British Trade, (London, Swan Sonnenschien, 1895), and M H Herby, The Trade Policy of Imperial Federation, (London, Swan Sonnenschien, 1892).

168. Cunningham, Christianity and Social Questions, op.cit, p.21. See Chapter 2, "Racial Differences", pp.21-45.

169. Cunningham, The Secret of Progress, op.cit, p.11. Also

see Kidd, Social Evolution, op.cit, Karl Pearson, Darwinism, Medical Progress and Eugenics, (London, University of London, 1912) and The Chances of Death and Other Studies in Evolution, (London, E Arnold, 1897).

170. Ibid. Also see Making the Most of Life, op.cit, pp.98-9; Christianity and Social Questions, op.cit, pp.21-40.

171. Cunningham, Christianity and Politics, op.cit, p.1, and Modern Civilisation in its Economic Aspects, op.cit, p.8.

172. Cunningham, The Secret of Progress, op.cit, and Audrey Cunningham, Cunningham, op.cit, pp.124-126.

173. Cunningham, Industry and Commerce, op.cit, p.881.

174. For a discussion of these commentators see Porter, Critics of Empire, op.cit, especially Ch.6, "The New Radicals", pp.156-206.

175. Cunningham, An Essay on Western Civilisation in its Economic Aspects, op.cit, p.262.

176. Ibid, p.267.

177. Cunningham, Tariff Reform and Political Morality, op.cit, pp.325-7; Case Against Free Trade, op.cit, pp.3-5.

178. Cunningham, Making the Most of Life, op.cit, p.92; also see pp.89-99.

179. Cunningham, Christianity and Social Questions, op.cit, p.45.

180. Cunningham, The Case Against Free Trade, op.cit, pp.135-136.

181. Ibid, p.3. On this point see Porter, Critics of Empire, op.cit, pp.156-90.

182. Cunningham, Christian Civilisation with Special Reference to India, (London, Macmillan 1880) p.119. Also see The Moral Witness of the Church on the Investment of Money and the Use of Wealth, (Cambridge, CUP, 1909) pp.39-41.

183. Cunningham, Christianity and Social Questions, op.cit, p.43.

184. Cunningham, Making the Most of Life, op.cit, p.99; Western Civilisation in its Economic Aspects, op.cit, pp.260-76.

185. Cunningham, British Citizens and Their Responsibility to God, (London Society for Promoting Christian Knowledge, 1916), p.8.

186. Cunningham, Christianity and Social Questions, op.cit, p.44; The Cure of Souls, op.cit, pp.121-133; Christian Civilisation with Special Reference to India, op.cit.

187. Ibid, p.120. In his 1882 tour of India, Cunningham had become most aware of the problems confronting missionaries and his views were often critical. "There can be no doubt that if other agencies are as powerful in overthrowing ancient institutions and habits, missionary effort is the most actively destructive force, and I have met more than one missionary who seemed to think that destruction was worth doing for its own sake". See his letter "From Delhi", Cambridge Review, 15/3/1882, pp.238-39.

188. Cunningham, Christianity and Social Questions, op.cit, pp.28-29.

189. Cunningham, Case Against Free Trade, op.cit, pp.4, 10, 15-17.

190. Cunningham, English Influence on the United States, op.cit, p.164.

191. Cunningham, Case Against Free Trade, op.cit, p.14.
192. Cunningham, Case Against Free Trade, op.cit, p.4.
193. Cunningham, Making the Most of Life, op.cit, p.45.

Chapter 9

W A S HEWINS : THE SELF-ACCLAIMED IMPERIALIST

INTRODUCTION

The greater part of Hewins' life was committed to reform, and as an educator, public commissioner and politician he sought to improve society.(1) The son of a middle-class Midlands metal merchant, Hewins considered himself one of England's foremost "radical and historical economists".(2) His first interest in economics was derived from the adverse impact of the 1870s downturn in trade and industry on his family's metal business. From an early stage in his reading of theoretical economics, Hewins rejected the accepted traditions and methodology of classical political economy:

> My practical interest in economic questions began with the depression of trade in the late seventies and the early eighties. This involved great hardships and I wanted to know the reason. From that time until I went to Oxford I read many economic books, but they did not help me. I disliked their theoretical outlook, their materialism leavened with sentiment and their remoteness from real events as I saw them in South Staffordshire. The 'economic man' made no appeal to me. There was little correspondence between the industrial system of the economic text-books and the industry that was being carried on around me and the men and women actually engaged in it.(3)

As a student at Lincoln College, Oxford, Hewins found the inspiration he wanted in the writings of Kingsley, Ruskin and Carlyle. Although he took mathematics in his finals, Hewins was most active in social science circles and he started the Social Science Club, the object of which was to find a solution to social difficulties by practical investigation. Upon graduating as a mathematician he decided upon economics as a career, and sought the advice of J E T Rogers who attempted to discourage him, so he decided to study history under Sir Charles Firth. In order to earn a living, he - like Ashley, Cunningham, and Hobson - taught as a University Extension Lecturer and wrote biographies for the Dictionary of National Biography.(4) In his autobiography, Apologia of an Imperialist, Hewins claimed that such research had "destroyed for ever in my mind the illusion that Adam smith and his successors represented the only English economic tradition".(5) Associating himself with economic historians, he cited Ricardo as the villain of English economic thought.(6) His biographical and economic study of English mercantilists - Malynes, Misselden, Mun, Newarck - suggested that their inductive and pragmatic approach was a superior model for British economics to follow than the abstractions of the classical school.(7)

During his early career as an extension lecturer, Hewins became more critical of economic orthodoxy:

> I did not think that political economy as then taught was particularly useful except as some sort of guide in the theoretical relations between the different branches of activity which formed the subject matter of economic investigation. Hasty generalisations had been made from presumed facts, not accurately observed or recorded and relating to one particular phase of social development. These pseudo-laws were extended in their application to nearly all social phenomena, and the 'economic man', a pure abstraction, was substituted for man as he actually is with all his social relations... We had to consider all the influences which bear on man in the economic, social, ethical, religious spheres. No sphere of human activity could be excluded, and we must widen the range of observation, and the first step in placing political economy in its right position was to describe accurately the structure and organisation of the society in which we lived, its great industries, its commercial enterprise and its international relations, and explain in order the steps by which we had reached that condition.(8)

Hewins attempted to invoke this approach in his first major published work, English Trade and Finance, (1892), which contained a reasoned defence of mercantilism as a policy appropriate to its stage of production.(9) To him mercantilism was a useful economic science and he asserted that Germany's industrial success was achieved by imitating Britain's earlier mercantilist policies. Like Ashley and Cunningham, he argued that under mercantilism, private interests were subordinated to public needs.(10) Mercantilism was wise national policy; it guaranteed the State's defence, provided plentiful food supplies and secured employment.(11) Towards the close of his life, Hewins advocated that the United Kingdom should return to mercantilism's central purpose, namely "the creation of an industrial and commercial state in which by encouragement and restraint imposed by the sovereign authority, private and sectional interests should be made to promote national strength and efficiency".(12)

Along with his extensive lecturing commitments for the

Extension Service and membership of Oxford's Economic Society, English Trade and Finance increased Hewins' academic standing amongst fellow dissenters.(13) He was briefly associated with Booth's survey of London's poor and he attempted to establish Toynbee Hall as a centre for historical economics, but failed.

After unsuccessfully contesting academic posts in London and Oxford, Hewins was appointed the first director of the London School of Economics. Sidney Webb had enlisted municipal support from the London County Council and with a bequest from another Fabian, Henry Hutchinson, established the LSE.(14) Hewins and Webb hoped to use the School to create an alternative economic tradition to that of Ricardo and Marshall.(15) Beatrice Webb noted that despite Hewins' political outlook being different from their own, as it sprang from "an instructive sympathy with medievalism", they agreed in their

> common dislike of the so-called Manchester School, of its unverified deductive reasoning and abstract generalisations, of its apotheosis of "the economic man", exclusively inspired by the motive of pecuniary self-interest, and of its passionate defence of the rights of property as against the needs of humanity. And, our common faith in the practicability and urgent necessity of a concrete science of society implemented through historical, personal observation and statistical verification.(16)

Hewins publicity of the LSE and advocacy of the historical method brought him into polite disagreement with Alfred Marshall, the leading professional economist of the time. Before the establishment of the LSE the two had corresponded, Marshall expressing an interest in Hewins' work.(17) However, Hewins' efforts, on behalf of the LSE, were extremely critical of Marshall's views, and Marshall requested him not to advertise the LSE by attacking Cambridge.(18) Whilst Hewins' letters to Marshall have not survived, rough drafts of his letters and notes are to be found in the Hewins Papers. These reveal a restraint and respect for the elder economist. By contrast, in a letter to Sidney Webb in 1898, Hewins enthusiastically noted their success in establishing a rival centre to Marshall's Cambridge for economics, and that "we seem to be getting a firm hold on the younger men".(19)

Although Hewins was not personally critical of Marshall's economics, he detested the deductive science and objected to the Ricardian economic tradition as it had neglected "the social needs of the nation". Ricardo was the root of both socialistic and Manchester economics.(20) He observed that "fundamentally all economics in England, with the exception of the historical school, are derived from the Ricardian system and under the pressure of modern developments tend to become more and more socialistic".(21)

To Hewins, only the historical method offered a viable

alternative to socialism. In an unpublished paper on methodology, Hewins elaborated his ideas on "the historical method", claiming it was "the only possible one for social science".(22)

> History alone can supply data for the investigation of the laws of wealth. Let us go to society and see what society had done in the past, and not try to compute its character from the character of its parts. Man is not the mere puppet of physical forces; he has a mind to control them: he is on a higher level. A mere physical organism has no knowledge of the type to which it is tending. Society can choose the type to which it shall conform and smooth the difficulties in the way.(23)

Hewins' paper began by considering the current state of political economy and enquired into why it had fallen into disrepute. He offered four reasons for the subjects' unpopularity: (i) the inexact reasoning and personal opinions which had obscured the economists' judgements; (ii) the inadequate and abstract methods of the Ricardian school; (iii) the attempt to give universal application to principles which had been deduced from assumptions out of correspondence with the real facts of life; (iv) the undue application of certain principles which had some validity for specific periods eg, the Malthusian law of population.

In notes at the end of the paper, Hewins made the following general remarks on the historical method which he attempted to employ throughout his written work and lectures:

> (1) Political economy in the past had made hasty generalisations from facts observed in one particular phase of society. (The Physiocrats, chief of whom is Quesnai (sic), were the first to make any attempt to perceive law in production and distribution of wealth, at the end of the eighteenth century).
> (2) These pseudo-laws of a merely mercantile economy were extended in their application to nearly all social phenomena and the "economic man", a Ricardian abstraction, was mistaken for man as he is with all his social relations.
> (3) These Ricardian laws are probably approximately true under certain conditions, but are no longer true when the conditions are changed.
> (4) But assuming their universal truth, the economists attempted a prevision of occurrences : in considering any measure, they would say "You must not do this : it is contrary to the law of supply and demand, to the law of the increase of capital, etc etc".
> (5) This prevision is outside the domain of political economy because you will have in the problem the unknown factor of human will, and what particular course this will take in certain assigned conditions cannot be ascertained with sufficient accuracy.

Political economists have gone wrong, then:

(a) In taking as their man a wretchedly maimed creature stripped of all his finest attributes.
(b) In limiting their observations to a short space of time and a narrow range of facts.
(c) In attempting this prevision.
Correct (a) by considering all the influences which bear on man in pursuit of wealth, social, ethical, religious, physiological and what not.
(b) Widen the range of observation, so that our generalisations shall be more true to the facts of human life, eg it is wrong to say that the tendency of population to increase beyond the means of subsistence is accountable for the present condition of the working classes. There have been many other reasons, eg The Statute of Labourers and similar legal enactments, the debasement of the currency, and confiscation of the Guild land by Henry VIII etc. There is, besides this, in all probability, a different law of population for every age, as Karl Marx says.
(c) Political economy must only explain the steps by which we have got to the present economical condition. It can only offer suggestions in dealing with the future, and must be supplemented by ethics and the like.

The sociological and the historical methods can go side by side, indeed must do so, because society is a physical organism and man is a physical organism, but they are both something more than this.(24)

As the director of the LSE, Hewins increased his contacts with the German historical school, and optimistically commented that "the transference of the 'centre of force' in economics from Germany to London is by no means impossible".(25) In 1899, Schmoller invited Hewins to write an article for his Jahrbuch on Britain's foreign trade. Hewins consented and wrote "Imperialism and its probable effects on the Commercial Policy of the United Kingdom" towards the end of 1899, and revised the article the following year.(26) Hewins' article is an extremely significant one, not only because of his distinction between three groups of imperialists, but also because it embodied his first concise statement of what he considered to be involved in a comprehensive imperial policy for the British empire. He contended that there were three important groups of imperialists which could be isolated from within conservative and liberal supporters (i) laissez-faire; (ii) political; and (iii) constructive imperialists.(27) Hewins firmly aligned himself with the third group, the constructive imperialists.

He pointed out that the laissez-faire imperialists had argued for the free development of the colonies, the granting of self-government and complete autonomy in financial policy. Whilst their party had achieved permanent results, if the policy was pursued, it would lead to the "disintegration of the Empire into a number of separate English-speaking States whose interests must inevitably clash in different parts of the world".(28) In contrast to the laissez-faire imperialists, the political imperialists viewed free trade not as an article of faith, but as a matter of expediency, which was dependent for its success on the existence of economic and political conditions which were not universally achieved. Since they confined their imperialism to political questions (eg imperial federation) their imperial policy was divorced from "an industrial, commercial and educational policy" and was "doomed to failure".(29) A purely political imperialism provided no security against the adoption of measures which would alienate the colonies by injuring their trade. Hewins predicted that the political imperialists would split into two parties, the laissez-faire imperialists and the "constructive imperialists".

> By "constructive imperialism" I mean the deliberate adoption of the Empire as distinguished from the United Kingdom as the basis of public policy, and in particular, the substitution in our economic policy of imperial interests for the interest of the consumer, those interests being measured, not necessarily by the immediate or even the ultimate gain of a purely economic character arising from a particular line of policy, but by the greater political or social stability, or the greater defensive power of the empire. But while imperialists of this school must undoubtedly contemplate the possibility of temporary economic loss as a consequence of their policy, they would look for a great increase of the wealth and productive power of the empire from the establishment of even closer commercial relations between the mother country and the colonies.(30)

To Hewins, Britain's naval power had been the essential condition for the empire's creation, and it had to remain "the principal guarantee of its permanence". Since an effective naval policy depended on the possession of great resources and the willingness of Parliament to spend money, it therefore involved:

> .... a financial and a commercial policy. But it involves far more. Steps must be taken for securing and maintaining the highest possible efficiency of the trades subsidiary to a modern navy, particularly the iron and steel industry in all its forms and the coal trade. The efficiency of these trades is not only closely bound up with the financial and commercial policy of the country but obviously requires drastic reform of the educational system of the country, particularly in relation to technical, professional and administrative education, and the further organisation of the methods of State regulation of the conditions of labour. Briefly we may say that a policy of constructive imperialism involves (i) an adequate scheme of imperial defence, naval and military; (ii) the determination of the conditions on which the colonies are to have a voice in

imperial affairs, and the provision of the machinery necessary to enable them to exercise the privilege; (iii) measures for promoting the commercial union of the United Kingdom and its colonies and dependencies; (he reorganisation of the system of public finance; (v) a transport policy; (vi) educational reform; (vii) a social and labour policy, particularly the State regulation of labour.(31)

Hewins' policy of constructive imperialism, once formulated, remained with him throughout his life-time.(32) Furthermore, he realised that while a comprehensive policy of imperialism involved "free trade within the empire", it could only be achieved by gradual stages and the co-operation of the self-governing colonies. Hewins' article was written during his directorship of the LSE, but his enthusiasm for the empire antedated that appointment.

> My enthusiasm for the British Empire was really born in the traditions of a district with which my family had been connected for many centuries, I mean the Vale of Evesham in the North Cotswolds. I had never visited it until 1888. Members of our family had gone from there in every generation since the days of Elizabeth to all parts of the British Empire.(33)

ALWAYS A PROTECTIONIST?

In contrast to Ashley and Cunningham, Hewins underwent no discernable conversion to protectionism.(34) Early in his academic career he undertook a close and systematic study of the leading mercantilist writers which, coupled with the failure of his father's metal business, exerted considerable influence on his protectionist beliefs.(35) He subsequently argued on historical grounds that mercantilism was a policy most appropriate to Britain's stage of development in the early twentieth century.(36)

Hewins claimed that he had undertaken a comprehensive review of free trade theory, but he merely noted that the classical assumptions of free mobility of labour and capital were no longer applicable to discussions on free trade and he unduly concentrated upon the proposition that free imports were a guarantee for cheapness.(37) He disputed the contention that the abolition of the corn laws reduced the price of English corn, mainly on the grounds that it was higher than in many countries.(38) Like Ashley and Cunningham, Hewins claimed that technical changes were primarily responsible for lower food prices throughout the United Kingdom:

> What made corn cheap in England was that the United States and other countries were opened up with roads and railways; machinery of all kinds was invented which made the cultivation of their land possible and profitable; and great ocean-going steamships were constructed which enabled them to send us the corn we wanted cheaply.(39)

Hewins approved of the corn laws, claiming that they formed but one of a variety of measures which were adopted to promote the growth of agriculture. He failed to specify any other measures, such as enclosures and technical changes, which had assisted the growth of agricultural productivity in the early nineteenth century. In this context he stressed the adverse effects of "the free trade policy in agriculture", which had driven thousands of people off the land into the cities, causing widespread congestion and the moral and physical deterioration of urban life.(40) He argued that free trade was the result of British development and not the cause: "Free trade as a policy, after 60 years of trial, has proved to be fatal to the continuance of British industrial supremacy and fatal to the maintenance of the Empire".(41)

Hewins asserted that a major adverse long-term effect of the repeal of the corn laws was that overseas producers flooded the British market with grain. He argued that the nation's food bill represented an economic loss from the circular flow of income and that the increased expenditure on imports injected more purchasing power into other countries, some of which were Britain's competitors. He ignored these countries' capacity to buy and the stimulus this afforded to the manufacturing sectors. He wanted a tax on foreign food which would increase food prices within the United Kingdom, and would be compensated for by an increase in wages.(42) He ignored the possibility that the stimulus to home production (resulting from import duties and the consequent rise in prices) might actually bring down prices, depending on the elasticity of supply.

Hewins' opposition to free trade was not based solely on a denial of the supposed benefits of the repeal of the corn laws. He firmly embraced protectionism in 1888 as a positive measure to combat foreign competition which he believed posed an increasing threat to British supremacy.(43) Through his extensive lecturing commitments for the Oxford University Extension Service he became increasingly aware of the impact of foreign competition on employment patterns in the industrial Midlands, where he spent a great deal of his lecturing time.(44) Throughout his publications, speeches and correspondence, he repeatedly referred to the effects of foreign competition on the structure of British industry, home employment and world leadership.(45) His systematic case studies of selected industries confirmed his opinions.(46) He was dismayed at the sudden decline and stagnation of numerous great industries, which had taken centuries to evolve and he even argued that it was better to maintain the iron trade at a financial loss than to allow the industry to be driven out of existence (with the subsequent loss of employment) as such an industry was a basic requirement of any strong nation.(47) Unfortunately, Hewins did not pursue this interesting comment. Britain had exported its goods and knowledge to so many parts of the globe, that now it faced the consequences of this policy.

We have in fact given away our trade and technical knowledge in the most reckless fashion, just as we have taught other nations how to compete with us, and they are now taking the trade right out of our hands; we have in fact put into their hands guns with which to shoot at us.(48)

Hewins certainly recognised the role that imported technology played in the growth of developing countries, although he believed that it contributed to Britain's industrial decline. "Our trade is passing from our hands into the hands of numerous other peoples".(49) The remedy to this situation was to introduce protection for the manufacturing sector, and so return to "sanity". It must not be thought that he viewed the adoption of tariffs by other nations as a "ridiculous policy"; quite the contrary. The high tariffs of other countries were the 'reflex' of Britain's one-sided free trade policy. In electing to establish tariffs, other nations entered a "perfectly natural course of development", for Britain's industrial strength had evolved under the Navigation Acts and the restrictions of mercantilism. He accepted List's argument and considered tariffs to be appropriate to various stages in a nation's development.(50)

Hewins asserted that he was the first economist to convert J S Mill's infant industry argument to cover the United Kingdom's declining industries, for he turned Mill's infant industry case into an argument of protection for Britain's 'senile' industries.

By protection in the modern sense is meant the use by the Government of special forms of regulation or restraint, particularly import duties and analogous fiscal expedients, in order to encourage or to maintain essential industries which must be determined by the requirements of public policy.(51)

Hewins stressed that in a protectionist policy political objectives could be of overriding importance, with economic forces secondary. In contrast to Marshall, he argued that the net economic welfare effects would be greater with protection than free trade, for "the protectionist policy, properly administered, will bring about a balance of economic activity, involving a higher maximum of efficiency to the community as a whole and a more equitable distribution between the economic groups".(52)

Though it could be argued that Hewins unintentionally touched upon a 'theory of protection' this was not his purpose. He wanted to keep Britain strong, and argued that the main justification for tariffs was to be found in the socio-economic and political conditions which governed the development of various stages, though he gave no specific examples to directly support this contention:

The actual policies of countries are the expressions of the living activities of great societies as they have been determined by their history and the powers and functions which they have developed, and they never follow the lines of an abstract theory divorced from the facts of development.(53)

Hewins strongly believed that it was necessary to impose tariffs to revive British industry and to consolidate the empire, and felt that they would secure the virtual monopoly of the home market, even if they did not restore British world monopoly:

> The British monopoly is destroyed forever; henceforth the United Kingdom will be, at best, one amongst a group of countries all carrying on production by machinery, whose wealth and progress will depend on the abundance of their natural resources, the scientific skill with which they can use them, the wisdom of their policy and the efficiency of their organisation.(54)

THE 'ANONYMOUS ECONOMIST' AND THE 1903 FISCAL CONTROVERSY

Between June and September 1903, Hewins published a series of articles on the fiscal controversy for The Times signing them as "An Economist".(55) Hewins adopted this anonymous title because of his "delicate" position as the first director of the London School of Economics.(56) The Fabians were seriously divided on the issue of tariff reform and since Sidney Webb feared that Hewins' active participation in public debate could embarrass the School, Hewins signed the articles, "An Economist". Hewins' anonymity aroused a considerable degree of curiosity, and Marshall was pleased to report to Bretano his discovery of "An Economist".(57)

Hewins' disagreement with the Webbs over imperial issues surfaced at the Co-efficients Club, which was organised by the Webbs in November 1902. The co-efficients were a small coalition of Liberal imperialists and progressive unionists selected by the Webbs to spread their Fabian ideas.(58) The original members besides the Webbs and Hewins were R B Haldane (the liberal imperialist barrister), Sir Edward Gray, H J Mackinder (Reader in Geography at Oxford), Clinton Dawkins, Bertrand Russell, Leo Maxse, Pember Reevers, Leo Amery, and H G Wells. J L Garvin joined shortly afterwards.(59) Hewins was the chief advocate of preference within the empire and at the third meeting of the club, he launched a full-scale debate on preferential tariffs. Apart from Amery and Maxse, no-one else "genuinely supported" Hewins' views, though Garvin and Mackiner were sympathetic to his arguments.(60)

Amery, a Fellow of All Souls and a correspondent for The Times, persuaded Hewins to write a series of articles on tariff reform. A meeting was arranged with Chamberlain on 12th June 1903, and after discussing the rift inside the Cabinet and the fiscal question, Chamberlain stated "But, I do not pretend to be an economic expert. I once read Mill and tried to read Marshall. You must supply the economic arguments".(61) Hewins agreed, and on 15th of June the first in his series of articles appeared. Originally six articles were planned, but these developed into seventeen and spanned four months. The articles surveyed the growth of British supremacy, the corn laws, the free trade movement, the rise of foreign competition and the wisdom of an imperial policy.(62)

The Times wanted the leading academic economist of the day, Alfred Marshall, to enter into public correspondence with Hewins over the question, but he refused.(63) During this period, Hewins was exceptionally busy and he did not revise one of The Times' articles, nor read a proof version of any. He sent Chamberlain a weekly report on the progress of the controversy and wrote regularly for the Saturday and Fortnightly Review, and the Morning Post.(64)

In his numerous newspaper publications, Hewins aligned himself with the leader of the tariff reform movement, Joseph Chamberlain, whom he had admired for some years. Their association had begun in 1900 when Hewins wrote to Chamberlain concerning the course of Britain's imperial policy, but it began in earnest after Hewins publicly, though anonymously, declared his support for Chamberlain's proposals. Throughout the latter half of 1903, Chamberlain frequently sought Hewins' advice on questions of economic theory and tariff reform proposals. Their long and frequent correspondence was invariably concerned with the progress of the tariff reform campaign, the most effective way of changing the free trade system, colonial developments towards imperial preference, and the implications of the adoption of preferential tariffs by Britain.(65) Chamberlain also arranged for Hewins to provide him with a weekly digest of his opponents' speeches together with suggested replies.(66)

Finally, the establishment of the Tariff Commission in the closing months of 1903 deserves our attention. Hewins appreciated Chamberlain's fears that government departments were unprepared for the framing of tariffs, and with the possibility of obstruction in the House of Commons to inadequately formulated tariff legislation, the achievement of tariff reform could be lost.(67) In November Hewins stated his reservations to Sir Cyril Pearson and Sir Vincent Caillard and stressed that tariffs could not be hastily established. On November 4th, after a long meeting with Pearson who outlined Hewins' concerns, Chamberlain decided to establish an official Tariff Commission. The following day, Pearson invited Hewins, on Chamberlain's behalf, to become the Secretary of the Commission.(68) Hewins accepted and drafted his own terms of reference, which were accepted without any important modifications by Chamberlain:

It should be clearly understood that the aim of the Committee is to work out in detail the first draft of a practicable scheme.

The outline already submitted to the country by Mr Chamberlain should be taken as the basis of the inquiry. This supplies perfectly definite points upon which the various trades can be consulted.

Invitations to serve on the Committee should, if possible, be signed by Mr Chamberlain, or at any rate issued in his name.

The Committee would be far too large if it included representatives of all of the important trades. But it should be as far as possible National, or rather Imperial in character.

It is of the greatest importance that representatives of Colonial interests should be included.

The inquiry should proceed by trades, not by commodities.

The trades should be grouped as far as possible in the order of their organisation; schedules of the commodities which will be affected should be worked out for each complete group; and the effect, cumulative and in detail, of the suggested duties can be examined.

All trades, if possible, should be examined.

Much relevant information which must be abstracted and considered by the Committee is contained in British and foreign official reports, economic works, trade journals and reports.

Evidence must further be obtained by the issue of properly constructed forms of inquiry.

The construction of such forms involves some preliminary examination of the trade and interest concerned and consultation with experts.

In this connection it is of the greatest importance that all the members of the Committee should be acquainted with the technical features of different trades and businesses.

Wherever there is a trade organisation it should be consulted and its co-operation invited.

Witnesses should represent such authoritative organisations and typical firms.

On certain points valuable evidence can be given by trade unions, co-operative societies, etc.

Evidence should be obtained both for and against the proposed policy.(69)

Chamberlain's critics charged that the Commission was nothing but a lobby for protectionists and that it included all the nation's leading opponents of free trade. In response, Hewins claimed that the Commission was impartial and that the issue of free trade versus protection was never raised at meetings. "We devoted ourselves solely to obtaining information as to what were the conditions under which firms had to carry on their trade".(70) Under Hewins guidance till 1910, when he resigned to enter Parliament, the Commission produced 13 volumes of reprints, 47 memoranda on industries and undertook a detailed investigation of the agricultural sector.(71)

TARIFF REFORM 1903-1914

Once he became publicly involved in the campaign for tariff reform, Hewins never retreated from his stance and worked until his death for the implementation of an imperial policy throughout the empire. He was convinced that a system of imperial preference was the means whereby the empire could be consolidated.(72) It was the centrepiece of his inadequately formulated imperial policy, which was too ambitious and too general to be acceptable to either the British public or the colonists. Essentially, it involved imperial defence arrangements, some unspecified colonial share in imperial defence, a commercial union, and a social and labour policy - effectively all the aspects he outlined in his "Imperialism and its probable effects on the Commercial Policy of the United Kingdom".(73)

As with Joseph Chamberlain, imperial preference was to be the provider and maintainer of this imperial policy. But amazingly Hewins wrote little on the nature and form of imperial preference. Nevertheless, some indication of his ideas emerged after his trip to Canada in 1905 which brought home to him the close relationship between the tariff policy of a member of the empire (Canada), the constitutional issues involved and the significance of treaty negotiations.(74) It also revealed on what principles and within what limits the tariff preferences should be arranged. However, he failed to outline these principles clearly, simply noting three general points: (i) There was a great deal of mutual trade between Great Britain and Canada which would be unaffected by preferential tariffs; (ii) there was a grave need to militarily defend the various parts of the empire, and revenue was urgently required for this purpose; (iii) each part of the empire had a natural and 'inherent' right to preserve such trade as was necessary for complete development of its resources.(75) Beyond this, Hewins merely noted that the implementation of preferential arrangements would not be difficult, since no part of the empire 'could at present live by itself'. The colonies had initiated schemes of imperial preference, and it was now up to the mother country to respond.(76) Like Ashley and Cunningham, Hewins did not explain his imperial preference scheme in detail as he was concerned more with winning acceptances for the general ideas than with particular proposals.(77)

Once Hewins and Chamberlain were allied in the common cause of tariff reform, they never separated and were in constant and frequent communication till the latter's death in 1914. Hewins saw a great deal of Chamberlain during the year following the latter's heart attack and in July, Chamberlain confessed to Hewins, "I am a wreck".(78) Hewins also became an adviser to Chamberlain's son, Austen, and in 1913 along with Selbourne, Wyndham, Ridley, Amery and Lloyd George, dined with Austen to consider the future of the Tariff Reform League.(79)

In addition to his extensive correspondence with Chamberlain, Hewins' expertise on trade policy was increasingly sought by A J Balfour, especially after 1903. From the commencement of the campaign in May 1903 to the end of 1904, Balfour was constantly engaged in "subtle dialectics", so as to maintain fiscal views which could be interpreted in numerous ways by the factions within his own party.(80) In the latter half of 1906, Balfour saw a great deal of Hewins and took a "new and unexpected interest in the work of the Tariff Commission".(81) As Amery suggests, Hewins' account of their talks certainly suggests that Balfour's earlier differences with the tariff reformers (which Hewins had noted in 1903-4) sprang more from fear of Chamberlain's personality and methods than from any question of policy.(82) Hewins' correspondence with Balfour reveals the latter's keen interest in imperial questions and willingness to consider Hewins' economic and political arguments on "fiscal issues" and related questions of tariff reform.(83)

By January 1907 there was mounting pressure within the Unionist Party from Chamberlainites such as Leo Amery, Bonar Law, J L Garvin and Leo Maxse, for Balfour to make a firm stand in favour of tariff and social reform.(84) The party wanted a statement on tariff reform which would refer sympathetically to closer union with the colonies as well as acknowledgement that social reform would only be paid for by finding new sources of revenue. Balfour did not weaken to the internal pressures of his party, but to the "urbane and flexible influences of Professor Hewins, whom he was consulting at this time".(85) On 11th February, Hewins supplied Balfour with a definition of tariff reform which he could unreservedly accept:

> I should define the new policy as the deliberate adoption of the Empire as distinguished from the United Kingdom as the basis of public policy, and, in particular, the substitution in our economic policy of Imperial interests for the interests of the consumer, those interests being measured not necessarily by the immediate or even the ultimate gain of a purely economic character arising from a particular line of policy, but by the greater political or social stability, or greater defensive power,

of the Empire.(86)

In the letter Hewins specifically advocated freer reciprocal trade within the Empire and ruled out the possibility of an imperial council or an imperial zollverein. He also demonstrated that nationalism in the self-governing colonies, eg Canada, was so strong that it would be impossible to establish an imperial council or a formula for contributions to imperial defence. Finally, Hewins discussed the position that food taxes could be avoided in preferential arrangements, arguing that the corn duty was "the most powerful engine for securing preference". Given that the colonial supply was "unlimited", a duty on foreign corn would not raise the price to the British consumer. He contended that politically direct taxation could not be increased so as to yield large revenue increases, whereas indirect taxes could. He produced figures which showed that there was latitude for increasing the ratio of indirect to direct taxes.(87)

Several of these authoritative arguments were produced by Balfour nine days later in the House of Commons, and although he made no precise statement on the issue of food taxes, he insisted that Britain had to abandon the notion of either an imperial council or an imperial zollverein.(88) Britain had to acknowledge that the self-governing colonies had proposed imperial preference, as well as the difficulties in uniting the separate self-governing colonies for the benefit of themselves and the United Kingdom.(89)

On another occasion Balfour also accepted Hewins' suggestion that tariff rates might be fixed at 0%, 2 1/2% 5% 7 1/2%, 10% ad valorem, and that every article should be placed in one of these groups.(90) The following year, in 1908, Hewins wrote to Balfour confidentially arguing that it appeared as if the United States was about to adopt a maximum/minimum system of tariffs in place of a single general tariff, which was also under consideration.(91) Hewins thought that the effects of this action would be as follows: (i) the United States would attempt to 'bluff' the United Kingdom by saying that if Britain adopted a preference policy then it could be discriminatory and they would have the right to introduce the maximum tariff; (ii) the United States would be in an excellent bargaining position with Canada which would consequently give the United States most-favoured-nation treatment. Once again, Balfour uncritically accepted Hewins' arguments and advice.(92) Furthermore, Balfour frequently wanted to speak to Hewins about the subject matter before the Political Economy Club, so that he would be better "prepared to appreciate arguments and counter-arguments".(93)

As an aspiring politician, Hewins' political manifestos were always related to imperial questions and the general issue of tariff reform. Moreover, he appealed to his constituents to "think of the union of the British family whenever 'they cast a vote".(94) After his election to the House of Commons Hewins' maiden speech on the Minimum Wages Bill predictably contained a digression on the benefits of empire unification.(95) However, interest in the economic and political consolidation of the empire in the House of Commons was minimal in the few years preceeding the outbreak of the Great War, and Hewins' occasional speeches did not attract much attention. The outbreak of the War sparked off a revival of Imperialist sentiment both domestically and in the empire, much as the Boer War had done fifteen years beforehand. Before the end of 1914, Hewins was advising British industrialists, through his information from the Tariff Commission, where they could buy alternative sources of scarce raw materials. The following year, he worked on the Unionist Business Committee, under the chairmanship of Walter Long. Supported by Amery, Hewins argued the necessity of mobilising the nation's resources as well as those of the empire, both for victory in the war and sustained economic and political influence after the successful completion of the conflict. To Hewins, the War also provided the opportunity to overturn the free trade system. On the 15th September 1915, the Cabinet decided that duties had to be introduced on selected and non-essential articles. Nine days later the autumn Budget imposed duties of 33 1/3 per cent on motor cars, cameras, clocks, watches, and other luxury goods.(96) Gleefully, Hewins noted that they had "smashed the Free Trade system at last".(97) In January 1916, he tabled the following motion:

> that with a view to increasing the power of the Allies during the war, HMG should enter into immediate consultation with the Governments of the Dominions in order with their aid to bring the whole economic strength of the Empire into co-operation with our Allies in a policy directed against the enemy.

Whilst Hewins spoke on co-operation for the "present war", he was more concerned with post-war economic co-operation. Surprisingly, as Amery suggests, the government met his motion by appointing a Committee on post-war trade relations, with three terms of reference:

> To consider the commercial and industrial policy to be adopted after the war with special reference to the following points:

> (a) What industries are essential to the future safety of the nation and what steps should be taken to maintain or establish them?

> (b) What steps should be taken to recover home and foreign trade lost during the War and to secure new markets?

> (c) To what extent and by what means the resources of the Empire can and should be developed so as to render it

independent of foreign supplies.(98)

Hewins was most determined that the Committee should agree a set of resolutions to be submitted to the imperial leaders. After a great deal of intensive lobbying, he was successful and the Committee unanimously agreed the following resolutions:

(1) In the light of experience gained during the war we consider that special steps must be taken to stimulate the production of foodstuffs, raw materials and manufactured articles within the Empire wherever the expansion of production is possible and economically desirable for the safety and welfare of the Empire as a whole.

(2) We therefore recommend that HM Government should now declare their adherence to the principle that preference should be accorded to the produce and manufactures of the British overseas dominions in respect of any customs duties now or hereafter to be imposed on imports into the United Kinddom.

(3) Further, it will be necessary to take into earliest consideration as one of the methods of achieving these objects, the desirability of establishing a wider range of customs duties which would be remitted or reduced on the produce and manufactures of the Empire and which would form he basis of commercial treaties with allied and neutral powers.(99)

The Committee's Report came before the Cabinet on the 11th April and fifteen days later, the Imperial War Cabinet discussed preference and, after considerable deliberations, unanimously accepted the principle of mutual preference within the empire. This decision might not have been taken had Hewins not pushed the committee to agree the three resolutions which were subsequently submitted to the Cabinet.(100)

In addition to his parliamentary activities, Hewins was a member of influential societies whose aims included the economic unification of the empire. The Tariff Reform League frequently accepted his advice on preferential tariffs and more general opinions on colonial policy.(101) He opened numerous discussions at the Political Economy Club on the general topic of tariff reform.(102) His involvement in imperial organisations continued well after the fiscal controversy, and in 1923 he was appointed Chairman of the Economic Development Union, a body whose primary theme was that the unification of the empire was the only means to relieve the growing unemployment.(103)

CONCLUSION

Hewins was not a theoretical economist, for his sympathies lay with inductive methods and practical applications, and he argued that economic theory should be relevant to time and place. Consequently, he asserted that free trade was not a policy to be pursued for ever, and he fully supported the tariff reform campaign of 1903. Undoubtedly Hewins was very active and influential in the fiscal controversy, but this is not to say that his activities were more significant than those of either Ashley, Cunningham or Marshall. Hewins' case for tariff reform was listened to with great respect, but he "lacked authority or experience when it came to the great issues of Imperial Policy".(104) A self-proclaimed "constructive imperialist", Hewins devoted an enormous amount of time and energy towards providing solutions to the problems - as he perceived them - of the British Empire and, like Ashley, his discussion of imperial questions focused on the issue of tariff reform and protection.(105)

NOTES

1. See his autobiography, W A S Hewins, The Apologia of an Imperialist, (London, Constable, 1929).
2. See Box Mss 158 in Hewins Papers, Sheffield University Library, Sheffield.
3. Hewins, Apologia, op.cit, pp.14-15.
4. See notes in Boxes Mss 141-143, Hewins Papers, op.cit.
5. Hewins, Apologia, Vol.1, p.23.
6. Ibid, pp.31, 33.
7. See Box Mss 142, Hewins Papers and his first book, English Trade and Finance, (London, Methuen, 1892), p.93.
8. Hewins, Apologia, op.cit, p.18.
9. Hewins, English Trade and Finance, op.cit, esp. p.130. It was during the period of writing the book that Hewins contributed numerous biographies on the mercantilists for the Dictionary of National Biography.
10. See Box Mss 158, Hewins Papers, op.cit.
11. It was in reference to Hewins and other economic historians that the Germans coined the term, "neo-mercantilist". See F A Hayek, "The London School of Economics, 1895-1914", Economica, NS XIII, February 1946, p.4.
12. Hewins Apologia, op.cit, p.53.
13. See Boxes Mss 158-159, Hewins Papers, op.cit.
14. On the establishment of the LSE, see S Caine, The History of the Founding of the London School of Economics, (London, Bell, 1963), and Janet Beveridge, An Epic of Clare Market: Birth and Early Days of the LSE, (London, G Bell & Sons, 1960).
15. Hayek, "The London School of Economics, 1895-1914", op.cit, p.5.
16. B Webb, Our Partnership, edited by Barbara Drake and

Margaret Cole, (New York, Longmans, Green & Co, 1948). F A Hayek suggested that if Hewins and Webb had been guided by one conviction in the foundation of the LSE it was their belief that "the theoretical and individualist economics of Ricardo and Mill had kept their dominant position too long and that it was time to give other schools a chance", p.5.

17. See Box Mss 34, p.34 in Hewins Papers, op.cit.

18. See A W Coats, "Alfred Marshall and the Early Development of the London School of Economics: Some Unpublished Letters", Economica, November 1967, pp.408-417.

19. Hewins to S Webb, 22/10/1898. Quoted in Beveridge, Epic of Clare Market, op.cit, p.39. Also see Box Mss 24, Hewins Papers.

20. Hewins, Apologia, op.cit, p.31. He told Bernard Shaw that since the socialist and Manchester economists had the same economic origin, the rejection of the one, necessitated the repudiation of the other. Ibid.

21. Ibid. p.33.

22. See his "Notes on Methodology" in Box Mss 198, Hewins Papers, op.cit, pp.436-443.

23. Ibid, p.440.

24. Ibid, pp.442-443.

25. Hewins to S Webb 22/9/1898, quoted in Beveridge, Epic of Clare Market, op.cit, p.39.

26. The article was never published in an English journal, but copies were printed for private circulation. See Box Mss 19, Hewins Papers.

27 Hewins, "Imperialism and its probable effects on the Commercial Policy of the United Kingdom", op.cit, pp.2-7.

28. Ibid, p.4.

29. Ibid, p.4-5.

30. Ibid, pp.6-7.

31. Ibid, pp.11-12.

32. Hewins, Apologia, Vol.I, op.cit, p.viii.

33. Ibid, p.121.

34. See the discussion in Ch.8, pp.185-188, 197-201.

35. See Boxes Mss 201-6, Hewins Papers; Hewins, English Trade and Finance, op.cit, p.130.

36. He felt that Germany's expansion in the late nineteenth century was the result of the imitation of British policies in the eighteenth century. See Hewins Papers, op.cit, Box Mss 201.

37. See Boxes Mss 160-1, 201-5, Hewins Papers, op.cit.

38. See Hewins' letter to The Times, 16/7/1903, p.4.

39. See Hewins' draft notes for The Apologia, Hewins Papers, Boxes Mss 161-2, p.211.

40. On this general question, See E J T Collins, "Migrant Labour in British Agriculture in the Nineteenth Century". EHR, Vol.29, No.1, 1976, pp.38-59.

41. Box Mss 162, p.64, Hewins Papers, op.cit.

42. Hewins failed to state if the increase would be in real or money wages. See his letter to The Times, 25/6/1903.

43. See his notes written on 26/5/1888 in Box Mss 141,

Hewins Papers, op.cit.

44. See his letter to The Times, 3/8/1903, p.17.

45. For his general position regarding foreign competition see Boxes Mss 160-1, Hewins Papers, and his article in The Times of 27/7/1903, p.8, and 3/8/1903, p.12.

46 For his study of the wrought-iron industry see Box Mss 141, Hewins Papers, op.cit, and his article in The Times 3/8/1903, p.12.

47. Hewins, "The Fiscal Problem", Fortnightly Review, October 1903, Vol.80, pp.590-97, especially p.594, and his article in The Times, 3/8/1903, p.12.

48. Hewins, Return to Sanity, (Published anonomously, London, The Patriotic Press, 1903), p.21.

49. Ibid, p.22.

50. Ibid, pp.17-21. Also see English Trade and Finance, op.cit, and Trade in Balance, op.cit.

51. See Boxes Mss 160, p.182, Hewins Papers, op.cit.

52. See Boxes Mss 160, Hewins Papers for a letter on the subject of protectionism written for the Encyclopedia Britannica of 4/7/1929, pp.183-184.

53. See Box Mss 160, p.199, Hewins Papers, op.cit.

54. Hewins, The Fiscal Problem, op.cit, pp.593-4.

55. For notes on the fiscal controversy see Ch.3, pp.25-31.

56. See letter from Sidney Webb to W A S Hewins, 30/5/1903 in Box Mss 161, Hewins Papers and Hewins Diary, in Hewins Papers, Box Mss 195, pp.22-38. Also see A W Coats, "Political Economy and Tariff Reform", op.cit, pp.223-224.

57. See H W McCready, "Alfred Marshall and Tariff Reform", JPE, Vol.63, pp.259-67.

58. See J Amery, Joseph Chamberlain, Vol.5, op.cit, pp.286-287.

59. Semmel, Imperialism and Social Reform, op.cit, p.170.

60. Hewins, Apologia, Vol.I, op.cit, pp.61-65. Also J Amery, Joseph Chamberlain, op.cit, p.86.

61. Hewins, Apologia, Vol.II, op.cit, p.60. In Imperial and Social Reform, Semmel incorrectly asserts that Hewins was more responsible than any other individual for convincing Chamberlain to campaign for tariff reform. (see pp.81-82.) Whilst correspondence began in 1900, there was virtually no personal contact till after Chamberlain launched the campaign in May 1903. For a different position from Semmel see A W Coats, "Political Economy and Tariff Reform", op.cit, p.187.

62. See Hewins Diary in Box Mss 195, Hewins Papers, pp.28-30. Also see The Times, June 15, 22, 25, 29; July 4, 11, 16, 20, 28; August 3, 8, 17, 20, 28; September 4, 14, 19.

63. See Hewins Diary in Box Mss 195, Hewins Papers, op.cit, p.29.

64. Ibid, op.33-34.

65. See Boxes Mss 60-64, 211, Hewins Papers for their fascinating correspondence. See especially Box Mss 211, letter from J Chamberlain to Hewins, 5/9/1900. Also see A W Coats, "Political Economy and the Tariff Reform", op.cit, pp.188-190. Also see

Hewins' anonymously published paper, "Imperialism and its probable effect on the Commercial Policy of the United Kingdom", op.cit.

66. See J Amery, Joseph Chamberlain, Vol.6, op.cit, p.479.

67. Ibid, pp.529-530.

68. Ibid, p.530. Also see Coats "Political Economy and Tariff Reform", op.cit, p.205.

69. Box Mss 61a, Hewins Papers, op.cit. Also see Amery, Joseph Chamberlain, op.cit, pp.530-531.

70. Hewins, Trade in Balance, op.cit, p.11.

71. See Box Mss 61a, Hewins Papers, op.cit.

72. See Boxes Mss 205-6, and the clippings taken from Public Opinion, 14/10/1904. Hewins Papers, op.cit.

73. See Box Mss 205, Hewins Papers, op.cit, p.27.

74. Hewins, Tariff Reform and Home Rule, op.cit, p.15; Box Mss 24, Hewins Papers, op.cit, pp.33-36.

75. Hewins, Trade in Balance, op.cit, pp.16-19.

76. See Hewins Papers, Box Mss 24 and his article in The Times 9/2/1906, p.38. Hewins also wrote, "Only by binding ourselves to our real national and Imperial needs can we suppose that these new methods will provide for the large increases of social reform long overdue, increased naval expenditure, more generous provisions for education, the development of agriculture, industrial insurance, and other great objects of public policy upon which all parties are more or less agreed". See Box Mss 24, the letter to the editor of The Standard, 7/1/1911, p.48.

77. Imperial preferential schemes, per se, were never fully specified, detailed or delineated. More often than not, questions of imperial preference were inter-related to Tariff Reform proposals, eg Joseph Chamberlain's proposals. See Semmel, Imperialism and Social Reform, op.cit, pp.83-97, and The Liberal Magazine, of August 1908, Vol.16, p.467. The Tariff Reform League supported imperial preference only on the condition of a general reform of free trade policy. See Tariff Reform League Leaflets, Nos.270-279. In the Tariff Reform League itself, there were increasing disagreements over the concept of preference for imperial consolidation. See Semmel, Imperialism and Social Reform, pp.123-5. In 1914 the preferential aspects of Tariff Reform were abandoned by the Leauge, primarily to ally fears over high food prices. One Tariff Reform League Specimen Leaflet even attempted to appeal to British tea drinkers by claiming that only imperial preference would reduce the free trade tax on tea, London, Tariff Reform League, 1903, No.1 and the Monthly Notes on Tariff Reform, July 1904.

78. Hewins, Apologia, Vol.I, p.172. Also see Vol.II, op.cit, pp.220-222.

79. Amery, Joseph Chamberlain, Vol.6, op.cit, p.984.

80. See Coats, "Political Economy and Tariff Reform", op.cit, pp.182-183.

81. Hewins, Apologia, Vol. II, op.cit, pp.185-189.

82. Amery, Joseph Chamberlain, Vol.6, op.cit, p.914; Hewins, Apologia, Vol.I, op.cit, p.187.

83. See Hewins' letters to A J Balfour in Box Mss 52, pp.153-5,

Box Mss 196, pp.3-95, Hewins Papers, op.cit.

84. See D Judd, Balfour and the British Empire: A Study in Imperial Evolution, 1874-1932, (London, Macmillan, 1968), p,.140.

85. See Peter Fraser, Joseph Chamberlain, Radicalism and Empire, 1868-1914, (London, Cassel, 1966), p.283.

86. See letter from Hewins to Balfour, 11/2/1907 in Balfour Private Papers - British Museum Add Ms 49779.

87. Ibid.

88. See Balfour's speech on 20/2/1907 in Hansard, 4th Series, Vol.169, 20/2/1907. Cols. 865-73.

89. Ibid, Cols. 872-4.

90. See Box Mss 196, p.72, Hewins Papers, op.cit, Leter from Balfour to Hewins, 25/8/1907.

91. See Box Mss 52, pp.153-5, Hewins Papers, op.cit, Letter from Hewins to Balfour, 30/11/1908.

92. Ibid, p.156. See Balfour's reply to Hewins.

93. See Box Mss 52, p.84, Hewins Papers, op.cit, Letter from A J Balfour to Hewins, 8/9/1908.

94. See Box Mss 206, especially the clippings on the Middleton Election, Hewins Papers, op.cit.

95. See Box Mss 69a, Hewins Papers, op.cit.

96. See Amery, Joseph Chamberlain, Vol.6, op.cit, pp.1002-1004.

97. Hewins, Apologia, Vol.II, op.cit, p.53.

98. See Amery, Joseph Chamberlain, Vol.6, op.cit, p.1004.

99. Hewins, Apologia, Vol.II, op.cit, p.115.

100. See Amery, Joseph Chamberlain, Vol.6, op.cit, pp.1007-1008.

101. See Box Mss 196, Hewins Papers, op.cit.

102. Ibid, pp.101-103. On 25/10/1910, Hewins argued at the Club that the survival of the Catholic faith was at stake in the empire.

103. See Box Mss 211, Hewins Papers, op.cit, and also The Yorkshire Post Trade Review, 13/1/1923.

104. Amery, Joseph Chamberlain, Vol.6, op.cit, p.1000. It was said that Hewins looked like Tenniel's drawings of the Mad Hatter in Alice in Wonderland, and Amery suggests, that perhaps this meant he was never taken quite seriously.

105. For Ashley's views see Ch.8, pp.185-191.

Chapter 10

J A HOBSON : THE SELF-CONFESSED HERETIC

INTRODUCTION

J A Hobson's classic work, Imperialism: A Study has received
widespread attention by commentators and his accompanying
economic theory of imperial expansion outlined in the work, has been
frequently re-interpreted, extended and criticised.(1) Whilst
Hobson's theory of imperialism is widely known, the evolution of his
ideas and writings in numerous journals in the years prior to the first
publication of Imperialism in 1902 is still relatively unknown.
Despite Bernard Porter's discussion of this development in Critics of
Empire, and P J Cain's recent article, Hobson's perspectives,
thoughts and more general contributions to discussions on a range of
imperial topics, including the two leading political imperial issues of
the 1880s and early 1900s - schemes for imperial federation and
imperial preference - have virtually been ignored.(2) This chapter
aims, amongst other things, to demonstrate that Hobson discussed
such topics with a substantial degree of balance and objectivity,
though he had strong personal feelings on the matters. Additionally,
it seeks to point out and note Hobson's ideas and opinions on a diverse
range of ethical, social, economic and political aspects associated
with the possession and governing of a diverse empire, such as that
commanded by the United Kingdom.

THE 'ECONOMIC HERETIC'

During his long life (1858-1940) which spanned unparalleled
achievements in British industrial supremacy and imperial expansion,
Hobson produced some 53 books and scores of periodical and
newspaper articles on a wide range of economic, social, political,
philosophical and ethical topics.(3) Born in Derby in 1858, Hobson
received his early education there and later went up to Lincoln
College, Oxford and studied the classics.(4) At Oxford in the late
1870s not only was 'political economy' in transformation, if not
decline, but there was also an extraordinary wave of interest in
reforming society; it was the period of T H Green, Jowett and Arnold
Toynbee.(5) As an undergraduate, Hobson did not undertake any

formal study of economics, claiming in later life that while a student he was most influenced by J S Mill's work On Liberty and Spencer's Study of Sociology.(6) Upon graduating, he taught in public schools in Faversham and Exeter for eight years from 1880 to 1887, when he became an extension lecturer in English and Economics from 1887 to 1897. As an extension lecturer, Hobson co-authored The Physiology of Industry with A F Mummery.(7) Published in 1889, the book was a scathing attack on orthodox economics, a denial of the Mill-Say law of markets and contained a thesis that oversaving was a possibility.

Hobson's attack on an accepted law of orthodox economics brought him the rancour of a diverse range of economists, and lost him two extension lecturing posts.(8) He never attained a university appointment and perhaps this was a consequence of his rejection of the Mill-Say law.(9) On the other hand, he did not actively seek a university teaching or research position, for he was primarily interested in journalism and from 1907 to 1923 was a regular contributor to the current economic and political column of The Nation.

Despite his considerable publications in 'economics', Hobson was never accepted as a professional economist. His books received poor reviews from economists, and he rarely published in the established economic journals, such as the Economic Review and Economic Journal.(10) Alfred Marshall, the leading economist of the period, 1870-1914, paid him incidental attention and Hobson's contribution to economic theory was comparatively neglected until Keynes praised him in the General Theory.(11)

Economics

Hobson's and Mummery's over-savings and over-investment theory in The Physiology of Industry was based on the notion that there is some technically fixed limit to the amount of capital employable or that "in a given condition of the productive arts, each labourer can only efficiently cooperate with a certain maximum amount of capital; if there could be brought into existence more forms of capital than sufficed to furnish the maximum for every labourer, the surplus must be waste".(12) Although Mummery was the leading partner in the work, Hobson retained the underconsumptionist position throughout his life.(13) However, in The Physiology of Industry there is virtually no mention of what became the key element in Hobson's underconsumption analysis - the maldistribution of income. Although there is mention of the unequal distribution of income in Hobson's The Evolution of Modern Capitalism (1894), the first substantial exposition of the problem appeared in 1896 in The Problem of the Unemployed.(14) Subsequently, he made numerous re-formulations of his basic ideas, particularly in The Industrial System.(15) In 1900, Hobson broke further from economic orthodoxy with the publication of his Economics of Distribution, in which he attacked marginal productivity theory, and sustained his criticisms in a series of articles thereafter.(16) The outcome of these articles was Hobson's refusal to recognise the logic behind the marginal productivity theory.(17)

From the publication of Imperialism in 1902 to the end of World War I, Hobson tended to play down his underconsumptionist thesis, save in The Industrial System, though he produced three "theoretical" works in economics - An Economic Theory of Investment, Gold, Prices and Wages and Work and Wealth.(18) After the termination of the war, Hobson produced a series of books - from Taxation in the New State (1919) to Property and Improperty (1937) - which laid considerable stress on his underconsumptionist hypothesis.(19)

As was the case with most of the economists in the nineteenth century Hobson had no professional training in economic theory. Nevertheless, his books contain references to major classical economists, as well as to W Ashley, J B Clark, W S Jevons, A Marshall, K Marx and A Toynbee. Various underconsumptionists - Sismondi, Lauderdale, Malthus and Wakefield - are given no citation, though reference to Malthus occurs in The Physiology of Industry, The Evolution of Modern Capitalism and Confessions of an Economic Heretic. However, there is a pregnant reference to Malthus and Lauderdale in the Preface to The Problem of the Unemployed.(20)

Hobson's prolific writings covered a far greater range of disciplines than economics, and he made contributions to philosophy, sociology, and political theory and ethics. His economic writings (e.g. those referred to above) are not in a rigorously theoretical style like, say Jevons' Political Economy or Marshall's Principles, but combine many thoughts and disciplines, distractions and excursions. It is therefore extremely important to note those vital influences which shaped Hobson's general philosophy.

Philosophy

As an extension lecturer, Hobson had become extremely interested in, and a keen adherent to, John Ruskin's writings, and throughout the rest of his life he was intensely concerned with social reform in a broader sense than mere economic reform. This belief, plus his unorthodox economics, led him to write mostly for the 'popular' press. His emphasis on the non-material development of society, coupled with his desire to change society, stemmed from the deep influence of men whose biographies he wrote - Ruskin, Cobden, Hobhouse and Veblen.(21) Of these, Ruskin exerted the greatest influence on the development of his ideas.

Hobson believed that the real scope of economic science had been misunderstood and divorced from the service of humanity. He denied the separability of the social sciences, and particularly of economics and ethics. "Ethics do not 'intrude' into economic facts;

the same facts are ethical and economic".(22) From John Ruskin he learnt "the necessity of going beyond the current monetary estimates of wealth, cost, and utility, to reach the body of human benefits and satisfactions which gave then a real meaning".(23) He agreed with Ruskin's main charge against orthodox political economy, namely that it "had deliberately and systematically degraded the true and formerly accepted meaning of such terms as "wealth", "value", and "profit" by putting them to the narrow service of the business mentality".(24) Hobson followed Ruskin's re-definition of wealth as: "A truly valuable or availing thing or that which leads to a life with its whole strength".(25) In 1898 in a monograph on Ruskin, Hobson maintained "the true 'value' of a thing is neither the price paid for it nor the amount of present satisfaction it yields to the consumer, but the intrinsic service it is capable of yielding by its right use".(26) In short, wealth could not be measured against some ethical standard.(27)

In The Social Problem, Hobson re-iterated his case against classical political economy, particularly the classical economists' assumptions that an invisible hand guaranteed that the free play of enlightened self-interest would automatically promote the good of the community. Accepting Ruskin's arguments, Hobson advocated a new political economy on a scientific basis, which looked to organic and evolutionary science for its inspiration. He distinguished between positive and normative economics, and argued that the new political economy should not merely review what is, but what ought to be.(28) Furthermore, it must recognise the essential interaction and interdependence of different parts of the social mechanism and must take into account qualitative distinctions between different kinds of goods. In combination, this constituted the "standard of value" which he labelled "social utility" which was neither liberal nor anti-individualistic.(29)

> The right ordering of work of an individual member of society ... will be determined by harmonious adjustment of the needs and capacities of his individual nature, and those of his social nature as interpreted and directed by the needs of society.(30)

From Ruskin, Hobson derived his opinions on the necessity of abandoning the old individualism and formulating a political philosophy on a more "social" basis which was dependent on two related biological concepts: "organism and evolution".

> The individual feeling, his will, his ends and interests, are not entirely merged in or sacrificed to public feeling, will and ends, but over a certain area they are fused and identified, and the common social life thus formed has conscious interest and ends of its own which are not merely instruments in forwarding the progress of the separate individual lives, but are directed primarily to secure the survival and physical progress of the community regarded as a conscious whole.(31)

Hobson believed that all individual action had a social import and that arrangements between individuals should be made with the good of the whole society in mind.(32) Similarly, he liberalised his "evolutionary" concept by making it "rational". Social evolution would be expedited when society learned to "bring its conscious will to bear upon the work of constructing new social and industrial forms to fit the new economic conditions".(33) Evolution was the process whereby the struggle for survival in the industrial field was replaced by industrial cooperation, with individual enterprise being free to devote itself to higher activities.

If ... we regard human life as comprising an infinite number of activities of different sorts, operating upon different planes of competition and educating different human 'fitnesses', we shall understand how the particular phase of industrial evolution we are considering is related to the wider philosophic view of life. All progress, from primitive savagedom to modern civilisation, will then appear as consisting in the progressive socialisation of the lower functions, the stoppage of lower forms of competition and of the education of the more brutal qualities, in order that a larger and larger proportion of individual activity may be engaged in the exercise of higher functions, the practice of competition upon higher planes, and the education of higher forms of fitness.(34)

Hobson's hopes for progress and social reform were rooted in his belief in man's ability to consider his own rational interests and act accordingly. Man must "use his reason to adapt his society to the machine age".(35) Throughout his life, Hobson retained his faith in rationality. Despite the ravages of the first World War he wrote in 1931: "Man is not a very reasonable animal, but (barring such temporary outbursts as the Great War) he becomes continuously more reasonable".(36)

Many of Hobson's ideas were discussed with fellow members of the 'South Place Society' and the 'Rainbow Circle', both of which exerted a strong influence in the formation of his social, philosophical and imperial views, as well as bringing him into contact with other radical thinkers of the late nineteenth century.(37) The South Place Society was part of the ethical movement, which was primarily a secularist 'religious' association for humanists.(38) Hobson originally joined the London branch of the movement in the late 1880s, but transferred his allegiance to the South Place Society in 1897. He said that the London society was "excellent in its assertion of discussion"; but it was unfortunately "committed so strongly to the stress on individual moral characters, as the basis of social progress, as to make it the enemy of that political-economic democracy which I was coming to regard as the chief instrument of social progress and justice ".(39) In contrast, the South Place Society emphasised the promotion of human welfare, considered in the broadest ethical terms. "Progress, to be permanent, must proceed, as far as possible, similtaneously in the material, intellectual, moral, aesthetic and social (sphere)".(40) Hobson was in sympathy with this position and his association with the South Place Society lasted for forty years and "acted as a stimulus for clarifying my thought and enlarging my range of interests in matters of social reconduct".(41)

The Society organised lectures and discussions on a range of topics, especially social and political questions. More importantly, the Ethical movement inaugurated in 1898 a new weekly paper, the Ethical World, which was edited by the minister of the South Place Society, Stanton Coit. The following year, Hobson shared the editorship with Coit for eleven months and in association with other prominent men of the Ethical movement, in particular Ramsay MacDonald, G H Perris and J M Robertson, he made the Ethical World the vehicle for the first published statements of their opinions on political, social and imperial questions.(42)

The Rainbow Circle, founded in 1893 as a progressivist political discussion group, encompassed all shades of political opinions from liberal - imperialism to socialism. Ramsay MacDonald was its secretary and other members, besides Hobson, included Herbert Burrows, William Clarke, G P Gooch, Russell Rea, J M Robertson and Charles Revelyan. Despite their diversity these men professed the simple aim of providing "a rational and comprehensive view of political and social progress, leading up to a consistent body of political and economic doctrine which could be ultimately formulated in a programme of action, and in that form provide a rallying point for social reformers so much needed in the present chaotic state of opinion".(43)

The Circle sought to discuss the reasons why the old Philosophical Radicalism and the Manchester School of Economics could no longer be applied in the political sphere as well as the ethical, economic and political bases of the newer politics. Like the Ethical movement, the Circle launched its own journal, the Progressive Review, in 1896. Despite its short period of publication, the journal made significant contributions to imperial discussions, with Hobson the co-ordinator of economics.(44)

THE ECONOMIC THEORY OF IMPERIALISM

Origins

In 1902 Hobson's Imperialism: A Study was published. In this popular work he synthesised a substantial amount of his earlier work on the nature of economics, the reasons for and effects of late nineteenth century expansion, as well as his personal experiences in the empire (South Africa). His economic theory of imperialism was not entirely the result of his unorthodox views on savings and investment, as some commentators argue.(45) It is difficult to date precisely Hobson's first interest in the empire and the era of 'new imperialism', although it appears that in the mid 1890s he was deeply involved in discussions on imperial questions. During this period, he was an active participant in the South Place Society and the Rainbow Circle and it was in the latters' journal, Progressive Review, that he published his first article on empire.(46)

Hobson's first significant article delineating his economic theory of imperialism, "Free Trade and Foreign Policy", was written in relation to the debate as whether "trade followed the flag", which re-emerged in the late 1890s.(47) From the 1880s onwards, commentators were concerned to discredit the position propounded by imperialists that political domination led to economic domination. In 1896, for example, the Increased Armaments Protest Committee, whose secretary was the Ethicist G H Perris, issued a pamphlet to specifically demonstrate that colonies were not actually an outlet for surplus goods. The pamphlets presented statistics to show:

> That the total of British Trade has not by any means advanced in proportion or direction with the area and population of the Empire, that in brief, trade does not follow the flag ... That by far the greatest proportion of our trade always has been and still is, not with our colonies, but with foreign countries ... That the proportion and in some important cases the amount, of colonial trade is not increasing; and that recent acquisitions which have involved so heavy a political and financial burden, have only infinitesimally increased that trade...(48)

In reply to those who demanded imperial expansion for commercial reasons, Lord Farrer re-iterated the same argument that trade did not follow the flag. Farrer's article in the pacifist journal, Concord, in 1898, was one of many in the controversy over the economics of foreign trade which raged in numerous different monthlies through 1898-99, during which period Hobson produced his first complete statement of the surplus capital theory of imperialism.(49) Hobson's article was also a comment upon the economic and political aspects of Chinese trade which were made more urgent by the events at the beginning on 1898. In November 1897, the Kaiser had seized Kiaochow and in March 1898 the Russians occupied Port Arthur. In Britain, there was considerable discussion as to what action, if any, the British government should specifically take, and whether British commercial interests were being jeopardised by such expansionist activities by other nations. Generally speaking, there were two different viewpoints in the commercial discussion over China. Firstly, the Liberal opposition advocated a noninterventionist policy, hoping that despite foreign competition the "Open-Door" practice could be maintained. Secondly, there was agitation for the government to annex or proclaim "spheres" of influence in China, thus compensating Britain for a trade loss to Germany and Russia.(50)

To Hobson, the advocacy of protecting free trade by force was a contradiction in terms. In "Free Trade and Foreign Policy" he argued that the Open-Door policy was not in the interests of free trade and attempted to reinstate the pacifist and internationalist aspects of Cobdenism.(51) The utilisation of force in the interests of trade and commerce was "a direct repudiation both of the logic and utility of Free Trade" and he denied that trade benefits could be secured by force, claiming that trade did not follow the flag. Furthermore, the annexation of territories was a heavy financial burden on the economy and (here Hobson went beyond Cobden) he argued the position that "our national prosperity depends on constant expansion of external markets" was false.(52) To Hobson, expansion occurred because manufacturers were demanding foreign markets for their produce. The home market should suffice, but it did not. To explain why this was so Hobson returned to his underconsumptionist heresy:

> Though a potential market exists within the United Kingdom for all 'goods' that are produced by the nation, there is not an 'effective' demand, because those who have the power to demand commodities for consumption have not the desire, since their material needs are amply satisfied, while those who have the desire have not the power.(53)

The upper and middle classes, not wanting themselves to consume more, and finding an insufficient home market among the underpaid workers, "are compelled to struggle with the classes of other nations in the same predicament for foreign markets, which seem to them limited in extent at any given time".(54) Thus, Hobson argued that the maldistribution of wealth meant that there was domestic underconsumption, which led to the existence of surplus capital - the cause of imperialism. Hobson had formulated his economic theory of imperialism in the concluding pages of this 1898 article but his explanation was ignored in the ensuing months, and the greater part of his article, which dealt with the topical question "did trade follow the flag", was pursued.(55) However, a dynamic emphasis was given to Hobson's thesis by events in South Africa in the following year.

During the summer and autumn of 1899, Hobson spent several months in South Africa, working as a journalist for the Manchester Guardian.(56) Hobson's experiences in South Africa and his personal observations of the inter-play of social, economic and political factors associated with the Boer War, confirmed his theory of imperial expansion. On his return to England, he wrote The War in South Africa, in which he mentioned the application of the "new imperialism" by the various Cape ministers to South African affairs.(57)

The early chapters of the book were impressions of what he saw and heard upon the eve of the Boer War. The latter part of the volume was chiefly devoted to an economic and political analysis of the factors in the situation which would shed light upon the possibilities of a stable settlement at the termination of the war. He believed that a plain account of the personal and economic forces which were operative in the Transvaal was essential to an understanding of the war. He viewed the outbreak of the Boer War as the "simplest example of the interplay of the political and economic motives of Imperialism".(58)

In addition to writing The War in South Africa, Hobson also published a series of articles in the Ethical World from mid July 1900 to early 1901. These articles were combined to form a book, The Psychology of Jingoism (1901) which was a "scathing account of the forces of irrationalism which seemed to him to be dominant in Britain during the War".(59) He contended that whatever professed causes were claimed for the war, Britain was fighting "in order to place a small international oligarchy of mine-owners and speculators in power at Pretoria". To Hobson, the Jews were the international financiers:

> Not Hamburg, not Vienna, not Frankfurt, but Johannesburg is the New Jerusalem ... the industrial and agricultural future of the foreigners...Englishmen will surely do well to recognise that the economic and political destinies of South Africa are, and seem likely to remain, in the hands of men most of whom are foreign by origin, whose trade is finance, and whose trade interests are not chiefly British.(60)

Out of the working example of capitalistic imperialism in South Africa, Hobson formulated a general principle:

> The full significance of this evil business in South Africa is only understood when it is recognised as a most dramatic instance of the play of modern forces which are world-wide in their scope and revolutionary in their operation. Those who see one set of problems in Egypt, another in China, a third in South America, a fourth in South Africa, or trace their connexion merely through the old political relations between nations, will be subjected to a rough awakening as their calculations, based on this old Separatist view, are everywhere upset. Without seeking to ignore or to disparage the special factors, physical, economic, and political, which rightly assign a certain peculiarity to each case, I would insist upon the supreme importance of recognising the dominance everywhere exercised by the new confederacy and interplay of two sets of forces, conveniently designated by the titles International Capitalism and Imperialism.(61)

In the articles and books Hobson wrote in the period 1899-1901, "underconsumption" is scarcely mentioned; rather, he concentrated almost exclusively on the tangible connection between capitalism and war, and this led him to devote scathing attacks on a small group of "cosmopolitan Jew" financiers. None of this particular line of reasoning was unique, for a large number of 'pro-Boer' Liberals claimed that the South African war was a 'financiers' war' and pointed to the same conspiracy in the Rand.(62) In a series of articles in the Progressive Review between November 1896 and June 1897, William Clarke, a fellow traditionalist and colleague of the Rainbow Circle, attributed the imperialistic policies of the early 1890's to the international financiers.(63)

In 1902 Hobson's Imperialism: A Study was published. It combined into a single book, Hobson's imperial theory developed in the preceding four years.(64) The first part of the work - The Economics of Imperialism - The Politics of Imperialism - dealt with the ethical justification of empire. In this section we are primarily interested in outlining the key elements in his economic theory of imperialism.

Intensely interested in this late nineteenth century expansion, Hobson offered his economic theory of imperialism as an explanation for the period of "new imperialism".(65) Like Cunningham and Giffen, Hobson attempted to delineate those regions affected by British expansion.(66) Whilst not as thorough as Giffen's tabulation on the empire's area and population, Hobson's statistics were far more detailed than popularist writers like Froude, George and Egerton who also attempted to quantify the physical attributes of the empire.(67)

Disutility of Empire

Population Hobson's argument on the economic disutility of empire is similar to that propagated by the economists writing in the 1860s - Cairnes, Rogers and Goldwin Smith.(68) While they concentrated on the self-governing colonies (Australia, Canada, New Zealand), Hobson was concerned to demonstrate that those regions acquired by the "new imperialism" were economically useless to the country as a whole. In Imperialism, Hobson reiterated his August 1898 article on the unprofitability of the 'new imperialism', arguing that the idea that the United Kingdom required areas for her surplus population and products was "delusion".(69) In contrast to Cairnes, Fawcett and Smith, Hobson denied that the United Kingdom was overpopulated. However, like them, he also wanted to demonstrate that most British emigrants went to the United States, although he differed in arguing that the tropical lands acquired by Western Europe made no significant contribution to the areas for emigration.(70) Writing with the hindsight of a century of censuses which revealed an easing of population growth and a reduction in the birth rate, Hobson was more optimistic concerning future rates of British growth than many of his predecessors.

It is true that our manufactures and commerce may not continue to grow as rapidly as in the past, though we have no clear warrant from industrial statistics for the judgement: but if this be so, neither is our population to increase so fast. Of this we have clear statistical evidence of the diminution of the rate of growth of our population, as disclosed by the latest consensus, is such as to justify the conclusions that, if the forces continue to operate the population of Great Britain will be stationary by the middle of the century.(71)

Hobson totally rejected the Malthusian theory of population, arguing that there was no general necessity for a policy of imperial expansion to provide an outlet for overpopulation, "present or prospective". He did not accept the view that British domestic poverty could be solved by merely sending people to the colonies, implicitly ruling-out Wilmot-Horton's and Wakefield's colonisation schemes.(72) Having rejected the Malthusian population argument, Hobson never reversed his position. In Wealth and Life he argued that if emigration occurred from an overpopulated to an underpopulated country, there would not be an immediate increase in the birth rate of the former country which would restore the equilibrium.(73)

In contrast to Hobson, Cairnes, Fawcett, Rogers and Smith were adherents to the Malthusian population doctrine. However, they wrote some forty years earlier than Hobson, and their concern was to discredit the contention that the self-governing colonies were outlets for the mother country's surplus population.(74) They referred to migration statistics which demonstrated that most British emigrants travelled to the United States, not to the British colonies.(75) Although Hobson wanted to demonstrate the uselessness of empire, like the 1860 economists, his population theory was more in keeping with the nineteenth century heretical stances of Cunningham, Hewins and Jevons.(76)

Trade Hobson rejected the view that 'trade followed the flag' and utilised figures, based on Giffen's work, to demonstrate: that "over the period 1870-1900 imperial trade was a small and diminishing proportion of total commerce; trade with foreign countries was increasing to a far greater extent; new tropical acquisitions were "the smallest, least progressive, and most fluctuating in quantity".(77)

Essential to Hobson's position was his conviction that foreign trade as a whole was unimportant, compared with domestic trade. It was only a small proportion of the 'real income' of the nation, which was diminishing per head of the population.(78) He rejected the assumption that home demand was a fixed amount and claimed that goods in excess of this must either find foreign markets or remain unsold:

There is no natural limit to the quantity of wealth which can be produced, exchanged, and consumed within Great Britain except the limits imposed by restricted natural resources and the actual condition of the arts of industry, provided that the productive power is disposed in industries which meet the rising demands of the consumer.(79)

Given such a situation, Hobson sought to answer why there was such pressure on the British government to expand its territorial control. Since he was a rationalist, he rejected all irrational explanations, postulating "that the only possible answer is that the business interests of the nation are subordinated to those of certain sectional interests that usurp control of the national resources and use them for their private gain".(80) To Hobson, these certain sectional interests were divisible into three groups. Firstly, there were special commercial industries and political interests like the armed services and aristocracy who wanted positions for their sons.(81) Secondly, there were home investors who could not find profitable domestic investments and demanded government protection for overseas investment.(82) Thirdly, there were the financial houses, who were composed of "men of a single and peculiar race".(83)

In sum, Hobson argued that the era of modern imperialism was the result of pressure placed on governments by financiers, investors and capitalists to find profitable fields for their surplus capital. These classes found that there were insufficient markets for capital or goods to absorb their trade surplus. Hence, they sought outside areas for investment and the markets which went with them.(84)

> Everywhere appear excessive powers of production, and excessive capital in search of investment. It is admitted by all businessmen that the growth of the powers of production in their country exceeds the growth in consumption, that more goods can be produced than can be sold at a profit, and that more capital exists than can find remunerative investment.(85)

Solutions to Imperialism It is exceedingly difficult, if not impossible, to keep Hobson's diagnosis separate from his remedies, for much of his writing is infused with a strong moral element. Generally speaking, Hobson provided both an economic and political solution to the 'complex problem of imperialism'. He contended that because the power of production in Britain had outstripped the rate of consumption, new investment opportunities had to be found for the 'recent and massive capital accumulation' of the rich. To this phenomenon, he offered two solutions. Firstly, the oversaving of the rich could be eliminated by taxes for commodity goods and transforming their oversaving into higher wages. The resulting redistribution of consuming power would, he maintained, remove the cause of imperialism. Even given such a change in income distribution, foreign trade would still be important, but "the domestic pressure would be the wholesome pressure of the consumer anxious to buy abroad what he could not buy at home. Not the blind eagerness of the producer to use every force or trick of trade or politics to find markets for his surplus goods".(86)

Secondly, domestic social reform, brought about by monetary and fiscal measures, would direct surplus wealth to uplifting general living standards. Consequently, the home markets would be most capable of indefinite expansion and there would be no requirement for the export of capital:

> An economy that assigns to the "possessing" classes an excess of consuming power which they cannot use, and cannot convert into really serviceable capital, is a dog-in-the-manger policy. The social reforms which deprive the possessing classes of their surplus will not, therefore, inflict upon them the real injury they dread; they can only use this surplus by forcing on their country a wrecking policy of Imperialism. The only safety of nations lies in removing the unearned increments of income from the possessing classes, and adding them to the wage-income of the working classes or to the public income, in order that they may be spent in raising the standard of consumption.(87)

Hobson also offered a political solution to imperialism:

> The power of the imperialist forces within the nation to use the national resources for their private gain, by operating the instrument of the State, can only be overthrown by the establishment of a genuine democracy, the direction of public policy by the people, for the people, through representatives over whom they exercise a real control. Whether this or any other nation is yet competent for such a democracy may well be matter of grave doubt, but until and unless the external policy of a nation is 'broad-based upon a people's will' there appears little hope of remedy.(88)

This remedy was identical to Cobden's:

> If you had a thorough representation in Parliament, you could not persuade the people of this country to spend half the money that is now spent under the pretence of protecting them, but which is really spent in order that certain parties may get some sort of benefit out of it.(89)

Reactions to Imperialism: A Study Intellectual reaction to Hobson's Imperialism was virtually immediate. Soon after its publication, Paul S Reinsch regretted that Hobson "did not develop more fully his evidence as to the existence of an international group of capitalists who mould public opinion and direct public action in order to be able to profit by fluctuations in the stock market".(90) Eight months earlier, the Edinburgh Review had complained of Hobson's 'palpable exaggerations'.

Five years after the publication of Imperialism, Hobson's close friend and former colleague in the Rainbow Circle, Ramsay MacDonald, wrote Labour and Empire.(91) Whilst MacDonald took a more practical approach to imperial problems, his broad line of argument was similar to Hobson's. He shared with Hobson the spectrum that imperialism was not necessarily an evil. However, he rejected Hobson's social efficiency thesis.(92)

In Imperialism: The Highest Stage of Capitalism, Lenin accepted Hobson's theory of imperialism in toto though it be that of a "frankly pacifist and reformist Englishman, Hobson". He accepted both the political and economic analysis of imperialism by Hobson.(93) Lenin also adopted, with generous acknowledgements, Hobson's arguments which related imperialism to capitalism. However, he went beyond Hobson and moulded them into a theory which identified imperialism with late, or declining, capitalism. He introduced inevitability into Hobson's thesis, systematising the whole argument into a deterministic form, which excluded any chance of rational choice and argued that imperialism was the "monopoly stage of capitalism".(94)

Lenin had forced Hobson's Imperialism into a mould for which Hobson did not intend it. Although he never replied directly to Lenin's thesis, he admitted in 1938 that he had been led "to an excessive and too simple advocacy of the economic determination of history"; he had "not yet gathered into clear perspective the nature of the interaction between economics, politics, and ethics, needed for anyone who might wish to claim the title of Sociologist".(95) Perhaps it is also true that Hobson was guilty of an "intellectual conjuring trick" in implying that the coincidence of increasing overseas investment and imperial expansion pointed to a causal connexion between the two.(96) On the other hand, Hobson never denied that the greater proportion of foreign investment still went to the United States, South America, and the self-governing colonies (Australia, Canada, New Zealand).(97) He quoted overseas investment figures to demonstrate that it had doubled in two decades, and that therefore capitalists sought foreign markets and this implied that there was domestic pressure for external markets.

Hobson's Imperialism ran three editions during his life-time, and despite the criticism and acclaim his thesis received, he made no re-statement of his theory and there were no substantial changes in the 1905 and 1938 editions, although he wrote a new introduction for the third edition. Furthermore, there was no lengthy discourse on his 1902 thesis in any of the books published after Imperialism and it would appear that he held to his 1902 thesis till his death in 1940.

Nevertheless, there are some subtle changes in his more general theory of expansion in the post-1902 publications.(98) Commenting on the causation of World War I, he felt that the chief "secret" driving force was the demand by industrialised countries for the control of those countries which could supply their raw material requirements. He claimed that his thesis was verified by "the Allies' scramble for the mandatory areas" and he re-iterated that only sectional interests gained from imperialism.(99) Hobson's post-1914 writings seem to place more stress on non-economic factors in imperial expansion. In Wealth and Life (1929), while he generally agreed with "those socialists" who insisted that imperialism was the result of capitalist forces, he criticised their total rejection of "the sentimental and genuinely moral support accorded to the policy by the people".(100)

Towards the end of his life, Hobson extended his 1902 thesis in an attempt to explain world poverty and wealth. In Poverty and Plenty (1931), he argued that international imperialism was the instrument responsible for the mal-distribution of the world's wealth and the debasement of the "moral currency" which resulted in "genuine missionaries and government officials" pleading for imperialism.(101) He suggested that there existed an international imperialism by which capitalist organisations of several countries in co-operation "mark-down backward countries for an economic exploitation which definitely worsens the distribution of the enlarged world-problem, by converting large low-producing but self-sustaining populations into the low-paid tools of a high productivity".(102)

Costs and Benefits of Empire

Hobson investigated a range of ethical, philosophical, political and social aspects associated with empire, not only in Imperialism but also in numerous other books and articles. In these works, there is no comprehensive account of the cost and benefits of empire. Rather, there is the juxtaposition of a diverse range of opinions and ideas, which (for purposes of illustration) will be considered under the following headings: threat to World Peace; absorption of Lower Races; general benefits.

Threat to World Peace Nowhere is Hobson's belief in Cobdenite philosophy more apparent than in his detestation of militarism and advocacy of world peace.(103) To Hobson, imperialism was inextricably linked with militarism, for expansionism was warlike and the retention of control in conquered lands involved military presence.(104) Subsequently, he argued that the imperialistic activities of the late nineteenth century had been a contributory factor to World War I.(105) Prior to the War, he had contended that imperialism would encourage wars and all the dangers associated with war - military expenditure, arms competition, militarism and conscription.(106) After the war, he firmly maintained that if the various struggles of rival imperialistic nations continued then there could be no serious hopes for a lasting world peace. He believed that the solution to such a situation was by an organised "economic internationalism", which could be achieved by obtaining mutual agreement of industrial and financial groups in different countries, thus extending their organisations across their national barriers. Competitive economic imperialism was the greatest barrier to world peace.(107)

On the economic side, the 'national' struggles for new resources such as oil, rubber, copper, the deficiency of foreign markets adequate to take the export surpluses which depressed trades in industrial countries could produce, the visible waste of manufacturing power thus revealed, the raising of tariff walls and other aids to home industries at the expense of foreigners, the payment of war-debts by poorer nations to richer, the harassing fluctuations of foreign exchanges - all these factors feed international fears, suspicions, envies, and hatreds. The only escape from these moral and economic wastes and perils is by way of organised economic internationalism.(108)

Absorption of Lower Races In Imperialism Hobson devoted a lengthy chapter to the impact of the advanced countries on what he calls the "lower races".(109) Hobson thought that the sudden arrival of imperialistic powers in societies which had remained virtually unchanged for thousands of years could be 'incredibly destructive'. This was especially so when foreigners attempted to suddenly "enforce white standards of hygiene, decency, or morals" which had - and still could - disintegrate "primitive groups standards and lead to extermination".(110) In this context he deplored pleas to "take up the white man's burden', (such as those made by Cunningham) as nothing more than a "pretence" in the name of "the conquest of imperialism".(111)

Thinking along similar lines to the colonial reformers and 1860s economists he demanded self-government for all peoples on the grounds that everywhere political rights were the indispensable condition of civil rights, without which there could be no "security of life, liberty and property for an inferior race or class".(112) He pointed out that in the vast majority of countries, Britain bestowed no real powers of self-government and had no intention of doing so.(113) Hobson asserted that this was a 'gross' contradiction, as the United Kingdom was self-governing and he argued that the authoritarian rule of foreign land by a self-governing democracy was an irreconcilable contradiction.(114)

The long-term implication of British despotism would be the rise of nationalist movements demanding self-government. In short, Hobson argued that the interaction of 'advanced' and 'backward' countries involved considerable exploitation; both of labour for 'efficient' production and the "deliberate education of new wants for the benefits of exporting manufacturers at home".(115) Such exploitation, coupled with the "unavoidable penetration of Western political ideas and movements", produced unrest and suspicion towards the rulers, and nationalist movements for political and economic self-government evolved.(116)

In summary, Hobson believed that imperialism had slowed-up the progress of co-operation and order between and amongst nations. It was obstructive to international democracy in its denial of self-government to the subjected races and, "by poisoning the democratic atmosphere of the country wielding this coercive power over the life and labour of weaker peoples".(117) National democracy was inextricably linked with personal freedom for all its citizens, but the limited freedom of subject peoples, caused by imperialism, was inconsistent with personal freedom. Most ominous of all was imperialism's inconsistency with democracy and social reform. It maintained a despotism abroad which was irreconcilable with popular government at home; in order to meet military expenditure, it drained the public of money which might be spent on social reform; it diverted public resentment from domestic grievances.(118)

To Hobson, British rule of India encountered the two essential problems associated with any imperialism - the destruction of culture and the government of a conquered people. Generally speaking, he believed that while a century of British rule in India had been conducted with sound ability and goodwill, it had not materially assisted the chronic starvation amongst the poor. Nevertheless, he felt that there was "one real and indisputable success" of British rule in India (and throughout the empire) - the maintenance of "order and prevention of war".(119) Despite the drawbacks of British rule, Hobson was pleased with British achievements in India:

> We have established a wider and more permanent internal peace than India had ever known from the days of Alexander the Great. We have raised the standard of justice, of fair and equal administration of laws; we have regulated and probably reduced the burden of taxation, checking the corruption and tyranny of native princes and their publicans. For the instruction of the people we have introduced a public system of schools and colleges, as well as a great quasi-public missionary establishment, teaching not only the Christian religion but many industrial arts. Roads, railways and a network of canals have facilitated communication and transport, and an extensive system of scientific irrigation has improved the productiveness of the soil; the mining of coal, gold and other minerals has been greatly developed; in Bombay and elsewhere cotton mills with modern machinery have been set up, and the organisation of other machine industries is helping to find employment for the population of large cities. Tea, coffee, indigo, jute, tobacco and other important crops have been introduced into Indian agriculture. We are gradually breaking down many of the religious and social superstitions which sin against humanity and retard progress, and even the deeply-rooted caste system is modified wherever British influence is felt. There can be no question that much of this work of England in India is well done.(120)

In acclaiming British rule in India, Hobson was consistent with all economists from J S Mill to Alfred Marshall and William Cunningham. Without exception, they believed Britain had brought peace and order to a once warring nation, though they agreed this was at a sacrifice to Indian culture.(121)

General Benefits Hobson was not totally opposed to the exploitation of resources in those regions under the control of the lower races. On the contrary, he maintained that tropical development was both right and necessary for two reasons. Firstly, if people within a given area failed to utilise their resources, a more 'progressive' power could do so for the "general good of nations".(122) He explicitly denied that any backward race had the right to refuse to other peoples the use of natural resources in its territories which it was unable to develop.

He re-iterated Cobden's position that the resources of the world should be available for those who were best suited to exploit them.(123) Moreover, Hobson felt it was impossible to stop the exploitation of the tropics by imperialistic powers and even if all governments abstained, private adventurers would not. Thinking along similar lines to Cunningham, Hobson argued if the United Kingdom abandoned its rule of the tropics, then these regions would become the prey of armed groups.(124)

> If organised Governments of civilised Powers refused the task, they would let loose a horde of private adventurers, slavers, piratical traders, treasure hunters, concession mongers, who, animated by mere greed of gold or power, would set about the work of exploitation under no public control and with no regard to the future.(125)

Given such a situation, nations had both a duty and a right to interfere with the "lower races". For Hobson, the only problem was how this should occur. He agreed that in the present pattern of relationships a good measure of exploitation was involved. To avoid this, Hobson recommended the establishment of a mandatory authority, which should have two broad guidelines: (1) To aim at the good of the whole world, (2) To benefit the nations involved and respect "the services of nationality, as a means of education and of self-development".(126)

The Political and Economic Unification of the Empire

Imperial Federation Hobson considered the majority of issues associated with imperial federation comprehensively and fairly, despite his strong opposition to any scheme.(127) He had not always been opposed to the imperial federation movement, and in 1888 claimed it was "the only secure protection against the otherwise inevitable decay which history teaches us is the lot of nations which have reached the proud position England now occupies".(128) He wanted the initiative for unification to come from the colonies, but if this did not occur the mother country would have to intervene.(129) However, after his visit to the United States in 1888 he came to regard the idea as too grandiose and the cause a 'hopeless one'.(130)

Despite his rejection of the idea, he nevertheless carefully outlined his conception of imperial federation in The War in South Africa, The Crisis of Liberalism and Imperialism. He regarded freedom of the constituent members as absolutely esssential to the formulation of an imperial parliament.

> Federation of States in South Africa as elsewhere, must be based upon the clear recognition of a community of interests and feelings; what is called a "union of hearts". Where and when this condition is lacking, no real federation is possible. A scheme of federation imposed as a result of military conquest cannot endure; coming into being by the sword, it will either perish by the sword or collapse from internal impotence.(131)

Hobson maintained that as each colony grew in population and wealth it persistently asserted larger rights of independent government, and he accurately stressed that colonies wanted to develop their own natural resources for their advantage and to be guided by purely national, as against imperial, aims in all important aspects of policy. He greatly welcomed the political diversity of the empire and he appreciated the practical difficulties in formulating a feasible policy of imperial unification.(132) Arguing in a similar manner to Marshall, Hobson considered, albeit briefly, the economic factors associated with political unification arguing that the self-governing colonies would not enter into an association of imperial federation which involved them in large new expenses out of mere sentimental regard for the British empire, and asserted that even if they did join a federation they would be unwilling to pay for the defence of the empire. Hobson was also interested in the manner in which the "new imperialism" had affected the relations between the United Kingdom and the self-governing colonies. In this he extended the customary arguments for imperial federation, contending that any 'proper' schemes of political unification should include all territories under British control and not simply the self-governing colonies.(133)

Hobson considered that it was important to present a systematic and thorough treatment of the issues relating to an imperial political federation of empire. This sprang from his concern about the "new imperialism" and his keen interest in international politics. Moreover, he explicitly stated what was involved in a true and proper federation of the empire - a federation of all the diverse races and forms of government and not simply the self-governing ones. Hobson also appreciated colonial sentiments and the national aspirations of the colonies and rightly asserted, as did Goldwin Smith, that the self-governing colonies would not federate into an imperial union if it involved costs and sacrifices on their part.(134)

Imperial Preference   An alternative to imperial federation which Hobson considered in the 1890s was the idea of an imperial zollverein, which he viewed as "one of the greatest possibilities of the future".(135) In 1896 he listed three difficulties associated with any scheme of imperial preference: food prices would rise, it would threaten world peace and the colonies would have to be persuaded to forfeit their tariffs.(136) He did not pursue the question again in detail till his tour of Canada in 1905, by which time he was firmly committed to the Cobdenite free trade position.(137) He recorded his impressions of Canada in a series of articles in the Daily Chronicle and afterwards in a small book, Canada Today. Later he wrote that his trip revealed to him the "beginnings of imperial protectionism in the form of preferences which had begun to operate in 1898".(138) In Canada Today, he argued that the Canadian preference of 1897 which gave Britain a reduction of 33 1/3% on import duties could not seriously be regarded as the "beginnings of an enduring fiscal policy, still less as the foundation stone of an imperial system of preferential trade".(139) He correctly maintained that the general course of Canadian trade, both import and export, had remained basically the same as before the preference: namely, that the trend was towards the United States. He conceded that the preference did have some apparent influence in checking the rate of decline in the growth of British as compared with American imports into Canada; however, he argued that the Canadian preference was generally ineffective.

In his brief policy discussion Hobson demonstrated a keen appreciation of colonial sentiment, especially when he noted that there "was no intention in Canada to allow impediments to be placed in the development of her own rising manufacturers by allowing the free competition either on British or American imports".(140) Although he appreciated these sentiments relating to imperial preferential arrangements between Canada and the United Kingdom, Hobson failed to advance any of the theoretical arguments for or against imperial preference and this task was left to the Marshallians.(141)

Conclusion

In addition to his thesis about imperial expansion, Hobson wrote on a range of imperial topics and presented a systematic and thorough treatment of the leading imperial issues of his time. Hobson's interest in imperial questions was largely the result of the wide spectrum of his intellectual pursuits and his broad conception of the topics which economics should encompass. Together with a small group of other intellectuals, journalists and academics - for example, Hobhouse and Robertson - Hobson adhered to a set of principles which owed much to the work of T H Green and J S Mill.

His breadth of learning incorporated the ideas on empire were well within the British tradition of thinking on the subject. There is a sharp resemblance between his ideas and those of Adam Smith. For example, like Smith he attempted to demolish the belief that there was overall profit in the colonies, claiming imperial profits accrued to special interest groups. Moreover, he was a firm adherent to, and upholder of, Smith's free trade principles. Identifying with the views of Jeremy Bentham and James and John Stuart Mill, he was anxious to demonstrate that Britain's withdrawal from her occupied areas would lead to worse ends.(142) Finally his ideas closely correspond to those of Cobden and Goldwin Smith who also feared that the possession of colonies undermined Britain's own inner security.(143)

NOTES

1.   J A Hobson's Imperialism: A Study ran three editions during his lifetime. (1st ed, 1902; 2nd ed, (revised), 1905; 3rd ed, (revised), 1938). Unless otherwise stated, all future references are to the 1st ed. His thesis of imperialism has been extended eg, by J Ramsay MacDonald in Labour and Empire, (London, George Allen, 1907), re-interpreted by V I Lenin in Imperialism: the Highest Stage of Capitalism, (new revised translation, New York, International Publishers, 1939) and criticised by D K Fieldhouse in "Imperialism: An Historical Revision", EHR, 2nd Series, Vol.24, December 1961, pp.187-209. Recently, P J Cain in "J A Hobson, Cobdenism and the Radical Theory of Economic Imperialism, 1878-1914", EHR, 2nd Series, vol.31, No.4, November 1978, pp.565-584, has examined and evaluated Hobson's ideas from 1898 to 1914.

2.   See B Porter, Critics of Empire, (London, Macmillan, 1968) and P J Cain, "J A Hobson, Cobdenism and the Radical Theory of Economic Imperialism", op.cit.

3.   On Hobson's life see his autobiography Confessions of An Economic Heretic, (London, Allen & Unwin, 1938), N Brailsford, The Life Work of J A Hobson, (London, OUP, 1948) and G D H Cole, "John A Hobson: 1858-1940", EJ, Vol.50, 1940, pp.315-60. On his economics see Nicholas Merkowick, "John A Hobson's Economics", Indian Journal of Economics, Vol.23, 1942, pp.175-185; W M Hamilton, "Economic Theory and Social Reform: Work and Wealth", JPE, Vol.23, 1915, pp.562-84 and E E Nemmers, Hobson and Underconsumption, (Amsterdam, North-Holland, 1956). Recently two doctorates have been written on Hobson: A J F Lee, "A Study of the Social and Economic Thought of J A Hobson", (Unpublished PhD Thesis, University of London, 1970) and J Townsend, "J A Hobson and the Crisis of Liberalism", (Unpublished PhD Thesis, University of Southhampton, 1973). Also see the recent article by W H Richmond, "John A Hobson: Economic Heretic", American Journal of Economics and Sociology, Vol.37, July 1978, pp.2830294.

4.   As Hobson commented, he was, "Born and bred in the middle stratum of the middle class of a middle-sized industrial town

of the Midlands", Confessions, op.cit, p.15.

5.   See Melvin Ritcher, The Politics of Conscience: T H Green and His Age, (Cambridge, Mass, MUP, 1964).

6.   Hobson was strongly influenced by Spencer in his youth - Hobson, Confessions, op.cit, p.23. Hobson's "first definite approach to economics" was as a student in the Cambridge Extension Course in Economics in 1875, Confessions, p.23.

7.   See J A Hobson and A F Mummury, The Physiology of Industry, (London, John Murray, 1889).

8.   See Hobson, Confessions, op.cit, pp.30-31, N Brailsford, The Life Work of J A Hobson, op.cit, pp.9-10 and T W Hutchison, A Review of Economic Doctrines, (Oxford, OUP, 1953), pp.118-119. Edgeworth, a leading orthodox economist wrote an acerbic review of The Physiology of Industry in Education, and the economic historian and self-proclaimed "radical economist", W A S Hewins, vigorously attached Hobson's heresy. See Hewins Papers, op.cit, Box Mss.55.

9.   See Hutchison, Review of Economic Doctrines, op.cit, pp.188-119, Hobson wrote, "In appearing to question the virtue of unpardonable thought, I had committed the unpardonable sin", Confessions, pp.31-2.

10.   See, for example, A W Flux's "Review of The Economics of Distribution", EJ, Vol.10, 1900, pp.380-385, and J M Keynes, "Review of Gold, Prices, and Wages", EJ, Vol.23, 1913, pp.393-398.

11.   Keynes wrote: "Theories of underconsumption (after Malthus) hibernated until the appearance in 1889 of The Physiology of Industry, the first and most significant of many volumes in which for nearly fifty years Mr Hobson has flung himself with unflagging, but almost unvailing, ardor and courage against the ranks of orthodoxy. Though it is so completely forgotten today, the publication of this book marks, in a sense, an epoch in economic thought". See J M Keynes, General Theory of Employment, Interest and Money, (New York, Harcourt Brace, 1936), pp.364-5. Keynes had also paid tribute to Hobson's work in his A Treatise on Money, (New York, Harcourt Brace, 1930), Vol.1, p.179.

12.   Hobson, The Physiology of Industry, op.cit, p.128.

13.   See T W Hutchison, A Review of Economic Doctrines, op.cit, p.122 and E E Nemmers, Hobson and Underconsumption, op.cit, p.26.

14.   Hobson, The Evolution of Modern Capitalism (1st ed, 1894, revised ed, 1906 - London, Walter Scott, 1906) and The Problem of the Unemployed, (London, Methuen, 1904).

15.   Hobson, The Industrial System, (London, P S King, 1927 ed).

16.   Hobson, The Economics of Distribution, (New York, Macmillan, 1903); "Marginal Units in the Theory of Distribution", JPE, Vol.12, 1904, pp.449-72; "Marginal Theory of Distribution: A Reply to Professor Carver", JPE, Vol.13, 1905, pp.587-90; "Marginal Productivity", ER, Vol.20, 1909, pp.301-10, 673-86.

17.   Nemmers, Hobson and Underconsumption, op.cit, p.22.

18.   Hobson, The Industrial System, op.cit, An Economic Theory of Investment, (London, Financial Review of Reviews 1911) Gold, Prices and Wages, (London, Methuen, 1913), Work and Wealth,

(New York, Macmillan, 1914). Cain claims Hobson became a Cobdenite in the period 1902-1914. See Cain, "J A Hobson, Cobdenism and the Radical Theory of Economic Imperialism, 1898-1914", op.cit, p.565.

19.   Hobson, Taxation in the New State, (London, Methuen, 1919), Property and Improperty, (London, Victor Gollance, 1937).

20.   Hobson, The Problem of the Unemployed. op.cit, Preface.

21.   See Hobson, John Ruskin, Social Reformer, (London, James Nisbet, 1893) Richard Cobden: The International Man, (London, T Fisher Unwin, 1918). With M Gunsberg, L T Hobhouse, His Life and Work, (London, Allen and Unwin, 1931), and Veblen, (London, Chapman, 1936). For a discussion of Hobson's Liberal idealogy see Michael Freeden, The New Liberalism: An Ideology of Social Reform, (Oxford, Clarenden, 1978) and Peter Clarke Liberals and Social Democrats, (Cambridge, CUP, 1978).

22.   Hobson, The Social Problem, op.cit, p.69. Hobson's view sharply contrasts with W S Jevons' position that not only was there separability in social sciences, but within economics.

23.   Hobson, Confessions, op.cit, p.42.

24.   Ibid, p.39.

25.   J Ruskin, Unto This Last, (London, Library ed, 1905), p.84, for which Hobson wrote and introduction.

26.   Hobson, John Ruskin, op.cit, p.79.

27.   Hobson (ed), Unto This Last, op.cit, p.ii, John Ruskin, op.cit, pp.78-79.

28.   Hobson, The Social Problem, op.cit, Bk.1, Ch.III, pp.17-32. Also see Chapter VI, "Society as Maker of 'Values'", pp.141-154.

29.   Ibid, Ch.VII, "Distribution According to Needs", pp.155-173.

30.   Ibid, p.22.

31.   Hobson, "A Restatement of Democracy", CR, February 1902, pp.265-6.

32.   Hobson, The Social Problem, op.cit, p.219.

33.   Hobson, The Evolution of Modern Capitalism, op.cit, pp.351-2.

34.   Ibid, p.364.

35.   Ibid, p.351.

36.   Hobson, "The State as an Organ of Rationalisation", Political Quarterly, Vol.II, No.1, (1931), p.34.

37.   See B Porter, Critics of Empire, op.cit, p.160.

38.   See Gustov Spiller, The Ethical Movement in Great Britain, A Documentary History, (London, Farleigh, 1934).

39.   Hobson, Confessions of an Economic Heretic, op.cit, p.56.

40.   South Place Magazine, Vol.I, (1896), p.103.

41.   Hobson, Confessions, op.cit, p.57.

42.   See Porter, Critics of Empire, op.cit, pp.162-162.

43.   Quoted in Porter, Ibid, p.164. J M Robertson, like Hobson was a staunch free trader. See The Tariff Swindle, (London, Cobden Club, 1911); Chamberlain: A Study, (London, Watts, 1905). Furthermore, he was an underconsumptionist. See The Fallacy of Saving: A Study in Economics, (London, Swan Sonnenschein, 1892).

Though The Fallacy of Saving was not published till 1892, it was written before Hobson's Physiology, see pp.105-118.

44. Porter, Critics of Empire, op.cit, p.166.

45. See eg, E E Nemmers, Hobson and Underconsumption, op.cit, p.33; T Kemp, Theories of Imperialism, (London, Dobson, 1967), pp.30-44; B Semmel, The Rise of Free Trade Imperialism, (Cambridge, CUP, 1970), pp.226-28.

46. Hobson, "The Ethics of Empire", (published under "Nemo"), PR, August 1897, No.11, pp.448-64. Also see Porter, Critics of Empire, op.cit, pp.162-64.

47. Hobson, "Free Trade and Foreign Policy", CR, August 1898, pp.177-9.

48. Empire, Trade and Armaments: An Exposure, (published by the Armaments Protest Committee, 1896), pp.16-17.

49. For a discussion on this matter see Porter, Critics of Empire, op.cit, p,p.190-99.

50. See J A Grenville, Lord Salisbury and Foreign Policy, (London, Athlone, 1964), p.143.

51. See Cain, "J A Hobson, Cobdenism, and the Radical Theory of Economic Imperialism", op.cit, pp.568-9.

52. Hobson, "Free Trade and Foreign Policy", op.cit, pp.176-77.

53. Ibid, pp.177-78.

54. Ibid, p.178.

55. However J M Robertson, a fellow nationalist echoed Hobson's ideas. See Robertson's Patriotism and Empire, (London, Grant Richards, 1899).

56. It was L G Hobhouse, then a leader-writer on the Manchester Guardian who encouraged the paper's editor, C P Scott, to send Hobson to South Africa. See Hobson, Confessions, op.cit, p.60.

57. Hobson, The War in South Africa: Its Causes and Effects, (London, James Nesbet, 1900).

58. Hobson, Confessions, op.cit, p.59.

59. See Porter, Critics of Empire, op.cit, p.203. The Psychology contained in this work was based on Le Bon's Psychologie des Foules, 1895. Hobson accepted some of Le Bon's conclusions, and even then with reservations. Generally speaking, he agreed with Le Bon's position that men were in the irrefrangible grip of heredity and unconscious psychological forces.

60. Hobson, The War in South Africa, pp.190, 104, 197.

61. Hobson, "Capitalism and Imperialism in South Africa", CR, Jan 1900, p.1.

62. See Porter, Critics of Empire, op.cit, pp.205-206.

63. "The Liberal Leadership", PR, I, pp.97-110; "The Genesis of Jingoism", PR, I, pp.397-406; "Is Democracy a Reality?", PR, II, pp.20-9; and "The Reign of Force", PR, II, pp.211-18. All these articles were published anonymously. "The Genesis of Jingoism", however, was published again under Clarke's name in H Burrows and J A Hobson (ed), William Clarke, A Collection of His Writings, op.cit.

64. Imperialism, was, in many ways, a work of political propaganda directed against certain contemporary events. It was essentially written in the form of separate articles contributed to a

number of different journals, eg, Chapter IV first appears as "The Commercial Value of Imperialism", in the Speaker, New Series, Vol.V, No.109, pp.124-26, November 1901; Chapter VI as "The Economic Taproot of Imperialism" in the CR, Vol.82, August 1902, pp.219-232. As Porter in Critics of Empire (p.216) maintains "Only later, and probably hurriedly, was it patched together in the form of a book with some pretensions to logical consistency".

65.   Hobson's economic theory of imperialism has received widespread attention and analysis. See, eg, Porter, Critics of Empire, op.cit,   pp.207-238;   E E   Nemmers,   Hobson   and Underconsumption, op.cit, Ch.IV, pp.33-59; T Kemp, Theories of Imperialism, op.cit, pp.30-44.

66.   See Ch.7, pp.162-166 and Ch.8, pp.195-197.

67.   Ser H E Egerton, A Short History of British Colonial Policy, (Oxford, Clarendon, 1903); J A Froude, Oceana, (London, Longmans Green etc, 1886); H George, Statistical Account of the British Empire, (London, Methuen, 1904).

68.   See Ch.4, pp.45-50, 59-61 and Ch.5, pp.74-76.

69.   See Imperialism, op.cit, p.76 and "Free Trade and Foreign Policy", op.cit.

70.   Hobson, Imperialism, op.cit, pp.48-50; The Social Problem, op.cit, pp.86-98.

71.   Ibid, p.48. Also see "The Population Question 1", Commonwealth, April 1897, pp.105-6 and "The Population Question 2", Commonwealth, June 1897, pp.170-1.

72.   Ibid, p.50. On these schemes see Ghosh Classical Macroeconomics and the Case for Colonies, op.cit.

73.   Hobson, Wealth and Life, op.cit, pp.370-72.

74.   See, for example, Ch.4, pp.45-48, 57-58, Ch.5, pp.80-86.

75.   Most emigrants did in fact, travel to the United States. See I Ferenczi and W F Willcox, International Migrations, (New York, National Bureau of Economic Research, 1929), Vol.I, pp.627-8, 636-7.

76.   See, for example, Ch.6, pp.102-104.

77.   Hobson, Imperialism, op.cit, p.42.

78.   Hobson, Imperialism, op.cit, pp.30-34.

79.   Ibid, p.32.

80.   Ibid, p.51.

81.   Ibid, pp.53-5. Also see "Capitalism and Imperialism in South Africa", op.cit, p.1.

82.   Hobson, Imperialism, op.cit, pp.56-61.

83.   Ibid, pp.66-7.

84.   Ibid, pp.62, 66-7, 86-9, 102-3, 242-3; Confessions, op.cit, pp.78-83, 182-5.

85.   Hobson, Imperialism, op.cit, p.86.

86.   Ibid, pp.77, 85-89.

87.   Ibid, p.95.

88.   Ibid, p.382.

89.   Cobden, speech at Rochdale, 29 October 1862; quoted in John Bright and J E T Rogers (ed), Speeches on Question of Public Policy by Richard Cobden, MP, (London, Macmillan, 1878), Vol.II,

pp.336-337.

90. Paul S Reinsch, "Review of J A Hobson's Imperialism", PSQ, Vol.18, 1903, pp.531-533. Also see the comments in the Edinburgh Review, Jan 1903, pp.268-269.

91. J R MacDonald, Labour and Empire, (London, Allen, 1907).

92. MacDonald, "The Propaganda of Civilisation", IJE, Vol.XI, No.4, 1901, pp.455-68. On the relationship between MacDonald and Hobson, see Porter, Critics of Empire, op.cit, pp.185-190.

93. V I Lenin, Imperialism: The Highest Stage of Capitalism, op.cit, p.127.

94. Ibid, pp.83, 92, 94.

95. Hobson, Confessions, op.cit, p,p.63-4.

96. D K Fieldhouse, "Imperialism: An Historiographical Revision", op.cit, p.190.

97. See Harvey Mitchell, "Hobson Revisited", JHI, Vol.26, No.3, (1965), p.412.

98. Recently P J Cain in "J A Hobson, Cobdenism, and the Radical Theory of Economic Imperialism", op.cit, has argued that Hobson's Imperialism was "only a snapshot of his views at the turn of the century, a interim statement of his position which was to be modified drastically thereafter", (p.565). Whilst Cain demonstrates the considerable changes in Hobson's thinking on the role of foreign trade from that stated in Imperialism (and there is no intention to discuss this in the present work) he does not, in our opinion, demonstrate how Hobson's thesis of imperialism was drastically modified as a consequence. Since Cain covers Hobson's thinking on foreign trade and imperialism over 1902-1914, there is - in the present section - no discussion of Hobson's thought in this period. Also see Cain's "International Trade and Economic Development in the Work of J A Hobson Before 1914", HOPE, Vol.II, No.3, Fall 1971, pp.406-424.

99. Hobson, Problems of a New World, (London, George Allen & Unwin, 1931).

100. Hobson, Wealth and Life, op.cit, p.391.

101. Hobson, Poverty and Plenty, op.cit, pp.75-77.

102. Ibid, p.77. Also see his Democracry and a Changing Civilisation, (London, John Lassw, 1934), p.126.

103. For an outline of Cobden's anti-militarism position, see Porter, Critics of Empire, op.cit, pp.10-16.

104. Hobson, Imperialism, op.cit, p.137.

105. Hobson, Problems of a Changing World, op.cit.

106. Hobson, Imperialism, op.cit, pp.135-146.

107. Hobson, Wealth and Life, op.cit, pp.401-402.

108. Ibid, p.401.

109. Hobson, Part II, Chapter IV, "Imperialism and the Lower Races", in Imperialism, op.cit, pp.235-304. Also see his "Imperialism of the Lower Races, 1, 2, 3" in British Friend, March 1902, pp.53-5, April 1902, pp.81-3, June 1902, pp.129-32, respectively.

110. Hobson, Wealth and Life, op.cit, p.336.

111. Hobson, Democracy and a Changing Civilisation, (London, John Lane, 1931).

112. Hobson, Crisis of Liberalism, op.cit, p.245.

113. Hobson, Imperialism, op.cit, p.120.

114. Ibid, p.129.

115. Hobson, Wealth and Life, op.cit, p.xxviii.

116. Ibid.

117. Hobson, Democracy and a Changing Civilisation, op.cit, p.140.

118. Hobson, Imperialism, op.cit, pp.123, 140, 147-61, 382-3.

119. Ibid, pp.313-323.

120. Ibid, p.307.

121. On this matter see for example, Ch.2, pp.10-13, Ch.6, pp.120-121, 132-134.

122. Hobson, "Socialistic Imperialism", op.cit; Imperialism, op.cit, p.246.

123. See N Brailford, The Life of J A Hobson, op.cit, pp.26-7.

124. For Cunningham's views see Ch.8, pp.201-204.

125. Hobson, Imperialism, op.cit, p.242.

126. Ibid, pp.245-7.

127. For a discussion of imperial federation see Ch.3, pp.32-35.

128. Hobson, "Notes", Derbyshire Advertiser, 6/4/1888, p.8.

129. Hobson, Derbyshire Advertiser, 22/11/1889, 4/4/1890, p.8.

130. Hobson, Derbyshire Advertiser, 24/8/1888, p.8, 7/8/1890, p.8.

131. Hobson, The War in South Africa, op.cit, p.393.

132. Hobson, The Crisis of Liberalism, op.cit, pp.238-39.

133. Hobson noted that many of the politicians and businessmen he spoke with wanted to strengthen the bonds between the mother country and the colonies but were opposed to all ideas which resulted in a diminution of their powers of government. See Hobson, Canada Today, (London, T Fisher Unwin, 1906) pp.22-23.

134. For Smith's position see Ch.4, pp.48-50.

135. Hobson, Derbyshire Advertiser, op.cit, 10/4/1891, p.8. For a discussion of imperial preference see Ch.3, pp.25-31.

136. Hobson, Derbyshire Advertiser, op.cit, 12/6/1896, p.8.

137. On this point see Cain, "J A Hobson, Cobdenism and the Radical Theory of Economic Imperialism", op.cit. Also see Hobson's "The Approaching Abandonment of Free Trade", Fortnightly Review, Vol.71, 1902, pp.434-44.

138. Hobson, Confessions, op.cit, pp.64-5. Also see "The Effects of Preferential Duties Upon Prices", Westminster Gazette, 10/9/1903, pp.1-2.

139. Hobson, Canada Today, op.cit, pp.64-70, 119-20, 132-4.

140. Hobson, Confessions, op.cit, p.65.

141. On this point see the discussion and references in Ch.6, pp.121-132.

142. See R N Ghosh, Classical Macroeconomics and the Case for Colonies, op.cit, pp.42, 104, 246-68, and D Winch, Classical Political Economy and Colonies, op.cit, pp.25-38, 61-4, 135-43.

143. See Klaus E Knorr, British Colonial Theories, op.cit, pp.117-25, 122-34, 166-74, 350-65 and Ch.4, pp.48-50.

Chapter 11

CONCLUSION

This study reveals that the economists were certainly not out of their depth in dealing with imperial and colonial issues, although such questions were considered by some late nineteenth century economists to be beyond the proper scope of their discipline. The preceding discussion on the economists' insights and comments on a vast range of factors associated with such a complex topic as "empire" overturns Wagner's position that economists writing after 1860 were unsympathetic to the concept of empire.(1) The literature considered in this study reveals the tremendous fertility, adaptability and durability of Adam Smith's system of ideas, which was evidently open to a variety of legitimate interpretations.(2) The 1860s economists (Cairnes, Fawcett and Rogers) acclaimed Adam Smith's free trade philosophy, whilst Ashley, Cunningham and Hewins pointed out his exceptions to the general principle of laissez-faire and emphasized his inductive approach. Nicholson admired Smith's "Project of Empire" and scheme of imperial federation, which he interpreted in terms of the problems and issues confronting Britain around the turn of the twentieth century. Hobson was a strong defender of Smith's free trade principles and an exponent of his liberal philosophy. And, despite the varied and numerous challenges to Smith's system of political economy, his prime policy prescription - free trade - survived throughout the period.

The study also lends weight to the position that the Mill-Say law of markets was less important to classical and neo-classical economics and the general development of economics than some commentators have claimed.(3) Nevertheless the law has some relevance to the economists and empire over the period 1860-1914. Although there was virtually no theoretical discussion or controversy over Hobson's rejection of the doctrine, he was attacked by some members of the profession, for by the time he was writing, the Mill-Say law of markets was generally accepted as a logical and indispensable component of an economist's set of beliefs.(4)

As a background to the thesis the two phases of classical political economy and the empire were summarized in Chapter Two.(5) In the period under study there are also two general phases,

1860 to 1880 and 1880 to 1914. The first covers the 1860s, a decade somewhat like the period 1776 to the 1820s, when economists were highly critical of British colonial connections and stressed the economic and political disutility of the empire. By contrast, between 1880 and 1914 there was enthusiastic support for the empire from such authors as Ashley, Cunningham, Hewins and Nicholson, although it was also the period of that important critic of empire, J A Hobson, who constituted the leading dissenting voice.

For the purposes of illustration and comparison it is possible to identify two loosely defined "groups" of economists, each of which expressed broadly similar attitudes on imperial questions, namely, the economists of the 1860s (Cairnes, Fawcett and Rogers - group one) and those of the post 1880 period (Ashley, Cunningham and Hewins - group two). Despite some variations of views within each group on a range of imperial matters (these have been considered in the preceding chapters and they defy neat classification) a number of sharp and important differences emerge between the two groups, for example, the differences in their underlying values, methodological beliefs and political biases.(6) The group one economists were against government participation in social and economic life; they treated free trade and laissez-faire as articles of faith, and denounced J S Mill's support for protection in the case of infant industries.(7) By contrast, the economic historians argued that the government ought to assist in the management of the national economy and they urged the mother country to follow the selfgoverning colonies and adopt protectionist policies for their mutual benefit.(8) The group one economists viewed the empire as a burden to the United Kingdom, while the group two economists contended that it was a means of supporting the nation's industrial leadership. The group one economists relied on elementary theoretical considerations and dogmas derived from classical political economy. Despite their predilection for theory - often of an elementary or popular kind - they utilized "facts" in an effort to disprove the contentions that the colonies were outlets for the mother country's surplus population, capital and goods, thereby overlooking the consideration that facts alone cannot disprove theories. By contrast, the group two writers, like other post 1880 economists, were less concerned to establish whether, for example, labour, capital and goods flowed to the empire or to verify and test classical imperial theories. Instead, together with Marshall and Nicholson, they grappled with the complex process of industrialization in Britain and elsewhere.

The leading ideas of the two groups may appear to bear a close parallel to the traditional framework for discussing the history of Victorian imperialism, i.e. with the shift from a position of separation, advocated by the group one economists, to support for expansionism in the period 1870 to 1900 by the group two economists. However, on closer examination this superficial dichotomy breaks down and the study lends support to the "new framework" for discussing nineteenth century British imperialism stemming from Gallagher and Robinson's work. According to this view there was a fundamental continuity in British overseas trade and territorial expansion throughout the nineteenth century, occurring in uneven bursts and for different reasons at different times, which was associated with a free trade policy that was considered the indispensable means of maintaining Britain's world supremacy.(9) Apart from the group two economists, the majority of economists throughout the period under investigation believed that free trade had been a most successful policy for Britain and asserted that its retention was the means whereby British industrial leadership could be assured. Without exception, all the selected economists were proud of British achievements in India and the spread of Anglo Saxonism around the globe. More particularly, the two groups shared common concerns over Britain's place in world affairs, her military strength in relation to the new industrializing nations, and the threats to Britain's industrial and political supremacy.

However, the analyst should not confine attention merely to these two rather loose groupings and it is significant that in the second phase, the dominant figure of orthodox economics, Marshall, strongly opposed any reversal of Britain's external trading policy.(10) This was also the case with the leading dissenter, Hobson, the only economist to offer a new thesis of imperial expansion. Although he was a critic of empire, the originator of a thesis of imperialism and a self-confessed "heretic", Hobson was - like Marshall - an upholder of free trade principles.(11)

A brief overview of the selected economists' analysis of the leading imperial themes offers further insights into the classical economists' influence on their work, and provides a basis from which to evaluate the extent, or lack, of progress in their ideas during the period 1860 to 1914. In contrast to the classical economists, the post-1860 economists devoted little attention to the broader questions of emigration in their published works, although Sidgwick discussed the problems associated with emigration, colonisation and late nineteenth century imperial expansion.(12) Apart from Jevons, those who considered migration issues in the 1860s demonstrated little analytical skill in using the migration statistics, or in drawing inferences from the fact that the colonies provided an inadequate outlet for the mother country's surplus population.(13) Apart from Merivale, they failed to examine the interrelationships between fluctuations in economic activity and the flow of emigrants.(14) Generally speaking, they neglected various problems considered by earlier economists, particularly Wakefield, such as the role of labour in economic development, the relationship between the urban and rural population at home and/or overseas, and the effects of emigration on the rate of growth of population at home and abroad.(15) Marshall's unpublished attempts at a cost-benefit analysis of the effects of migration, and his treatment of wage differentials between the United Kingdom and her colonies, were the only penetrating discussions of this complex question.(16)

Nevertheless, there were discernible developments in the patterns of ideas, in the perceptions of events, and the appreciation of the changing volume and direction of emigration over the period 1860 to 1914. Before 1860 there were few dissenters from the Malthusian theory of population, but this was not the case thereafter, when Jevons, Hewins, and Hobson disavowed the Malthusian doctrine.(17) Falling birth rates and indications of an easing in the growth of population drastically reduced fears of overpopulation, and the belief that there was an inevitable and growing surplus of labour, which had to emigrate, gave way to a more agnostic position.

There were also new developments in the pattern of ideas and the interpretation of events concerning the nature of, and reasons for, imperial trade and capital movements over the period. Whereas the group one economists provided no new insights into these matters, Jevons, Marshall, and Hobson made significant contributions to the analysis of capital movements.(18) All the post-1880 economists appreciated that the empire, particularly the self-governing colonies, would come to occupy an increasingly important role in British trade and overseas investment. Although the economists investigated in this study did not take into account the effects of imperial trade and capital exports on the aggregate balance of payments, Giffen, Marshall and Hobson attempted to identify those regions that absorbed British capital and goods.(19) There was an increasing recognition of the statistical trends of imperial capital and trade throughout the period, with Giffen undertaking extensive statistical research in this area.(20) Over the period there was a discernible move away from the concerns of the group one economists, such as the destinations of capital and goods flows, towards a broader interest in the process of industrialization, the rise of foreign competitors, and their challenge to Britain's leading position in the world economy.(21)

Like the classical economists, the selected economists made no systematic analysis of the financial costs and benefits of empire. Nor did they concentrate solely upon economic factors in evaluating the empire's worth, either to the mother country or the world. On the contrary, like the classical economists, non-economic factors figured prominently in their discussions of the topic, and they included such factors as the spread of Anglo-Saxonism throughout the globe in their overall estimation of the advantages of the British imperial connection.(22)

In the period of classical economics there had been few challenges to the theory of free trade. However, as the nineteenth century drew to a close an increasing number of commentators expressed reservations about this doctrine, with the group two economists no longer upholding all the acclaimed theories and benefits of free trade.(23) Yet, the selected economists made no significant analytical advances in trade theory and policy apart from Marshall, who was the only economist to make significant contributions to the theory of international exchange and tariffs.(24) In relation to the colonies, apart from Marshall's work, nothing was specifically written on a number of topics that were to become of interest to later economists such as differential or uniform taxes, the optimum levels of trade, direct subsidies and taxes on consumption or production of traded goods, and multiple exchange rates.

Intertwined with the debate over tariff reform which erupted in the early years of the twentieth century (after rumblings in the previous three decades) were schemes for the introduction of imperial preferential trade and imperial federation in the empire. Generally speaking, it would appear that the economists' attitude towards free trade governed their approach to the imperial preference issue. Thus, those who sought reforms in Britain's external trading relations and/or the adoption of a protective system warmly embraced imperial preferential schemes; those who wished to retain free trade, necessarily opposed differential trading arrangements.(25) However, two vociferous advocates of the benefits of free trade, Giffen and Nicholson, reluctantly came to advocate the adoption of imperial preference essentially for political reasons.(26) Only Marshall made any significant analytical contribution to the theory of preferential tariffs in the period. By contrast, all the group two economists who advocated imperial preference were uninterested in pursuing international trade thoery, for they were primarily concerned with achieving rather vague political, economic and social goals; and they were in any case a minority within the economics profession.(27) Moreover, apart from Hobson and Marshall, the selected economists ignored the fiscal and financial considerations associated with imperial federation.

But did the economists make a distinctive contribution to the public's understanding of imperial issues, particularly those associated with questions relating to free trade, preferences and imperial federation? While at a theoretical level Marshall made advances in trade theory, superficially it would appear that the economists did not increase the public's general understanding, as the controversy in which the economists were involved reduced the effects of their ideas. However, the public's general appreciation of the complexity of the issues was enhanced and those who followed the discussion should have been made aware of the lack of simple agreed solutions to the question, the disagreements among the "experts", and the readiness of some politicians to consult economists. Although Hewins and Marshall, two of the selected economists whose advice was sought by politicians, influenced individual politicians' thinking, their contribution appears to have made little difference to British imperial trade policy over the longer term.(28)

The study also draws attention to certain changes in the economic thought of the period and supports the view that the late nineteenth century witnessed an increased professionalization of economics and a narrowing of the range of economists' interests. However, the development of marginal analysis in the period, to which historians of economic theory have devoted so much attention, had no obvious impact on the economists' discussions of the empire.(29) After 1870 there was the narrowing of the range of issues considered in the formal body of economic analysis.(30) Professional economists became less inclined to make statements about some of the broader issues which had been near the centre of the clascial economists' interests, such as long term growth and shifts in macro-economic distribution.(31) While Marshall, for example, was interested in imperialism, he did not consider it to be within the range of the professional economists' research.(32) However, not all the economists thought along these lines, and neither the group two economists nor Hobson considered the empire beyond the bounaries of their intellectual and professional investigations. Hobson in particular, had a radically different conception of the nature and significance of economics from the other economists and his extensive interest in philosophy and politics meant that he pursued his line of argument into areas where his contemporaries were reluctant to follow.(33)

While the economics of the empire had been part of economics, though a subordinate one, from Adam Smith's writings on the subject till the 1870s, it was inevitable that an issue which involves socio-political and philosophical problems and perspectives, would attract writers like Hobson and the group two economists who were less concerned with the rigorous, analytical developments of economic science. Hence, there are two general reasons why there was a general lack of economic analysis over imperial topics. Firstly, the economics of the empire was not one of the primary areas of economic research pursued by the economists during the period which witnessed the increased professionalization of the discipline, and some division of labour and interests between (a) those who were interested in analysis per se - static analysis of marginal changes - and found little potential with imperial questions to apply to such analysis, and (b) those economists who either were not interested in or competent in marginal analysis. The very nature of such a diverse and amorphous topic as empire, of itself, hindered the pursuit of rigorous economic analysis. Secondly, amongst the majority of economists, the period witnessed a shift away from classical aggregate analysis to a fascination with marginalism and mathematical concepts, with a resulting loss of interest in some questions hitherto considered as central to the discipline such as the changing long term relationship between population and resources.(34) Nevertheless, the writings of the selected economists reflect an awareness of the economic and political implications of imperial preference and imperial federation, and their comments on imperial trade, capital movements and labour's role in economic development demonstrate their familiarity with the classical economists' discussions of these matters.

In addition to the subjects considered in this thesis there is a need to investigate trends in the economists' opinions on a number of other 'applied' topics in the period 1860-1914 before it is possible to reach more definite conclusions concerning the relevance of their ideas to contemporary affairs.(35) Such a study or studies would necessarily have to include the works of lesser known economists such as Cliffe Leslie or Fawcett, as indicated by the accounts of their views in earlier pages. But this, like the post 1914 discussion of empire, lies beyond the scope of this thesis.

NOTES

1. See Ch.1, p.1.
2. Smith's work still is open to a variety of legitimate interpretations. In Britain's Economic Problem: Too Few Producers (London, Macmillan, 1st ed. 1976), W A Eltis and R Bacon extend and apply Physiocratic and Smithian concepts to produce an analysis of contemporary British economic problems. The persistence of Adam Smith's influence in the so-called Ricardian period has been increasingly recognised in recent years notably, for example, in D P O'Brien's volume on J R McCulloch: A Study in Classical Economics (London, Allen and Unwin, 1970).
3. After the publication of The General Theory there was a tendency to subdivide economists into two categories, those who anticipated Keynes, and those who did not. Often economists were assembled according to their support or rejection of the Mill-Saw law of markets. See, for example, E E Nemmers, Hobson and Underconsumption, op.cit.
4. See Ch.10, pp.236-238.
5. See Ch.2, pp.7-15.
6. See, for example, Ch.4, pp.45-49, 56-60, Ch.5, pp.73-76, 77-80, and Ch.8, pp. 181-188, 193-197, Ch.9, pp.220-230.
7. See, for example, Ch.4, pp.45-48, 58-59, Ch.5, pp.74-76, 80-92.
8. See Ch.8, pp.181-188, 197-201, Ch.9, pp.214-220.
9. See the brief discussion in Ch.3, pp.35-37.
10. See Ch.6, pp.121-132.
11. See Ch.10, pp.236-241, 253-255.
12. See Ch.6, pp.108-110.
13. See Ch.6, pp.103-106.
14. See Ch.4, pp.46-48.
15. See the brief discussion in Ch.2, pp.7-10.
16. See Ch.6, pp.116-120.
17. See, for example, Ch.6, pp.105-106 and Ch.10, pp.245-246.
18. See, for example, Ch.6, pp.110-120.
19. See, for example, Ch.6, pp.116-121, Ch.7, pp.162-166, Ch.10, pp.245-250.
20. See Ch.7, pp.162-166.
21. See, for example, Ch.4, pp.45-48, Ch.8, pp.197-201, Ch.9, pp.214-223.
22. See, for example, Ch.2, pp.10-13, Ch.4, pp.48-50, 61-63,

Ch.6, pp.110-112, 132-134, Ch.7, pp.156-160, Ch.10, pp.250-253.

23. See, Ch.8, pp.185-191, 197-201, Ch.9, pp.220-226.

24. See Ch.6, pp.121-132.

25. See, for example, Ch.6, pp.121-132, Ch.8, pp.185-191, 197-201.

26. See Ch.7, pp.153-160, 166-172.

27. See, for example, Ch.6, pp.121-132, 197-201, and Ch.9, pp.220-230.

28. See, Ch.6, pp.121-132, Ch.9, pp.223-230.

29. See G J Stigler, "The Adoption of the Marginal Utility Theory", in Black, Coats and Goodwin (eds) The Marginal Revolution in Economics, op.cit, pp.305-320.

30. See D Winch, "Marginalism and the Boundaries of Economic Science", Ibid, pp.59-77. Winch forcibly makes the point about the narrowing of the range of issues considered by economists after 1870. Also see the brief discussion in Ch.3, pp.16-18.

31. See J J Spengler, "The Marginal Revolution and Concern with Economic Growth", Ibid, pp.203-232.

32. See Ch.6, pp.115-116.

33. See Ch.10, pp.236-241.

34. See Spengler, "The Marginal Revolution and Concern with Economic Growth", op.cit.

35. An example of such a study is A Petridis, The Economic Analysis of Trade Unions by British Economists, 1860-1930, op.cit.

SELECT BIBLIOGRAPHY

PRIMARY SOURCES

(i)   Manuscript Sources
(ii)   Parliamentary Debates, Papers and Reports: Government Publications.
(iii) Periodicals, Serials, Society Publications.
(iv) Newspapers
(v)   Unpublished Dissertations.
(vi) Contemporary Sources.

SECONDARY SOURCES

1.   Primary Sources

1.1   Manuscript Sources

W H G Armytage, Goldwin Smith: Some Unpublished Letters, Nuffield College Library, Special Collection, Ca 86.

W J Ashley, Testimonials in Favour of W J Ashley MA. A Candidate for the Drummond Professorship of Political Economy in the University of Oxford, Oxford Bodleian Library, Bd 23149e69, 232e641(2).

W A S Hewins, "Papers and Correspondence" in the Hewins Papers, Sheffield University Library, Boxes Mss 24, 36, 43, 52, 55, 60-65, 69, 69a, 127-133, 141-4, 158-9, 160-2, 168-169, 195-199, 201-206, 211.

A Marshall, "Marshall Papers", Marshall Library, Cambridge University.

J E T Rogers, Papers Relating to the Rogers 1868 Re-election to the Chair of Political Economy, Bodleian Library, Oxford, Oxon, c 84(402) Scrap Book, Bodleian Library, Oxford, Bd 232d188 (1884-1894).

Goldwin Smith, The Professorship of Political Economy: To Members of Convocation. Remarks on the circulation of a paper criticising Professor Rogers' political and theoretical utterances upon his seeking re-election to the Professorship, Bodleian Library, Oxford, Ox 84(408).

1.2   Parliamentary Debates, Papers and Reports: Government Publications.

"British Foreign Trade and Industry", Parliamentary Papers XXXI, (Cd 1761) 1903.

Fifth Interim Report of the Commission on Depression in Trade and Industry 1888.

"Final Report of the Royal Commission on Natural Resources", Parliamentary Papers (Cd 5745) 1917.

Hansard   Third Series   Vol.CLXIX   p.96   1863
                           Vol.CCI   p.1164   1884
                           Vol.CCVIII   pp.932-940   1891
                           Vol.CCXV   p.153   1898
           Fourth Series   Vol.CXXII   pp.5-67   1903
                           Vol.CXXIII   pp.568-70   1914

House of Lords Debates, 15th, 20th May 1873.

"Minutes of the Proceedings of the Colonial Conference 1907":
Parl. Papers LV (Cd 3523) 1907.

"Minutes of the Proceedings of the Colonial Conference
1911": Parl. Papers LIV (Cd 5745) 1911.

Parliamentary Papers

1887	LVI	Cd 5091	pp.213-230
1888	LXVIII	Cd 5304	pp.21-29
1890	XIX	Cd 5979	pp.xxiv
1901	XXXIX	Cd 607	p.255
1903	XLIV	Cd 1597	p.1
1903	XL	Cd 5745	pp.36-75
1905	LIII	Cd 2326	p.4441

"Report of the Inter-Departmental Committee on Migration
Policy", Parl. Papers, 1933-1934, X Cd 4689.

"Report of the Secretary of State for Dominion Affairs on the
Inter-Departmental Committee on Migration Policy", Parl. Papers,
1933-1934 X Cd 4689.

The Colonial Office List (London, Harrison, 1870).
The Colonial Office List (London, Harrison, 1910).

1.3   Periodicals, Serials, Society Publications

Cobden Club - List of Members 1872 (London, Rupert, 1872).
Free Trade Union - Handbook to the Tariff Question (London,
Free Trade Union 1908).
Free Trade Union - Pamphlets, 1903.
Journal of the Imperial Federation League, 1888-1893.
Liberal Association - Tariff Reform Simply Explained, (London,
1911)
Liberal Magazine, August 1908, Vol. XVI.
Political Economy Club - Revised Report of the
Proceedings of the Dinner of May 31st, (London, 1876).
Report of the British Association, 1903.
Tariff Committee on Trade and Empire, Report No. 14.
Tariff Reform League
        "Food and Work Under Tariff Reform" 1910.
        "Leaflets", Nos. 270-279, 1903.
        "Leaflets", Nos. 1-11, 1909.
        "Monthly Notes", July 1904.
        "The Tariff Reformers Enquire Within", 1914.
The British Association for the Advancement of Science
Local Oxford Programme, Bodleian Library, Oxford, 1894.

United Empire Trade League Publications, New Series, London, 1897.

1.4   Newspapers

General Daily News, 1861-1863.
Guardian, 1903-1905.
Morning Chronicle, 1847,1911.
National Review 1894.
Pall Mall Gazette, 1869.
Public Opinion, 1904.
Rochadale Times, 1911.
The Star, 1869.
The Times 1869, 1877, 1881, 1887, 1888, 1889, 1903, 1905, 1907.
The Yorkshire Post Trade Review, 1923.

1.5   Unpublished Dissertations

Edward R. Kittrell, The Development of the Theory of Colonization in English Classical Political Economy, (Chicago University, Doctoral Dissertation, 1962).
G M Koot, The English Historical School of Economics, 1870-1920; Economic History, Social Reform and Neo-Mercantalism, (New York State, Doctoral Dissertation, Stony Brook Library, 1972).
A J F Lee, A Study of the Social and Economic Thought of J A Hobson, (University of London, Doctoral Dissertation, 1970).
A Petridis, The Economic Analysis of Trade Unions by British Economists, 1870-1930, (Duke University, PhD Dissertation 1970).
J Remenyi, Core-Demi-Core Interaction in Economics (Duke University, PhD Dissertation, 1976).
J Townsend, J A Hobson and the Crisis of Liberalism, (University of Southhampton, Doctoral Dissertation, 1973).

1.6   Contemporary Sources

G Armitage-Smith, The Free Trade Movement and its Results (London, Blackie and Son, 1903).
W J Ashley, An Introduction to English Economic History and Theory, 2 Parts, (London, Longmans Green and Co. 1902 ed.) Part I 1888 and Part II 1893.
W J Ashley (ed), British Dominions (London, Longmans Green and Co, 1911).
"Industry and Commerce" in the Handbook of the British Association for the Advancement of Science, (Birmingham Cornish, 1913).
W J Ashley, Introduction to J S Mill's Principles of Political Economy, (London, Green and Co, 1905).
W J Ashley, Introduction to the Commercial Year Book of the Birmingham Chamber of Commerce, (London, Penrose and Derby, 1905).
W J Ashley, "James Edward Thorold Rogers", PSQ, Vol.14,

Sept, 1899, pp.381-407.

W J Ashley, Political Economy and the Tariff Problem, (London Macmillan, 1905).

W J Ashley, "Review of W A S Hewins: English Trade and Finance", PSQ, Vol.8, 1893, pp.543-547.

W J Ashley, Surveys: Historic and Economic, first published in 1900 (New York, Augustus M Kelly, 1966).

W J Ashley, The Adjustment of Wages, (London, Longmans Green and Co, 1903).

W J Ashley, "The Argument for Preference", EJ, Vol.14, June 1904, pp.1-10.

W J Ashley, "The Canadian Sugar Combine", University Quarterly, Toronto, Feb. 1890, pp.361-377.

W J Ashley, The Economic Organisation of England, (London, Longmans Green and Co, 1949).

W J Ashley, "The Enlargement of Economics", EJ, Vol.18, June 1908, pp.181-204.

W J Ashley, (ed.) The Origins of Property in Land, (London, Swan Sonnenschien, 1891).

W J Ashley, "The Present Position of Political Economy", EJ, Vol.17, 1907, pp.467-489.

W J Ashley, The Progress of the German Working Classes in the Last Quarter of the Century, (London, Longmans, Green and Co, 1904).

W J Ashley, "The Rehabilitation of Ricardo", EJ, Vol.1, Sept, 1891, pp.474-89.

W J Ashley, The Tariff Problem, (London, P S King, 1903).

W J Ashley, The War in its Economic Aspects, (London, OUP, 1916).

R D C Black (ed.), The Papers and Correspondence of W S Jevons, (London, Macmillan, Vol.2, 1973, Vols.3-7, 1977).

R D C Black and R Könekamp (eds), The Papers and Correspondence of W J Jevons, Vol.1, (London, Macmillan, 1972).

J Bonar, Theories of Population from Raleigh to Arthur Young, (London, George Allen and Unwin, 1931).

A L Bowley, "Statistical Methods and the Fiscal Controversy", EJ, Vol.13, September 1903, pp.303-312.

J Bright and J E T Rogers, (eds), Speeches by Richard Cobden (London, Macmillan, 1878).

Edwin Burgis, Perils to British Trade. How to Avert Them, (London, Swan Sonnenschein, 1875).

J E Cairnes, Essays in Political Economy: Theoretical and Applied, (London, Macmillan, 1873).

J E Cairnes, Lectures Delivered before the Dublin's Young Men's Christian Association, (Dublin, Hodge, Smith and Co., 1865).

J E Cairnes, Political Essays, (London, Macmillan, 1863).

J E Cairnes, Slave Power, (London, Macmillan, 1863).

J E Cairnes, Some Leading Principles of Political Economy, (London, Macmillan, 1884). First published in 1874.

E Cannan, The Economic Outlook, (London, T Fisher and Unwin, 1912).

E Cannan, History of the Theories of Production and Distribution, (London, Perival, 1903).

W Cunningham, "A Plea for Pure Theory", ER, Vol.2, pp.25-41.

W Cunningham, An Essay on Western Civilization in its Economic Aspects, (Cambridge, CUP, 1900).

W Cunningham, Christiananity and Social Questions, (London, Duckworth, 1910).

W Cunningham, "Economists as Mischief Makers", ER, Vol.4, pp.1-23.

W Cunningham, "English Imperialism", The Atlantic Monthly, Vol.84, July, 1899, pp.1-7.

W Cunningham, English Influence on the United States, (Cambridge, CUP 1916).

W Cunningham, Hints on the Study of Economic History, (London Society for Promoting Christian Knowlege, 1919).

W Cunningham, Making the Most of Life, (London, Society for Promoting Christian Knowledge, 1920).

W Cunningham, "Nationalism and Cosmopolitanism in Economics", Section F of the British Association for the Advancement of Science, 1891, pp.723-34.

W Cunningham, Politics and Economics, (London, Paul Trench, 1885).

W Cunningham, Richard Cobden and Adam Smith, (London, Tariff Reform League, 1904).

W Cunningham, Tariff Reform and Political Morality, (London, Macmillan, 1905).

W Cunningham, The Causes of Labour Unrest and the Remedies for it, (London, John Murray, 1912).

W Cunningham, The Case Against Free Trade, (London, John Murray, 1911).

W Cunningham, The Common Weal, (Cambridge, CUP, 1902).

W Cunningham, The Cure of Souls, (Cambridge, CUP 1902).

W Cunningham, "The Good Government of Empire", The Atlantic Monthly, Vol. 84, Nov. 1899, pp. 654-660.

W Cunningham, The Growth of English Industry and Commerce. First published in 1882, 2 Vols., (Cambridge, CUP, 2nd ed., 1892, 3rd ed., 1903, 4th ed., 1907, 5th ed., 1910).

W Cunningham, The Growth of English Industry and Commerce in Modern Times, 6th ed., (Cambridge, CUP 1919).

W Cunningham, "The Failure of Free Traders to Attain their Ideals", Section F of the British Association for the Advancement of Science, 1903, pp.750-51.

W Cunningham, "The Perversion of Economic History", EJ, Vol.2, 1892, pp.491-506.

W Cunningham, The Progress of Capitalism in England, (Cambridge, CUP, 1916).

W Cunningham, "The Relativity of Economic Doctrine", EJ Vol.2, March, 1892, pp.1-16.

W Cunningham, The Rise and Decline of the Free Trade Movement, (Cambridge, CUP, 1912).

W Cunningham, The Secret of Progress, (Cambridge, CUP, 1918).

W Cunningham The Use and Abuse of Money, (London, John Murray, 1891).

W Cunningham, The Wisdom and the Wise: Three Lectures on Free Trade Imperialism, (Cambridge, CUP, 1906).

W Cunningham, "Unconscious Assumptions in Economics", Section F of the British Association for the Advancement of Science 1905, pp.466-472.

H Cunynghame, "The Effects of Export and Import Duties on Prices and Production Examined by the Graphic Method", EJ, Vol.13, 1903, pp.313-323.

George T Denison, The Struggle for Imperial Unity, (London, Bingay, 1909).

C W Dilke Greater Britain, (London, Macmillan, 1868).

Geoferey Drage, The Imperial Organisation of Trade, (London, Smith, 1911).

W Farrer Ecroyd, Suggestions Towards the Consolidation of the Empire and the Defence of its Industries and Commoners, (London, Hamilton, Adam and Co, 1879).

F Y Edgeworth, "Disputed Points in the Theory of International Trade", EJ, Vol.11, December 1901, pp.582-595.

H Elliot (ed), Letters of J S Mill, (London, Longmans, 1910).

H Elliot (ed), Protection of Infant Industries, (Reprint by the Cobden Club, 1911, London, Cobden Club).

C Litton Falkiner, "A Memoir of the Late John Kells Ingram", Journal of the Statistical and Social Inquiry Society of Ireland, Vol.12, 1908, pp.105-124.

Lewis R Farnell, An Oxonion Looks Back, (London, Martin Hopkins, 1934).

Henry Fawcett, Economic Position of the British Labourer, (London, Macmillan. 1865).

Henry Fawcett, Free Trade and Protection, (London, Macmillan, 1878).

Henry Fawcett, Manual of Political Economy, (London, Macmillan, 1863), 3rd ed, 1869.

Henry Fawcett, Pauperism: Its Causes and its Remedies, (London, Macmillan, 1871).

Henry Fawcett, Speeches on Indian Finance (London, W Tweedie, 1872).

Henry Fawcett, Speeches on Some Current Political Questions, (London, Macmillan, 1873).

Henry Fawcett, State Socialism and the Nationalism of Land, (London, Macmillan, 1883).

Henry and M G Fawcett, Essays and Lectures on Social and Political Subjects, (London, Macmillan, 1872).

A W Flux, "Britain's Place in Foreign Markets", EJ, Vol.14, 1904, pp.356-371.

A W Flux, "The Commercial Supremacy of Great Britain", EJ, Vol.6, 1896, pp.173-83.

A W Flux, "The Commercial Supremacy of Great Britain", EJ, Vol.9, 1899, pp.457-67.

A W Flux, "Review of J A Hobson's The Economics of

Distribution", EJ, Vol.10, 1900, pp.380-385.

H S Foxwell, "The Economic Movement in England", QJE, Vol.11, Oct. 1887, pp.84-103.

J A Froude, Oceana, (London, Longmans Green, 1886).

Francis Galton, "Considerations Adverse to the Maintenance of Section F", JRSS, September, 1877, pp.468-73.

H George, Historical Account of the British Empire, (London, Methuen, 1904.

R Giffen, Essays in Finance, (First Series, London, George Bell, 1880).

R Giffen, Essays in Finance, (Second Series, London, George Bell, 1886).

R Giffen, "Further Notes on Economic Aspects of the War", EJ, Vol.11, March 1901, pp.1-11.

R Giffen, "Imports Versus Home Production", EJ, Vol.15, 1905, pp.483-93.

R Giffen, Nationalism, (London, P S King and Son, 1919).

R Giffen, "Our Trade Prosperity and Outlook", EJ, Vol.10, Sept, 1900, pp.295-309.

R Giffen, "Protection and Manufacturers in New Countries", EJ Vol.8, 1898, pp.3-16.

R Giffen, "Some Economic Aspects of the War", EJ, Vol.10, June 1900, pp.194-207.

R Giffen, Statistics, (ed. by Henry Higgs, London, Macmillan, 1913).

R Giffen, Stock Exchange Securities, (London, George Bell and Sons, 1877).

R Giffen, The New Protection Cry, (anonomously published, London, Imfield, 1879).

R Giffen, The Progress of the German Working Classes in the Last Quarter of the Nineteenth Century, (London, G Bell and Sons, 1884).

R Giffen, "The Relative Growth of the Component Parts of the Empire", Journal of the Royal Colonial Institute, No.6, Series 1, Feb. 1898, pp.1-21.

W P Greswell, "The Growth and Administation of the British Colonies, (London, Black and Son, 1898).

H L Hastings, Small Families, (London, H L Hastings, 1893).

W E Hall, Foreign Jurisdication of the British Crown, (Oxford Clarendon, 1894).

E E G Hatch, In Support of Free Trade, (London, Unionist Free Trade Club, 1906).

M H Herbey, The Trade Policy of Imperial Federation, (London Swan Sonnenschien, 1892).

W A S Hewins, English Trade and Finance, (London, Methuen and Co, 1892).

W A S Hewins, Protection (in the Encyclopaedia Britannica, 1929).

W A S Hewins, Tariff Reform and Home Rule, (London, The Tariff Reform League, 1912).

W A S Hewins, The Apologia of an Imperialist, (London,

Constable, 1929).

W A S Hewins, "The Fiscal Problem" in the Fortnightly Review Oct 1903, Vol.80, pp.590-97.

W A S Hewins, The Return to Sanity, (Published anonymously: London, The Patriotic Press, 1903).

W A S Hewins, Trade in Balance, (London, Philip Allan and Co, 1924).

F W Hirst, From Adam Smith to Philip Snowden. A History of Free Trade, (London, Fisher, Unwin, 1925).

F W Hirst, An Economic Interpretation of Investment, (London, Financial Review of Reviews, 1911).

J A Hobson, "Can England Keep Her Trade", National Review, 1891, p.6.

J A Hobson, Canada Today, (London, T Fisher, Unwin, 1906).

J A Hobson, "Capitalism and Imperialism in South Africa", in the CR, 1900, pp.1-17.

J A Hobson, Confessions of an Economic Heretic, (London, George Allen and Unwin, 1938).

J A Hobson, Co-operative Labour on the Land, (London, Swan Sonnenschien, 1895).

J A Hobson, Democracy and a Changing Civilisation, (London, John Lane, 1934).

J A Hobson, Economics and Ethics, (London, D C Heath, 1929).

J A Hobson, Economics of Distribution, (New York, Macmillan 1903).

J A Hobson, Economics of Unemployment, (London, George Allen and Unwin, 1922).

J A Hobson, "Expansion in the Light of Sociology", Ethical World, Nov. 1898.

J A Hobson, Free Thought in the Social Sciences, (London, George Allen and Unwin, 1926).

J A Hobson, "Free Trade and Foreign Policy", CR, August 1898, pp.177-9.

J A Hobson, Gold Prices and Wages, (London, Methuen, 1913).

J A Hobson, Imperialism: A Study, (London, James Nisbet, 1st ed. 1902, 2nd ed. 1905, 3rd ed. 1938).

J A Hobson, Incentives in the New Industrial Order, (London, Leonard Parsons, 1922).

J A Hobson, International Trade. An Application of Economic Theory, (London, Methuen, 1904).

J A Hobson, "Issues of Empire", in Ethical World, July, 1899.

J A Hobson, John Ruskin: Social Reformer, (London, James Nisbet, 1898).

J A Hobson, Morals of Economic Internationalism, (New York, Houghton, 1920).

J A Hobson, "Neo-Classical Economics in Britain", PSQ, Vol.XL, No.3, Sept, 1925, pp.337-383.

J A Hobson, Poverty in Plenty, (London, George Allen and Unwin, 1931).

J A Hobson, Problems of a New World, (London, George Allen and Unwin, 1931).

J A Hobson, Problems of Poverty, (London, Methuen, 1891).

J A Hobson, Property and Impropery, (London, Victor Gollance 1937).

J A Hobson, Rationalization and Unemployment, (London, George Allen and Unwin, 1937).

J A Hobson, Richard Codben - The International Man, (London, T Fisher, Unwin, 1918).

J A Hobson, Taxation in the New State, (London, Methuen, 1919).

J A Hobson, The Condition of Industrial Peace, (London, George Allen and Unwin, 1927).

J A Hobson, The Crisis of Liberalism, (London, P S King and Son, 1909).

J A Hobson, The Economics of Distribution, (New York, Macmillan, 1900).

J A Hobson, "The Ethics of Empire" (published under 'Nemo'), The Progressive Review, August 1897, No.11, pp.448-64.

J A Hobson, "The Ethics of Internationalism" in the International Journal of Ethics, Vol.17, 1906, pp.16-28.

J A Hobson, The Evolution of Modern Capitalism, (London, Walter Scott, 1906).

J A Hobson, The Industrial System, (London, P S King, 1927).

J A Hobson, The New Protectionism, (London, T Fisher Unwin, 1916).

J A Hobson, The Problem of the Unemployed, (London, Methuen, 1904).

J A Hobson, "The Pro-Consulate of Milner" in the CR, Oct. 1900, pp.54-55.

J A Hobson, The Psychology of Jingoism, (London, Richards, 1901).

J A Hobson, "The Scientific Basis of Imperialism" in PSQ, Vol.17, 1902, pp.460-89.

J A Hobson, "The Testimony from Johannesburg", in CR, May 1900, pp. 656-69.

J A Hobson, The War in South Africa: Its Causes and Effects, (London, James Nisbet, 1900).

J A Hobson, Towards International Government, (London, George Allen and Unwin, 1915).

J A Hobson, "Underconsumption: An Exposition and a Reply by J A Hobson. A Reply to Mr Hobson by E F M Dubbs. A Rejoinder", Economica, Nov. 1933, pp.402-427.

J A Hobson, Work and Wealth, (New York, Macmillan 1914).

J A Hobson and A F Mummery, Physiology of Industry, (London, John Murray, 1889).

W S Jevons, Investigations in Currency and Finance, (London, Macmillan, 1884).

W S Jevons, Methods of Social Reform, London, Macmillan 1883).

W S Jevons, Money and the Mechanism of Exchange, (Iowa, Meridith, 1875).

W S Jevons, On the Conditions of Metallic Currency in the United Kingdom, (London, Harrison and Son, 1868).

W S Jevons, The Coal Question, (1st ed. 1865, 3rd ed. by A W Flux, London, Macmillan, 1906).

W S Jevons, The Principles of Economics, (London, Macmillan, 1905).

W S Jevons, The State in Relation to Labour, (London, Macmillan, 1882).

W S Jevons, The Theory of Political Economy, (1st ed. in 1871, 4th ed. edited by Harriet Jevons in 1911, London, Macmillan).

J M Keynes, A Treatise on Money, 2 Vols., (New York, Harcourt Brace, 1930).

J M Keynes, General Theory of Employment, Interest and Money (London, Harcourt Brace, 1936).

J M Keynes, (ed.), Official Papers of Alfred Marshall, (London, Macmillan, 1926).

J N Keynes, The Scope and Method of Political Economy, (London, Macmillan, 1917 ed.).

T E Cliffe Leslie, Essays in Political and Moral Philosophy, (London, Longmans Green and Co, 1879).

T E Cliffe Leslie, Introduction to Fredrich List's National System of Political Economy, (Philadelphia, I P Lippincott, 1856).

T E Cliffe Leslie, Land Systems and Industry and Economy of Ireland, England and Continental Countries, (London, Longmans and Green, 1890).

T E Cliffe Leslie, Trade Unions and Combinations in 1853, (Dublin, 1853).

Sir George Cornwall Lewis, The Colonies of England. An Essay on the Government of Dependencies, (London, John Murray, 1841).

J R McCulloch, A Description and Statistical Account of the British Empire, (London, Longmans, Brown, Green and Longmans, 1847, 2 vols, 3rd ed.).

J Ramsay MacDonald, Labour and Empire, (London, George Allen 1907).

T R Malthus, An Essay on the Principle of Population, (London, Macmillan, 1926, 1st ed. report 1798; London, J Johnson, 1803, 2nd ed, London, J Murray, 1826, 6th ed.).

T R Malthus, Principles of Political Economy, (London, LSE Reprint, 1936).

Alfred Marshall, Elements of the Economics of Industry, (London, Macmillan, 1899, 3rd ed.).

Alfred Marshall, Industry and Trade, (London, Macmillan, 1919).

Alfred Marshall, Money, Credit and Commerce, (London, Macmillan, 1923).

Alfred Marshall, Official Papers of Alfred Marshall, ed. by J M Keynes, (London, Macmillan, 1926).

Alfred Marshall, Principles of Economics, (London, Macmillan, 1st ed. 1890, 8th ed. 1920).

Alfred Marshall, The Pure Theory of International Trade, (London, LSE Reprint (1879), 1930 reprint).

Alfred Marshall and Mary Paley Marshall, The Economics of Industry, (London, Macmillan, 1879).

J C Meekins, Parliamentary Reform, Should the Colonies Be

Represented? (London, Macmillan, 1859).

Herman Merivale, Lectures on Colonization and Colonies, (London, Cass 1967 reprint, delivered at Oxford during 1839-41).

Herman Merivale, "On the Colonial Question", Fortnightly Review, Vol.7, New Series, 1870, pp.154-158.

Herman Merivale, "On the Utility of Colonies as Fields for Emigration", Journal of the Statistical Society, 6/10/1862, pp.491-96.

James Mill, Elements of Political Economy, (London, Henry H Bohen, 1844, 3rd ed).

J S Mill, "Essay on Representative Government" in A D Lindsay (ed) Utilitarianism, Liberty and Representative Government, (London, A M Dent, 1826).

J S Mill, An Essay on Some Unsettled Questions of Political Economy, (London, London School of Economics Reprint, 1884).

J S Mill, Principles of Political Economy, (Ashley, ed, London, Longmans and Green, 1909).

Arthur Mills, Colonial Constitutions, (London, Stanford, 1891).

Francis E Mineka and Dwight N Lindley, The Late Letters of J S Mill, (Toronto, TUP 1972, Vol.16).

J S Nicholson, A Project of Empire, (London, Macmillan, 1909).

J S Nicholson, Elements of Political Economy, (London, A and C Black, 1909).

J S Nicholson, Historical Progress and Ideal Socialism, (London, A and C Black, 1894).

J S Nicholson, Introduction to Adam Smith's Wealth of Nations (London, T Nelson and Son, 1884).

J S Nicholson, Introduction to F List's National System of Political Economy, (London, Longmans Green, 1904).

J S Nicholson, Money and Monetary Problems, (London, Blackwood, 1888).

J S Nicholson, Principles of Political Economy, 3 vols, (London, A and C Black, Vol.1, 1902; Vol.2, 1903; Vol.3, 1908).

J S Nicholson, "Review of W J Ashley's The Tariff Problem, EJ, Vol.14, March 1904, pp.63-65.

J S Nicholson, Strikes and Social Problems, (London, A and C Black, 1896).

J S Nicholson, "The Economics of Imperialism", EJ, Vol.20. June 1910, pp.155-172.

J S Nicholson, The Neutrality of the United States in Relation to the British and German Empires, (London, Macmillan, 1915).

J S Nicholson, The Tariff Question with Special Reference to Wages and Employment, (London, A and C Black, 1903).

J S Nicholson, War Finance, (London, P S King and Son, 1917).

A C Pigou (ed), Memorials of Alfred Marshall, (London, Macmillan, 1925).

A C Pigou (ed), Protective and Preferential Import Duties, (London, Macmillan, 1906).

A C Pigou (ed), "Pure Theory and the Fiscal Controversy", EJ, Vol.14, March 1904, pp.29-33.

A C Pigou (ed), The Riddle of the Tariff, (London, Macmillan, 1903).

A C Pigou (ed.), Wealth and Welfare, (London, Macmillan, 1912).

L L Price, "Some Economic Consequences of the South African War", EJ, Vol.10, September 1900, pp.323-329.

L L Price, "The Economic Possibilities of an Imperial Fiscal Policy", EJ Vol.13, December 1903, pp.486-504.

David Ricardo, Principles of Political Economy and Taxation, Vol.1 of The Works and Correspondence of David Ricardo (ed) P Sraffa and M H Dobb, (Cambridge, CUP, 1951-55).

J M Robertson, Chamberlain: A Study, (London, Watts, 1905).

J M Robertson, Overpopulation: A Lecture, (London, L Forder 1890).

J M Robertson, Patriotism and Empire, (London, Grant Richards, 1899).

J M Robertson, The Collapse of Tariff Reform, (London, Cassell, 1911).

J M Robertson, The Fallacy of Savings, (London, Swan Sonnenschien, 1892).

J M Robertson, The Great Question: Free Trade or Tariff Reform, (London, Pitman, 1909).

J M Robertson, The Tariff Swindle, (London, Cassell, 1911).

J M Robertson, Trade and Tariffs, (London, A and C Black, 1908).

J A Roebuck, The Colonies of England, (London, Parker, 1849).

J E T Rogers, A History of Agriculture and Prices in England from 1259-1793, (Oxford, Clarendon, 1866).

J E T Rogers, Address to the Electors of the Division of Bermonsdey, (London, Bean Webely and Co, 1895).

J E T Rogers, Cobden and Modern Political Opinion, (London, Macmillan, 1873).

J E T Rogers, England's Industrial and Commercial Supremacy, (London, T Fisher Unwin, 1892).

J E T Rogers, Manual of Political Economy, (Oxford, Clarendon 1st ed. 1863; 2nd ed. 1869).

J E T Rogers, Manual of Political Economy for Schools and Colleges, (Oxford, Clarendon, 1868).

J E T Rogers, "Review of T E Cliffe Leslie's Essays in Philosophy", The Academy, No.370, Jun. 7, 1829, pp.489-491.

J E T Rogers, Six Centuries of Work and Wages: The History of English Labour, (London, Swan Sonnenschien, 1884).

J E T Rogers, The British Citizen: His Rights and Privileges, (London, Society for Promoting Christian Knowledge, 1885).

J E T Rogers, "The Colonial Question" in Cobden Club Essays, (London, Cassell, 1872), pp.403-459.

J E T Rogers, The Economic Interpretation of History, (London, T Fisher, Unwin, 1888).

J E T Rogers, The Free Trade Policy of the Liberal Party, (Manchester Guardian, 1868).

J E T Rogers, The Irish Land Question, (Oxford, E H Aldi, 1881).

J E T Rogers, The Relation of Economic Science to Social and Political Action, (London, Cassell, 1872).

J R Seeley, The Expansion of England, (London, Macmillan,

1883).

N W Senior, An Outline of the Science of Political Economy, (London, Library of Economics, 1938 reprint).

Arthur and Eleanor Sidgwick, Henry Sidgwick: A Memoir, (London, Macmillan, 1906).

H Sidgwick, Elements of Politics, (London, Macmillan, 1897).

H Sidgwick, Principles of Economics, (London, Macmillan, 1883, 1901 reprint).

H Sidgwick, "The Wages-Fund Theory", Fortnightly Review, New Series, Vol.CLIII, September 1897, pp.401-413.

Adam Smith, An Inquiry into the Nature and Causes of the Wealth of Nations, (E Cannan ed., New York, Modern Library 1937).

Goldwin Smith, Empire, (Oxford, John Henry and James Parker, 1863).

Goldwin Smith, Essays on Questions of the Day, (New York, Macmillan, 1893).

Goldwin Smith, "Imperialism in the United States", CR, Vol.XLVII, March 1885, pp.620-8.

Goldwin Smith, Reminiscences, (ed by Arnold Hamilton, New York, Norwood, 1910).

Goldwin Smith, "The Disorganisation of Democracy", CR, Vol.XLVII, March 1885, pp.315-33.

Goldwin Smith, "The Political Aspects of Imperial Federation", Saturday Review, Vol.LXXXIII, February 1897, pp.287-88.

Goldwin Smith, The Schism of the Anglo Saxon Race, (New York, New Coy, 1887).

Goldwin Smith, Two Lectures on the Study of History, (Oxford, Parker, 1861).

J W Taylor, On the Diminishing Birth-Rate, (London, Baillieve, Tindall & Co, 1904).

A Toynbee, Lectures on the Industrial Revolution in England, (London, Revingtons, 1884).

E G Wakefield, England and America: A Comparison of the Social and Political State of Both Nations, 2 Vols., (London, Richard Bentley, 1833).

A S White (ed), Britannica Confederation, (London, George Philip & Co, 1892).

2.   Secondary Sources

D H Aldcroft and H W Richardson, The British Economy, 1870-1939, (London, Macmillan, 1969).

S Ambirajan, "Economics and Economists in the Formulation of a Monetary Policy for India, 1873-1893", HOPE, Vol.9, No.1, Spring 1977, pp.122-43.

American Economic Association, Index of Economic Journals and Index of Economic Articles, 1886-1967, (Illinois, Richard D Irwin, 1961-69).

R T Appleyard, British Emigration to Australia, (Canberra, Australian National University, 1964).

Anne Ashley, William James Ashley - A Life, (London, P S King and Son, 1932).

T S Ashton, "The Relation of Economic History to Economic Thought" in N B Harte (ed.) The Study of Economic History (London, Cass. 1971), pp.161-180.

W Ashworth, An Economic History of England, 1870-1939, (London, Methuen, 1960).

R Bacon and W A Eltis, Britain's Economic Problems: Too Few Producers, (London, Macmillan, 1st ed, 1976).

Philip S Bagwell and G E Mingay, Britain and America. A Study of Economic Change 1870-1939, (London, Routledge and Kegan Paul, 1970).

W J Barber, British Economic Thought and India 1600-1858, (Oxford, Clarendon, 1975).

H E Bateson, A Select Bibliography of Modern Economic Theory, 1870-1929, (London, Routledge and Kegan Paul, 1930).

G M Baqir, Economic Historicism, (New Delhi, New Book Society of India, 1968).

Hugh Bell, Our Iron and Steel Industries Under Free Trade, (London, City of London Free Trade Committee, 1910).

E A Benians, "Adam Smith's Project of Empire", Commonwealth Historical Journal, 1925, No.3, pp.349-83.

George Bennet (ed.), The Concept of Empire: Burke to Atlee, 1774-1949, (London, Adam and Charles Black, 1953).

Rowland Toppan Berthoff, British Immigrants in Industrial America 1790-1950, (Cambridge, CUP, 1953).

W Beveridge (ed), Tariffs: The Case Examined, (London Longmans, 1931).

R D C Black, Economic Fashions, (Belfast, The Queens University, 1963).

R D C Black Economic Thought and the Irish Question 1817-1870, (Cambridge, CUP 1960).

R D C Black, "Jevons and Cairnes", Economica, New Series 27, 1960, pp.214-32.

R D C Black, "W S Jevons and the Foundation of Modern Economics", HOPE, Vol.4, No.2, 1972, pp.364-378.

M Blaug, Economic Theory in Retrospect, (Illinois, Richard D Irwin, 1968).

M Blaug, "Kuhn Versus Lakatos or Paradigm Versus Research Programmes in the History of Economics, HOPE, Vol.7, No.4, 1975, pp.399-433.

M Blaug, Ricardian Economics: A Historical Study, (New Haven, Conn. 1958).

M Blaug, "Was There a Marginal Revolution?", HOPE, Vol.4, No.2, Fall 1973, pp.269-280.

A I Bloomfield, "Adam Smith and the Theory of International Trade", in Essays on Adam Smith (eds) Andrew S Skinner and Thomas Wilson, (Oxford, Clarendon, 1975), pp.455-81.

G A Bodelsen, Studies in Mid-Victorian Imperialism, (Copenhagen, Glydendalen, 1924).

G F Bowen, Thirty Years of Colonial Government ed. by

S Lane-Poole, 2 Vols., (London, Macmillan, 1889).

C W Boyd, Speeches of Joseph Chamberlain, (London, Constable, 1914), Vol.2.

H Henry Brailsford, The Life Work of J A Hobson, (London, OUP, 1948).

Earl Brassey, Seventy Years of Progress Under Free Trade, (London, Free Trade Union, 1914).

C Briece, The Broad Stone of Empire: Problems of Crown Colony Administration, 2 Vols., (London, Macmillan, 1910).

Martin Bronfenbrenner, "The Structure of Revolutions in Economic Thought", HOPE, Vol.3, Spring 1971, pp.136-151.

Martin Bronfenbrenner, "Trends, Cycles and Fads in Economic Writing", AER, Vol.LV, (2), May 1966, pp.539-552.

B H Brown, The Tariff Reform Movement in Great Britain, 1881 -1895, (New York, Columbia, UP, 1943).

Lucy Brown, The Board of Trade and the Free Trade Movement, (Oxford, OUP, 1958).

M B Brown, After Imperialism, (London, Heinemann, 1963).

M B Brown, The Economics of Imperialism, (London, Penguin, 1974).

R C Buck and R S Cohen (eds.) Boston Studies in the Philosophy of Science, Vol.3, (Dordrecht, Reidel, 1971).

A L Burt, The Evolution of the British Empire and Commonwealth from the American Revolution, (Boston, D C Heath, 1956).

A Cairncross, Home and Foreign Investment 1870-1913, (Cambridge, CUP, 1953).

A Caldecott, English Colonization and the Empire, (London, John Murray, 1897).

Cambridge History of the British Empire, (Cambridge, CUP, Vol.1, 1929, Vol.2, 1940; Vol.3, 1959; Vol.4, 1932; Vol.5, 1933; Vol.6, 1959).

E Cannan, History of the Theories of Production and Distribution, (London, Riverton, Perival and Co, 1903).

Walter F Cannon, "The Uniformitarian - Catastrophic Debate", ISIS, Vol.51, 1960, pp.55-58.

C E Carrington, The British Overseas, (Cambridge, CUP, 1950).

W A Carrothers, Emigration from the British Isles with Special Reference to the Overseas Dominions, (London, P S King, 1929).

S G Checkland, "Economic Opinion in England as Jevons Found It" in Manchester School of Economic and Social Studies, Vol.19, May 1951, pp.143-169.

S G Checkland, The Rise of Industrial Society in England, 1815-1885, (London, Longmans Green and Co, 1969).

R A Church, The Mid-Victorian Boom 1850-1873, (London, Macmillan, 1975).

Randolph Churchill, Winston Churchill, (London, Macmillan, 1975).

J H Clapham An Economic History of Modern Britain, (Cambridge CUP, Vol.1, 1830; Vol.2, 1932; Vol.3, 1938).

J H Clapham, "Obituary: Sir William Ashley", EJ Vol.27, Dec.

1927, pp.678-684.

Peter Clarke, Liberals and Social Democrats, (Cambridge, CUP, 1978).

H. Clinton, Suggestions Towards the Organization of the British Empire by Realizing the Parliamentary Representation of all Home and Colonial Interests, (London, Smith Elder and Co, 1856).

R H Coarse, "Marshall on Method", JLE, Vol.XVIII, April, 1975, pp.25-32.

A W Coats, "Adam Smith and the Mercantile System", in Essays on Adam Smith, ed. by A S Skinner and T Wilson, (Oxford, Clarendon, 1975), pp.218-236.

A W Coats, "Adam Smith's Conception of Self Interest in Economic and Political Affairs", HOPE, Vol.7, No.1, Spring 1975, pp.132-136.

A W Coats, "Alfred Marshall and the Early Development of the London School of Economics: Some Unpublished Letters", Economica, Vol.36, Nov. 1967, pp.408-17.

A W Coats, "Is there a Structure of Scientific Revolutions in Economics?", Kyklos, Vol.22, Fasc 2, 1969, pp.289-294.

A W Coats, "J E T Rogers", International Encyclopaedia of the Social Sciences, (London, Macmillan and the Free Press, 1968), p.154.

A W Coats, "Political Economy and the Tariff Reform Campaign of 1903", JLE, Vol.II, April, 1968, pp.181-229.

A W Coats, "Research Priorities in the History of Economics", HOPE, Vol.1, No.1, Spring 1969, pp.6-18.

A W Coats, "Sociological Aspects of British Economic Thought 1880-1930", JPE, October 1967, pp.706-29.

A W Coats, "The Appointment of Pigou as Marshall's Successor", JLE, 1973, pp.478-95.

A W Coats, (ed.), The Classical Economists and Economic Policy, (London, Methuen, 1971).

A W Coats, "The Economic and Social Context of the Marginal Revolution of the 1870s", HOPE, Vol.4, Fall, No.2, 1972, pp.303-24.

A W Coats, "The Historicist Reaction in English Political Economy, 1870-1890", Economica, NS, May 1954, pp.143-53.

A W Coats, "The Interpretation of Mercantilist Economics: Some Historiographical Problems", HOPE, Vol.5, No.2, Fall 1973, pp.485-95.

A W Coats, "The Origins and Early Development of the Royal Economic Society", EJ, Vol.78, June 1968, pp.349-71.

A W Coats, "The Role of Authority in the Development of British Economics", JLE, Vol.7, 1964, pp.85-106.

A W Coats, "Value Judgements in Economics", Yorkshire Bulletin of Economic and Social Research, Vol.16, 1964, pp.53-67.

A W Coats and S L Coats, "The Changing Composition of the Royal Economic Society and the Professionalization of British Economics", British Journal of Sociology, Vol.24, No.2 June 1973, pp.165-88.

G D H Cole, British Trade and Industry, (London, Macmillan, 1932).

G D H Cole, "John A Hobson 1858-1940", EJ, Vol.50, pp.315-60.

G D H Cole and Raymond Postgate, The British People 1746-1946, (New York, Alfred A Knopf, 1947).

D C Coleman (ed.), Revisions in Mercantalism, (London, Methuen, 1969).

E J T Collins, "Migrant Labour in the Nineteenth Century", EHR, Vol.29, No.1, 1976, pp.38-59.

W M Corden, The Theory of Protection, (Oxford, Clarendon Press, 1971).

W M Corden, Trade Policy and Economic Welfare, (Oxford, Clarendon Press, 1974).

W H B Court, British Economic History 1870-1914: Commentary and Documents, (Cambridge, CUP, 1965).

Colin Cross, The Fall of the British Empire 1918-1968, (London, Hodder and Stoughton, 1968).

Audrey Cunningham, William Cunningham, Teacher and Priest, (London, Society for Promoting Chirstian Knowledge, 1950).

J H Dales, The Protective Tariff in Canada's Development, (Toronto, TUP, 1966).

P A David, Technical Choice, Innovations and Economic Growth, (Cambridge, CUP, 1975).

Albert Demangeon, The British Empire, (London, George Harrop, 1925).

Richard V Eagley (ed), Events, Ideology and Economic Theory, (Detroit, Wayne State University Press, 1968).

C C Eldridge, Victorian Imperialism, (London, Hodder and Stoughton, 1978).

W A Eltis, "Adam Smith's Theory of Economic Growth" in Essays on Adam Smith, (ed.) by Andrew S Skinner and Thomas Wilson, (Oxford, Clarendon, 1975), pp.426-44.

W A Eltis, "Francois Quesnay: A Reinterpretation. 1. The Tableau Economique", OEP, Vol.27, July 1975, pp.167-200.

W A Eltis, "Francois Quesnay: A Reinterpretation. 2. The Theory of Economic Growth", OEP Vol.27, November 1975, pp.327-351.

Henry Fawcett, "Professor Cairnes", Fortnightly Review, Vol.II, Jan-June 1878, pp.149-54.

C R Fay, Great Britain from Adam Smith to the Present Day, (London, Longmans Green, 1956, 5th Edition).

I Ferenczi and W E Willcox, International Migration Vol.1, (New York, National Bureau of Economic Research, 1929).

Herbert Feis, Europe - The World's Bankers, (New Haven, Yale UP, 1930).

D K Fieldhouse, Economics and Empire, (London, Weidenfeld and Nicholson, 1973).

D K Fieldhouse, "Imperialism: An Historical Revision", EHR, 2nd Series, Vol.24, December 9, 1961, pp.187-209.

D K Fieldhouse, The Colonial Empires: A Comparative Study from the Eighteenth Century, (London, Weidenfeld and Nicholson, 1966).

M Freeden, "J A Hobson as a New Liberal Theorist: Some Aspects of his Social Thought Until 1914", JHI, Vol.34, 1973, pp.421-423.

H S Foxwell and Lilian Knowles, "Obituary: Archdeacon Cunningham", EJ, Vol.29, September, 1919, pp.382-390.

Carl Fuchs, The Trade Policy of Great Britain and Her Colonies Since 1860, (London, Macmillan, 1905).

J Gallagher and R Robinson, "The Imperialism of Free Trade", EHR, 2nd series, 1953, pp.1-15.

J L Garvin, The Life of Joseph Chamberlain, (London, Macmillan, 1932-4).

R N Ghosh, Classical Macroeconomics and the Case for Colonies, (Calcutta, New Age, 1967).

D V Glass and D E C Eversly (eds.) Population in History: Essays in Historical Demography, (London, Edward Arnold, 1965).

D F Gordon, "The Role of Economic Thought in the Understanding of Economic Theory", AER, Papers and Proceedings, Vol.55, May 1965, pp.96-99.

F Gottheil, "An Economic Theory of Colonialism", JEI, March 1977 pp.73-82.

William D Grampp, The Manchester School of Economics, (London, OUP, 1960).

William D Grampp, Economic Liberalism, (New York, Random House, 1965, 2 Vols).

J A Grenville, Lord Salisbury and Foreign Policy, (London, Athlone, 1964).

G W Guillebaud, "Marshalls Principles of Economics in the Light of Contemporary Economic Thought, Economica, Vol.21, May 1952, pp.111-30.

E Halevy, A History of the English People in the Nineteenth Century, (New York, Peter Smith, Vol.5, 1949 and Vol.6, 1952).

A R Hall (ed), The Export of Capital From Britain 1870-1914, (London, Methuen, 1968).

W K Hancock, A Survey of British Commonwealth Affairs, (London, Royal Institute of International Affairs 1937-42, 3 vols).

W K Hancock, Wealth of Colonies, (Cambridge, CUP, 1950).

N B Harte (ed), The Study of Economic History: Collected Inaugural Lectures, 1893-1970, (London, Cass, 1971).

E E G Hatch, In Support of Free Trade, (London, Unionist Free Trade Club, 1906).

G R Hawke, "The United States Tariff and Industrial Protection in the late Nineteenth Century", EHR, Vol.27, No.1, 1975, pp.84-99.

Eli F Hechscher, Mercantilism, (London, Allen and Unwin, 1934).

W O Henderson, The Genesis of the Common Market, (London, Cass, 1962).

Henry Higgs, "J S Nicholson", JRSS, Vol.XC, Part IV, 1927, pp.811-13.

F Hilgeratt, Industrialisation and Foreign Trade, (London, Longmans, 1945).

Rita Hinden, Empire and After: A Study of British Imperial Attitudes, (London, Essential Books, 1949).

History of Economic Thought Newsletter, Autumn 1977, No. 19, pp.7-8.

C K Hobson, The Export of Capital, (London, Constable and Co,

1914).

S Hollander, "Malthus and the Post Napoleonic Depression", HOPE, Vol. 1, No. 2, Fall 1969, pp.306-38.

Richard S Harvey, "The Origins of Marginalism", HOPE, Vol.4, No.21, Fall 1972, pp.281-302.

T W Hutchinson, A Review of Economic Doctrines 1870-1929, (Oxford, Clarendon, 1953).

T W Hutchinson, "Bentham as an Economist", EJ Vol.66, June 1956, pp.288-306.

T W Hutchinson, "Berkeley's Querist and Its Place in the Economic Thought of the 18th Century", British Journal for the Philosophy of Science, May 1953, pp.52-77.

T W Hutchinson, "Economists and Economic Policy in Britain After 1870", HOPE, Vol.1, No.2, Fall 1969, pp.231-55.

T W Hutchison, Positive Economics and Policy Objectives, (London, George Allen, Unwin, 1964).

T W Hutchison, "The 'Marginal Revolution' and the Decline and Fall of English Political Economy", HOPE, Vol.4, No.2, Fall 1972, pp.442-68.

A H Imlah, Economic Elements in the Pax Britannica, (Cambridge, Massachussets UP, 1958).

Harry Jerome, Immigration and Business Cycles, (New York, National Bureau of Economic Research, 1926).

Harriet W Jevons (ed), Letters and Journal of W Stanley Jevons, (London, Macmillan, 1886).

N Jha, The Age of Marshall, (Patna, Novelty and Co, 1963).

S C Johnson, Emigration from the United Kingdom to North America from 1763 to 1912, (London, George Routledge, 1913).

A E Kahn, Great Britain and the World Economy, (London, Pitman, 1946).

M C Kemp, "The Mill - Bastable Infant Industry Dogma", JPE, Vol.68, February 1960, pp.65-67.

Tom Kemp, Theories of Imperialism, (London, Dobson, 1968).

J M Keynes, "Alfred Marshall, 1842-1924", EJ, Vol.34, No.135, September 1924, pp.311-72.

J M Keynes, "Henry Sidgwick", EJ, Vol.10, 1900, pp.585-91.

C P Kindleberger, Economic Development, (New York, McGraw Hill, 1958).

C P Kindleberger, "Foreign Trade and Economic Growth : Lessons from Britain and France 1850 and 1913", EHR, Vol.14, 1961-2, pp.289-385.

Edward R Kittrell, "The Development of the Theory of Colonization in English Political Economy", SEJ, Vol.31, January 1965, No.3, pp.189-206.

Paul Knaplund, British Commonwealth and Empire 1900-1955, (London, Hamish Hamilton, 1956).

Klaus E Knorr, British Colonial Theories, (Toronto, Frank Cass, 1963).

Richard Köebner and Helmut Dan Schmidt, Imperialism : The Story and Significance of a Political Word, 1840-1910, (London, CUP, 1964).

G M Koot, "T E Cliffe Leslie : Irish Social Reform and the Origins of the English Historical School of Economics", HOPE, Vol.7, No.3, pp.312-37.

I Kravis, "Trade as the Handmaiden of Growth", EJ, Vol.80, No.320, December 1970, pp.850-70.

Thomas Kuhn, The Structure of Scientific Revolutions, (Chicago, CUP, 1962).

I Lakatos, "Changes in the Problem of Inductive Logic" in The Problem of Inductive Logic, (Amsterdam, North Holland Publishing Co., 1968).

I Lakatos and A Musgrave (eds), Problems in the Philosophy of Science, (Amsterdam, North Holland Publishing Co, 1968).

William L Langer, The Diplomacy of Imperialism, (New York, Alfred A Knopf, 1935, 2 vols).

S J Latsis (ed), Method and Appraisal in Economics, (Cambridge, CUP, 1976).

B Mallet, British Budgets, (London, Macmillan, 1913, 1st Series, 1887-1888 to 1912-13).

John Maloney, "Marshall, Cunningham and the Emerging Economics Profession", EHR, 1976, pp.440-51.

N B de Marchi, "Mill and Cairnes and the Emergence of Marginalism in England", HOPE, Vol.4, No.2, Fall 1972, pp.344-63.

N B de Marchi, "On the Dangers of Being Too Political an Economist : Thorold Rogers and the 1868 Election to the Drummond Professorship", OEP, No.3, November 1976, pp.364-80.

Peter Mathias, The First Industrial Nation : An Economic History of Britain, 1700-1914, (London, Methuen, 1969).

Nicholas Mikowick, "John A Hobson's Economics", Indian Journal of Economics, Vol.25, 1942, pp.170-85.

B R Mitchell and P Deane, Abstract of British Historical Statistics, (Cambridge, CUP, 1962, Second Abstract, 1971).

E C Moore, The Spread of Christianity in the Modern World, (Chicago, Heinemann, 1919).

J Morley, The Life of William Ewart Gladstone, (London, Lyold, 1908, 2 vols).

H W McCready, "Alfred Marshall and Tariff Reform", JPE, Vol.63, pp.259-67.

Oliver MacDonald, A Pattern of Government Growth 1800-1860, (London, Mac Gibbon, 1961).

Hla Myint, "Adam Smith's Theory of International Trade in the Perspective of Economic Development", Economica, Vol.44, 1977, pp.231-248.

Hla Myint, "The Classical Theory of International Trade", EJ, Vol.68, 1958, pp.317-31.

J A La Nauze, Political Economy in Australia, (Melbourne, Melbourne UP, 1949).

E E Nemmers, Hobson and Underconsumption, (Amsterdam, North Holland, 1956).

A P Newton, A Hundred Years of the British Empire, (London, Duckworth, 1940).

Walter Nimmocks, Milner's Young Men, (London, Hodder and

Stoughton, 1970).

R Nurkse, Equilibrium and Growth in the World Economy, (Oxford, OUP, 1961).

D K O'Brien, "The Longevity of Adam Smith's Vision : Paradigms, Research Programmes and Falsibility in the History of Economic Thought", Scottish Journal of Political Economy, Vol.23, No.2, June, pp.133-51.

D P O'Brien, J R McCulloch : A Study in Classical Economics, (London, Allen and Unwin, 1970).

D P O'Brien, The Classical Economists, (Oxford, Clarendon Press, 1975).

W Page (ed), Commerce and Industry, (London, Constable and Co, 1919).

Sir George Paish, "Great Britain's Investments in Other Lands", JRSS, Vol.71, September 1909, pp.456-80.

R Pares, "The Economic Factors in the History of the Empire", EHR, Vol.7, No.2, May 1937, pp.119-144.

E Parret, Sixty Years of Protection in Canada, (Toronto, TUP, 1961).

Ellen Frankel Paul, "W S Jevons : Economic Revolutionary", Journal of the History of Ideas, Vol.40, No.2, April-June 1979, pp.267-283.

Anastosis Petridis, "Alfred Marshall's Attitudes to and Economic Analysis of Trade Unions : A Case of Anomalies in a Competitive System", HOPE, Vol.5, No.1, Spring, 1973, pp.165-198.

Michael Polanyi, Personal Knowledge : Towards a Post-Critical Philosophy, (Chicago, CUP, 1958).

O Popescu, "On the Historiography of Economic Thought : A Bibliographical Survey", Journal of World History, Vol.7, No.1, 1964, pp.168-181.

K Popper, Conjectures and Refutations : The Growth of Scientific Knowledge, (London, Routledge and Kegan Paul, 1963).

K Popper, The Logic of Scientific Discovery, (New York, Hutchison, 1968).

B Porter, A Short History of British Imperialism, (London, Longmans, 1975).

B Porter, Critics of Empire, (London, Macmillan, 1963).

John Rae, Life of Adam Smith, (London, Macmillan, 1895).

Barrie M Ratcliffe, Great Britain and the World, (Manchester, MUP, 1975).

A Redford, Manchester Merchants and Foreign Trade, (Manchester, MUP, 1956).

A Redford, Labour Migration in England 1800-1850, (Manchester, MUP, 1964).

Melvin Ritcher, The Politics of Conscience : T H Green and His Age, (Cambridge, Mass, HUP, 1964).

J E Rippy, British Investments in Latin America, (Minesota, MUP, 1959).

L Robbins, Robert Torrens and the Evolution of Classical Economics, (London, Macmillan, 1958).

Ronald Robinson, John Gallagher and Alice Denny, Africa and

the Victorians : The Climax of Imperialism in the Dark Continent, (New York, St. Martins, 1961).

E Roll, A History of Economic Thought, (London, Faber and Faber, 1938).

N Rosenberg, "Adam Smith on Profits - Paradox Lost and Regained", in A Skinner and T Wilson (eds), Essays on Adam Smith, (Oxford, Clarendon, 1975).

W W Rostow, British Economy in the Nineteenth Century, (Oxford, OUP, 1948).

Seldon Rothblatt, The Revolution of the Dons : Cambridge and Society in Late Victorian England, (London, Faber and Faber, 1960).

G W Rusden, The History of New Zealand, (London, Chapman and Hall, 1923).

R Russel, Imperial Preference : Its Development and Effects, (London, Empire Economic Union, 1974).

Warren Samuels, The Classical Theory of Economic Policy, (New York, New World, 1969).

Paul Samuelson, "International Trade and the Equalisation of Factor Prices", EJ, Vol.58, pp.163-84.

Paul Samuelson, "Review of Hla Myint's Theories of Welfare Economics", Economica, New Series, Vol.16, November 1949, pp.371-4.

K Saville (ed), Studies in the British Economy - Special Number of the Yorkshire Bulletin of Economic and Social Research, Vol.17, 1965, 64.

S B Saul, Studies in British Overseas Trade, (Liverpool, LUP, 1960).

W Schlote, British Overseas Trade from 1700 to the 1830's, (London, Blackwell, 1952).

Bernadotte E Schmitt (ed), Some Historians of Modern Europe, (Chicago, Heinemann, 1942).

C B Schedvin, Australia and the Great Depression : A Study of Economic Development and Policy in the 1920's and 1930's, (Sydney, SUP, 1970).

R L Schulyer, The Fall of the Old Colonial System : A Study in British Free Trade, 1770-1870, (New York, OUP, 1945).

J A Schumpeter, A History of Economic Analysis, (New York, OUP, 1954).

J A Schumpeter, Imperialism and Social Classes, (Cambridge, Massachusetts, Harvard UP, 1951).

Pedro Schwartz, The New Political Economy of J S Mill, (London, Weidenfeld and Nicholson, 1968).

W R Scott, "William Cunningham 1849-1919", Proceedings of the British Academy 1919-1920, London, 1920.

Ben B Seligman, "The Impact of Positivism on Economic Thought", HOPE, Vol.1, No.2, Fall 1969, pp.256-78.

B Semmel, Imperialism and Social Reform, (London, George Allen and Unwin, 1959).

B Semmel, The Rise of Free Trade Imperialism, (Cambridge, CUP, 1970).

B Semmel, "Sir William James Ashley as 'Socialist' of the Chair", Economica, Vol.24, November 1957, pp.343-53.

Richard Shannon, The Crisis of Imperialism, (London, Hart Davis, 1934).

A G L Shaw, The Story of Australia, (London, Faber and Faber, 1954).

D C Sommerville, English Thought in the Nineteenth and Twentieth Centuries, (London, Macmillan, 1929, 2nd edition).

Joseph J Spengler, "Discussion" in AER Papers and Proceedings, Vol.XLIII, May 1953, pp.269-71.

H Spiegel, Growth in Economic Thought, (New York, Prentice Hall, 1971 edition).

G Spiller, The Ethical Movement in Great Britain, (London, Farleigh, 1934).

Leslie Stephen, "Henry Sidgwick", Mind, Vol.10, New Series, January 1901.

Leslie Stephen, Life of Henry Fawcett, (London, Smith Elder and Co, 1885).

G J Stigler, "Does Economics Have a Useful Past?", HOPE, Vol.1, Spring 1969, pp.217-30.

G J Stigler, Essays in Economic Thought, (Chicago, CUP, 1965).

G J Stigler, "Textual Exegesis as a Scientific Problem", Economica, New Series, Vol.32, No. 128, November 1965, pp.447-50.

W F Stopler and P A Samuelson, "Protection and Real Wages", in Readings in the Theory of International Trade, (London, Allen and Unwin, 1950), pp.333-57.

Thomas Sowell, Classical Economics Reconsidered, (Princeton, PUP, 1974).

Thomas Sowell, Says Law, (Princeton, PUP, 1972).

Eric Stokes, English Utilitarians and India, (London, OUP, 1959).

Paul Sturges (ed), Economists Papers 1750-1850 : A Guide to Archive and Other Manuscript Sources for the History of British and Irish Economic Thought, (London, Macmillan, 1975).

Brinley Thomas, International Migration and Economic Growth, (Paris, United Nations Scientific and Educational Organisation, 1961).

Brinley Thomas, Migration and Economic Growth, (Cambridge, CUP, 1st edition 1954, 2nd edition 1973).

Brinley Thomas, Migration and Urban Development, (London, Methuen, 1972).

Stephen Toulmin, Human Understanding, (Oxford, Clarendon, 1972, 2 vols.).

M E Townsend, The Origins of Modern German Colonialism 1871-1885, (New York, Columbia, 1921).

W Tuckwell, Reminiscences of Oxford, (London, Cassel, 1900).

J E Tyler, The Struggle for Imperial Unity 1868-95, (London, Longmans, 1983).

A Viallete, Economic Imperialism and Economic Relations, (Paris, Collins, 1923).

J Viner, Studies in the Theory of International Trade, (New York, Harper and Brothers, 1937).

Elisabeth Wallace, Goldwin Smith - Victorian Liberal, (Toronto, TUP, 1957).

D O Wagner, "British Economists and the Empire 1", PSQ,

Vol.46, 1931, pp.248-276.

D O Wagner, "British Economists and the Empire 2", PSQ, Vol.47, 1932, pp.53-74.

R S Walshaw, Migration to and from the British Isles, Problems and Policies, (London, Jonathon Cape, 1941).

Ian D S Ward, "George Berkeley : Precursor of Keynes or Moral Economist on Underdevelopment", JPE, Vol.67, February 1959, pp.31-40.

Charlotte M Waters, The Economic Development of England and the Colonies 1874-1914, (London, Noel Douglas, 1926).

A Williamson, British Industries and Foreign Competition, (London, Simpkin, Marshall, Hamilton, Kent and Co, 1894).

James A Williamson, A Short History of British Expansion, (London, Macmillan, 1922).

D Winch, Classical Political Economy and the Colonies, (London, G Bell, 1965).

D Winch, Economics and Policy, (London, Hodder and Stoughton, 1969).

D Winch, "Marginalism and the Boundaries of Economic Science", HOPE, Vol.4, No.2, Fall 1972, pp.325-343.

Robin W Winks (ed), British Imperialism - Gold, God, Glory, (New York, Holt Rinehart and Winster, 1965).

E M Winslow, The Pattern of Imperialism, (New York, Harper and Row, 1962).

J K Whittaker (ed), The Early Writings of Alfred Marshall 1867-1890, (London, Macmillan, 1975, 2 vols.).

J C Wood (ed), Alfred Marshall: Critical Assessments, (London, Croom Helm, 1982, 4 Volumes).

J C Wood, "Alfred Marshall and the Tariff Reform Campaign of 1903", JLE.

J C Wood, "Henry Fawcett and the British Empire", The Indian Economic and Social History Review, Vol.XVI, No.4, December 1979, pp.395-414.

J C Wood, "J A Hobson and British Imperialism", American Journal of Economics and Sociology, Forthcoming.

Cecil Woodham-Smith, The Great Hunger : Ireland, 1845-1849, (New York, Harper and Row, 1963).

L S Woolf, Economic Imperialism, (London, The Swaryhmore Press, 1920).

Harrison M Wright, The New Imperialism, (Boston, D C Heath, 1968).

W S Woytinsky and E S Woytinsky, World Commerce and Government, (London, Allen and Unwin, 1953).

G M Young, Early Victorian England, 1830-1865, (London, OUP, 1934).

INDEX

Printed in the United States
by Baker & Taylor Publisher Services